THE SPAIN OF
FERDINAND AND ISABELLA

The
SPAIN
of
Ferdinand and Isabella

BY JEAN HIPPOLYTE MARIÉJOL

Translated and Edited by

BENJAMIN KEEN

Rutgers University Press

New Brunswick, New Jersey

The editor and the publisher are greatly indebted to the Museum and Library of the Hispanic Society of America, the New York Public Library, and the News Bureau of the Spanish National Tourist Department for their invaluable aid in the search for appropriate illustrations for this book.

Editor's Preface

The age of Ferdinand and Isabella was Spain's spring-
time, a spacious time of heroic deeds, of creative ardor,
of cascading national energies. Under these talented and
energetic monarchs Spain emerged from her medieval
isolation to assume the first place among the powers of
Europe. The turbulent Castilian nobility was tamed, the
Moors were expelled, the Spanish kingdoms united in the
pursuit of common goals. Industry and trade were encouraged, and Spanish literature and art were launched
on a glorious course. In the same period, America was
discovered under Castilian auspices, the Caribbean became a Spanish lake, and Spanish explorers and adventurers, by the end of the era, were at the approaches to
the great Indian empires of Mexico and Peru. The Spanish people saw the joint realms of Castile and Aragón
marching from triumph to triumph, and were filled with
pride; the Spanish commoner forgot his hard lot in daz-
zled contemplation of *la Grandeza Española*.

Small wonder that monarchs who presided over such
victories became for succeeding generations the objects
of a national cult and legend. The nostalgia inspired by
their memory was deepened by consciousness of the contrast between their rule and that of their successors. Spaniards who suffered under the negligent government of the

Hapsburgs, who groaned under the burdens imposed by the unprofitable foreign wars of Charles I and Philip II, wistfully recalled Isabella's economical ways and Ferdinand's prudent, realistic diplomacy.

A story told by the official historiographer Prudencio de Sandoval at the end of the sixteenth century suggests how strong was the national sense of loss. He relates that one day, while hunting in the woods near Toledo, the Emperor Charles missed his way and finally met a peasant who failed to recognize him. The two fell into conversation. "The peasant said that he had lived to see five kings in Castile, and when asked which of them he considered the best and which the worst, replied that Ferdinand the Catholic was unquestionably the one, and the present sovereign the other." [1]

Spanish literature testifies to the powerful hold of the Catholic Sovereigns upon the imagination and affection of the Spanish people. In Lope de Vega's splendid drama, *Fuente Ovejuna,* the monarchs are portrayed as champions of the poor and humble, as defenders of the peasantry against arrogant feudal lords. In the decaying and misery-ridden Spain of the seventeenth century the great satirist Francisco de Quevedo wrote with implied reproach of Ferdinand's successors that "Ferdinand the Catholic knew how to be a king himself, and how to teach others to be kings." For the philosopher and novelist Baltasar Gracián, Ferdinand exemplified the hero in action; Gracián asserted that "one hundred kings could be forged from one Ferdinand the Catholic, and there would still be enough substance left for as many more."

The flow of eulogy continued in the eighteenth and nineteenth centuries. Spanish liberals as well as conservatives claimed the heritage of the Catholic Sovereigns for their own. The historian Diego Clemencín (1765 to 1834), who fought against the royal absolutism that Fer-

dinand and Isabella had established in Spain, wrote that
"if the succeeding ages had followed the paths indicated
to them by the example of Isabella, and had progressively
perfected her maxims with the aid of experience and
learning," then "Spain would have possessed the naval
power of England." [2] The unanimity of Spanish opinion
in regard to Isabella impressed the American historian
Prescott. "Even in relation to the Inquisition," he wrote,
"her countrymen would seem willing to draw a veil over
her errors, or to excuse them by charging them to the
age in which she lived." [3]

Today, in the second half of the twentieth century, the
vein of eulogy in Spanish comment on Ferdinand and Isabella is not yet exhausted. A great Spanish scholar, Ramón Menéndez Pidal, has summarized with a moving sincerity the symbolism of Isabella for the Spanish people.
"The happy reign of that queen was recalled with longing
by Spaniards under the degenerate Hapsburg rulers; in
later centuries the figure of Isabella continued to symbol-
ize the happiest epoch in the history of the nation; and
the wheel of that memory yet continues to turn and arouse
nostalgia in the minds of all who yearn for a return of
'that divine mode of governing.' " [4]

For some historians, to be sure, the fame of the Catholic Sovereigns has lost part of its luster. Time and the
findings of recent historical study have not dealt altogether kindly with the political and even the moral repu-
tations of Ferdinand and Isabella. Leading Spanish
historians today confirm the verdict of Isabella's contemporaries that the establishment of the Inquisition and the
expulsion of the Jews had a disastrous effect on Spain's
economy. These historians also attribute to the agrarian and pastoral policies of the Catholic Sovereigns the
growth of such evils as deforestation and land monopoly,
which led to a terrifying food crisis at the end of the

reign; they even minimize the industrial achievements of the monarchs. To the scandal of some Spaniards, a revisionist trend in Spanish historical writing brands Isabella a usurper, a principal in an unholy plot to wrest the throne of Castile from its rightful heir, the injured Juana, la Beltraneja.

What the figures of the Catholic Sovereigns have lost in ideal perfection through the revelation of blemishes on their record, they have gained in actuality, in human interest. They continue to loom large against the baroque background of their violent and ambiguous time, a time of difficult transition from the feudal to the modern world. The Spanish people honor them for their services to national unity, for their hard-working devotion to the common good as they understood it. The contradictions in their policies, the incorrect decisions that nullified some of the sound part of their work, resulted from more than personal errors of judgment; they reflected the antagonisms, the structural weakness, the backwardness of Spanish society, as it emerged from seven centuries of struggle against the Moor.

The Spain of Ferdinand and Isabella is the starting point of American history. From the land of the last knights-errant and the last crusade Columbus sailed in search of the Emperor of Cathay and the gold-roofed temples of Cipango. Palos holds as large a place as Plymouth in the story of our beginnings. Yet the American reader who would learn about the life and manners of Isabelline Spain finds little to satisfy his curiosity. Historians have reconstructed in elaborate detail the panorama of English life in the age of colonization.[5] Until now, no book in English has offered a comparable insight into the intricate and colorful Spanish world in which Columbus moved.

More than one hundred and twenty years ago a distinguished American historian, William Hickling Prescott, wrote *The Reign of Ferdinand and Isabella the Cath-olic* (1838). His book was so well conceived and so surely executed that it remains a standard work. The themes of war, court intrigue, and diplomacy, however, were most congenial to Prescott's romantic bent; he did not neglect social and economic developments, but he relegated them to the background of his picturesque canvas. The lower orders of Spanish society, and the round of daily life, he excluded almost completely from his field of vision.

Some eighty years after the appearance of Prescott's book, the late Roger Bigelow Merriman devoted a volume to the reign of the Catholic Sovereigns in his *Rise of the Spanish Empire* (1918 to 1934). Merriman dedicated his work "to the honored memory of William Hickling Prescott"; and in the preface to his first volume he paid tribute to "the profound learning, deep insight, and . . . unfailing honesty" of that master historian. Merriman himself displays the sterling qualities he ascribed to Prescott. The Harvard professor moved easily amid a sea of sources; he had a gift for lucid expression and synthesis; his judgments were even more studiously impartial, measured, and massively documented than those of Prescott. However, Merriman was above all a writer of military, political, and diplomatic history. His volume on the Catholic Sovereigns has an admirable chapter on the institutional side of their reign, but the life of Isabelline Spain is missing from his work. Two pages of comments dispose of the art and literature of the period. It was not within the scope of Merriman's book to offer a rounded survey of life and manners in the Spain of Ferdinand and Isabella.

Meanwhile, a young French scholar, Jean Hippolyte Mariéjol,[6] had published a book that achieved this objective with conspicuous success. *L'Espagne sous Ferdinand et Isabelle: Le Gouvernement, les Institutions et les Moeurs* (Paris, 1892) is in a great tradition of French historical scholarship, the tradition of Michelet and Renan. It represents a brilliant fusion of history and literature, of scientific method and sensibility. Mariéjol wears the strong armor of his erudition so lightly that the reader overlooks its presence. His style is fluent and expressive, sometimes lyrical, with occasional flashes of quiet wit. Mariéjol is a historian of the scientific school; but a pleasing romanticism, a warmth that seems to derive from the Midi, flavors his outlook. He is a nineteenth-century liberal who carefully puts aside his liberal preconceptions when treating such a passion-laden subject as the Spanish Inquisition, but he is not indifferent to moral issues. Mariéjol is so steeped in the sources of the period that he has entered completely into its life; this identification of the author with his subject is evident in the section on social life, notably in the delightful chapter on "The Spaniards," with its imaginative and altogether convincing evocation of the men, the manners, the very soul, of fifteenth-century Spain.

Merriman, who drew copiously on Mariéjol's book for his own volume on the Catholic Sovereigns, described it as "by all odds the best general picture of the political, social, and administrative system of the Spanish kingdoms in the period of the Catholic Kings," adding that "the book is so entertainingly written that the casual reader might be deceived into thinking it superficial; careful perusal, however, will speedily reveal the sound and thorough scholarship which forms the basis for the entire work." [7]

Almost seventy years have elapsed since the publication of Mariéjol's work. The book is as fresh, as vivid, as pulsing with life, as in the year of its appearance. In the main, its conclusions require no revision. However, historical scholarship does not stand still. During the long interval some new material has been discovered, and old materials have been scrutinized from new points of view. Conspicuous among the new interpretations are those bearing on the accession to the throne of Isabella the Catholic, the Spanish Inquisition, and the economic and social policies of the Catholic Sovereigns.

The older historians were not content to proclaim the contributions of Isabella to the unity and greatness of Spain. They must clothe her not only with beauty and talent but with all the private virtues; they strove to banish the least doubt concerning the legitimacy of her royal title. Since Isabella came to the throne in the sequel to a dynastic quarrel and war of succession, these historians had to deal harshly with her chief opponents, her half-brother, King Enrique IV, and his daughter Juana. Briefly, this is the account of the traditional history.

Enrique IV was a weak, incompetent ruler, unable to cope with the feudal anarchy and violence that engulfed Spain under the last Trastamaras. This was not all. "The personal aspect and private life of the new monarch," says Merriman, "were calculated . . . to enhance the dissatisfaction created by his career." [8] "Having been addicted from his earliest youth to debauchery," says Prescott in a finely turned phrase, "when [Enrique IV] had lost the power, he retained all the relish, for the brutish pleasures of a voluptuary." [9] His daughter Juana, born in 1462, was probably illegitimate, the fruit of a liaison between the queen and the royal favorite, Beltrán de la Cueva. Popular discontent with the sway of the unmanly king combined with baronial discontent at the overweening influence of the queen's lover to produce rebellion. The outraged nobles proclaimed, first, the king's brother

Alfonso, a child of eleven, and, after his death, the Infanta Isabella, as legal heir to the crown of Castile. By the pact of Toros de Guisando (1468) the king formally recognized Isabella as legal heiress of the realm and tacitly admitted the illegitimacy of his daughter.

The king's efforts to annul the concessions he had made, and to prevent the marriage of Isabella to Ferdinand, son of the King of Aragón, proved unsuccessful. Ferdinand, stealing romantically across hostile territory to Isabella's side, was married to her on October 19, 1469. The death of Enrique IV brought Isabella to the throne of Castile (1474). A dynastic war (1475 to 1479) in which Portugal supported the claims of Juana, known in history as la Beltraneja, ended in victory for Ferdinand and Isabella and ushered in a glorious reign.

One or another of the older historians had voiced an occasional doubt as to the validity of this version of the succession struggle. In the twentieth century the doubts grow stronger, and the subject began to be intensively explored. The historian J. B. Sitges upheld the claims of Juana in a scholarly work, *Enrique IV y la Excelente Señora* (Madrid, 1912). The late Gregorio Marañón, a physician as well as a historian, concluded on the basis of the available medical evidence that Juana was probably legitimate.[10] Most recently, the noted historian Orestes Ferrara brought the revisionist movement to its climax with a remarkable book, *L'Avènement d'Isabelle la Catholique* (Paris, 1958). Subjecting the familiar sources to a rigorous criticism, Ferrara placed the succession struggle in a challenging new light. The force of his arguments is often difficult to resist. Ferrara's thesis may be summarized as follows:

The struggle over the succession was an incident in a complex sociopolitical revolution that pervaded all Europe. Enrique IV was neither a weakling nor a sexual degenerate; he was a brave and astute ruler whose chief faults were an excessive generosity and an ill-timed desire to avoid the shedding of blood. Enrique's misfortune was to reign in a time of transition when the forces making for the triumph of royal absolutism over feudal anarchy had not matured; Isabella, coming to the throne under more favorable circumstances, rode "the wave of history" to success. The Castilian grandees were menaced in their privileges by the king's efforts to create a new loyal nobility and a personal army that could keep order in the kingdom; that is why they schemed to bring to the throne a weak successor who should be their cat's-paw. This was the meaning of their successive proclamations of the child Alfonso and the youthful Isabella as legal heirs to the throne.

Fraudulent charges of impotence against the king and of illegitimacy against his daughter Juana were made to justify this usurpation. Yielding to superior force, at Toros de Guisando the king recognized Isabella as heiress of the realm, but he never admitted his daughter Juana to be illegitimate; this charge is based on interpolation or destruction of official documents, and on the distortions of Isabella's official chroniclers, Hernando del Pulgar and Alonso de Palencia.

At the center of the spider-web of baronial conspiracy was Juan II of Aragón, plotting to add Castile to his son Ferdinand's heritage through marriage of the prince with Isabella. By supporting this marriage project the Castilian grandees unwittingly prepared their own downfall. They defeated Enrique IV only to fall into the strong and energetic hands of the Catholic Sovereigns.

Not content with branding Isabella a usurper, Ferrara exposes as illusions some of the most cherished notions of patriotic Spaniards. The marriage of Ferdinand and Isabella was no love match: "One cannot speak of love between two young people who, without any previous acquaintance, reach the marriage bed after having seen each other twice." Isabella had no choice in the matter; the marriage was willed by the powerful Aragonese faction in Castile, on which rested all Isabella's hopes for attaining the throne. Neither party to the marriage cherished noble dreams of Iberian unity. "At this period the possibility of a union of the two crowns, not to speak of the two states, inspired fear rather than joy on both sides of the frontier." [11]

Ferrara's book serves to correct an apparent historical injustice to Enrique IV—as tragic and complex a figure as may be found in the history of the time; to his high-spirited, lusty wife; and to their daughter Juana, who is shown defending her claims with an admirable courage, dignity, and constancy. The book has the additional merit of sweeping away some of the romantic haze that obscures our view of the Catholic Sovereigns, of reducing them to life-size figures, of calling attention to the forces of social and economic change that made possible their constructive work. Ferrara seeks to give Isabella her due; he recognizes her "implacable energy"; he concedes that under her scepter "Castile was pacified, the Moors were expelled from the Peninsula, and the Spanish people acquired a certain degree of homogeneity. Spain appeared in its unity, and America was discovered." [12] To have presided over events of such magnitude is a sufficient claim to greatness.

Mariéjol's chapter on the Spanish Inquisition represents a serious effort to explain, without justifying, the religious policies and climate of opinion of Spain under the Catholic Sovereigns. It strikes telling blows at the *leyenda negra* of Spanish cruelty and intolerance. Its thesis, once revolutionary, is now a familiar and widely accepted one. We must not condemn the Catholic Sovereigns, urges Mariéjol, for not holding the viewpoint of a more enlightened time. Spaniards regarded the Jews and Moslems as alien elements within the Spanish nation; heresy they regarded as the most heinous of crimes. The forced conversions, the expulsions, the burnings, were so many devices for cementing the political and religious unity of the Spanish people.

This explanation contains a large element of truth, but it does not fit all the complex facts of the case. More than a passion for religious and political unity, or a wish to placate popular fanaticism and resentment of Jewish wealth, determined the religious policies of the Catholic Sovereigns.

To begin with, religious intolerance and racial hatred were not ingrained or ancestral Spanish traits. The "ancient hates" of which Mariéjol speaks were really not very ancient. H. C. Lea[13] has shown that down to the close of the thirteenth century the relations between Jews, Christians, and Moslems in Christian Spain were so close and neighborly as to provoke protests on the part of the Church. These relations began to deteriorate markedly in the fourteenth century. Efforts by the clergy to arouse ill-will toward the Jews played a part in this process, as did also popular resentment, at a time of rapid growth of a money economy, of certain specialized Jewish economic activities, such as usury and tax farming, which caused severe hardship to peasants and other groups. The rise of anti-Semitism was reflected in the adoption of repressive legislation by the crown and especially in a wave of great pogroms.

A recent writer, M. J. Aragoneses, has called attention to another factor, that of class rivalry, in the development of Spanish anti-Semitism.[14] Spanish monarchs of the late Middle Ages faced difficult economic problems. The growing complexity of the machinery of government, the needs of the new standing army, required large revenues. Meanwhile the royal income tended to decline because of the growing social and political power of the nobility, who obtained lavish grants of lands and fiscal rights from the kings. The Cortes, in which the towns played a decisive role, jealously guarded its control over taxes and strictly limited the size of its subsidies.

In this situation, the crown attempted to meet its growing financial needs by developing new sources of revenue that did not require parliamentary approval—export and import duties, state monopolies, and the like. The success of this new fiscal policy required the cooperation and prosperity of the crown's numerous Jewish subjects. In the first place, their tribute payments composed a large portion of the crown income. In the second place, the kings preferred to employ Jews in the collection of taxes and in other fiscal capacities, not so much because of their special talents in this direction as because they were politically reliable. The creation of a new state apparatus required loyal collaborators. The crown could not rely on the nobility and the burghers, whose class interests ran counter to the royal program of centralized absolutism.

The growing role and influence of Jews in the government aroused bitter resentment on the part of the privileged classes, the nobles and the burghers. When the power of the Jews was broken or seriously diminished by the great pogroms and the repressive legislation of the fourteenth and fifteenth centuries, a new social class, the *conversos,* or Jewish converts to the Catholic faith, arose to take their place. The *conversos* achieved an extraordinary prosperity and influence as tax farmers, court physicians, councilors, ambassadors, and in many other capacities. Unhampered by feudal traditions, intellectually curious, intensely ambitious, the *conversos,* like their un-

converted brethren, had to incur the hostility of the medieval Church, nobility, and burghers. Whether heretics
or not, they posed a threat to the old ruling classes and
a feudal order based on landed wealth and hereditary
status. "The principle of social stratification," says Aragoneses, "was being shattered."

This process helps to explain the policy of the Catholic
Sovereigns toward the Jews and *conversos;* it helps to explain why monarchs who had surrounded themselves with
Jewish and *converso* advisers established the Inquisition
and expelled the Jews from Spain. When the crown had
tamed the feudal nobility and subjected the towns to its
will, when it had acquired large new sources of revenue,
its dependence on the Jews and *conversos* was reduced:
These groups became dispensable. The sacrifice of the
Jews and *conversos* sealed the alliance between the absolute monarchy and the feudal Church and nobility.

The *conversos* were the first to feel the blows of religious persecution, with the establishment of the Inquisition in 1480 and 1481. These blows nearly coincided with
the passage at the Cortes of Toledo of the great Act of
Resumption, by which the nobles surrendered and the
crown gained an annual revenue of 30,000,000 maravedís. The Jews had a breathing space of twelve years.
"The war with Granada was calling for large expenditures, to which the Jews were most useful contributors,
and the finances were in the hands of two leading Jews,
Abraham Senior and Isaac Abravanel, to whose skillful
management its ultimate success was largely due." [15] The
surrender of Granada brought near the liquidation of the
Jewish problem. "With the accession of a rich territory
and an industrious Moorish population, and the cessation
of the drain of the war, even Ferdinand might persuade
himself that the Jews were no longer financially indispensable." [16] After some hesitation, the sovereigns yielded

to pressure from feudal forces and signed the edict of expulsion of the Jews on March 30, 1492.

The experience of the Moriscos, or converted Moors, provides additional evidence that a passion for religious and political unity was not the only determinant of Spain's religious policy at this period. Although many Moriscos were Christian in name alone, and lived in coastal areas exposed to Moslem invasion from Africa, the mass of this alien population was not disturbed for more than a century after the conquest of Granada. Not until 1609 did an order for the expulsion of the Moriscos from Spain go forth. According to Professor Earl J. Hamilton, however, the failure of wages and prices to reflect the expulsion of 1609 to 1614 "strongly suggests that few Moors were expelled." [17] In this case, it appears, the nobility subordinated religious and political ideals to economic advantage by shielding their Moorish tenants and farm laborers against expulsion.

The economic consequences of the Inquisition and the expulsion of the Jews undoubtedly contributed to the picture of economic decay that Spain presented by the close of the sixteenth century. The blows struck at the Jews and *conversos* fell on a large and important segment of Spain's merchant and manufacturing class, the group that in other lands was transforming economic life and preparing the way for the Industrial Revolution.[18] The anti-Semitic policies of the Catholic Sovereigns led to a mass flight of Jewish and *converso* capital from Spain, and thus conflicted with other royal dispositions in favor of trade and industry. Moreover, the *conversos* were the basic artisan class of Spain, and their exodus forced the sovereigns to issue edicts (1484) encouraging foreign artisans to settle in the country.[19]

For Spanish science and thought in general the consequences of the religious policies of the sovereigns were no less serious. The Inquisition blighted the spirit of free inquiry and discussion in Spain at a time when the Renaissance was giving an extraordinary impulse to the play of intellect in all fields.[20] The Catholic Sovereigns, who laid the foundations of Spain's greatness in so short a time, bear no small part of the responsibility for its premature decline.

Mariéjol's chapter on economic policy is a concise, informing, yet readable and even sprightly treatment of what in other hands might prove an arid topic. He rightly praises the sovereigns' reform of the currency, their removal of barriers to internal trade, their encouragement to domestic industry, shipping, and foreign commerce. However, in discussing the woeful consequences for agriculture of the policy of favoring the Mesta, the powerful sheep raisers' corporation, he shifts most of the blame to later rulers. He does not discuss the economic repercussions of the religious policies of the Catholic Sovereigns. The chapter closes on a eulogistic note. "The country was prosperous and happy. As if the very elements had conspired to smile upon the sovereigns, after their time Spain ceased to enjoy the genial seasons and abundant harvests that had favored the reign of Ferdinand and Isabella."

Mariéjol wrote before the intensive investigations of Julius Klein, Earl J. Hamilton, and other students had shed new light on various phases of Spanish economic history. Modern Spanish historians, basing themselves on these studies and on careful rereading of contemporary sources, view less favorably the economic policies of the Catholic Sovereigns. The criticism of these historians centers on the agrarian policies of the sovereigns. Older writers tended to attribute the depopulation of the Spanish countryside, the rise of a horde of vagrants and beggars, and other undesirable conditions that became glaringly manifest in the seventeenth century, to the work of Hapsburg princes. Recent summaries of Spanish economic history find the roots of these conditions in the era of the Catholic Sovereigns.[21]

Of decisive importance, in the view of recent writers, was the bias shown by the sovereigns in favor of the economic and social interests of the aristocracy. This bias becomes more understandable when it is recalled that Ferdinand and Isabella were linked by a maze of blood ties with the Enríquez and other great noble clans of Castile and Aragón. If the aristocracy lost its political power under the Catholic Sovereigns, nothing of the kind happened in the economic and social spheres. One estimate vividly suggests the economic and social predominance of the aristocracy: Around 1500 this class, numbering about 2 or 3 per cent of the population of Spain, owned some 95 per cent of the soil of the country.

In Catalonia, to be sure, Ferdinand intervened in the fearful struggles between the serfs, the *payeses de remensa*, and their feudal lords, to bring about a solution relatively favorable to the peasantry. His arbitral sentence of Guadalupe (1486) ended serfdom in Catalonia and enabled 50,000 peasants to become small landowners.

In Castile, however, no agrarian reform took place; on the contrary, concentration of landownership markedly increased under the Catholic Sovereigns. The Cortes of 1480, which compelled the nobility to surrender the lands and revenues usurped from the crown since 1464, explicitly authorized the nobles to retain the vast holdings acquired prior to the reign of Enrique IV. "Since these usurpations were the most important ones," says Professor Jaime Vicens Vives, "we may affirm that the law of 1480 only ratified the absolute predominance of the noble class over the State and the rest of the country." Other developments favorable to the growth of land monopoly were the institution by the Catholic Sovereigns of *mayo-razgo* or entailment (Leyes de Toro, 1505); the fusion of the lands of great noble families through marriage; and a policy of distribution of conquered lands that assigned a lion's share to the grandees. Thus, after 1492, when Granada was conquered from the Moors, most of the land passed into the hands of the nobility; only in the western portion of the kingdom were small tracts allotted to members of the middle and lower classes who had fought in the campaign.

As concerns the freedom of movement of the Castil-ian peasantry, the Catholic Sovereigns confirmed (1481) the right of the *solariegos* to leave the land. But since the nobility owned virtually all the land, the liberty of the peasants, as Professor Vicens remarks, was the liberty "to die of hunger."

The policy of the Catholic Sovereigns which has come under the most severe attack was their pastoral policy. By the law of *posesión*, which Klein describes as "by far the most pernicious, and unfortunately the most lasting contribution of Ferdinand and Isabella to the supremacy of the pastoral industry over agriculture," Mesta members secured undisturbed permanent occupancy of the fields of landowners, sometimes on the flimsiest of pretexts. The privilege granted the shepherds to cut enough branches from trees to make corrals, fences, or fuel, to trim or even fell trees whenever pasturage was scarce, and the practice of burning the trees in autumn to provide better spring pasturage, had the most devastating results. "This reign was indeed the critical period in the history of Castil-ian forestry," says Klein, "and the desolation which was wrought on the wooded areas of the kingdom had its be-ginnings in the uncompromising partiality of Ferdinand and Isabella for the pastoral industry." [22]

Klein ascribes the pastoral policies of the sovereigns

to their desire to secure large quantities of gold and other economic advantages from abroad through the export of wool. Professor Vicens adds a closely related motive: the need to overcome the financial crisis faced by the crown from 1484 as a result of the flight of *converso* capital and the subsequent exodus of the Jews. "Quick remedies were needed, and the export of wool was nearest to hand." This comment again brings into focus the intimate relation between the religious and the socioeconomic policies of the sovereigns.

Those policies had their natural result in the form of a devastating food crisis toward the end of the reign. The contemporary chronicler Andrés Bernáldez, in his *Historia de los reyes católicos,* paints in darkest colors the conditions in the Castilian countryside during the famines of 1502 to 1503 and 1506 to 1507. "Many places were depopulated . . . , and fathers and mothers wandered down the roads carrying their children, dead of hunger, on their backs." Only massive importations of foreign grain checked the ravages of the Great Hunger. Vicens emphasizes that the famine of 1506 was the result, not of a series of adverse climatologic circumstances, but of a faulty economic structure produced by such factors as excessive protection for sheep-raising, the expulsion of the Moriscos of Granada, and, above all, a policy favorable to the growth of large landed estates.

The traditional history taught that the Catholic Sovereigns gave a great stimulus to Spanish industrial advance. "I must confess," says Professor Vicens, "that I do not find evidence to support this assertion." Santiago Sobrequés Vidal believes that the importance of the so-called industrial "renaissance" should not be exaggerated, since in most cases it amounted to the production of luxury goods in small quantities or production for a local market. The only true industries of the era, says Vicens, were the iron industry of the North and the cloth manufactures of the Castilian central zone. The silk industry of Granada enjoyed a certain prosperity, but only until the revolt of the Moriscos in 1503, after which it fell into decline. Shortages of capital and skilled labor, aggravated by the anti-Semitic measures of the sovereigns, acted as a decisive brake upon industrial expansion.

Spanish industry in this period was typically carried on in the home, and usually with the aid of only a small number of paid workers. Vicens notes that whereas before 1475 the Castilian monarchs had been hostile to guilds, under the Catholic Sovereigns the guild system on the rigid Catalan model was introduced into the Castilian towns, under crown auspices. In this the sovereigns did Castilian industry no service, for they fastened the strait jacket of guild organization upon it precisely at the time when the discovery and colonization of the New World, the influx of American gold and silver, and the resulting economic upsurge challenged Spanish industry to transform its techniques, lower costs, increase output and quality, and thereby establish Spanish economic as well as political supremacy in Europe.

This translation of Mariéjol's book seeks to be faithful to the meaning of the French original and to retain its attractive stylistic qualities. In the course of my work, however, it became obvious that certain changes in the text were needed to increase the book's interest and usefulness for the modern reader. Mariéjol sometimes assumes more knowledge of the facts of Spanish and European history than the average reader possesses. I have elaborated some of his offhand allusions to make them more informative; I have explained more difficult references in notes bearing the abbreviation "Ed." I have also used notes to define some terms not given in the Glossary of Terms, or to call attention to the controversial or doubtful character of some of Mariéjol's statements. I have corrected errors of dating and have revised a few statements not in conformity with present-day scholarship. I have not, however, undertaken to annotate every statement from which one or another modern specialist might dissent. Both the Glossary of Terms and the Glossary of Persons are my own additions.

Mariéjol attempted in many cases to translate sums of Spanish money into equivalent sums of francs of his time. I have omitted these equivalents and have not tried to supply counterparts in American dollars. However, my Glossary of Terms defines the coins mentioned in the text and gives their value in pre-1934 gold dollars. The reader may also gain some idea of the value or purchasing power of Isabelline coins from these facts: The ducado, or ducat, fixed at 375 maravedís by the Ordinance of Medina del Campo of 1497, would pay the wages of a skilled mason or carpenter for about eight days, of a common laborer for about twenty days; or it would purchase 187 pounds of bread of fair quality in normal years, or about 20 pounds of veal of medium grade. Food and lodging at an inn seems to have cost a minimum of 9 maravedís a day. It may also be of interest to recall that in 1487 Columbus was given a retaining fee of 12,000 maravedís a year—$83 in U. S. pre-1934 dollars. This, says Samuel E. Morison, "was the pay of an able seaman, enough to support a man of Columbus's simple tastes, if paid regularly."

Benjamin Keen

Nutley, New Jersey
August 1960

Contents

Part Three
SOCIAL LIFE

Part Four
INTELLECTUAL LIFE

Maps and Tables

THE SPAIN OF
FERDINAND AND ISABELLA

Introduction

Until the fifteenth century Spain participated only from afar in the general movement of European affairs. The different kingdoms sharing the Peninsula were individually too weak to pursue an energetic foreign policy. The marriage of Ferdinand of Aragón and Isabella of Castile, and the union of these two most powerful Spanish states, were needed to make a place for Spain in the Christian world.

War against the infidel had been the great if not the only preoccupation of the Spanish mind. When the Gothic empire fell under Moslem blows on the plains of the Guadalete (711), the remnants of the defeated army took refuge in the mountains of Asturias and took Pelayo for their leader and king. Whereas the majority of the Christian population accepted the yoke of the Arab and Berber conquerors, this little band engaged the invaders in a war that was marked by astounding successes and terrible reverses; and that ended after seven centuries in the liberation of all the conquered territory. This long crusade explains the principal traits of the Spanish character: the somber fanaticism of the people, its military qualities, its impotence in practical matters, and its heroism. The configuration of the land, the immense extent of

the mountain chains to the north, which served as a retreat for the fighters for independence, favored the development of separate centers of resistance and conse-
quently the formation of numerous states: Portugal,
Castile, León, Navarre, Aragón, Catalonia.

For three centuries the pace of the Gothic advance was
slow. This was the brilliant epoch of the Caliphate.
The Ommiads (756 to 1031) joined the arts to the
glory of empire in their court at Córdoba; a careful
husbandry enriched the soil. The raids made by the
mountaineers hardly disturbed the quiet of the Moorish
conquerors, living amid a delightful climate, wealth,
and grandeur; they responded with raids of their own,
burning down Christian houses and villages. But the
good fortune of the Caliphate passed with the passing of
its able princes. The Moslems were not immune to that
pervasive influence which in the Middle Ages destroyed
the authority of the central government, partitioned sovereignty, and limited the purview of each kingdom to the
narrow horizon of an ignorant population. The *walís*
(governors) proclaimed themselves independent and
took the title of king at Córdoba, Seville, Málaga, Granada, and elsewhere. These divisions hastened the progress of the Christians, whose forward march never
ceased. The Moslems appealed for the aid of the Almohades or the Almorávides, but to no purpose, for their
powerful intervention only postponed the day of ruin.
Softened by the sweetness of their sky, weakened by their
discords, the Moslems had to succumb before the irresistible advance of the Spaniards.

While the infidels employed all their energy in fighting each other, the Christians redoubled their efforts.
Ferdinand I, who united Castile and the Kingdom of
León under his rule, overwhelmed the Moors at Coimbra, in Portugal. His son, Alfonso VI (1072 to 1109),

conquered Toledo and the kingdom of that name. The King of Aragón and Navarre, Alfonso I, the Battler, seized the important town of Zaragoza (1118). Some years later another Alfonso, Affonso Henriques, son of Count Henri of Burgundy, captured Lisbon and had himself acknowledged as King of Portugal at the Cortes of Lamego.[1] Thus, while the Castilians and the Portuguese occupied the whole line of the Tagus, the Aragonese seized the two banks of the Ebro. The victory of Las Navas de Tolosa (1212) shattered the last great effort of Islam and consolidated all the earlier Christian conquests. From that moment it was perfectly clear what race and what religion were to possess the Peninsula.

The definitive union of León and Castile (1230) inaugurated a new period of successes. Ferdinand III, the Saint, King of Castile, contemporary and emulator of St. Louis, captured Córdoba, the principal bastion of the Arab empire, in 1236. He crossed the Guadalquivir, took Écija, Baena, and Jaén in 1240; and in 1248 he entered Seville, which gave him control of the mouth of the river and communications with the sea. By the time St. Ferdinand died in 1252, he had rolled the ancient masters of Spain back upon that massif of the Sierra Nevada from which they withstood for two centuries the assault of their enemies. Reduced to the defensive, blockaded on the east by Valencia, on the north by Córdoba, Seville, and Jaén, they could only prolong their occupancy without hope of regaining a lost supremacy. The Castilian monarch died just as he was preparing to cross the sea to occupy the African ports from which arms, provisions, and soldiers were sent to Málaga and Gibraltar. When Ferdinand's death halted this effort at isolation and blockade, the empire of the caliphs had been reduced to the Kingdom of Granada.

The strength of its position, and, above all, the dissensions of the Christians, preserved for two centuries this remnant of a vast empire. Hardly had fear of the Moslems subsided when divisions broke out within the Christian camp. The kings had leaned for support on the towns and nobility, but they had paid dearly for this aid. A turbulent aristocracy claimed for itself all the royal prerogatives, the rights of administering justice and making war; in order to augment the number of their subjects the nobles despoiled the king. The military orders, who constituted the most energetic and warlike part of the nation, joined in the defense of their privileges at the expense of every other part, not excepting the king. The towns, harassed by the lords, lacking adequate protection by the crown, formed defensive brotherhoods (*hermandades*) that often were as much to be feared as the leagues of the nobles. The clergy had the merit of having grafted patriotism on religion and placed faith at the service of the nation, but it made only too plain its determination to be exempt from the laws and the common burdens.

Amid this anarchy Alfonso the Sage, successor to St. Ferdinand, affirmed in the code of the Siete Partidas the omnipotence and divine right of kings.[2] The lords, leagued with his son Sancho the Brave, drove him from Castile and forced him to seek refuge among infidels. The same conflict arrayed sovereigns against subjects in Aragón. Pedro III, who wanted to make foreign policy without consulting the nation, was compelled by a union of burghers and nobles to confirm the ancient liberties of the country. His promise to summon the Cortes every year, and his extension of the powers of the *justicia*,[3] consecrated the victory of the confederates. A counter-offensive by the crown met with varying success in the two kingdoms. In Aragón, Pedro IV, victorious over his subjects at Epila (1348), contented himself with abolishing the right of confederation among the nobility, together with the arrogant privilege which they had claimed of "making war on the king, dethroning him if it were necessary, and choosing another king in his place, though that other be a pagan." In Castile, Pedro the Cruel or the Just, incapable of controlling his ambition and grudges, rained terror and punishments on his Castilian nobles. The day came when he was abandoned by all and fell into the hands of his half-brother Enrique de Trastamara, who killed him with a dagger (1369) and ended the legitimate line of Pelayo.

The reign of this dynasty, begun with a fratricide, was the golden age of the aristocracy. Enrique II, its founder, was skillful enough to maintain order at the price of numerous concessions. Besides, the prestige of success and bitter memories of the cruelties of his predecessor protected Enrique against his turbulent nobles. Under his successors, Juan I and Enrique III, the Sickly, factions raised their heads. Yet it is apparent that the principle of royal authority was continually growing in influence. The crown commanded such respect that the different factions disputed the influence attached to the privilege of being the royal favorite. Thus, by a contradiction not infrequent in history, the crown was never so weak as at the moment when its supremacy ceased to be contested. The Condestable Álvaro de Luna, who in the reign of Juan II tried to turn to his own advantage this movement of opinion, raised all the great lords against himself. He was defeated and paid with his head for his stern exercise of power. Juan II, who had long been under his favorite's influence, abandoned him to the victors of the day. This monarch made up for his weakness by the dignity of his manners, his delicate tastes, and his literary culture.

His son, Enrique IV, had none of these qualities: Not

content with handing the government over to his favorites, he admitted them to the intimacy of his queen,
Juana of Avis, and dishonored himself by a compla-
cence that appeared to be the result of calculation. The
nation regarded him as impotent; though he had a
daughter, Doña Juana, public opinion assigned her paternity to Beltrán de la Cueva, crony and habitual guest
of the king, who made him Duke of Alburquerque. By
her weaknesses this ardent, flirtatious queen may have

served her husband's unscrupulous desire for an heir. This shameful business, joined to the familiar causes of disorder, caused almost all Castile to rise. On the plains of Ávila the lords proceeded solemnly to depose a scorned king and to proclaim as king his brother Don Alfonso. The death of the pretender saved Enrique IV. His enemies, remaining under arms, turned to his sister Isabella and proposed that she assume the role of Alfonso. This intelligent, beautiful, and energetic daughter of Juan II had too strong a respect for the principle of royal authority to compromise herself in a revolt, but she utilized the general discontent to extract from her brother acknowledgment of herself as presumptive heiress and a formal repudiation of la Beltraneja. The hardpressed king consented to ratify his own dishonor; he disavowed his wife's child and assured the throne to Isabella.

However, he could not resign himself to this humiliation; the talents of this inconstant prince were next devoted to annulling the concessions that the Cortes had solemnly ratified. Now he negotiated the marriage of his alleged daughter to a foreign prince, now he granted the hand of Isabella to one or another unworthy aspirant, such as Pedro Girón, Grand Master of Calatrava. Enrique IV was intent on denying his sister the aid of an intelligent energetic husband and the support of a powerful state in order to ensure the triumph of Doña Juana, whom he insisted on regarding as his own flesh and blood. The friends of the Princess of Asturias, on the other hand, were interested for a variety of reasons in securing for her a husband in a neighboring kingdom, some young man of great promise. Ferdinand, son of the King of Aragón, satisfied all their wishes. He was Isabella's cousin, and of about the same age. Although barely nineteen, he had already shown a good deal of courage and prudence. His father,

Juan II, had made himself sadly memorable by his clashes with Don Carlos de Viana, his son by a first wife, Blanche of Navarre. On the death of his mother, Carlos had claimed the Kingdom of Navarre, but Don Juan refused to surrender it. The Navarrese and the Catalans embraced the cause of Don Carlos out of hatred for the King of Aragón, who respected neither their liberties nor their particularist tendencies. Thus the history of Aragón and that of Castile presented a remarkable parallelism; the insurrection of the subjects of the crown of Aragón corresponded to the revolt of the Castilian lords; the struggle of Juan II with Don Carlos reproduced in tragic proportions the differences of Enrique IV and Isabella.

Juan II, married a second time to a Castilian lady, Juana Enríquez, had only a tepid affection for the child of his first bed, and a jealous stepmother fought even that lukewarm attachment. Juana Enríquez, Ferdinand's mother, grieved to see her own son reduced to the position of a cadet of the blood royal. The death of Don Carlos carried Ferdinand to the steps of the throne (1461). Juan II had as much love as his wife for this child of his old age. Not satisfied with leaving Aragón and Sicily to his son, he dreamed of adding Castile thereto by a marriage. The ambitions of the old king and the fears of Isabella's friends were at one in urging a union of the presumptive heirs. The efforts of Enrique IV to frustrate this project failed. Ferdinand, alive to the pleasure of winning a wife and a kingdom at one stroke, journeyed in disguise to Valladolid, where the marriage took place (1469).

It was a great event. The death of Enrique IV in 1474 and the coming of Isabella to the throne, the death of Juan II of Aragón (1479) and the accession of Ferdinand to the throne, gave it its full significance. The two most powerful Spanish kingdoms were to act in concert for the first time. Before the reign of Ferdinand and Isabella each of the different states of the Peninsula had its own history. With the new reign their interests were joined, and the general history of Spain began. In both kingdoms the crown gained strength in its struggle against disturbers of peace of every rank and origin. In Aragón, separatist agitation no longer had a future; in Castile, the nobility threw its last forces into a war of succession. Everywhere the aristocracy was combated, order re-established, the royal power consolidated. But these benefits came only after terrible ordeals in which the Catholic Sovereigns (that was the name given to the royal pair) had to display extraordinary qualities of bravery, vigor, and pitiless severity. It was no easy work to stamp out the anarchy bred by a half-century of veritable interregnum.

Part One

THE REIGN OF
FERDINAND AND ISABELLA

I

The End of Anarchy

The foreign policy of the Catholic Sovereigns is the most
brilliant and celebrated aspect of their reign. The Italian
Wars involved so many European governments, the rise
of Spanish power was linked to so many international alliances, marriages, and conflicts, that the names of Ferdinand and Isabella, praised or damned, appear on almost every page of the history of that period. Their
domestic policy is not so well and universally known,
because it concerned Spain alone. Yet this side of their
work is of capital importance; internal peace explains
their foreign efforts and successes. The restoration of
royal power, the pacification of the country, the repression of disorder of every kind, offer a spectacle as moving as the establishment of Spanish power in Italy.

When Enrique IV of Castile died, the situation was
singularly troubled. This prince left to his successors not
only the heritage of a half-century of factional struggles,
of feudal anarchy, but a war of succession. The kingdom
had first of all to pronounce concerning the rival claims
of Doña Juana, daughter of Enrique IV, and Isabella,
sister of the same king. Isabella, strong in popular approval, boldly seized the vacant throne and had herself
and her husband Ferdinand proclaimed as rulers of Cas-

tile. A part of the aristocracy pronounced against the young queen and allied itself with Affonso, King of Portugal, on the pretext of defending the rights of the infanta; actually it only sought to augment its privileges and increase the disorder that it found so profitable. A Portuguese invasion merged with the civil war to add to the miseries of Castile.

These evils were of very ancient date. The story of aristocratic violence had long constituted almost the whole history of the kingdom. Murders, robberies, arson, injuries, riots, tumults, challenges, brawls, conspiracies —such are the words that accumulate under the pen of the contemporary chronicler, Hernando del Pulgar; according to him they were the only words capable of describing the state of the kingdom under Isabella's predecessor. The countryside had become a desert; feudal bandits terrorized the highways; a private person was in constant danger of his life. "And all this because the office of king is vacant, as it were (*y esto porque falta el oficio del Rey*)." [1]

The absence of that moderating force was truly the great evil of Spain. There were factions which struggled for power; there was no government. To rescue Castile from the abyss into which it had fallen thanks to the weakness of Juan II and the inertia of Enrique IV required strong hands and an energetic effort. Isabella and Ferdinand were equal to the task. It would be a mistake to represent Isabella as an amiable, gentle person inclined to be merciful to the guilty. This portrait is not verified by history, which shows her to be more inclined to severity than to mercy, and moved to wrath by vice and crime. The goodness of monarchs is all too often a manifestation of their apathy; the queen was not indifferent to social injustices that caused private griefs and ruin to the state. The difficulties of the first days of her reign obliged her to put off the day of retribution, but it was no less exemplary for coming later.

Galicia had been enslaved by lords who secularized the revenues of the churches, terrorized the towns, and devastated the countryside. The villages paid tribute to these brigands of noble blood, whereas the royal officials were never obeyed and had not managed to collect taxes since the reign of Juan II; a hundred tyrants had replaced the lawful master.[2]

In 1481 Ferdinand and Isabella sent to this province a soldier, Don Fernando de Acuña, and a member of the royal council, Garcí López de Chinchilla, with full powers to restore the rule of justice. The troubles were so ancient, the country so accustomed to the domination of the lords and the impotence of the royal government, that the deputies of the towns and cities of Galicia who were assembled at Santiago de Compostela hesitated to furnish the royal envoys with the resources needed to restore order. They told these envoys that they would have to have powers from the King of Heaven as well as from the earthly king to punish the oppressors of the land. But Acuña and Chinchilla were energetic men of the kind who inspire confidence by the vigor of their first blows. They struck down the guilty without mercy. Taxes began to enter the royal treasury instead of aiding the army of disorder. Forty-seven castles were razed to the ground. An inquest was made into past events, and several persons of note, such as Pedro de Miranda and the Marshal Pedro Pardo de Cela, were executed. These "great days" of Galicia inspired such salutary terror in criminals that more than fifteen hundred thieves and assassins fled a province where such strict justice prevailed.

To Seville the queen had proceeded in person;[3] her presence was an indication of the number and quality of the culprits. Andalusia was a prey to two factions, one headed by the Duke of Medina Sidonia, the other by the Marquis of Cádiz.[4] These powerful grandees, who between them shared almost the whole territory of the province, contended for power in armed struggle. Begun in 1471 in the streets of Seville, it had spread throughout the whole country. Even the governors of fortresses had joined the quarrel in disregard of the royal wishes. The civil war had attracted adventurers and thieves under its banners; it had fired passions, given license to every appetite, and provoked violent men to murder and assassination. As a result, when Isabella began to give audience to the oppressed, complaints came thick and fast. At her Friday assizes, she redressed injuries, punished crimes, returned homes and fields to persons who had been despoiled of them. She passed two entire months in the work of reparation, but investigation brought ever new crimes to light. The acts of violence, the murders, the thefts, "were so numerous that in my opinion there were few persons in Seville free of fault: some for having committed some offense, others for having kept it silent, still others for having committed that same offense in another manner and in other circumstances." [5]

The queen would not stop punishing until she had seized every guilty party. More than four thousand persons of uneasy conscience left the city and took refuge in Portugal and even among the Moors. Only the solemn supplications of the Bishop of Cádiz, Alonso de Solís, surrounded by the notables of Seville and followed by a weeping throng composed of the wives of the fugitives, at last succeeded in calming the sovereign's wrath. She consented to publish a general pardon, but excepted from the amnesty certain categories of criminals whom she condemned to exiles of varying length or even to perpetual punishment.

To make these examples effective, to prolong the terrible impression made by the executions, required a system of vigilant police ready to strike at all points and at all hours.

The towns, with their fortified *enceintes,* were in a measure protected from sudden attack, but the countryside, the villages, the roads, remained at the mercy of evildoers of every rank. Moved by the sight of such great misery, two men, Alonso de Quintanilla, Chief Royal Auditor (Contador Mayor de Cuentas), and Don Juan de Ortega, General Vicar of Villafranca de Montes de Oca, proposed to the sovereigns that they form a Hermandad of the towns.[6] This was not a new thing; in the twelfth and thirteenth centuries a number of municipal councils had joined forces to hunt down brigands. These leagues or brotherhoods united all the citizens of a single town or associated several towns in a common enterprise. Quintanilla and Ortega proposed to revive and extend throughout the kingdom, under the official patronage of the crown, an institution that hitherto had been limited to a single district or province and had always operated outside the sphere of royal authority.

After obtaining the consent of the sovereigns, they communicated with the most influential personages of Burgos, Palencia, Medina del Campo, Olmedo, Ávila, Segovia, Salamanca, and Zamora. The Cortes of Castile convened at Madrigal in April 1476 gave its hearty support to the project. The sovereigns responded by promulgating (April 27) a plan of organization. The next question was one of securing the formal adherence of the towns. Their deputies held a meeting at Dueñas. At first nothing was heard but a chorus of complaints about the unhappy state of Castile. Each man proposed a different remedy, and the assembly, unable to reach a decision, was about to break up when Quintanilla heaped shame upon it for its impotence, assured it of the royal protection, and showed the enterprise to be both useful and easy of accomplishment. What was needed for success? Money; a well-armed force under good commanders; an effective constitution.

The assembly allowed itself to be persuaded, and voted the establishment of a brotherhood for three years. On the basis of the plan outlined in the ordinance of April 27, the Junta of Dueñas drafted its charter, which the monarchs sanctioned on August 13.[7] The jurisdiction of the Santa Hermandad extended to all the territory of the crown of Castile. The nobles, who were interested in maintaining the state of anarchy, were annoyed to see the towns place all their forces at the service of the crown. However, after the Condestable of Castile, Don Pedro Fernández de Velasco, the greatest lord of Old Castile, had instructed his vassals to cooperate with the Hermandad, the other lords reluctantly followed his example.

The Hermandad had as its principal object the suppression of brigandage and the surveillance of the roads and the countryside. To this end all the towns, from the largest to the smallest, raised and maintained at their expense a force designed to perform the role of a rural police. Every inhabited place contributed according to its resources and population; every hundred *vecinos,* or householders, had to equip and maintain one horseman. Strong companies of three hundred, two hundred, or one hundred lances were placed under the command of eight captains. There was a standing body of two thousand troops. The supreme command was assigned to a natural brother of Ferdinand, Alonso de Aragón, Duke of Villahermosa. A treasury supported by fines and municipal taxes supplied the necessary funds. The Hermandad did more than maintain order; its jurisdiction was very extensive. It exercised high and low justice over several types of offenses. To avoid conflicts between ordinary judges and those of the Hermandad the cases falling within its jurisdiction were carefully defined. Five classes of crimes were subject to these extraordinary tribunals.[8] They were:

1. Robbery and murder committed in the open country, in deserted places, and in hamlets of less than one hundred householders; the burning of homes, of harvests, and of vineyards.

2. The same offenses perpetrated in towns and villages if the criminal, having committed a crime, fled across country or took refuge in another place.

3. Housebreaking.

4. Rape.

5. An act of rebellion against the central government.

To settle questions of jurisdiction there was a Supreme Junta composed of a deputy from each province and presided over by Don Lope de Rivas, Bishop of Cartagena. This *diputación general* in turn had in each province a delegate who was a judge of first instance, and who was also responsible for collecting the taxes due to the Hermandad. Ferdinand and Isabella would entrust only to their own agents, Quintanilla and Ortega, the responsibility of deciding the contribution due from the different members of the brotherhood, of choosing the best means of collecting this tax, and of designating the collectors and treasurers. From afar and from on high they directed the administration of the new militia.

By the rapidity of its movements the Hermandad was designed to strike terror in the malefactor. As soon as notice of an act of violence was received, the archers departed in pursuit of the criminal. In all the places through which they passed they raised a hue and cry and were joined by other archers who quickly responded to the alarm. For five leagues these human bloodhounds followed on the criminal's tracks, and when they stopped, the furious chase was taken up by fresh comrades of other towns and villages and ever renewed, lap on lap, until the fugitive had been caught or driven out of the kingdom. There was no refuge for him in the whole extent of the kingdom. The towns had to open their gates to the troops of the Hermandad; the strongholds, once asylums for assassins, could not refuse search. The lords were obliged to receive four or five soldiers empowered to see everything, to visit and inspect everywhere.

A speedy justice and punishment increased the dread inspired by the Hermandad. After being apprehended by the archers, the fugitive was led back to the place where the crime had been committed. There, in a space of three days, the *alcaldes* of the Hermandad, alone or assisted by *alcaldes* of the chief judicial seat of the district, reviewed the facts, pronounced sentence, and ordered it carried out. The penalties meted out were ferocious: For a theft of 500 to 5,000 maravedís, the loss of a leg; for the majority of crimes, death. The execution took place in open country. The formalism of an ancient law, in its naïve cruelty, minutely regulated the details: "The malefactor will be tied to a straight post; this post should not be permitted to take the form of a cross, but the culprit will be fastened to the middle of the post with bonds of wood and his feet made fast with a piece of wood; then his body shall be taken for a target and arrows will be shot at him until he dies." [9] Ferdinand and Isabella dared not abolish this barbarous provision; however, they ordered that in the future criminals should be hanged before being shot. The spirit of humanity was satisfied—but was not the spectacle of a dead man executed a second time even more revolting?

Such great severity moved even contemporaries to

comment. The next generation, which inherited domestic peace without knowing its cost, had some difficulty in reconciling its veneration for Isabella with the memory of her rigors. Francisco López de Villalobos, physician to both Ferdinand and Charles V, well conveys this attitude of a more peaceful time. "In the time of the Catholic Sovereigns of glorious memory, the judges displayed such great severity that it appeared to be cruelty; but then it was necessary, for the kingdoms were far from peaceful and the tyrants and proud men had not yet been abased. That is why veritable butcheries of men were carried out. The executioners cut off feet and hands, shoulders and heads, neither sparing nor veiling the rigor of justice." Villalobos borrows from the surgeon's art a strikingly effective name for these executions, which he calls "terrifying and horrible vivisections." [10]

The Santa Hermandad caused grumbling among its own members for very different reasons. The towns found burdensome the support of an army and an administration. After three years of strenuous effort they demanded its dissolution. But the Portuguese war (1476) and the struggle against the Moors provided the sovereigns with arguments strong enough to convince the Juntas Generales of the necessity of continued sacrifices. During the last crusade to free Spain from the Moslem yoke, archers of the Hermandad campaigned at the side of the feudal contingents, and the brotherhood furnished considerable aid in beasts of burden and money.[11] The institution had changed in object; now it was simply an all-purpose instrument in the royal hands, an ingenious means of securing troops without loosening the royal purse.

As long as Ferdinand and Isabella confronted the menace of the Moors and the great lords they maintained the Hermandad, but they were too jealous of their power

to permit the indefinite existence of a league which could become very dangerous under a weaker sovereign. The desire of lightening the burdens of their subjects and the counsels of prudence pointed in the same direction. Accordingly, in 1498, amid general satisfaction, they suppressed the Supreme Junta, the supreme judges, the captains, and the officers, who received wages in money and in kind. The association was thereby decapitated. The sovereigns left to the members of the Hermandad the election of the *alcaldes* and the platoon leaders (*cuadrilleros*), as well as the responsibility for maintaining the safety of the roads.[12] The Hermandad was thus reduced to the modest proportions of a citizen militia charged with policing the countryside.[13]

The organization of the Santa Hermandad, the suppression of crime, were only expedients, after all, and Ferdinand and Isabella would have shown a total lack of foresight if they had not sought to prevent a return of the same evils. Spain suffered from an excess of vitality and force; the towns, the clergy, and the nobility enjoyed privileges and independence incompatible with social order. These private powers neutralized the royal power and prevented it from exercising its moderating role. As Pulgar rightly observed, all the misfortunes of Castile stemmed from the powerlessness of the crown. Ferdinand and Isabella undertook to impose recognition of their supremacy on all classes; and they reached their goal without brusque changes, without dangerous innovations, without arousing doubt in the Spanish people concerning the import of the changes taking place.

In the struggle against anarchy, the towns had been their loyal allies, but several considerations aroused in the sovereigns a desire to acquire some influence in the municipal councils: the extent of the municipal liberties, the importance and large resources of certain cities, the existence of aristocratic factions which turned city streets and squares into battlefields, the egotistical and limited views of these little centers that could see no farther than their boundary marks and were ready to sacrifice the general advantage to local interest—all the vices and dangers of autonomy, in short. Some of their predecessors, notably Alfonso XI of Castile, had already attempted to restrict the municipal liberties; the anarchy that arose under his successors halted these encroachments.[14]

From the beginning of their reign Ferdinand and Isabella renewed the design of placing royal agents at the head of the municipalities. As early as 1476 the Cortes of Madrigal complained that the kings were sending *corregidores* (such was the title of these agents) into the towns without having consulted their wishes.[15] The deputies of the towns also observed that according to the laws of the kingdom a *corregidor,* appointed for one year, could be renamed for one more year; but they objected that if a *corregidor* stayed longer, he might be drawn into taking sides with one faction or another. The sovereigns were not strongly enough entrenched to risk the displeasure of the towns; they replied that they would conform to the laws. But once they had overcome their first difficulties, they returned to their project. In 1480 they named *corregidores* to all the towns and cities, thus placing them under the royal tutelage.[16]

They employed other means to weaken the independent spirit of the *ayuntamientos* (municipal councils). The action taken by Isabella at Cáceres shows this policy of subordination in practice.[17] At Cáceres, as everywhere else, there were feuds between families and wards. As a result, the annual election of councilmen (*regidores*), of the administrators of the communal properties (*mayordomos*), and of the commissioners of weights and measures (*fieldades*) gave rise to riots and murders. To correct these abuses the queen ordained that no more elections should be held at Cáceres and that its municipal magistrates should henceforth hold office for life. She ordered that these magistrates should be chosen by lot and herself invested them in office, reserving for herself the right of filling all future vacancies. Isabella found that this system, already tried by her predecessors, had the double advantage of securing a council less liable to impulsive acts and of suppressing together with the elections a constant source of disorders. She prescribed the qualifications for eligibility in many places where elections were retained.[18] The royal agents also attempted to weaken the aristocratic element in the municipal councils. In order to secure a more tractable *ayuntamiento,* the *corregidor* of Madrid, Juan de Bobadilla, proposed to admit taxpayers (*pecheros*) into the body. He was disavowed by the sovereigns; but his proposal suggests the liberties that a royal agent might allow himself in regard to the towns.

No less interesting are the relations between Church and state. Isabella, so ardent in her piety, always dis-

played the liveliest solicitude for the clergy and the greatest veneration for the Holy See, but she would never
abandon the crown's rights and prerogatives. The sovereigns gave evidence of their desire to justify their title
of "los Católicos" by the respect with which they surrounded priests and monks, by the high posts that they
gave to bishops in their government, and still more by
their zeal in reforming the Church. When the Cortes of
Toledo (1480) compelled restitution by the great lords
who had managed to wrest so many domains and revenues from the weak Enrique IV, Isabella sanctioned as
definitive the donations made to monasteries and charitable establishments.[19] In Galicia she forced the nobles to
return to the churches the benefices that they had secularized.[20] But although Ferdinand and his wife regarded
this benevolence as the noblest manifestation and use of
their authority, they also believed that Spain's eternal
struggle against the Moslems gave the Kings of Castile
a privileged position among Christian princes, and they
availed themselves of this privileged status to dominate
the clergy and repulse encroachments of the Papal Court.

There is only one recorded case of their allowing an
invasion of their rights. This was at Alcalá de Henares,
whither they came to pass the winter of 1485. As soon as
the monarchs entered the town, the court *alcaldes*
sought, as was the rule, to substitute their courts for all
others, and to subject to their jurisdiction the town and
countryside for five leagues around.[21] Now, Alcalá de
Henares formed a part of the rich ecclesiastical principality which Cardinal Pedro González de Mendoza administered in the name of the Archbishop of Toledo.[22]
The cardinal claimed that royal justice must halt at the
boundaries of his diocese. The queen vainly alleged her
prerogative; nothing would move the stubborn prelate.
To get her way the queen would have had to humiliate

a man who had rendered the greatest services to the royal cause. This time the queen chose to leave the question undetermined while she submitted it for study to a number of legists.

She had no reason, however, to display a like tolerance toward the people of Trujillo when they provoked a similar conflict.[23] The *corregidor* of this town had jailed a man convicted of a crime. The offender demanded trial before an ecclesiastical court on the grounds that he had taken the tonsure. The magistrate refused to release him. Then some priests raised a mob; Cross in hand they went through the streets and incited the people to march on the prison and break in to rescue the prisoner. At this news Isabella sent a considerable body of troops to Trujillo; the principal rebels were hanged and their homes razed. The priests who had instigated the rioting were banished forever from Castile and Aragón.

Ferdinand and Isabella displayed the same firmness in their dealings with the ruling pontiffs. The chair of St. Peter was occupied in this period by unworthy vicars: Sixtus IV, Innocent VIII, Alexander Borgia. Their vices were in glaring contrast with the purity of Isabella; compelled to acknowledge her moral superiority, they felt unable to resist her. Ever since the monks of Cluny had introduced into Spain the maxims of Papal supremacy, the Popes had gradually assumed the right of making appointments to all vacant benefices; they assigned the richest abbeys and the meanest prebends as the interests of the Church or their own whims dictated. The kings often protested against scandalous nominations; but Rome always measured the value of their protests by their power, and the princes of the fifteenth century were anything but powerful. The Cortes had never ceased to protest against the usurpations of the Roman Curia; the national assembly did not obtain satisfaction till the time of Ferdinand and Isabella. In 1482 the see of Cuenca became vacant; the Pope appointed Cardinal San Giorgio to the position.[24] Now the crown was worn by sovereigns jealous of their prerogative. They protested the nomination and sent ambassadors to Rome to explain that their title of Defenders of the Faith gave them patronage of all benefices and that vacant sees must not be filled without their consent. The security of Spain required that only Spaniards should have bishoprics, for there were many fortresses in their jurisdiction, and it was only just that these bastions of Christianity should not be entrusted to foreigners.

Sixtus IV would not heed these remonstrances; Isabella and Ferdinand then ordered all their subjects to leave Rome and threatened the Pope with a summoning of a general council. The Vicar of Christ was hardly in a condition to submit to the scrutiny of the universal Church. He sent a legate who by conciliatory tactics succeeded in reopening negotiations. An agreement was reached (1482). The Pope acknowledged Isabella's right to "supplicate" him in favor of the worthiest candidate in the event of a vacancy among the important sees. It was a major concession.[25]

It is true that the compromise of 1482 reserved for the pontiff control of the smaller benefices. But even in this area his control was gradually whittled away. Sometimes the queen responded to unpalatable nominations by seizure of the benefice; sometimes she finally obtained by her importunities the right of appointment for a certain period. Once she had gotten permission, she hurried to fill all vacancies. In a single day she filled twenty prebends.[26] It is easy to see that in these conditions the authority of the Pope was becoming extremely small. That is why the successor of Sixtus IV attempted to take back the concessions that had been made. In 1485 the Archbishop of Seville, Don Íñigo Manrique, died. In spite of the accord, Innocent VIII named as successor his vice-chancellor, the famous Rodrigo Borgia.[27] But the sovereigns protested, and the Pope yielded again. Two years later the same pontiff granted them patronage of all the churches of the Kingdom of Granada. This assured the future conquerors of the Moslems of control over all benefices in the conquered territory. The Spanish Church, like the towns, was now securely in the hands of the sovereigns. Religion and morality suffered no loss thereby.[28]

But the great, the true, enemy of the crown was the independent and anarchical spirit of the nobility. Its opposition had continued for several centuries without the least profit to the country. No national gain resulted from this struggle; the nobles had no more constructive idea than to hatch league after league that did not even secure their own interests. Their mischievous agitation devastated Spain without making any contribution to the country's future.

At the death of Enrique IV the aristocracy was divided into two hostile parties. One declared for Isabella, the other for La Beltraneja. This last party summoned to its aid the King of Portugal, Affonso V. Taught by experience, Ferdinand and Isabella strove to make impossible the return of factions. They achieved their ends by a blend of energy and diplomacy. It was no easy task to inculcate in the grandees the idea of obedience. More than one example had to be made: The most illustrious families learned by experience, one after the other, to respect the royal wishes. The Duke of Medina Sidonia and the Marquis of Cádiz, whose feud had troubled all Andalusia, were banished from Seville. Córdoba was forbidden to the Marquis of Aguilar and the Count of Cabra for the same reason. A Manrique was Adelantado Mayor of Castile; at the Cortes of Toledo the sovereigns received the complaints of the deputies of the towns against his *alcaldes*. The Duke of the Infantado, head of the house of Mendoza, was sharply rebuked when he dared protest against the establishment of the Santa Hermandad.

The Enríquez', who had blood ties with Ferdinand of Aragón, were treated with no less severity.[29] Don Fadrique Enríquez had a quarrel with another gentleman, Ramiro Núñez de Guzmán. When Isabella learned of the dispute, she ordered the adversaries seized and gave Ramiro Núñez a letter of safeconduct. However, several days later Ramiro Núñez was attacked by three masked men who gave him a beating with sticks. News of this ambush threw the queen into the greatest wrath. She instantly ordered the Almirante Mayor, father of Don Fadrique, to deliver the culprit up to her. Because he pleaded inability, she made him surrender to her his castles of Simancas and Medina de Ríoseco. This show of contempt for the royal authority, and the fatigue caused by her rapid march to take possession of these gages, shattered her frail health. Asked the cause of her illness, she replied: "My body is lame from the blows that Don Fadrique gave yesterday in despite of my safeconduct." When the admiral perceived the queen's wrath, he realized that only total submission could atone for his son's offense; he personally led him to court. Isabella refused to see the young man; she ordered a court *alcalde* to lead him prisoner through the plaza of Valladolid and thence to the castle of Arévalo, where he was kept in close confinement; sometime later she banished him to Sicily (1481).

An order of her council compelled the Duke of Alba to return the town of Miranda, which he had taken from its lawful possessor.[30] She gave another lesson to this proud house of Toledo. The *alcalde mayor* of the duke and the

governor (*alcaide*) of Salvatierra had abused and struck
a royal officer charged with collecting a duty on migratory herds of cattle. A court *alcalde,* Diego de Proano,
secretly left for Salvatierra, surprised the governor, and
hanged him in the very spot where the offense had been
committed. The *alcalde mayor* was brought before the
chancillería of Valladolid, which condemned him to loss
of a hand and banished him from the kingdom.[31] These
examples, made upon such notable persons, "struck
fear into the evil and caused joy in the good."

Together with measures to impose obedience, Isabella took steps to rebuild the crown domains at the
aristocracy's expense. Enrique IV had alienated almost
all the revenues of the crown. So great were the needs of
this prince and so poor was his credit that to obtain
1,000 maravedís in cash he had to assign to the lender
an equal revenue from the public receipts. The grandees
had profited by the king's weakness to secure land grants,
pensions, and the right to collect certain taxes.[32] Thus,
when Ferdinand and Isabella came to the throne, they
found themselves despoiled. During the first years of
their reign they closed their eyes to this spoliation, but in
1480, at the Cortes of Toledo, they welcomed if they did
not actually inspire the protests of the deputies of the
towns.[33] For reasons of tact they summoned the grandees
and explained to them the extreme distress of the royal
treasury.

The aristocracy was not happy over the sacrifices
asked of it, but to refuse was impossible. Cardinal Mendoza and the queen's confessor, Hernando de Talavera,
were entrusted with conducting an inquest into the origins of the royal grants. Sometimes they had been a reward for services rendered, sometimes a scandalous gift.
The arbiters were to be guided by these distinctions in
deciding whether to diminish, maintain, or annul the

grants. Admiral Enríquez had to surrender 240,000 maravedís in revenue; the Duke of Alba, 575,000; the Marquis of Cádiz, 573,000.[34] The Mendoza lost even more, as if the cardinal wished to attest thereby his impartiality and disinterest. The old favorite of Enrique IV, Beltrán de la Cueva, Duke of Alburquerque, suffered most because he had been most favored; he renounced a pension of 1,400,000 maravedís.

The sovereigns struck an even harder blow at the nobility by taking away from it control of the military orders. The grand masterships, the commanderies of Alcántara, Calatrava, and Santiago, gave the grandees of Castile large revenues; the benefices and prebends in their gift gave them a powerful means of influence over the petty nobility. The military orders were a source of danger not only to royal authority but to public peace, for every vacancy provoked fierce rivalry that often degenerated into civil war. It was most important to subordinate this power to the crown. The first step was taken in 1476. The Grand Master of Santiago, Don Rodrigo Manrique, had just died. At this news the queen left Valladolid, where she was staying, and reached Ocaña in three days. When she arrived, night had fallen; however, the queen continued her journey to the convent of Uclés, where the thirteen dignitaries of the chapter were assembled. She claimed for the crown the right of administering these great orders, whose jurisdiction included many border fortresses; she informed the chapter that she had applied to the Pope for a bull of investiture, and closed by inviting the chapter to suspend the election.[35]

The fear she inspired drew a favorable response from the knights; the Grand Master designate, Don Alonso de Cárdenas, Grand Commander of León, withdrew his candidacy. But the concession was made so grudgingly

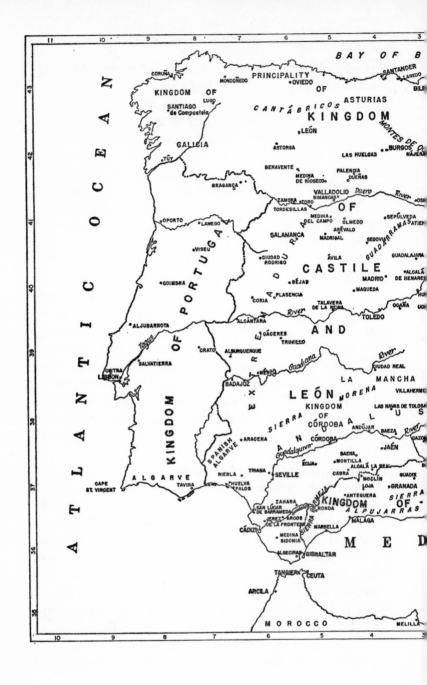

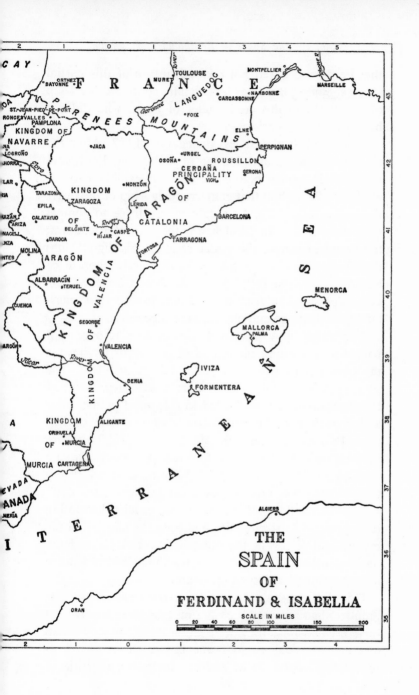

that Ferdinand dared not take advantage of this partial success. Some years later he officially conferred headship of the order on this commander of León, who did not belong to the high aristocracy.[36]

Ferdinand displayed less delicacy in 1487. After the election of the Grand Master of Calatrava, Ferdinand appeared in person before the chapter, exhibited to the electors a Papal bull that conferred headship of the order upon him, and did not hesitate to use force to compel their obedience.[37] In 1494 it was the turn of Alcántara; the grand master of this order resigned his dignity into the king's hands in exchange for the archbishopric of Seville. Finally, in 1499, on the death of Cárdenas, Ferdinand presented himself as candidate for the grand mastership of Santiago and obtained the succession.

The crown now possessed considerable resources; it had at its command the means of buying or paying for the devotion of the nobility, both high and low. The sovereigns had nothing left to fear; step by step, they had taken all the measures needed to safeguard public order and transform the turbulent lords of the time of Enrique IV into obedient subjects. It was forbidden to use firearms or to take justice into one's own hands. Private wars were prohibited, on pain of the most severe penalties. Dueling was regarded as a capital crime; the challenger, the challenged, and the witnesses all risked losing their heads. The strongholds had been the base of all the revolts and terror in the countryside. Isabella ordered the destruction of all fortresses which she did not judge necessary for the safety of the country.[38]

Nor did she spare the pride of the aristocracy. The grandees had assumed the right of quartering a crown on their escutcheons; they were attended by mace-bearers and had a naked sword borne before them; they borrowed the regal style of address, inscribing the title of their dignity at the head of their letters. Like the king, they wrote to their vassals: *Es mi merced* (it is my will) and *so pena de la mi merced* (on pain of my displeasure). An act passed at the Cortes of Toledo forbade all these usurpations, and reminded the nobility that between it and the crown existed other differences than those of power.[39] The very favors accorded by the sovereigns to the nobility served to abase it. Court life in Spain dates from the reign of Isabella; the queen loved to surround herself with gentlemen and ladies, to play with pomp and glitter her role of majesty. One chronicler reproves her taste for having noble servants, censuring as vanity her tendency to assign domestic offices to the members of the aristocracy.[40] Where some contemporaries saw pettiness, I am inclined to suspect a deep calculation. These court offices gave the holders no influence, but forced them to live under the eye of and, so to speak, in dependence upon the sovereigns. A luxurious and indolent existence, numerous favors, the habit of obedience, all tended to transform the grandees into contented spectators, into willing subjects, into docile instruments. Isabella ushered in this change; the presence of the most powerful nobles at court enhanced her dignity and served her policy.

To build a solid foundation for the edifice of absolute power, the sovereigns sought allies outside the aristocracy. Influence passed to another class, that of the legists (*letrados*). The study of the Roman law, in Spain as in France, had formed jurisconsults who scorned customary law and regarded the omnipotence of a Justinian as the ideal of the monarchy. The liberties of the towns, the privileges of the orders, they regarded as so many vexatious curbs on the royal prerogative. Unquestioning obedience was the principal dogma of the political religion of these legists. Their studies naturally fitted them to serve the monarchical cause; their origin made them its most faithful and reliable servants. Sprung from the ranks of the people or the lesser nobility, they owed all they were to the king, who could thrust them back into the shadows with a single word. The civil and political offices, the ecclesiastical benefices—power, in a word—passed from the grandees to men of middling condition. To the *caballeros* of Toledo, who resented having to obey men of low birth, Gómez Manrique, governor of the Alcázar, observed with some irony that their jealousy of parvenus was not very reasonable, for change was the law of the world, and the sole nobility was that of virtue.[41]

Diego de Mendoza, the penetrating author of the *Guerra de Granada,* saw very clearly that Ferdinand and Isabella had given the government a new orientation. "The Catholic Sovereigns," he wrote, "placed the administration of justice and power in the hands of the legists, a class intermediate between the great and the small and which could excite the envy of neither. Their profession was observance of the laws, modesty, discretion, truth; a life that reflected complete respect for the old customs—no visits, no acceptance of presents, no close ties, no sumptuous dress or trains." It was these discreet agents, who carefully hid their private lives from view and who were interested only in their duties, who quietly and systematically overcame every resistance as they won Spain for the sovereigns over the feudalism of the lords and towns and over the medieval Church.

II

The Spanish Inquisition

A spirit of passion pervades much that has been written on the Spanish Inquisition. Some writers, eager to justify the Church, see in the Inquisition only a political tribunal, a docile instrument of royal policy; they cite triumphantly the many occasions on which the Holy See evidenced displeasure and even hostility toward it. Others, wishing to blacken the Church, see only an institution whose cruelty to heretics has made it odious to mankind. The truth is not so simple. The apologists should remember that political trials were accidents in the history of the Holy Office, and that disloyalty to the crown was not one of the offenses subject to its jurisdiction. Foes of Catholicism might recall that the Inquisition was founded in 1480, and that at that date, when Luther and Calvin were not yet born, Ferdinand and Isabella could not have thought of destroying the doctrines and adherents of those great reformers. The complex fact is that originally, in the reign of the Catholic Sovereigns, the Inquisition was an ecclesiastical court charged with achieving an objective of interest to both religion and the state.

Restoration of order was not the only great problem facing the government. A graver problem demanded its attention: the assimilation of foreign peoples, Jews and

Moslems, whom a succession of conquests and that of Granada, finally, brought under the crowns of Aragón and Castile. What should be done with these people? The Jews aroused disquiet by their wealth and proselytism, the Moslems by their numbers. Should they be permitted to live and multiply as they pleased? Should they be driven out? Toleration, so honored in our time, was alien to the spirit of the age. Although religious prejudice was very intense, expulsion appeared a very barbarous proceeding, and men were not blind to the economic dangers of such a measure. Yet religion was so intimately linked to the idea of the state that it seemed unthinkable for a prince to allow adherents of Moses and Mohammed to live side by side with Christian folk. Racial differences represented a large obstacle to assimilation; but these were of secondary importance by comparison with the question of religious belief. Sincere conversion on the part of the vanquished removed the strongest prejudice of their conquerors.

We must remember, if we would be just, that during the French religious struggles of the sixteenth century it was more than once proposed to banish the Huguenots, and that Louis XIV finally expelled from France more than three hundred thousand Protestants. The fanaticism of Ferdinand and Isabella was as narrow but more excusable; they were confronted in each case with people of another race whose tenacious clinging to their faith seemed to make of them an enemy group within the Spanish nation. Convert or disappear—this was the motto of a policy which measured its success in the work of unification by the number of New Christians. What better proof could a man give that he had thrown off all feeling of hostility toward the people of which he was going to form a part than by abandoning a holy and cherished religious tradition, and one resistant to all assimilation?[1] In this campaign against alien elements the Church had the mission of preventing the spread of heretical doctrine throughout Christian society, and of preserving at all cost the victories won over the enemies of the Spanish religion and nationality.

The Jews, whose faith has preserved and sustained them amid all persecutions and ordeals, remain a nation wherever they may be; their religion is their fatherland. They were very numerous in fifteenth-century Spain. Their intelligence, their financial ability, won them the favor of princes and the hatred of the people. They formed a class devoted to the pursuit of wealth, and exploited every branch of the public revenue, farming the collection of tithes and sales taxes (*alcabalas*), and acting as collectors of tolls at city gates. To these profits of publicans, they joined those of banking and usury. About this financial aristocracy was grouped an industrious democracy of tailors, cordwainers, curriers, wool-shearers, peddlers, and silk workers. Through all these channels money flowed into Israelite purses. To be sure, now and again, acts of mob violence reminded the Jews that it was a mistake to be rich among a poverty-stricken multitude, a mistake to be faithful to the ancient law amid the fanatical adherents to the new law. Now in one town, now in another, the populace rose in riots against the Jewish quarters, combining pillage with massacre. So intense was popular hatred that in 1473 the inhabitants of Jaén murdered at the foot of the altar the Condestable Don Miguel Lucas, accused of sympathy for the Jews. That year similar disorders took place at Andújar, Córdoba, and many other points in Andalusia. Despite these bloody portents, calm and confidence soon returned to the ghettos. The Jews returned to their toil, resumed the patient accumulation of gain, put down to the account of inevitable accidents the periodic pogroms, the periodic storms of blood fury of the mob. Had they not reason to hope that the sun would again shine on the people of God . . . ?

This hope was not unfounded. Many Spanish nobles married the daughters of rich Israelites to increase or restore their estates. At the price of baptism these women gained entry into the most illustrious families and also a brilliant social situation. Many nobles had Jewish blood in their veins.² Descendants of these neophytes were to be found in the administration, in the court, and even in the Church. Alonso de Cartagena, Bishop of Burgos, Juan Arias Dávila, Bishop of Segovia, and Isabella's own confessor, Hernando de Talavera, did not have to search very far in their genealogical trees to find an ancestor of the ancient law.

Many *confesos* were sincere in their Christian faith, but the majority probably retained some degree of sympathy for the faith and ideas in which their forebears had been reared. Andrés Bernáldez, chaplain of the Grand Inquisitor Diego Deza, reproached the Jews for their pride; to hear them talk they were the best informed, the most judicious, the worthiest persons—in a word, a "Chosen People."³ Some *confesos* even continued to be proud of their Hebraic origin. One of them, Francisco Villalobos, physician to Charles V, wrote a letter in 1532 that reveals the extensive ramifications of these New Christians and the kindly sentiments which they felt for each other, whatever the class to which they belonged; the high opinion that the children of Abraham continued to have of themselves comes through, despite the writer's air of badinage. The Duke of Nájera had a daughter, Doña Guiomar, by a marriage with a Jewess. This girl had just made her debut in the court of Charles V, and her beauty and virtues had made the strongest impression there. The physician informed her

father of this happy event: "Not only is she as lovely a
lady as ever there was in the world, but she knew so well
how to talk with the other ladies and the Empress, when
to be silent and when to speak, all so discreetly, and with
such high authority and grace, that all of us direct a thousand benedictions *to the womb that bore her;* for it was the
mother who conceived her that we must thank and not
the father who engendered her; in fine, if some good
comes out of your family, it is *to us that credit is due,* we
who are the chosen sacerdotal race (*genus electum regale sacerdotium*), and not you others, the Manriques,
who come from the devil (*quia pars diaboli estis*). My
lord the Grand Inquisitor must pardon me if I reduce
him to dust, him who some day will reduce me to
smoke. In what concerns the health of this lady, my
cousin. . . ." [4]

If Villalobos, fifty years after the establishment of the
Inquisition, did not forget despite his baptism that he
was of Jewish race, how much keener must that memory
have been among the New Christians who lived at the
beginning of Isabella's reign, and who were numerous,
powerful, honored!

In 1391, after massacres that stained with blood the
principal towns of Castile, thousands of Jews renounced
their faith to save their lives and received baptism en
masse.[5] These conversions, inspired by fear, were not
very sincere; once the storm had passed many regretted
their weakness. They dared not defy the Draconic laws
against apostasy, but they made secret contact with their
brothers who had remained faithful. Though compelled
to attend mass and take part in the sacraments, they ab-
sented themselves as often as they could from these
odious comedies. At confession they admitted nothing
or only the lightest faults; they baptized their children,
but on leaving the ceremony they carefully washed

the parts anointed with the holy oil. Rabbis came in secret to instruct them. *Shohets* slaughtered according to the rites the animals and fowls used for food.[6] The *confesos* used oil to prepare meat, and ate pork only when it could not be avoided. Such were the practices of these converts, outwardly Christians but actually relapsed to the faith of Moses; they were called Judaizers. There was a great number of them in Andalusia; for the tolerance of the high clergy, among whom they had adherents, and of the nobles, to whom they were sometimes joined by ties of kinship, and the neglect or impotence of the kings, had permitted the increase of this apostate people, faithless alike to Christ and Moses. They did not secede from the Catholic community, but were all the more dangerous for that. Christian society, mined at its base, heard but could not see the sappers who prepared its ruin.[7]

However, the tolerance which they had enjoyed during the time of troubles under Enrique IV seems to have emboldened the Judaizers of Seville to relax the caution which hitherto had protected them. They felt secure because their coreligionists included some of the wealthiest and most prominent citizens of the city, and even some municipal magistrates. They forgot that nothing could sway Ferdinand and Isabella from a course of pitiless severity that they believed necessary. When the court moved to Seville in 1477, a Dominican, Fray Alonso de Ojeda, took advantage of the presence of the sovereigns and of the Archbishop, Pedro González de Mendoza, to bring complaints against the Judaizers. As a first step, the archbishop issued a charge in which he defined the obligatory beliefs and duties of a Christian, and called on the priests to indoctrinate their flocks and on fathers to instruct their children. A commission composed of Fray Alonso de Ojeda, the *corregidor* or *asistente* Diego de Merlo, the vicar general, and other priests and friars, was to enforce the charge and to induce heretics to return to the faith by preaching or secret admonitions.[8] At the end of two years, the commission reported that no change had taken place.

Aroused by the complaints of the clergy, the sovereigns had asked Sixtus IV to grant a bull for the establishment of an inquisition. The new tribunal thus differed in purpose from the ecclesiastical inquisition of the thirteenth century; the new instrument of death was aimed only at apostates, in fact, at a particular class of apostates—the Judaizers. The Pope granted the bull (dated November 1, 1478).

Three inquisitors came to Seville in 1480 and began their terrible purges. After a rapid inquiry, they ordered the arrest of the most open Judaizers and imprisoned them in the Monastery of San Pablo. This first cast of the net captured the richest and most influential members of the sect, twenty-four *jurados* (municipal officers), holders of bachelor's degrees, and legists. The number of arrested persons soon grew to the point where the monastery could receive no more prisoners, and it was necessary to hand over to the inquisitors the castle of Triana, where they established their jail and court. Then the executions began. Their site was a scaffold erected at Tablada and flanked at the corners by four statues of prophets. Sixteen persons, men and women, were burned on the first day. This was the first auto de fe. On this occasion the instigator of the persecution, Alonso de Ojeda, delivered a very moving sermon before the victims. Several days later three more men, of considerable rank and fortune, marched to their deaths. These blows, directed at such powerful persons, terrified the lesser sort. The Sevillanos fled the city en masse; the magistrates ordered the gates of the city closed. The plague drove away the inquisitors but did not dampen their zeal. At

Aracena, where they took refuge, they started out by sending twenty-three persons to their death. In eight years, the tribunal of Seville put seven hundred persons to death, and condemned five thousand to perpetual imprisonment or to severe acts of penance.[9]

Such were the beginnings of the Holy Office, of that fearful tribunal that brought to the work of persecution a rigorous method, firmness, and sang-froid. From Seville its operations were extended to Córdoba, then to other towns. Temporary inquisitorial commissions were first sent to the places where their presence was considered necessary. Later these missions were replaced by permanent tribunals in the most important towns. A supreme council sat near the sovereigns; its head was the grand inquisitor. Three prelates occupied this high office during the reign of Ferdinand and Isabella: they were Tomás de Torquemada, Prior of the Dominican Convent of Ávila (1483-1498); Diego Deza, Archbishop of Seville (1498-1507); Francisco Jiménez de Cisneros (1507 to 1516), Archbishop of Toledo. The bull of Sixtus IV limited the grand inquisitor's jurisdiction to Castile; but in 1485 Aragón was placed under his inquisitorial authority. Torquemada dealt especially with the Judaizers; Deza, with the Moriscos; Jiménez established the Holy Office in the Indies and in Africa.

Having arrived in a town, the inquisitors opened their hearings by publication of a general pardon, and announced a period of grace during which suspects could without fear of loss of life confess their faults and ask for reconciliation with the Church. When this period had ended, the arrests and investigations began. The judges sent hardened heretics to the stake without mercy; others they condemned to perpetual or temporary imprisonment. The majority were let off with acts of penance of varying severity. An auto de fe concluded the inquest.

On a day of great religious solemnity a long procession wound its way through the streets. The religious orders began the march; then came the actors in this lugubrious drama, the impenitent heretics being led to their punishment and the reconciled sinners being subjected to the menacing spectacle of a horrible death. The effigies and disinterred bones of dead Judaizers, destined for the fire, were also carried in the procession.

The reconciled were dressed in *sanbenitos,* chasubles of yellow cloth on which were painted red St. Andrew's crosses. A bonnet (*coroza*), closely resembling a magician's, completed this fantastic apparel. Relapsed heretics were marked out for the horror or compassion of spectators by having devils painted on their *sanbenitos.* The tribunal condemned some heretics to wear this infamous vestment for several years or even for life. No punishment seemed more severe to those who had escaped death; an object of laughter to some, of scandal to others, of hatred to all, the unhappy wearer of the *sanbenito* was henceforth a pariah in society.

During the fifteen years of Torquemada's administration, fifteen thousand relapsed heretics were reconciled with the Church; two thousand obstinate heretics were burned. The number of the victims of Jiménez and Deza is unknown.

The severity of this repression aroused censure even in Spain. Leaving aside the *confesos,* who complained of the constant suspicion under which they lived, and who accused even the inquisitors of personal hostility, there were generous souls, as the Jesuit Juan de Mariana asserted, who criticized such great harshness. Hernando del Pulgar, Isabella's secretary, recalled the famous letter in which St. Augustine judged death to be too cruel a punishment for the Donatists. But many more than Pulgar, while conceding the legitimate character of the repres-

sion, condemned the practices of the inquisitorial procedure. The examination as well as the judgment was secret; the name of the denouncer was carefully hidden;
there was no confrontation of witnesses. The scenes of
death, embellished with the name of "Acts of Faith,"
were less revolting to some than this impunity and encouragement offered to informers, this compelling of a
whole class of men to watch their words, gestures, emo-
tions. Fear killed confidence and suppressed all intimacy.

That the father's heresy stamped a brand of ignominy
on all his children, and that these innocent victims were
declared incapable of exercising any public employment,
also aroused indignation. Mariana himself considered
the measure barbarous; however, he added that the
fear of dooming one's descendants to infamy was a most
effective deterrent to apostasy.[10] Thus the Inquisition even
played upon paternal tenderness. Such casuistical refinements, even more than the number of its executions, have
made of the Inquisition a hateful legend.

Moreover, this terrible tribunal was not cruel to laymen alone. Among its first victims one finds an administrator of the property of the church of Seville, and four
friars, one of them a famous preacher. Nor did it spare
the high clergy. The Bishop of Segovia, Juan Arias
Dávila, was of Jewish origin. Heedless of the scandal that
such an action must arouse, the inquisitors ordered an
inquest into the orthodoxy of his dead parents. Don
Juan chased the commissioners out of his diocese, ex-
humed the beloved remains that they sought to burn,
hid them in a safe place, and left for Rome.[11]

The most celebrated of these fanatics was Diego Rodríguez Lúcero, inquisitor of Córdoba, a credulous sec-
tary ever ready to receive denunciations. Some Judaizers
of low condition denounced hundreds of persons, think-

oplas õloſſiete pecados moz
tales bechas poz el famoſo
poeta Juan de mena.

ing that the judges would take fright at the idea of hunting down such a multitude, and that they would thus
gain immunity. Lúcero did not hesitate to order the arrests and fill the jails of Córdoba. The process, suspended
by the accession and reign of Philip the Handsome, was
resumed after his death. An insurrection broke out; a
crowd led by the Marquis of Priego (October 6, 1506)
stormed the jails and liberated the prisoners. The movement soon spread throughout Andalusia. Ferdinand was
then in Italy; he perceived that Deza, the accomplice of

Lúcero's ragings, must be sacrificed. Jiménez was invested with the office of grand inquisitor (May 17, 1507). Lúcero got off with the loss of his job.

Jiménez could not punish severely an excess of inquisitorial zeal. Yet Lúcero had dared attack the most respected prelate of Spain, Hernando de Talavera, recommended by his title of Queen Isabella's confessor, by his virtue, and by his great age. This Archbishop of Granada was of Jewish origin on the distaff side; his brother, Alfonso de Oropesa, Prior of the monks of San Jerónimo at Segovia in the reign of Enrique II, had exposed an imposture of the monks of the Observance, who excited the people to massacre the Jews.[12] Talavera himself would use no other means to convert the Moors than that of opening up to them his home, his purse, and his heart. It was this aged man that Lúcero sought to convict of Judaism; in full daylight he ordered the arrest of the Archbishop's nieces, his sister, and his nephew, Don Francisco Herrera, Dean of the chapter of Granada. He would have dragged Hernando de Talavera himself off to the dungeons of the Inquisition if the bull of Sixtus IV had not formally reserved to the Pope the right of authorizing the arrest and trial of bishops.

Nevertheless, Lúcero had already commenced an inquest, when Deza took fright at his audacity. Julius II, compelled to intervene, entrusted the affair to his nuncio, Giovanni Ruffo, Bishop of San Bertinoro (in the Romagna), friend of Peter Martyr and a choice spirit who was repelled by violent and unseemly actions. The accusation rested on worthless reports made by informers of dubious character and carefully arranged and interpreted by Lúcero. On May 21, 1507, the Roman Curia handed down a sentence which declared Talavera innocent; but the strain of the long trial had exhausted the forces of the aged archbishop. Several days after the proclamation of his orthodoxy, this model of Christian charity and tolerance expired. "Alas for the poor!" exclaimed a contemporary.

Church and state spared no violence in order to prevent the spread of the disintegrative influence of the Judaizers throughout Christian society. They did not back from a still more radical step when, after ten years of terror, heresy had almost been extirpated. The Jews were now isolated amid the Catholic mass; no longer were they linked to it even through the mediation of apostates, those Christians in outward forms, Jews in heart and tradition. From the beginning of their reign, Ferdinand and Isabella had enforced the old ordinances which segregated the followers of Moses in certain quarters. The time of troubles and the indifference of earlier rulers had permitted the Jews to spill over these limits into the interior of the towns. There they built houses and synagogues. The Cortes of Toledo (1480) revived the whole ancient system of segregation. The Jews were allowed a space of two months to quit their homes and temples and re-enter the Jewries.[13] If a Jew settled in a Christian quarter, his property would be confiscated; his person would be at the disposition of the sovereigns.

Up to this point, the Jews had no basis, strictly speaking, for raising the cry of persecution; the laws being applied to them were existing laws. The establishment of the Inquisition in 1480 was not aimed at them; in the eyes of the fervent Jew the persecuted Marranos must have seemed unworthy of much pity or interest. The Christian state appeared to be defending the cause of two orthodoxies, Jewish and Christian, in harrying apostates from both religions. But the logic of the situation doomed the Jews after the Judaizers. To statesmen who placed the unity of the Spanish nation above all other interests the presence of this heterogeneous fraction constituted a danger; to the inquisitor it seemed necessary, having exterminated the Judaizers, to stop up the source of the perverse doctrines.[14] When the Holy Office began its operations, Isabella had already expelled from Seville and Córdoba the Jews who were settled there. This measure presaged a more radical step. On March 30, 1492, in conquered Granada, the Catholic Sovereigns issued an ordinance of proscription. They banished from the Kingdoms of Aragón and Castile all Jews unwilling to receive baptism. They gave them a space of six months in which to sell their goods.

This concession was sheer mockery; a buyer is never in a hurry to close when the seller is hard pressed. Besides, since they were forbidden to carry gold or silver out of the kingdom, there was no need to fear that these last transactions would bring them any profit. It is a remarkable fact, attested by witnesses above suspicion, that only a few men of lowest condition agreed to give up their religion. Almost all the Jews preferred exile with all its uncertainties and certain misery to apostasy. They tried to sell at the best possible price what they could not carry away; but the Christians took fullest advantage of their situation. A house had to go for an ass, a vineyard for a piece of cloth or linen. Before departing, the exiles married off all boys above the age of fourteen, all girls above the age of twelve, so that in case of need each should have a legitimate protector.

The exodus began the first week of July 1492. The Jews of Castile (theirs was the greatest number) set off for Portugal; those of Navarre and Biscay embarked at Laredo; the Andalusian Jews flocked to the port of Cádiz. The Aragonese and the Catalans sought refuge in Italy and in the Barbary states. The sufferings of these poor wretches were infinite; in Portugal they had to pay ransom; in Africa they were hunted down by the Arabs, who robbed them and slit open their bellies to search for gold. Some returned to Castile and asked for baptism. Their faith had received too severe a shock. Had they not hoped that God would be their guide and lead them as if by the hand to another promised land? [15]

Now it was the turn of the Moors. They were more numerous than the Jews, more valiant and formidable. Even in the Kingdoms of Léon and Castile, disciples of Mohammed were yet to be found here and there. According to Peter Martyr, in Valencia and Aragón there were more Moslems than Christians.[16] Annexation of the Kingdom of Granada added three hundred to four hundred thousand coreligionists to these scattered groups. The political peril was as great as the religious menace. By natural increase alone, what weight might this multitude come to have in the councils of the nation! Yet the treaties made with them were so explicit, the word of the sovereigns so solemnly pledged, and, above all, a rupture threatened such dangerous consequences, that the advocates of violence had to force the hands of the Catholic Sovereigns.

The latter had entrusted the political and religious administration of the conquered land to Don Íñigo López de Mendoza, Count of Tendilla, and to the virtuous Talavera. These men spared the feelings of the conquered Moors and sought to gain their confidence. Talavera, although eager to lead them to the Christian faith, displayed in the work of conversion a discretion worthy of his charitable spirit. Daily he brought together at his table the principal *alfaquíes,* and tried to dispel their mistrust or their ignorance. His goodness argued in favor of his doctrine; several times he pledged his silver to feed the Moors in time of drought. He caused some portions of the Gospels to be translated into Arabic, and dreamed of placing the whole Bible within the reach of the infidels. The Moors bowed in respect before the great *alfa-qui* of the Christians.

His methods did not satisfy the zealots; the pace of conversion was too slow for them. There were no innumerable crowds falling at the knees of the Apostles to seek baptism, as in the first days of Christianity. In 1499 Jiménez came to Granada, and the whole aspect of things changed. Although he paid tribute to the archbishop's virtue, he found fault with these slow methods of spiritual conquest. The translation of the Bible seemed to him almost a sacrilege; it was, he said brutally, to throw pearls before swine.[17] He marched to the conversion of the Moors like a captain of war to the storming of a stronghold, with enthusiasm and with no other thought than the glory of God. He harangued the Moslem priests like a ruler, but, full of unconscious scorn for their gross natures, he relied less on the effect of his speeches than on the presents which he heaped on them. But he did not hesitate to use force; he handed the Moor Zegri Azaator over to his chaplain, Pedro Ponce de León, to bring him to reason. A rain of blows tamed the obstinate miscreant; he cried out that nothing could resist this lion (León), and became a Christian.[18] These victorious ways had complete success: More than four thousand Moslems embraced Christianity. On December 18, 1499, a memorable scene took place; so great was the number of catechumens that they could not be baptized in the ordinary manner. Holy water was sprinkled on the prostrate multitude; Jiménez saw victory in sight; he ordered the burning of several thousand copies of the Koran and many other Arab manuscripts.

But he had misjudged the patience of this people. Of all the measures he had ordered, the most odious was the forcible taking of Moslem children. A last outrage caused an explosion of pent-up hatred. Two servants of Jiménez went into the quarter of the Albaicín to carry away a young girl; the cries of the child summoned a furious crowd who surrounded and massacred the attackers. The armed Moors soon moved on the house of Jiménez. Their attack was repulsed, but the revolt did not subside. Then the venerable Talavera proceeded to the Albaicín; barricades and chains fell before him. The Count of Tendilla offered to negotiate a pardon for the insurgents, surrendering his family to them as hostages.

News of the insurrection startled the sovereigns; Ferdinand heaped reproaches on the rash man who risked the frustration of such great efforts. Isabella herself was shaken. Jiménez hastened to their side; instead of defending himself, he explained to his masters that the Moorish rising freed them of all their obligations. The rebels of the Albaicín had torn up the Treaty of Granada (he forgot that he had first violated its clauses); there was nothing to do but seize the offered chance and convert by force one of the capitals of Islam. This shameful casuistry convinced his illustrious hearers; the Moslems of the city were offered a choice of death or baptism. Fifteen thousand Moors accepted baptism. These forced conversions should have aroused some misgivings; but Jiménez saw nothing but the glory of the state and the interest of the Church. For the rest, the Inquisition had effective means of inhibiting apostasy. The tribunal at Córdoba had under its jurisdiction the ancient capital of the Moorish kings.[19]

The Granadan affair had repercussions in the massif of the Alpujarras. There the mountaineers, convinced that the Christians sought to convert them by force, took to arms. But each tribe revolted at a time of its own choosing, without taking the trouble to reach a general accord with the others; as a result, they were easily crushed (1500). A more serious movement arose in the

Sierra Bermeja. There was a savage battle in which Don Alonso de Aguilar, elder brother of Gonzalo de Córdoba, and Francisco Ramírez, organizer of the Spanish artillery, lost their lives. The Moors soon tired of an unequal struggle, however, and asked for mercy; they were offered a choice between exile and conversion. Some passed over to Africa; the majority remained and embraced Christianity. Not a single unbaptized Moor remained in Granada. The Inquisition extended its vigilance to all these people of doubtful faith. In order to save them from the temptations of example, an edict of July 20 forbade the Moriscos (that was the name of these New Christians) all intercourse with their unconverted brethren of Castile. It was the story of the Jews and the Judaizers all over again.

The logic of the situation led to a further act of violence. On February 13, 1502, an order expelled from the Kingdoms of León and Castile all unbaptized male Moors more than fourteen years of age, and all the women of twelve or over. In order not to increase the number of their enemies, the sovereigns forbade the exiles to go to the Sudan or other parts of Africa at war with Spain. Another order of September 12, 1502, further restricted their choice to Portugal and Aragón. In the hereditary states of Ferdinand the worship of Islam was tolerated until the reign of Charles V.

The great number of the neophytes, the peculiar mode of their conversion, the numerous causes of relapse, opened the widest possible field to the activity of the inquisitors. Heirs of the ancient Inquisition, they had many other foes to combat with the appearance of the Reformation; but apostasy always remained the offense most especially commended to their vigilance. Actually, Protestantism made but a light impress on the Peninsula; Spain had already had its heresy, Judaism, and the heroic remedies employed to cure that disease were not to the taste of innovators. Thus the Holy Office could devote all its efforts to watching over the conscience of the New Christians, the Marranos and Moriscos. It had a second falling out with the latter. Not all the descendants of the Moors were transformed into true Spaniards. Assimilation of the races was slow; and under Philip III a new expulsion order was issued.

In this pursuit of an impossible fusion, the Santo Oficio had been the formidable instrument of a policy that pursued the national interest through the interests of the Church, or that even identified the two. This dual character of its repressive activity explains the contradictory judgments made concerning the Inquisition. In 1478 Pope Sixtus IV granted the bull which authorized establishment of the new Inquisition. In 1483, on the basis of complaints received from the Peninsula, he declared that advantage had been taken of his good faith. Some years later he entrusted a mission to Spain to a nuncio of whose good will Isabella assured herself, even before his departure, by rich gifts. The historian Llorente has some reason to suspect the sincerity of the Holy See; few counsels of humanity and few examples of morality came down from the apostolic chair in the reign of the Catholic Sovereigns.

The fact is that in Spain heresy was more than a religious question; it was also a political and national issue. Rome displayed greater tolerance toward the Moriscos and Marranos because, even in case of relapse, to her they were nothing more than hardened sinners. The Spaniards regarded them as both apostates and aliens. The clergy shared the passions of the multitude; the multitude breathed the fanaticism of the clergy. That is why the Holy Office, which left a deservedly odious memory in other nations, enjoyed a great popularity in

Spain. It was not from fear alone that nobles and commoners became familiars of the Inquisition. These connections gratified that jealous, exclusive, and somber patriotism which found satisfaction of ancient hates in a pitiless severity. When the Holy Office arrested a Judaizing prelate, Rome claimed the right to try the heretic by virtue of her religious supremacy. But the kings protested in the name of state interests; and Ferdinand did not hesitate to pronounce sentence of death *ipso facto* on whoever invoked the protection of a Papal bull to place himself outside the jurisdiction of the Inquisition.

III

The Spanish Supremacy

The marriage of Ferdinand and Isabella united most of the Iberian Peninsula in the hands of the royal pair. There remained outside the new state only the Christian Kingdoms of Navarre and Portugal and the Moslem Kingdom of Granada. Politics as well as religion doomed the latter to conquest. It was at Granada's expense that the Catholic Sovereigns made the first test of their strength. Hardly had they restored internal order and repulsed the Portuguese invaders when they demanded the tribute paid by the Moors to their predecessors. Muley Abul Hassan, who then reigned at Granada, proudly replied that his mints coined no longer gold, but steel.[1] Despite this provocative language the truce was renewed, but without much confidence in its continuance.

In 1481, with Abul Hassan's surprise attack on the fortress at Zahara, began the long war that was to complete the destruction of Moslem power in Spain. The ample resources of the Moors, and the ease with which they could defend their territory, explain the long duration of the struggle (1481 to 1492). The Emirs of Granada had in their pay seven thousand horse in addition to the militia, who could be assembled at a moment's notice. The capital alone could call out for each of its seven gates three thousand archers or lightly armed foot soldiers. The revenues of the Moslem king were considerably greater than those of Isabella. The country, with its steep mountains and impassable gorges, made for difficult campaigning. But the rulers of Granada were disunited; the jealousy of the Sultana, Aisha, of her rival, Zoraya, armed son against father, Boabdil against Muley Hassan. Henceforth there were two parties in the kingdom; and all the bravery of its leaders and soldiers could not make up for the evil of divided forces, energies, and wills. Stout walls and fortresses nested on heights fell under the pounding of Spanish artillery. The death of Muley Hassan did not restore peace; his brother, El Zagal, continued the struggle against both the Spaniards and Boabdil. When the fall of Baza induced El Zagal to treat with Ferdinand and hand over to him the towns which acknowledged his sway (1489), Boabdil was freed of a rival, but gained no resources thereby. In 1492 Granada opened its gates to the Catholic Sovereigns.

This brilliant conquest was above all the work of the Castilian Isabella. Her Aragonese husband had once proposed to quit the struggle in order to attend to the affairs of his own kingdom. It was the only disagreement between the spouses during the whole of their public life. The possession of Granada united the sovereigns of Aragón and Castile in a close and permanent community of views and allowed them to think of extending their frontiers, of establishing Spain as a great power. From that time on, moreover, the role of Aragonese diplomacy became preponderant. Isabella willingly followed Ferdinand's lead in foreign policy, influenced less by wifely tenderness than by a lively sense of Spanish grandeur. She might have attempted the annexation of Portugal, but that little nation was capable of defending itself. The victory of Toro (1476) had avenged the defeat of Aljubarrota (1385), but had not established Spain's unquestioned military supremacy. Navarre remained as an object of Spanish expansionist desires. Here the sovereigns ran into a formidable obstacle: France.

Until this time Castile had enjoyed the most amicable relations with France. The Castilian kings, preoccupied with civil wars or struggles against the Moors, gave no trouble to the French monarchs and cared little about events beyond their mountains. To these causes of amity was added the memory of mutual services. A lieutenant of Charles V of France, Du Guesclin, commanded French bands that helped materially to place Enrique of Trastamara on the throne. That prince and his successors acknowledged these good offices by the aid which they gave France during the Hundred Years' War. A Castilian fleet saved La Rochelle and defeated an English naval force. With each change of reign the Franco-Castilian alliance was carefully renewed. Never was France more generously repaid for so small a favor.

The marriage of Isabella to the King of Aragón changed these relations. The Aragonese and Catalan dwellers in the basin of the Ebro, contained in the Peninsula by Castilian power, had sought to expand in other directions. The great islands of the Mediterranean, Corsica and Sardinia, had fallen into their hands. When the rapacious and oppressive government of Charles of Anjou caused Sicily to rise in revolt (1282), an Aragonese prince, Pedro III, responded to a summons from the insurgent people and accepted the proffered throne. It was a first act of hostility against France. Viewed from nearby Palermo and Messina, Naples appeared very tempting to an enterprising folk. The Angevin princes soon had to contend with Aragonese pretenders. Alfonso V of Aragón conquered the Kingdom of Naples (1443) from René of Provence, heir designate of Jo-

anna II.[2] Although the French kings had often regarded
with indifference the misfortunes of the House of Anjou,
many of their subjects went to fight in Italy and helped to
establish a tradition of hostility between Aragón and
France.

This was not the only place where the past held the
germ of future struggles; along the whole frontier of
the Pyrenees the ambitions of the two peoples collided
head-on. Navarre was hauled and tugged about by the
rivals. Power had been exercised there for some years by
Don Juan II of Aragón and his daughter, Leonor de
Foix; but on their death, Madeleine, sister of the French
King Louis XI and mother of the young King François
Phoebus, restored the French predominance. Seeking to
redress the balance, Ferdinand and Isabella negotiated
the marriage of François Phoebus with their daughter, Doña Juana; then, following the death of Phoebus
(1483), they demanded the hand of Catherine of Navarre for their heir, Don Juan. All these intrigues failed;
the Estates of Béarn, having been consulted, pronounced
for the union of Catherine with Jean d'Albret (1484).
Navarre escaped Ferdinand's clutches.

He had many other scores to settle with France. In
1462 his father, Juan II, had alienated Cerdaña and
Roussillon to Louis XI as security for a loan of 300,000
crowns. The royal debtor soon repented of having given
a pledge which the French king was unlikely to return
even for repayment in cash; besides, Juan doubted his
ability to wring so large a sum out of his subjects. All his
efforts to recover his property without loosing his purse
strings were in vain; with deep chagrin he beheld Louis
XI consolidating his hold on the country and putting
down all resistance to his rule. France, mistress to the
west of passages that opened on the Basque provinces,
now occupied to the east the hills that led directly into

Catalonia. She held in her hands the keys to the Peninsula.

Thus the past bequeathed many difficulties. But the causes of conflict were much more numerous now that the union of Aragón and Castile added to old rivalries the ambition of a great power. Where would Spain make test of its might? Africa offered a large field for conquest and conversion. But the Castilian Jiménez was the only one who took this project seriously; no concerted effort was made in that direction. Aragón drew Castile after itself in an Italian and anti-French policy. Aragón recognized the pre-eminence of Castile, the true center of the monarchy, but Castile espoused the interests and hatreds of Aragón. The questions of Navarre, of Cerdaña and Roussillon, which until then had been secondary, assumed in Castilian views a major importance. Formerly relations with Portugal and the Moors had been of primary interest; now Castilian eyes were fixed on more distant prospects.

With the end of the Crusades the true enemy of Spain came into view across the frontiers to the north. And what motives there were for hatred! When Charles VIII of France set out to conquer the Kingdom of Naples, he proposed to confront across the straits of Messina adversaries who could hardly keep their hands from each other's throats the whole length of the Pyrenees. It does not adequately explain the foreign policy of the Catholic Sovereigns to say that they found France too powerful. There was more; Spain's national interests drove her against a power that closed off all her avenues of expansion. As if it were not enough that France blockaded Spain in the Pyrenees, French conquest of the Kingdom of Naples threatened to shut off to her that immense battlefield of Italy on which the nations of Europe met, fought, and were transformed.

The foreign policy of Ferdinand and Isabella was anti-French of necessity, and their relations with other powers were conditioned by the help that they hoped to obtain from those states in their struggle with France. The new diplomatic orientation took shape during the War of Granada.[3] However, some efforts were made to reconcile Castilian attitudes with the interests of the united kingdoms.[4] Cardinal Mendoza, raised in the tradition of the French alliance, intervened to bring about conclusion of a satisfactory peace between Louis XI and the Catholic Sovereigns.[5] But events overruled the wishes of men. War was resumed on the borders of Roussillon. So close were Aragonese interests to Ferdinand's heart that in 1484, at the height of the War of Granada, he was on the point of abandoning the struggle to hasten to Catalonia. Isabella shamed him out of his resolve but she in turn fell under his influence.

Unable to attack France openly, the sovereigns took advantage of her embarrassments and kept alive the discontents of the great French vassals. Spanish troops passed over to Brittany and placed themselves at the service of François II. When the succession to the dukedom fell vacant, Ferdinand reached agreement with King Henry VII of England on a common course of action; although he affected disinterest, he offered his son Don Juan as candidate for the hand of the heiress. Anne of Brittany preferred the imperial dignity to any kingdom; besides, she was unwilling to wait until the ten-year-old infante grew to manhood. Maximilian, King of the Romans and future Holy Roman Emperor, was chosen and was wedded to Anne by proxy (1490). The aspirants had left out of account Charles VIII, who intervened at a strategic moment and snatched away both wife and duchy (1491). This denouement inflicted a new humiliation on the Spanish sovereigns and added a province to France.

Ferdinand soon took his revenge. The son of Louis XI was a bold, willful, romantic spirit. His father left him a quarrel with Aragón; his marriage with Anne of Brittany and his dismissal of Margaret, daughter of Maximilian, wounded the feelings of the head of the House of Austria both as father and betrothed (I dare not say husband). The intrigues of the King of Aragón made Charles still another enemy in the person of the King of England, Henry VII. Although the current of previous relations pushed Charles VIII toward Italy,[6] he would have done better to do his modest duty on the plains of Flanders or in the mountains of Cerdaña than to embark on the brilliant Neapolitan adventure and to dream of Constantinople. It was a mistake on the part of Charles VIII—and one that reflects on his intelligence—to take seriously the conquest of Jerusalem, which was no more than a conventional theme of diplomatic correspondence. Artois and the Franche-Comté belonged of right to Margaret; he should have retained them while offering compensation. As for Cerdaña and Roussillon, he should have barred discussion of those subjects until the sum advanced to Juan II had been totally repaid. For the rest, several years of struggle would have been preferable to the loss of these lands, which were geographically French.

But passion for glory prevailed over all these considerations: Charles VIII preferred being a hero to a statesman. He signed with Henry VII the Treaty of Étaples (1492); with Maximilian, the Treaty of Senlis, which cost France two provinces (1493). The Treaty of Barcelona, concluded with the Spanish sovereigns (1493), freely returned to them Roussillon and Cerdaña.

Ferdinand had easily restored the ancient boundaries

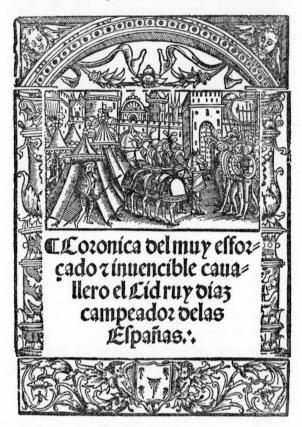

of the crown of Aragón. He had very skillfully exploited the enthusiasm of Charles VIII, the resentment of Maximilian, and the desire of Henry VII to secure by his complaisance the friendship of the Spaniards and Flemings. It was a peculiar gift of this great statesman to make the humors and ephemeral interests of his contemporaries serve his own permanent interests. For his part, he never yielded to the caprices of the moment; he sacrificed his allies without shame or scruple when their ardor upset his plans or went beyond his objectives. He kept his word only in the measure that this folly of honesty served his ends.

No man was cleverer than he when it came to discovering nullifying clauses in a convention. The Treaty of Barcelona guaranteed the French king, if not Ferdinand's aid, at least his benevolent neutrality. But Charles VIII had hardly reached Lyon when a Spanish ambassador presented himself and suggested that France abandon the Neapolitan enterprise.[7] Naples was a fief of the Holy See; the tender conscience of the King of Aragón forced him to respond to the appeals of Alexander VI. In this matter he was not bound by the Treaty of Barcelona, which explicitly reserved his freedom of action in the event of an attack on the Pope. Besides, Charles had renounced the benefits of the pact of Barcelona by failing to send within three months the adhesions of the "good towns" (note of July 1494).[8] These representations had a menacing character.

The rapid French advance prevented Ferdinand from giving effect to his implied threats. Charles was able to enter Rome and negotiate with the Pope a treaty that was violated as quickly as it was concluded.

In Venice a coalition of jealous powers was already forming against the conqueror. Ferdinand displayed great zeal in inciting Italian discontent. In June 1495, his ambassador, Don Lorenzo Suárez de Figueroa, arrived at Venice and obtained from the republic a commitment to take the initiative in a break with Charles. A Spanish fleet, commanded by Gonzalo de Córdoba, sailed for Sicily; two ambassadors, Antonio de Fonseca and Juan de Albión, met Charles VIII at the gates of Rome, on the road to Naples. They had several audiences in which they announced that Charles's acts of violence against the Holy See freed their sovereigns from all obligation toward him. In default of reigning princes, the throne of Naples belonged to no other than Ferdinand of Aragón. The French king must submit his claims to the scrutiny of the Pope. Charles VIII replied that he had gone too far to withdraw; he acknowledged no other judge of his rights than the Parliament of Paris. Then, it is said, in a burst of anger Fonseca tore up the Treaty of Barcelona and appealed from it to the judgment of God.[9]

The easy conquest of the Kingdom of Naples precipitated the formation of an anti-French alliance. At Venice a league was concluded for twenty-five years; it united the Pope, the King of the Romans, Maximilian, Ferdinand and Isabella, and the Duke of Milan. It was directed "against the aggressions of other potentates possessed of states in Italy."[10] Charles VIII, blockaded in his new kingdom, resolved to open a way for himself to the north, arms in hand. The Spanish fleet had already disembarked the King of Naples, Ferrante II, at Terranova in Calabria. Charles VIII learned in Tuscany, some days before Fornovo, of the victory won by his lieutenants at Seminara. But these two victories led to nothing. A rising delivered Naples into the hands of Ferrante II; meanwhile the Spanish sovereigns sent artillery into Roussillon and menaced Languedoc. Charles VIII, caught napping, sent to Spain M. de Clérieux, who signed an armistice (April 25 to November 1, 1497). It was the prelude to a general peace.

While Spanish diplomacy and arms snatched from Charles VIII the fruits of his efforts, Ferdinand pursued his political aims in another direction. Nature had blessed him with four daughters for whom he must provide. With the concerns of a paterfamilias the King of Aragón mingled calculations of larger interests. Since commonsense forbade him to dream of a conquest of Portugal, could he not prepare by means of marital alliances a happy chance that should unite in the same hands, by way of inheritance, Portugal, Aragón, and Castile?

In 1490 the Catholic Sovereigns married their eldest daughter, Isabella, to Affonso, the younger son of João II, King of Portugal. The infante died almost immediately after the celebration of his marriage. Despite feelings of repugnance, the young widow married the new presumptive heir, Manoel (1495). The death of Prince Juan (1497), which caused Ferdinand and Isabella such great dolor, nevertheless seemed to bring closer the fulfillment of their hopes. The passing of their only son transferred the succession to the wife of Manoel; the son that she had by him, Don Miguel, would inherit all the crowns of Spain. But this sickly child, who cost his mother her life, lived only a few months. These new afflictions, which indefinitely forestalled all designs on Portugal, prepared a still more brilliant future for the successor of the Catholic Sovereigns.

The check to Ferdinand's Portuguese combinations thrust to the fore of his program alliances which had not figured so largely in his original plans. To press upon France to the north and the east, and to distract it from Italy by a perpetual threat of invasion, Ferdinand had assured himself of the assistance of the King of England and of Maximilian. The marriage of his daughter Catherine to the son of Henry VII had for its sole aim the creation of a fulcrum for these alliances. The union bore the fruit hoped for by the lucky contriver; Henry VII and Henry VIII long remained under the influence of Spanish diplomacy. Another infanta, Doña Juana, had married the Archduke Philip, son of Maximilian, at the same time that the Prince of Asturias, Don Juan, was married to Philip's sister Margaret (1496). This double union linked the House of Aragón-Castile with that of Austria by the closest ties. Doña Juana, older than Catherine and more capable of comprehending and abetting her father's projects, was to serve as intermediary between the hostile houses of Tudor and Burgundy. Ferdinand hoped to use Philip the Handsome, master of Flanders and the Low Countries, in keeping France busy at home, while employing the King of the Romans to thwart her Italian designs.

The death of Don Miguel (1500) changed the character of these alliances. Doña Juana and Philip the Handsome, who were to receive the Austrian succession, found themselves elevated in addition to the dignity of heirs presumptive to the thrones of Aragón and Castile. The marriage directed against France was assuming the fantastic dimensions of a project of universal monarchy. Ferdinand, a practical genius, had dreamed only of unifying the Spanish Peninsula. Destiny, by the painful, overwhelming blows that she dealt him, prepared a result that was out of all proportion to his calculations and that may even have had no relation to his secret wishes.[11]

Be that as it may, Louis XII, successor to Charles VIII, had inherited his father's foreign policy; and as descendant of Valentina Visconti, he added thereto claims on the Milanese, of which he easily made himself master. The desire of obtaining the imperial dignity made him pay too dearly for the friendship of the King of the Romans, and his ambition entangled him in the snares of the King of Aragón. Even during the lifetime of Charles VIII, the Catholic Sovereigns had concluded with M. de Clérieux, the French ambassador, an agreement for common action against the Kingdom of Naples (Treaty of Alcalá de Henares, November 24, 1497).[12] They asked only for Calabria to compensate them for the expenses of the expedition. Louis XII naïvely renewed this project and signed with Spain a secret treaty of partition which assigned Apulia and Calabria to Ferdinand, and reserved for Louis the Terra di Lavoro and Naples (Treaty of Granada, November 11, 1500).

The conquest was easy; but the day after the victory the allies fell out over a question of boundaries. Louis XII demanded a province which had fallen to Ferdinand's lot, and hostilities began. The French at first had the better of it, and cooped Gonsalo de Córdoba up in Barletta. There the Spanish general and his troops suffered all the horrors of famine (July 1502 to April 1503). Before assuming the offensive he waited for reinforcements; these reached him at the beginning of April 1503 and enabled him to extricate himself. Even as he sent an army to Gonzalo, the astute King of Aragón was maneuvering to secure for himself the advantages of a good peace in case of defeat, while resolved to extract all possible advantage from a victory. The relations of Philip the Handsome with Louis XII were the foundations on which he built his shrewd calculations.

The Archduke Philip, the King of France, and Maximilian had already concluded in 1502, at Lyon (April 15, 1502) and Trent (October 13, 1501), treaties which stipulated the marriage of Claude of France with Charles of Luxembourg, son of Philip the Handsome. The House of Burgundy rejoiced at a marriage that gained for it in France the equivalent of what it had lost there.[13] So cordial had become the relations of Philip the Handsome with Louis XII that the archduke did not hesitate to cross France in order to pass into Spain when he and his wife went there to be recognized as heirs of the throne by the Cortes of Aragón and Castile.[14] The Catholic Sovereigns hoped to keep their daughter and son-in-law beside them for a prolonged period, but Philip would only stay a year (January 23, 1502, to March 1503). In March 1503 he departed for home by way of France. At that moment the Spaniards and the French were grappling in the Kingdom of Naples; Gonzalo de Córdoba had not yet broken the siege of Barletta. Philip hoped to settle the quarrel and reconcile the warring monarchs. However, he did not display the same complete trust as on his first journey and, probably at the urging of his father-in-law, did not risk setting foot on French soil until three princes of the blood had been sent to the Low Countries.

In what measure and on what conditions was he authorized to treat with Louis XII? It is difficult to say. Had he received a carte blanche? Isabella herself affirmed that she sent Philip full powers to negotiate.[15] In any case, the archduke believed himself authorized to sign a treaty of peace. He found Louis XII at Lyon, and on April 5 they agreed on the terms of the accord. The marriage of Claude of France with Charles of Luxembourg was the pledge of their reconciliation. The Capitanata,[16] an object of litigation, was to be placed in the hands of third parties and governed in the name of the young spouses. The Kings of France and Aragón were to keep the provinces that had been assigned to them by the treaty of partition. The historian Juan de Ferreras claims that the Abbot Boil, assigned to Philip as his mentor, unsuccessfully sought to dissuade him from signing; but the careful author of the *Anales de Aragón,* Zurita, confirms that this same Abbot Boil did not withhold his own signature.

Louis XII promptly sent his troops an order suspending hostilities. At that very moment Gonzalo de Córdoba, strengthened by the reinforcements he had received from Spain, found himself in a position to launch a vigorous offensive. One of his lieutenants, Fernando de Andrade, trounced Robert d'Aubigny at Seminara (April 21, 1503). Gonzalo himself went out to meet the Duke of Nemours. The French vainly hastened to notify the

Spaniards that peace had been concluded. The Great Captain replied that he was under orders to obey only a letter written in Ferdinand's own hand. The French, weakened and demoralized, were conquered at Cerignola (April 28). On May 14 the Spaniards entered Naples; soon the whole kingdom was in their hands. Louis XII cried perfidy; but the King of Aragón was not the man to be moved by such a reproach. The death of Alexander VI (August 18) and the defeat of the French on the Garigliano (December 27) ended all hopes of revenge. A three months' truce (March 31, 1504) left the Spaniards in occupation of all the conquered territory. Some months later the new master of Naples communicated to his unlucky rival the doubts that possession of his recent conquest inspired in him. To make peace with his conscience he offered to return the Kingdom of Naples to its legitimate lord, King Federico, if Federico's son would consent to marry Ferdinand's niece.[17] This was pushing the hypocrisy of benevolence to its utmost limits.

The death of Isabella the Catholic (November 23, 1504) suspended for some years the rivalry of the two sovereigns. The marriage of Doña Juana to the Archduke Philip, which had been intended to consolidate the Spanish-Austrian entente, for the moment only resulted in raising up a formidable rival to Ferdinand. Ferdinand fully expected that Philip the Handsome would be content with an empty title and would leave effective power to his father-in-law, but he failed to take into account the ambition of the prince and the resentment the Aragonese king inspired in the Castilian aristocracy. His situation was delicate in the extreme. He was completely unsure as to the attitude of Castile and had everything to fear from an alliance between Louis XII and the House of Burgundy. Several months before the death of Isabella,

Maximilian, King of the Romans, his son, and the King of France had concluded a union which was to make of the sovereigns "a single soul in three bodies." [18] The contracting parties engaged themselves not to negotiate any settlement touching the Kingdom of Naples with either Ferdinand or Federico without the consent of the others. The King of Aragón was not allowed to enter the alliance save on condition of turning over to the archduke control of the Kingdom of Naples. This pledge was to remain in the hands of Philip the Handsome until the marriage of Claude of France and Charles of Luxembourg, into whose hands it was to pass.[19]

These clauses were really portentous. Ferdinand had reason to fear a concerted action by his allies. Could he overcome a rising supported by Philip's troops and a simultaneous attack across the Pyrenees? [20] "It was believed that Philip had obtained permission to cross France with a small army. Other and more ominous rumors were current concerning the loyalty of the Castilian captains in command at Naples." It is certain that Ferdinand felt out the intentions of Gonzalo de Córdoba. In this extremity Ferdinand resolutely chose his course: He turned toward France. "His overtures came at an opportune moment; Louis XII, just recovered from a grave illness, began to feel the burden of the commitments he had made to the House of Austria. He reflected with terror that in marrying his daughter Claude to the Archduke Charles he would have to abandon to the spouses the two provinces of Burgundy and Brittany. An alliance with Ferdinand terminated the disastrous adventure of the treaties of Blois." Louis XII transferred all his rights to Naples to his niece Germaine de Foix, who became Ferdinand's second wife. The King of Aragón in turn pledged the crown of Naples to the children that he should have by this French princess and promised to indemnify the Angevin barons.

The Treaty of Blois of October 12, 1505, had advantages for both parties. Louis XII gave up hopeless claims, and Ferdinand dispelled an imminent and terrible danger at the cost of some uncertain promises. Philip the Handsome, surprised by the defection of Louis XII, consented to make peace with Ferdinand (the Treaty of Salamanca, November 24, 1505); father-in-law and son-in-law were to rule jointly. "But this equality in ruling was a chimerical conception which neither king took very seriously." Philip the Handsome had hardly disembarked at Coruña when he forgot his engagements. The Castilian aristocracy openly pushed him toward a rupture. Ferdinand was on the point of formally declaring war; he gave up the idea in order not to compromise the future. At Puebla de Sanabria and again at Remesal de Sanabria, Philip had interviews with the king which fixed the terms of their agreement. Ferdinand should keep the grand masterships and half the revenues of the Kingdom of Granada, but must withdraw into his hereditary estates. He immediately left for Naples. The idea of treason on the part of Gonzalo de Córdoba haunted him; he had been on the point of sending his natural son Alonso de Aragón, Archbishop of Zaragoza, to take all power into his own hands. A letter in which the Great Captain refuted all calumnies dissuaded Ferdinand from this desperate expedient, but did not completely remove his suspicions. In Spain events appeared to work in his favor. He had not yet arrived in Naples when he learned of the death of Philip the Handsome. He was in no hurry to return and continued his journey, persuaded that a few months of anarchy would make the Castilians more docile. His stay in Italy allowed him to hatch new intrigues; on the return journey he saw

Louis XII at Savona and prepared to wring all possible advantage from the French alliance. When he was not making war on Louis, he found ways of making Louis go to war, to Ferdinand's own great profit.

Julius II then occupied the chair of St. Peter. An ardent, overbearing spirit, he proposed to make the Papacy the most powerful seigniory in all Italy, and to use this power to drive the foreigner from the Peninsula. Venice was as hateful to the pontiff as the "barbarians"; she held Ravenna, Cervia, Faenza, Rimini, Imola, Cesena, which had belonged to the Holy See.[21]

Julius II had no trouble finding allies against the usurpers of his temporal domain. By their commerce, industry, and wealth, by their policy, at once bold and prudent, by their enterprises, ever crowned with success, the Venetians had raised against themselves the jealousy and hatred of foreigner and Italian alike. Maximilian mourned the loss of Verona, Padua, Vicenza, Treviso, and the Friuli, former lands of the Empire; Louis XII wished to round out his Duchy of Milan, which lacked Brescia, Crema, Cremona, Bergamo, the Ghiara de Adda; finally, as concerns Naples, the Venetians had compensated themselves for the help they had given Ferrante II and Federico against the French by occupying Trani, Otranto, and Gallipoli. The new ruler of Naples had no intention of leaving the ports of his kingdom in Venetian hands. All these greedy and discontented princes signed the League of Cambrai (December 10, 1508); they bound themselves to war against the Republic of Venice until the objectives of each had been completely attained. The French, who were the first to be ready, crossed the Adda and defeated the Venetian army at Agnadello; from there they fanned out as far as the lagoons.

The King of Aragón proposed to save himself the expenses of participating in a campaign whose fruits he intended to reap. The Venetians, occupied in resisting Louis XII and Maximilian, neglected to defend the ports of the Kingdom of Naples; Ferdinand retook them and stopped right there. In fact, he was inclined to deplore the excessive good fortune of his friends. The Austrian-French armies were really too successful. Almost all the mainland domains of the Venetian Republic had fallen into their power; Venice seemed doomed. Ferdinand had been quite willing for Louis XII to organize a diversion in Ferdinand's favor; but he did not like to see France work in her own interest. Yet, whatever ill will he might bear his allies, too rapacious to please him, he hesitated to violate openly the Treaty of Cambrai; he still needed Louis XII, who was trying to iron out Ferdinand's differences with the King of the Romans on the subject of Castile. He pushed forward his son-in-law, Henry VIII, King of England, who became the Republic's advocate before all the allied courts. Henry's representations enabled his father-in-law to put the Venetian question on the diplomatic agenda.[22] When the matter of the succession of Philip the Handsome had been settled to his entire satisfaction (December 1509), Ferdinand put away all scruples, and by way of rewarding the King of France for his good offices he organized a coalition against him.

The Pope was quite ready to lend an ear to Ferdinand's suggestions. Having satisfied most of his own territorial ambitions by ousting the Venetians from their cities in the Romagna, Julius II discovered, like the King of Aragón, that the French were very greedy. On February 25, 1510, he withdrew from the League of Cambrai and gave an absolution to the Venetians whom he had excommunicated. This defection foretold a break with France. Ferdinand neglected no means in order to stir up the pontiff's wrath against his former allies. He se-

THE
ITALIES
ABOUT
1494

KINGDOM
OF
HUNGARY

TYROL   CARINTHIA

INNSBRUCK

CARNIOLA
LJUBLJANA   ZAGREB
GORIZIA
TRIESTE
FIUME

OTTOMAN
EMPIRE

B. OF
TRENT
TRENT   BOLZANO
BELLUNO
FRIULI
UDINE

AOSTA
BIELLA
NOVARA
BERGAMO   VALDAGNO   TREVISO
GONADELLO   CREMA   BRESCIA   VICENZA
MILAN   VERONA   PADUA
COMO
VERCELLI   PAVIA   MANTUA   ESTE   VENICE
DUCHY
TURIN   PIACENZA   CREMONA
ASTI
ALESSANDRIA   PARMA
SALUZZO   REGGIO   FERRARA
SAVOY   GENOA   MODENA   FERRARA
SAVONA   EMILIA   BOLOGNA   RAVENNA
MONACO   SPEZIA   CARRARA   FAENZA   CERVIA
NICE   VENTIMIGLIA   PISTOIA   RIMINI
LUCCA   FLORENCE   REP. OF   CESENA
PISA   LEGHORN   SAN MARINO
REP. OF   URBINO
FLORENCE   ANCONA

DALMATIA
ZADAR

LIGURIAN   SEA

CORSICA
BASTIA
AJACCIO

ELBA

REP. OF
SIENA

SIENA
AREZZO

PERUGIA
ASSISI
UMBRIA   SPOLETO
ORVIETO
VITERBO   TERNI
PATRIMONY   AQUILA
TIVOLI
OF ST. PETER   ROME
OSTIA

THE   MARCHES
MACERATA
ASCOLI
TERAMO
PESCARA

ABRUZZI

MOLISE   CAPITANATA
CAMPOBASSO   FOGGIA
GAETA   SESSA   BENEVENTO   BARLETTA
CAPUA   CERIGNOLA   TRANI   BARI
NAPLES   ATELLA
SALERNO   APULIA
POTENZA   TARANTO
BASILICATA   OTRANTO
GALLIPOLI

ADRIATIC   SEA

KOTOR

SARDINIA
SASSARI

CAGLIARI

TYRRHENIAN   KINGDOM

SEA   OF   THE

COSENZA
CATANZARO

TWO   SICILIES
TERRANOVA
SEMINARA
REGGIO
MESSINA

MEDITERRANEAN

PALERMO
TRAPANI
MARSALA
SICILY
CALTANISSETTA   CATANIA
AGRIGENTO
RAGUSA   SYRACUSE

SEA

AFRICA

TUNIS

MALTA

cretly communicated to him a dispatch in which Ferdinand's ambassador in France, Jerome Cabanillas, reported (April 1510) that Louis XII was going to descend on Italy in full force to conquer the Papal States and cast the Pope in prison. So angry did Julius II become that he proposed to march in person at the head of his troops. The progress of the French arms in Italy, the French threat of an ecumenical council, only stoked the fires of his resentment. A Holy League was concluded in October 1511 between the Pope, Venice, and Ferdinand. On November 13, the adhesion of Henry VIII was obtained; several months later, that of Maximilian.

This time the King of Aragón had no intention of staying out of the fray. The forces of the Holy League were commanded by Ramón de Cardona, Viceroy of Naples, and Spanish infantry formed the backbone of the allied army. For a moment Louis XII appeared equal to meeting and overcoming this immense danger. A young hero, Gaston de Foix, brother of Ferdinand's wife Germaine, had inspired his troops with his own ardor. After taking and pillaging Brescia he advanced against the allies, who had invested Bologna. At his approach the besiegers abandoned their project and retreated as far as Ravenna. There a decisive engagement took place. The French artillery devastated the enemy ranks. The Italian contingents disbanded and fled, but a body of Spanish infantry fell back slowly, without panic or disorder. Gaston de Foix found intolerable a sight that appeared to diminish his triumph; he sought to break this last resistance, threw himself, followed by a few horsemen, against this impenetrable mass, and fell under a rain of enemy blows (April 11, 1512).

The battle was won; but the death of Gaston de Foix snatched away all the fruits of victory. The French commander, La Palisse, brave and methodical, lacked daring. A corps of twelve thousand Swiss joined the Venetian troops and compelled the French to fall back on the Adda River. A Spanish army entered Florence and restored the Medicis to power; Genoa abandoned the French side. All Italy was lost for France. The adroit Ferdinand had destroyed the only power capable of counterbalancing Spain in the Peninsula. The Holy League established Spanish domination in Italy.

This was not the only advantage secured by Ferdinand. He never neglected the affairs of Spain. Even as he joined with Julius II against Louis XII, he had negotiated with Henry VII and offered to conquer Aquitania for him if Henry would send him several thousand troops (note of November 17, 1511). An English army commanded by the Marquis of Dorset landed in Biscay and joined the Spanish forces. But the allies disagreed as to the conduct of operations. The Marquis of Dorset wished to follow the coast and strike directly at Bayonne. Ferdinand insisted that Navarre must be occupied before attacking Aquitania. We may safely assume that the conquest of Navarre was his only concern. During this debate the Duke of Alba, loyal executor of his master's secret designs, possessed himself of the whole kingdom up to Saint-Jean-Pied-de-Port. Jean d'Albret, King of Navarre, was excommunicated by Julius II as the instigator of the famous Council of Pisa, and deprived of his kingdom. A pontifical bull awarded Navarre to the victorious Ferdinand. This was the supreme culmination of his whole reign. The unity of the Peninsula was almost complete.

Ferdinand had shown himself quite unscrupulous in his choice of means, but none could dispute his ability. He had carefully refrained from pursuing wills o' the wisp after the French fashion. His policy, which never lost sight of its goals, never turned aside to pursue shadows, enabled him to consolidate conquests and score brilliant diplomatic successes. He knew just how far he should push his demands and did not seek to take excessive advantage of his good fortune.

Ferdinand, who had no liking for war, was always ready to conclude an agreement if it conformed to his interests. On April 1, 1513, he signed with Louis XII, at Orthez, a one-year truce that left him in possession of large gains pending the signing of a definitive treaty. He egged on Henry VIII and Maximilian to invade France; he received with satisfaction news of the defeat of the French at Novara (June 6) and at Guinegate (August 16, 1513), and of the entrance of the Swiss and the Imperials into Burgundy, but he would not budge. His son-in-law, Henry VIII, urged him to attack Guienne in order to draw a part of the French forces toward the south.[23] He objected that his conscience forbade him to launch an attack on the domains of Louis XII, but that he was willing to move against Béarn, a possession of the House of Albret. Henry VIII replied that Louis XII was not sufficiently concerned for the fate of the Albrets to risk the loss of his kingdom in their behalf. Ferdinand was very careful not to expose himself to any dangers in a foreign cause. He simultaneously welcomed the overtures of Louis XII and Anne of Brittany, who proposed a marriage of Renée of France with his grandson, the Infante Ferdinand.[24] Anne's death halted these parleys, but the truce of Orthez was renewed at Orléans (March 13, 1514).

The King of France was playing for time and preparing his revenge. He took advantage of the discontent of Henry VIII to effect a rapprochement. In the numerous treaties that the King of Aragón and the King of the Romans had signed with the King of England, it had been stipulated that Charles of Luxembourg should wed

Henry's sister Mary. Now, Charles had just reached his fourteenth year; Henry VIII demanded that the marriage take place. Ferdinand and Maximilian, who cherished the project of uniting their grandson with the heiress to the crowns of Hungary and Bohemia, replied with evasions that were regarded as affronts. Louis XII, perceiving an opportunity to break the solidarity of the enemy camp, asked, notwithstanding his advanced age, for the hand of the jilted young princess. His nuptials hastened his end, and his plan perished with him. His successor, François I, was a youth eager for glory and combat.

Ferdinand, who had reason to fear a new invasion of Italy, ably exploited the disquiet aroused by François. On February 12, 1515, the Pope, the Emperor, the Duke of Milan, the Medicis, the Swiss Confederation, and the King of Aragón and Castile formed a league against the young monarch. A place in the alliance was reserved for Henry VIII, whose adherence was not long delayed. Ferdinand died some months later (January 23, 1516), having created a coalition directed against François I. His last act summed up the idea that had inspired his whole policy: Close off Spain to the French, close off Italy to the French.

Ferdinand had two grandsons, both born to his daughter Doña Juana, Charles of Luxembourg and Ferdinand. Charles, who became Charles V, Holy Roman Emperor, had been raised in the Low Countries; Ferdinand, his brother, had never left Spain. He was the old king's favorite; he had lived by his side and received a completely Spanish education. This preference could not prevail over Charles's right as eldest son to succeed to the thrones of Castile and Aragón. It has been claimed, however, that the doting grandfather sought to get around the rule of succession.

King Ferdinand's extensive dominions already included Spain and the New World, and the Kingdom of the Two Sicilies. What an immense conglomerate would be formed by adding thereto the possessions of the House of Burgundy and the domains of the House of Austria! Should Charles, heir of both Maximilian and Ferdinand, unite in his hands rule over all these lands? Should he seek to reign over all these different peoples? Was it not possible to assign a share to the younger brother? We may be sure that Ferdinand's jealous tenderness, not to speak of his immense experience, had already posed the question. Would it not be better for Spain and the two Sicilies to have their own king than to be subjected to the rule of a cosmopolitan monarch? The historian Maurenbrecher maintains that this was Ferdinand's thought, and that only fear of France and the alarm caused by the victory of Marignano induced him to give up this cherished plan.[25]

Another German scholar, Bergenroth, has embroidered a very ingenious romance on this theme.[26] He angrily rejects as unworthy of Ferdinand the project ascribed to him of leaving Aragón and Naples to the Archduke Ferdinand and Castile to the Archduke Charles; but if he has no difficulty proving how unlikely was this partition, he soon shows that he is without a peer among the spinners of theories. He subordinates the whole policy of the grandfather to a single idea: the formation of an Italian kingdom for his youngest and best-loved grandson. Maximilian was to turn over to him the Italian provinces of the Trentino and the Tyrol; Ferdinand would give him the Two Sicilies and Sardinia; Genoa, Venice and Milan would have to be conquered. This powerful grouping would doubtless end up by absorbing Florence and the Papal States. France (so runs the argument) put herself in the way of this brilliant project; all the coalitions and leagues directed against her must have had as their sole object the gaining of French consent.

Regarded in this light, Ferdinand appears as the precursor of Cavour and Vittorio Emanuele. But Ferdinand was altogether too wise to conceive such a chimerical plan. True, the documents show him to have been intensely concerned with the future of his grandson. When Maximilian had recovered from Venice a part of the mainland provinces, the King of Aragón declared that Maximilian and he proposed to vest this territory in the Infante Ferdinand. But the reason he gave for this generous gift goes directly against Bergenroth's hypothesis: Should the infante become an Italian prince, he would be interested in defending the Duke of Milan against the French. Clearly, there was no thought here of despoiling the Sforza. The question of Naples was always kept clearly separate. The King of Aragón believed that his favorite child would gain more by securing the administration of the military orders than by having Naples. This was probably his secret thought. If there ever was a testament favorable to the Archduke Ferdinand (and there is some reason to doubt it), it could have had no other object than to assure him of the rich revenues and the exalted station of the Grand Masters of Calatrava, Alcántara, and Santiago.

Did the old king's ambitions for his favorite grandson go beyond this? We observe that the contemporary chronicler Galíndez does not ascribe to him the intention of bequeathing the crowns of Aragón, Castile, and Naples to Ferdinand; he simply says that the king intended to leave the administration of these kingdoms to Ferdinand. True, the official chronicler adds that the King of Aragón, without wishing to infringe the monarchical principle or to break the unity of the possessions of the House of

Burgundy, hoped that Charles would renounce living in
Spain, where he had not been raised, and would allow his
brother to act there, as it were, in the capacity of viceroy.[27]
This project was not unworthy of the old king's wisdom. A
partition was necessary, and later one came about through
the force of events; but there was an exchange of roles between the royal personages. Ferdinand went to reign over
the states of the House of Austria, and after the abdication
of Charles V he received the imperial crown. The successors of Charles V (Charles I of Spain) held, in addition
to the Low Countries, the Indies, Italy, and Spain. The
question arises, would not the Low Countries have fared
better in the hands of the Austrian dynasty, and would
not the Spaniards have been better off under a completely
Spanish prince, less interested in German affairs?

Even if it were well established that Ferdinand the
Catholic had dreamed of establishing a Spanish viceroy-
alty[28] for his favorite grandson, this fact would not diminish his greatness. Ever ready to heed the advice of his
counselors, ever ready to take the times into account,
he suppressed his inclinations in order not to weaken the
crown vis-à-vis the aristocracy by a possible competition
between the two brothers, and the kingdoms vis-à-vis
France by a division of resources among different
hands. Philip II had good reason to say that the Kings of
Spain owed everything to Ferdinand. He had been the
principal architect of the present and future greatness
of the monarchy. His good fortune helped him—but
what a large role his daring and foresight played! To Isabella, Spain owed the Kingdom of Granada and the New
World; to Ferdinand, her northern frontiers, her Italian
empire, and the fundamentals of her foreign policy.
When Isabella died, Spain had emerged from her isolation to join the ranks of the great powers. At the death
of Ferdinand, she had become the dominant state in

Europe without arousing a general resentment; she had not only successfully defended herself against France but had even managed to turn against France all the powers of Europe.

IV

The Indies

Spain in this period enjoyed the success that is the fruit of calculation, and the good fortune that is a bonus, as it were, awarded to ability. History records many a famous victory that was the fruit, not of foresight, but of a happy chance. But Fortune's darlings do not show themselves worthy of her gifts unless they make the most of their opportunities. Ferdinand and Isabella did this the day a foreigner of genius offered them a new world.

The desire to reach the Land of Spices, joined to knowledge of the roundness of the earth, sooner or later had to lead to the discovery of America. If the Portuguese sought their route to the East by going around Africa, others might be tempted to cut straight across the western seas. The stories of Marco Polo seem to have drawn the attention of the Italians toward this solution of the problem. The Italian cosmographers speculated that the Empire of Cathay (China) was not very far from western Europe. On June 25, 1474, eighteen years before Columbus departed on his memorable voyage,[1] the Florentine astronomer Paolo dal Pozzo Toscanelli wrote the Portuguese Fernão Martins: "I have formerly spoken with you about a shorter sea route *to the places of Spices* by ocean navigation than that which you are pursuing by way of Guinea. The most gracious King now desires from me some statement, or rather an exhibit for the eye, so that even slightly educated persons can grasp and understand that route. Although I am well aware that this can be proved from the spherical shape of the earth, nevertheless, in order to make the point clearer and to facilitate the enterprise, I have decided to display that route by means of a sailing chart. I therefore send to His Majesty a chart made by my own hands, upon which are laid down your coasts, and the islands from which you must begin to shape your course *steadily westward*." [2]

This was the plan that Columbus put into effect. The idea was not Toscanelli's own; it arose inevitably from men's knowledge of the shape of the earth. This fact does not detract from the fame of the Discoverer. He retains the glory of having undertaken a daring deed in which he risked life and honor on a hypothesis and, what required even greater courage, of having coolly braved the terrible unknown dangers of a mysterious ocean.

Christopher Columbus was the son of Domenico Colombo, a native of the Valley of La Fontanabuona in the Republic of Genoa. His father was a weaver; he himself was a wool-carder; he was born about 1446 at Quinto or at Terrarossa.[3]

Centuries later a writer of charm and conviction, Roselly de Lorgues, zealously labored for the canonization of the great navigator, and while waiting for the Roman Court to grant his client a place among the celestial aristocracy, sought to confer on Columbus membership in the nobility of this earth. History is not so exigent. It does not demand a saint, or a gentleman, or even a student grown wan with the study of learned tracts. Columbus's attendance at the University of Pisa is a tribute paid by the filial piety and vanity of his son Ferdinand to his

quick and penetrating intelligence. Reality is more elo-
quent than fiction. In 1473, Columbus was still at Genoa,
practicing his modest trade. We have no way of knowing whether prior to this date he had ever gone to sea.
His only school was the town of Genoa, rival of Venice,
where the needs of commerce caused the art of navigation and the scientific knowledge that goes with it to be
brought to perfection, where eminent cosmographers
recorded on portolani the results obtained to date and inspired thirst for new discoveries, where the sight of the
port, the endless horizon of the sea, the coming and going
of the ships, the quays burdened with merchandise, all
excited adventurous imaginations.

Columbus must have felt these powerful lures. In
1473 he departed for Portugal, where certain Genoese,
the Pessagno, had charge of all shipping and gave preference in employment to their countrymen. The wool-
carder became a seaman; he sailed to the fort of São Jorge
da Mina in the new Portuguese possession of Guinea;
he made a large number of voyages to the Levant, to
the north, and to the south. If at the time of his departure
from Genoa he had not yet set foot on a vessel, he was
quickly initiated into his new profession and became very
skilled in it. When did he begin to be haunted by the vision of a route to the Indies? One would like to think that
this dream already obsessed him in his father's shop in
Genoa, that he first went to sea in order to put himself in
the way of turning that dream into reality. If we could be
absolutely sure that he had not sailed before 1473 and
that he had knowledge as early as 1474 of Toscanelli's
letter to Fernão Martins, we might conclude that Columbus regarded his voyage as a mere prelude to and preparation for discovery; we might speculate that he first
came to Europe's extreme West to look out from the

coasts of Portugal and Guinea, as if from an outpost, upon that boundless ocean across which he proposed to open a way to the lands of Marco Polo.

Ten years later (1484) we find him in Spain. The Enterprise of the Indies obsessed him; he later wrote that he had broached his project to and received proposals from the Kings of France, Portugal, and England, but had rejected them all in order to enrich Castile. More likely he was the only one at that period who believed the enterprise to be easy and profitable. Like all dreamers, Columbus tended to give an external reality to his own imaginings. He must have confused his own overtures with the proposals of princes. At any rate, he had established himself in Castile. In the account book of the Royal Treasurer, Francisco González of Seville, we find the name of Christopher Columbus, "foreigner employed for certain matters in the service of Their Highnesses." [4]

His life is difficult to reconstruct. It appears that the sovereigns afforded him an opportunity to present and defend his ideas. To this end they assembled at Salamanca a council composed of members of the court, scientists, and mariners, and presided over by Fray Hermando de Talavera, the queen's confessor (1486 to 1487). According to an eyewitness, Columbus did not succeed in convincing his learned auditors. This may be the foundation on which arose the story of a solemn debate before the University of Salamanca. Possibly some professors of the university did attend the conference, but this is only a hypothesis.

Discouraged by this setback and neglected by the Catholic Sovereigns, who had more pressing cares (the crusade against the Moors), in 1489 Columbus decided to go to France; he was induced to stay by Luis de la Cerda, Duke of Medina Celi, who lodged him for two years at his castle at Puerto de Santa María, and even agreed to provide him with the caravels that he needed. Isabella, informed by the duke of his project, refused her authorization and ordered Alonso de Quintanilla to subject the enterprise to a new examination. Columbus came to the camp of Santa Fe, whence, angered by new delays, he departed with the firm intention of leaving Spain forever. He was sadly trudging back to Portugal, leading his son Diego by the hand, when, on arrival near the Convent of La Rábida, he came to the door to ask for bread and water for his little boy. A monk, Juan Pérez, noting his foreign accent, began to ask him questions. The traveler spoke, and spoke so well that he persuaded the friar. Pérez immediately wrote the queen, whose confessor he had been. He was summoned to the camp of Santa Fe, and succeeded in convincing his former penitent. Ferdinand and Isabella ordered Columbus to return. This time they were resolved to keep their word.

A new conference took place at Santa Fe in the last months of 1491. Cardinal Mendoza presided. The Italian Alessandro Geraldini, tutor of the infantes, relates that the majority of the Spanish prelates, basing themselves on the system of Nicolas de Lyra and of St. Augustine, saw a heresy in the ideas of Columbus: "I found myself by chance," says he, "behind Cardinal Mendoza and observed to him that Nicolas de Lyra and St. Augustine had unquestionably been excellent theologians but mediocre geographers, since the Portuguese had reached a point in the other hemisphere where the Pole Star could not be seen, and had discovered another star at the opposite pole, and had even found all the lands in the torrid zone densely peopled. . . ." St. Augustine was disregarded.

After all those years of waiting, of entreaties, of refusals, the unknown dreamer was at last given the opportunity to realize his audacious ideas. Isabella, ever economical, risked only 1,140,000 maravedís in the venture; she ordered the town of Palos to atone for some misdeed by providing the vessels needed for two months and the pay of the crews for four months. Columbus and his unknown protectors furnished 500,000 maravedís. Some able shipowners of Palos, the Pinzón brothers, sailed with him. He had under his orders two caravels of small tonnage and a small decked ship, carrying one hundred twenty men in all; the crews were largely recruited from the town's jail.[5] With this small fleet, accompanied by adventurers of all nations, the Genoese mariner departed for the Indies.

On Wednesday, August 3, 1492, the fleet left Palos, cleared the mouth of the Tinto River, and put out into the high seas. Columbus first set course for the Canaries. On September 8, the fleet left that archipelago. Beyond lay the unknown, a region peopled by sea monsters, a bottomless, boundless ocean. The crews had begun to murmur, the ship captains were on the verge of revolt, when, on the night of Thursday to Friday, October 11 to 12, Columbus himself descried a vague light that betokened land. At daybreak they saw an island, perhaps Guanahaní, which Columbus baptized with the name of San Salvador. They saw some naked Indians on the shore. After landing on several small islands of the Bahamas, on October 28 Columbus reached Cuba. He sailed down its coast, discovered Española and Tortuga, and was shipwrecked on Cap-Haïtien. Everywhere he found men of gentle and peaceable disposition; the pious Discoverer flattered himself that he could easily lead them to Christianity.

Leaving a small garrison in a fort constructed on the shore of Española, he hastened to return to Spain to announce his marvelous discovery. On March 15, 1493, he again crossed the bar of the Tinto. The sovereigns received him with extraordinary honors. They made him be seated and cover himself in their presence. News of the discovery spread rapidly among all European nations. The explorer gave the most enthusiastic accounts of the resources and beauty of the country, of the luxuriance of its vegetation, of the abundance of its gold, which could even be gathered from the sands of its brooks.

Bearing the titles of Admiral and Viceroy of the Indies, he sailed again on September 22 or 25, 1493. The fleet took a more southerly course; and new islands were discovered: Désirade, Dominica, Marie-Galante, Guadeloupe. The natives of this region were of savage disposition; they raided the other peoples of the islands, carried away their women, ate their prisoners, and fattened young boys for their inhuman feasts. On November 16, Columbus discovered Puerto Rico and then sailed for Española, where he found that the Spaniards left by him had been massacred by Indians. On the northern coast of the island he founded Isabela, the first town constructed in America by Europeans. Then he sailed for Cuba.

This island, whose northern coast stretches east to west a length of 720 miles, he believed to be a continent. He was convinced that he had at least reached the mysterious realms of Cathay and Cipango; he thought that he was only a hundred degrees from the Golden Chersonese (Malacca Peninsula).[6] So complete was his confidence that he resorted to a novel proceeding to implant conviction. He compelled every member of his crew "to declare before a notary, on pain of a hundred lashes and having the tongue slit if they ever gainsaid the same, that Cuba was the mainland." [7]

Thus Columbus was determined to join his discoveries to those of Marco Polo, end to end. He believed that he had reached by sea the lands that the illustrious Venetian had reached overland across the whole expanse of Asia. He was more fortunate than he knew. He had discovered the approaches to a world. He went on to discover Jamaica, but instead of pushing westward, which would have brought him to the Aztec Empire, he returned to Isabela, September 29, 1494. The cares of government and the revolt of the Indians of Española detained him on the island for two years. He did not see Cádiz again until June 11, 1496.

It was on his third voyage, begun from Sanlúcar, the port of Seville, on May 30, 1498, that Columbus finally set foot on the mainland. Leaving the Cape Verdes, he steered farther south than before, and on July 31 discovered Trinidad. He rounded it and encountered the powerful tidal wave that the Orinoco forms in its conflict with the ocean. This mighty current of sweet water convinced the explorer that it was the discharge of a continental stream. Sailing through the Boca de la Sierpe, he crossed the great Gulf of Paria, and went ashore in a harbor on the Paria Peninsula the fifth, sixth, or seventh of August.[8] He left the Gulf of Paria by the Boca del Dragón, and discovered Margarita. The natives received him without hostility; a superb and luxuriant nature spread itself before him. Columbus believed that the Orinoco was one of the rivers of Paradise, and that it had its source in the ancient Garden of Eden, from which mankind had been driven through the sin of our first parents. But on August 31, when he landed at the town of Santo Domingo, founded by his brother, he perceived that he had returned to an inferno. In Spain, the initial enthusiasm had given way to skepticism. The hope of finding infinite riches had proved vain; the fleets sent to Española did not even pay for themselves. The adventurers who had been drawn to Española by greed for gold, and who had experienced every possible misery, blamed the viceroy for their sufferings. The Alcalde Mayor, Francisco Roldán, had raised the standard of revolt against him.

All these developments, exaggerated by passion, swollen by distance, reached the ears of the sovereigns. The rumor flew about that the Columbus brothers were planning to make themselves independent. The court sent out Francisco de Bobadilla with the title of governor and with full powers to conduct an inquiry. As soon as he arrived at Santo Domingo, Bobadilla, without any investigation, clapped Christopher and Bartholomew Columbus in irons and sent them to Europe. In this state the discoverer of America made his third landing in Castile. It is said that the generous Isabella could not restrain her tears at the sight. The action of the governor was disavowed, Nicolás de Ovando was named in his place; but despite her show of tenderness the queen did not return to Columbus the administration of the colony.

Under the blows of these injustices Columbus's embittered spirit sought consolation on high; mingling his dreams with his spleen, he saw the end of the world as near and proclaimed the necessity of hastening the fulfillment of the grand designs that he had conceived. The mysticism of Columbus was an essential trait of his nature. His unshakable confidence in himself was derived therefrom. He believed himself to be the elect of God, one of those privileged servants whom Providence takes and directs by the hand both to honor them and for Its own glory. When he related to the Catholic Sovereigns the marvelous visions that consoled him for the miseries of reality, this plain sea captain rose on the wings of imagination and faith to a grand eloquence.

Lying off the coast of Honduras, abandoned by his crews, almost dying, he despairs: "In a trembling and weeping voice, I called several times to all the four winds, on the war captains of Your Highness, to ask for their aid; but they did not reply. Exhausted, I fell asleep while weeping; then I heard a compassionate voice saying: Oh! Senseless man and slow to believe and serve thy God, the God of all! Did He do more for Moses and for David His servant? From the day of thy birth, He ever took the greatest care of thee. When He saw that thou hadst reached the age that suited His design, He made thy name resound marvelously over all the earth. Those Indies that form one part of the earth, those rich Indies, He gave to thee, that thou mightest give them again to whomsoever pleased thee, and He empowered thee to do this. He gave thee the keys to the doors of the Ocean Sea, that were closed with such strong chains; thou hast been obeyed over so many lands and hast obtained a good and honorable name among the Christians. Did He do more for Israel when He led it out of Egypt? And for David, whom He raised from a shepherd to be king in Judea? Turn to Him and admit thy error, His mercy is infinite; thine old age will not hinder thee from attaining the greatest things; many very great inheritances are in His power to bestow. . . . I was half dead, yet heard all; but had no other reply to such just words than to weep at my errors. Then he who spoke, whoever it was, ceased to speak, saying: 'Trust and fear not, all these tribulations are written on marble, and not without cause.'" [9]

We should not ascribe the idea of the discovery to the penetrating intuition of his genius, or to the compact logic of his reasonings. His inspiration was elsewhere: He found his illumination in the prophecies of Isaiah. He was himself a prophet: The world would end in one hundred fifty years. It was necessary to hurry, to gather immense resources in order to deliver the Holy Sepulcher. He wanted to depart on another expedition that would provide the necessary treasure and that would be but a prelude to the last and supreme crusade.

Naturally, a prince as cool, as pragmatic, as calculating as Ferdinand would hesitate to risk a large investment on so problematical an adventure. He agreed to entrust a new fleet to Columbus, whose great navigational skill he recognized; but he doled out sparingly the necessary funds.

He gave him only three caravels and a ship of small tonnage, and expressly forbade the admiral to disembark on Española.

On this fourth voyage, after sailing to Española and from there past Jamaica, Columbus steered to the southwest, crossed the Caribbean, and came to the Bay Islands off the coast of Honduras, July 30, 1502. He ranged the coast, doubled Cape Gracias a Dios, and sailed as far south as the Chiriqui lagoons and the narrow isthmus that joins the two Americas. He believed himself to be a nineteen days' journey from the Ganges and did not suspect that he was so near another ocean. He resolved to return to Española. The return voyage was marked by every possible misfortune; he was cast away on Jamaica and waited for six months for aid that did not arrive; Nicolás de Ovando, jealous of his glory, left him in this perilous situation, exposed to the mutinies of his crew and the hostility of the local Indians. Finally, in June 1504, he arrived at Santo Domingo; in November 1504, he returned to Europe. His protectress Isabella was dead; his services and claims were regarded by Ferdinand as a burden. He passed the last two years of his life in soliciting favors whose grant was always put off, in demanding rights and privileges that the crown contested. He died at Valladolid, May 21, 1506.

He did not even leave his name to the continent that he

discovered. Explorers of lesser stature followed in the footsteps of the great navigator. Alonso de Ojeda, the pilot Juan de la Cosa, and the Florentine Amerigo Vespucci sailed in 1499 to those mouths of the Orinoco that Columbus had just visited.[10] They carried maps that he had prepared and followed in the wake of his ship, as it were, the length of the Venezuelan coast. Amerigo Vespucci wrote the history of this voyage; his account, diffused throughout Europe, gave its author the reputation of being the first European to tread the soil of the new continent. Yet Columbus had preceded him by a year in the same region.[11] In his *Cosmographiae introductio,* published at Saint-Dié in 1507, Martin Waldseemüller of Fribourg proposed the name "America" for the world that Amerigo Vespucci had surveyed.[12] The name caught on; and posterity has been powerless to correct its injustice.

Once the impulse had been given, the area of exploration grew day by day. First the broad expanse of the Caribbean was overrun. Sebastián de Ocampo sailed around Cuba, Juan Díaz de Solís and Vicente Yáñez Pinzón touched on the coast of Yucatán. Juan Ponce de León, he who sought the Fountain of Youth, discovered Florida. The establishments that Alonso de Ojeda and Diego de Nicuesa made on the Gulf of Darién were disastrous failures; but one of the survivors, Vasco Núñez de Balboa, crossed the Isthmus of Panamá and discovered the Pacific. Now there was proof that Columbus, in sailing toward the Indies, had the way closed to him by a continent. Its magnitude was revealed by Pinzón, who, in 1500, had seen the mouth of the Marañon, and who pushed on his new voyage as far as latitude 40° South without ever losing sight on his right of an uninterrupted line of coast.[13] Hoping to find a seaway between the two oceans, Ferdinand entrusted an expedition to one of Pinzón's companions; Juan Díaz de Solís set sail for the south, ventured into the mouth of the Plata, which he took for a large strait, and fell on the banks of the river under Indian blows. On the death of the King of Aragón (1516), Florida to the north, the Río de la Plata to the south, the Isthmus of Panamá to the west, marked the limits of exploration. But to the north, other Europeans had discovered other regions. John Cabot had landed on the North American continent even before Columbus disembarked in the Gulf of Paria.

It was lucky for the cause of civilization that Columbus directed his appeal to a country as powerful as Spain. Only a great state was capable of supplying the man power needed to colonize a world. If Portugal had been favored with Spain's good fortune, she would have had to be satisfied for the most part with establishing trading posts and forts on the American coasts; Brazil alone more than kept her busy. But Spain's abundant resources were not enough; she must establish an efficient administration.

The first difficulty arose from the commitments that the Catholic Sovereigns had made to the Discoverer. The day the sovereigns approved his project, they had concluded a treaty that assured him in case of success of enormous advantages and most extensive privileges. These were the famous capitulations signed April 17, 1492, in the town of Santa Fe. The sovereigns named Columbus Admiral, Viceroy, and Governor-general of the seas, coasts, islands, and lands that he should discover.[14] These dignities were made hereditary in his family, and gave him the right of presenting three candidates for any post of profit and emolument under him, from whom the sovereigns should select one. The magistrates that he should appoint would be the only ones competent to judge disputes and offenses relating to trade and

barter. He might contribute one eighth to the cost of any enterprise formed with a view to exploiting the new lands, receiving one eighth of the profits resulting from it. He collected a tenth of all cargoes sent out and a ninth of their proceeds.

These concessions cost the sovereigns little as long as the project remained speculative, as long as the most dazzling prospect was the discovery of some islands and the opening of a sea route to the lands which, on the authority of Marco Polo, men knew to be provided with governments capable of defending their independence. But the success of the enterprise exceeded all expectations: Columbus came to places that were, so to speak, masterless, and easy prizes to the first European occupier. With each voyage the area of discovery grew; it appeared limitless. Were the capitulations to be strictly observed, Columbus might become a vassal much more powerful than his sovereigns. Could one conceive of a man of Genoese origin governing half of Spanish America, having an interest in everything, and collecting a tenth of all revenues?

The interests of Spain required, if they did not justify,

an act of perjury. There is the whole secret of Ferdinand's "ingratitude" and "perfidy." [15] Isabella shared her husband's apprehensions, for she appointed and sent to the Antilles two governors, Bobadilla and Nicolás de Ovando, in despite of Columbus's rights. She went so far as to forbid Columbus to land on Española. When he died, his son Diego demanded all his hereditary rights and even began a suit at law before the Council of the Indies. Clearly, reasons of state and not any base feelings of jealousy inspired Ferdinand's attitude. "Listen, Admiral," he once said to Diego, "I would be glad to deliver to you your patrimony, but I cannot do it because of your sons and successors." To which Diego is said to have replied: "Sir, is it just that I should pay and suffer for the sins of sons and successors whom I may never have?" [16] A witty reply, indeed—but does it not reflect a failure to understand that Columbus's great power was transmissible only on condition of being diminished and ceasing to be a source of disquiet?

Nevertheless, in 1509, Diego, who had married a niece of the Duke of Alba, obtained on the recommendation of that powerful family the privilege of departing for the Indies in the capacity of governor. But he was allowed only two consecutive years of residence in the seat of his jurisdiction; all his time was passed in coming and going from Spain to the Antilles, from the Antilles to Spain. Assuredly, not all these journeys were pleasure trips. Although in 1520 Charles V returned to Don Diego the title of viceroy, the litigation between the crown and the descendants of the Discoverer dragged on. In 1536 it was settled by a compromise. Don Luis Columbus, third Admiral of the Indies, yielded all his claims in return for the Duchy of Veragua and an annual income of 10,000 ducats.

Several establishments were made under these first

governors. Española was first occupied by the Spaniards, and became the center of their empire in the Antilles. To the north of the island, Columbus had founded the town of Isabela. His brother Bartholomew preferred Santo Domingo, on the western coast, as the island's capital. Nicolás de Ovando sent an expedition to settle Puerto Rico. The beginnings of the colonization of Jamaica and Cuba were made during the first part of the administration of Diego Columbus (1509 to 1512). Don Diego Velásquez was charged in 1511 with the establishment of Spanish domination in Cuba. In the expeditionary force were two men who left very different imprints on the history of America. One, Hernando Cortés, was to overthrow one of the great civilized empires of the continent; the other, Bartolomé de Las Casas, would attract the admiration of the entire world by his spirit of charity. Diego Columbus did not carry his colonizing efforts any farther. If Alonso de Ojeda and Diego de Nicuesa occupied various points on the mainland from the Cabo de la Vela to Cabo Gracias a Dios, they did so without the approval or participation of the governor, and contrary to his rights.

It was not enough to found posts and towns; it was necessary to ensure their order and prosperity. Certain Franciscan and Dominican monks had undertaken to convert the natives; a number of monasteries were established; bishoprics were created at Santo Domingo and Darién; Ferdinand applied to Rome for the erection of a patriarchate of the Indies in behalf of Don Juan de Fonseca.[17] The judicial hierarchy was also founded. A decree dated at Burgos (October 1511) established at Santo Domingo a royal audience which had supreme jurisdiction over all the inferior tribunals of the island. In order to lessen delays, the judges, chosen by the governor, were empowered to act as judges of first instance even in cases involving the crown (*casos de corte*).[18] These organizational beginnings helped to stabilize the Conquest. The first Spaniards who came to America had been officials, soldiers, or adventurers. Now artisans were introduced; the colonists were urged to develop agriculture. Nicolás de Ovando introduced the culture of sugar cane, which became the principal business of the settlers in Española.[19]

Unfortunately, false economic principles led both sovereigns and subjects astray. Instead of seeking to promote the relations between the colonies and the mother country, the government at the outset planned to make all trade and exploration a state monopoly. It dared not go this far, however, and authorized shipowners who applied for the privilege to trade with the Indies on their own account. The state reserved profitable operations for itself, abandoning to private enterprise activity that involved great risks. But what precautions were taken to safeguard the interests of the royal treasury! The concessionaire must declare the nature and value of his cargo before sailing; the captain must carry long memoranda listing the most trifling items of the cargo.[20] The same formalities were repeated on the return voyage; the precautions were even greater, if that were possible, for gold was the principal merchandise imported from America. The customhouse officers visited and maintained a careful watch over every ship that entered port. In order that no precious gold might be lost to foreigners, Ferdinand ordered the Admiral and all other officials to provide all ships leaving the West Indies with victuals for eighty days.[21] In this way they could make the return voyage to Seville without having to replenish their stores at any Spanish or Portuguese island. To make easier and complete this jealous surveillance, Seville was the only authorized Spanish port for ships plying between the

New World and Spain. Needless to say, foreign merchants were strictly forbidden to trade with the Indies.
What is more, as long as Queen Isabella lived, only Castilians were authorized to go there. The Aragonese, the
Catalans, the Valencians, had not this right; and if they
were allowed to go to America, it was, as Ferdinand
affirmed, by virtue of a special license and despite their
origin.[22]

The Casa de Contratación (House of Trade), established at Seville, was the mainspring of the colonial enterprise, the indispensable go-between between the Indies
and Castile. Everything went through this control point;
not a single item left for America without having been
declared to the Casa; nothing came from the Indies
without being deposited in the Casa. For this purpose
the sovereign had constructed a building divided into
many rooms, a sort of warehouse where the imported and
exported merchandise was stored; there was a different
room for each kind of goods.

The officials attached to the Casa answered the needs
of the institution. The sovereign needed a capable business manager familiar with commercial affairs and the
prices of goods (the factor); a faithful agent to receive
and care for the wealth in gold or commodities deposited
there (the treasurer); finally, a constable (the *contador*
or *escribano*) to control and record the operations of the
other two officers. These three men directed the trade of
the colonies with the mother country; they kept themselves informed as to the needs of the American market,
and made ready beforehand the arms, foodstuffs, and
manufactured goods required by the colonists. They pro-
visioned all the ships that departed for the Indies. They
were expected to acquire all possible information about
the resources of the newly discovered lands.

In founding the Spanish colonies, the primary object

was not to foment the nation's trade and industry but to increase the revenue of the crown. In pursuit of this aim, the government accorded the greatest importance to the accumulation of precious metals. Columbus does not appear to have obtained a significant quantity of gold on his first voyage. The Indians knew nothing of mining; they gathered their gold on the surface of the earth.[23] The first explorers obtained some extraordinarily large nuggets by this same means, but once they had exhausted this source it became necessary to delve into the bowels of the earth in search of its hidden treasures. Instead of encouraging these efforts, the state was concerned only with obtaining the greatest possible immediate profit. It caused all gold to be brought to a designated place where the royal officials cast it, keeping one half for the crown.[24] But the extraction of gold was too difficult, and the returns too small, for the miners to be able to pay the crown such a large share. Nicolás de Ovando had to reduce the proportion from one-half to one-third, and from one-third to one-fifth.[25]

In this enervating climate, Europeans would not set their hands to manual labor. They would only direct agricultural enterprises, supervise the work of the mines, and introduce mining procedures somewhat less primitive than those of the natives. However, workers were still needed to apply these methods and perform common labor. The Indians were employed for this purpose. These soft, indolent people, whose agriculture consisted of a bare scratching of the soil, who were interested only in hunting and fishing, were led in gangs to the places where the presence of gold was suspected; there they were employed without rest in tasks that exceeded their strength by masters insensitive to their sufferings and their complaints. This deadly labor, joined to the wars, the killings on the battlefields, and massacres in cold blood, rapidly reduced the number of the inhabitants of Española, Cuba, and the other Antilles. The race that witnessed the first landing of the Spaniards did not leave a single descendant. The cruelty of civilized men puts that of barbarians in the shade.

As soon as the generous Isabella learned of this inhuman exploitation, she proclaimed the Indians freemen and forbade them to be forced to labor without payment of a reasonable wage. In the same human spirit she freed several hundred Indians that Columbus wished to sell as slaves in the markets of Seville.[26] In default of spices, gums, and gold dust, the Admiral proposed to inaugurate a trade in Indian slaves. But in the Indies, far from the eyes of Isabella, the regime of oppression of the Indians was hardly interrupted.

When Nicolás de Ovando perceived that the Indians, left to their own devices, were returning to their customary indolence, and that the Spaniards were abandoning the Indies for lack of labor, he suspended these salutary ordinances and forced the Indians to labor for a certain time in the mines or on the land. Bobadilla had set an example of granting the colonists one or more groups of Indians; the soil and its inhabitants were distributed among European masters whose lands were cultivated by Indian slaves. Ovando followed the same practice, contrary to the wishes of Isabella; but to give the appearance of complying with the law, he compelled the colonists to pay a nominal wage to these slave laborers.

A decree promulgated by Ferdinand in 1515 annulled the protective provisions of Isabella. The king declared that there was no reason to question the legitimacy of the *repartimientos*. Was he not absolute master of all the newly discovered lands? Had he not been declared their proprietor by two bulls of the Holy Father? Indeed, according to the ideas of the time, what rights could these non-Christian peoples have? Did God not destine these infidels to be slaves? In order to confirm his decree, and to close the mouths of opponents, Ferdinand gave thousands of Indian slaves to his favorites. The principal members of the Council of the Indies were abundantly provided with these human cattle.[27]

However, these outrages did not pass without protests. The Dominican Order, which had sent missionaries to America in 1510, undertook the defense of the oppressed.[28] The spirit of charity and the anti-absolutist doctrine of St. Thomas inspired these monks, and they opposed the rights of the human personality to the theories of the legists concerning the absolute power of kings.[29] As early as 1511, Fray Antonio de Montesino mounted the pulpit in the church of Santo Domingo and there, before the governor and a crowd of colonists, indignantly denounced the treatment accorded to the Indians. This sermon created an extraordinary excitement; the Superior of the Dominicans, Pedro de Córdoba, was called upon to censure the preacher; instead he extolled his boldness. Montesino again arose in the pulpit to lash with new vigor the conduct of the Conquistadores. The friars went even further; they refused absolution and communion to every owner of Indians. Agitation in the colony reached such a pitch that the affair was taken to the Royal Council. The theologians were consulted and pronounced in favor of the Indians, but Ferdinand made the cause of the slaveowners his own, and urged the friars to display greater moderation.

But the cause was not lost. Among the men who had come with Nicolás de Ovando to Española in 1500 was a Sevillano of noble family (perhaps of French origin), a graduate in law of the University of Salamanca, Bartolomé de Las Casas. He had traveled through Española and had borne arms. Then he took holy orders; and when Diego Velásquez sailed to colonize Cuba, Las Casas went along and received as his reward a large village of Indians, "with whom," as he ingenuously confesses, "the Father" (he is speaking of himself) "began to carry on agriculture and whom he exploited in the mines, taking more interest in these matters than in giving religious instruction to the Indians." [30] He had not the least doubt concerning the legitimacy of his rights when the Dominicans made their appearance. One day he went to confess to one of these missionaries; the latter refused to absolve him as an exploiter of Indians. He left, astounded and unconvinced; but doubts began to enter his spirit. His reflections on the subject, the books he read, caused the germination of the seed of charity and justice implanted in his generous heart by the preachings of the monks and by the refusal of absolution. What an irony of history! As Prescott observes, the same order that lighted the pyres of the Inquisition in Spain, raised up in America a defender of oppressed races, the patron and apostle of the Indians!

As soon as Las Casas discovered the truth, he gave up his unjust possessions. But his ardent soul was incapable of lukewarm acceptance of a cause. Cuba, where he lived, was being depopulated with the same speed as Española and for the same reasons: war, forced labor, massacres. To these causes must be added hunger, which dried up the milk in the breasts of the Indian women and killed several thousands of suckling infants in the arms of their helpless mothers. Las Casas, encouraged by the Dominicans, resolved despite snares and threats to return to Spain (September 1515) and defend there the interests of these miserable people. He found Ferdinand weakened by age and illness, surrounded by representatives of the colonists and by the powerful slaveowners of the Council of the Indies. Introduced into the king's presence, December 23, 1515, he presented to him a memorial in which he revealed the state of affairs in America; but the king was dying. He probably did not read this writing, and Las Casas did not see him again. Undiscouraged, he turned to Adrian, Dean of Louvain, and to Jiménez, men who could understand him. The cardinal was appalled by his recital of atrocities. He at once brought together Las Casas and Dr. Juan López de Palacios Rubios, a man known for his humane sentiments. The two drew up an ordinance which restored liberty to the Indians without excessive injury to the interests of the Spaniards. Jiménez adopted the plan, but did not place its execution in the hands of government officials. Only to friars would he entrust the tutelage and protection of these childlike peoples. A happy idea, all in all, for it saved the miserable remnants of the native races, if not in the West Indies, at least in South America. Anglo-Saxon civilization destroyed the Indian in the North. The Indians of Central and South America have lived under the paternal domination of the friars, without enjoying a notable intellectual development, it is true, but at least they have survived.

Since the Dominicans and Franciscans appeared to the cardinal to be excessively involved in the struggle, and he wanted to offer the colonists disinterested arbiters, he chose commissioners from among the Jeronymites, and gave them their instructions.[31] Their principal object was to attach the Indians to the soil, to regulate the system of property, and to group the scattered native population in small centers; thereby it would be easier to convert and civilize them. A religious or priest was to serve each group or village; a hospital would take care of the sick; a part of the resources of the community would be used to maintain the poor and infirm. The labor of the mines was carefully regulated. Only one-third of the Indians in a village was to be called up to the mines at one time, and only for a period of two months. Youths up to the age of twenty and adults above the age of fifty were excused from this forced labor. The cardinal did not go so far as to abolish the *repartimientos,* but he forbade the Indians to be treated like slaves; he ordered the workers to be assured of sufficient food and several hours of rest, and he especially recommended to the monks the progressive emancipation of the Indians who appeared capable of living in freedom. It may have been his thought to achieve by this careful recruitment the formation of a free class under an aristocracy of Conquistadores.

To ensure the effectiveness of these measures, Las Casas was named by Jiménez, "Procurator of the Indians." The Jeronymite brothers, however, proved to be excessively good politicians, their desire to appease every interest caused them to respect every abuse. Las Casas knew that one could not count on the good will of men, and that all the counsels of charity and moderation would fall without effect on selfish and egotistic souls. He resolved to sail again for Castile to denounce to Jiménez the lukewarm and partisan conduct of his agents. He found Jiménez on his death bed, and now put all his trust in Charles V. During all of a long lifetime he never ceased to try to right this great injustice. Theologians acknowledged the validity of his views; statesmen thought him mistaken. Posterity credits him with zeal, if not with success. Yet it is comforting to reflect that there were generous souls to shed tears over the vanquished and to deplore the extermination of a race.

Christopher Columbus, Las Casas—these two names give luster to the history of the Caribbean. Between the mystic and the apostle stand a swarm of conquerors, explorers, adventurers, some of superhuman stature. If we may banish for a moment the memory of ferocious executions, what a multitude of truly remarkable men Spain produced at this epoch: mariners like Juan de la Cosa and Antonio Alaminos; adventurers like Ojeda and Ponce de León; knights like Vasco Núñez de Balboa! Hernando Cortés and the Pizarros have already stepped on the stage of history, they who with a few hundred soldiers destroyed the empires of the Aztecs and the Incas. This rich flowering of individualities, each remarkable in a different way, seems to me the chief blessing and the most enviable good fortune of the reign of the Catholic Sovereigns; for if the glory of the Conquest was great, its profits were small. Castile depopulated itself for the New World; the fleets and expeditions did not repay their expense. The gold obtained was far outweighed by the mass of suffering it caused; yet, despite all these inevitable evils, to Spain remains the honor of having placed its stamp on the majority of the restless young peoples of Greater America. One of her navigators loosened the bonds of Ocean, discovered a new world, and shifted the geographic axis of world civilization and history.

Part Two

THE INSTITUTIONS

Fernãdᵒ rex hyspania

I

The Crown

A knowledge of political institutions casts a strong light on the history of men and events. If we would judge of the wisdom and foresight of a government, we must know what means of governing it found at hand. Merit is measured by the difficulty of the task. Sovereigns like Philip III and Philip IV of Spain inherited from their predecessors an administrative machine all of whose parts were judiciously meshed. In response to an impulse given from above, the wheels began to turn, and each part performed its proper function. There was no question as to the identity of the man who was destined to direct the whole machine as long as he lived; no question as to the aid to be given him by the ministers he had chosen. Everything moved along effortlessly, without shocks; if anything was to be feared, it was not a failure of correspondence and reciprocal action of the different parts, but a general breakdown of an instrument weakened by old age and long use.

It was not so in the time of Ferdinand and Isabella. The crown had just emerged from a terrible crisis; it had beaten off the last assault of the feudal world. The struggle of the aristocracy against the kings, of the kings against the aristocracy, the turbulence of the grandees,

the independent spirit of the towns, had created traditions and habits which were not always compatible with
good government. A firm will was necessary to restore
order, to fix the institutions, the governmental hierarchy,
and to place at the summit of the administrative organization a power that would be preponderant if not absolute.

The crown derived most of its prestige from its own
past. Without going all the way back to the Visigothic
monarchs who sought to revive in Spain the phantom of
the Roman Empire, we may recall that after the defeat
of the Guadalete (711) the chiefs of the vanquished
people had regarded the conduct of war against the Moslems as their first duty. The authority of the war captain,
the glory of the conqueror, were added to the respect inspired by royalty. The king was in all eyes the symbol of
national and religious aspirations. As a result, whatever
rebellious spirit might exist among the nobility, the Castilians were regarded as loyal subjects.

"All are warned," said the Fuero Real,[1] "that the life
and health of the king are confided to their guard and
ardent loyalty; that they must strive as much as they can
to increase in every way the personal honor of the king
and that of his sovereignty. And that none must dare to
proceed in deed, word, or counsel against the king, or
his sovereignty, or to incite to any revolt or tumult either
against the king or his kingdom, either in his land or
without, or to make common cause with his enemies or
give them arms or aid them in any way whatsoever. And
whoever does these things or any of these things should
be held unworthy to live and be condemned to capital
punishment." [2]

The influence of the Roman law only increased this
fund of respect and veneration for the king. "It is necessary," says the Siete Partidas, "to refrain from touching

him in order to kill him, strike him, or seize his person. For in seeking his death one would go against the act of God and against His order; against His act, for one would be killing him whom God Himself placed on the throne as His representative; against His order, for He Himself forbade hand to be laid on His earthly and temporal vicar. One would be committing an attack on the kingdom itself, for one would be removing the head that Providence gave to it, and the very life by means of which the kingdom lives in unity." [3]

Loyalty was not given without necessary restrictions. The Partidas itself recommends to subjects that they should protect the king from himself and others who might lead him into error. When Juan de Mariana, in a work dedicated to the son of Philip II, discussed if it were lawful to kill a tyrant, he drew unconscious inspiration from those old Castilian ideas that attached certain conditions to obedience. [4] With these reservations, the crown was a respected institution. The people spared neither their blood nor their treasure in the royal service, but their masters had to conduct themselves in such a way that the sacrifice be made easy and the devotion honorable.

This doctrine of conditional obedience was a delicate matter, and, unfortunately, the laws concerning the transmission of power were so uncertain that they often offered pretexts or reasons for rebellion. It is generally agreed that under the Goths the monarchy was elective. The bishops and the grandees, assembled in council, made and unmade kings. The choice was restricted to the members of a single family, but this rule was more than once set aside. When the battle of the Guadalete delivered Spain to the Arabs, the Christians who found refuge in the mountains of Asturias elected Pelayo, an alleged kinsman of Don Rodrigo, the last Visigothic king, as their ruler. F. M. Marina claims that for several centuries the nation that was forming in the shelter of mountains, and was gradually to advance into the plains of Old Castile, had the right to select its sovereigns.[5] These rulers were above all military leaders who could be deposed as punishment for incapacity or bad fortune. At the opening of the twelfth century, according to this same author, there was as yet no stable tradition on this important point of the succession to the throne.

It appears that beginning in the twelfth century the monarchy became hereditary. The representatives of the nation continued to assemble for each coronation, but one should not assign too much importance to this fact. If their assent was requested, that assent was not so much an expression of supremacy as recognition of an accomplished fact. When, under the vaults of the cathedral of Reims, the heralds called out to know if the assembled onlookers accepted so-and-so for King of France, it was well known that the newly elected monarch had long exercised supreme authority. The master was simply asking for applause and acclamations. The same was true of the Cortes of Castile. They gave their assent to the regular transfer of power and accorded the sovereign the moral support of their sympathy.

Yet this act of consultation still had some importance. It proved that the Castilians had not forgotten the origins of the royal power. The people may have abdicated its rights once for all into the hands of a single family, but it was aware that sovereignty emanated from itself. Historical facts served to confirm men in this opinion by multiplying cases of disputed succession. When Enrique I of Castile died at an early age, the representatives of the nation chose his younger sister, Doña Berenguela, to succeed him, over his elder sister, Blanca of Castile, whom they rejected as the wife of a foreign prince (Louis VIII of France). The Cortes designated as heir apparent to Alfonso the Sage his younger son, Don Sancho, instead of the legal heir, Alfonso de la Cerda, grandson of the Scholar King, in order to avoid the difficulties of a long minority. Enrique of Trastamara, though a bastard, wrested the crown of Castile from his half-brother, the sanguinary Don Pedro, with the complicity of the people and the aristocracy. The daughters of Don Pedro were also shunted away from the throne. Such intervention, repeated century after century, inspired in princes themselves a proper appreciation of the rights of the nation.

In the reign of Enrique IV (1454 to 1474), the lords and the towns intervened in a more delicate question and called up a debate which continues to agitate historians to this day. Enrique IV was believed to be impotent; his wife, who was of a spirited disposition, gave birth to a daughter of whose legitimacy the most serious doubts were entertained. The grandees compelled the king to recognize his sister as presumptive heiress, to the prejudice of this child. The Cortes, assembled at Ocaña (1468), confirmed the arrangements that secured the throne to Isabella, "because they had been informed by witnesses worthy of credence of the adultery of the queen and the impotence of the king." Thus, because of the king's weakness, the audacious deputies of the nation forced their way, as it were, into the royal bedchamber; the spirit of party did not shrink from trying to resolve the most difficult of problems. To the end of his life, Enrique IV vainly protested the legitimacy of his daughter; in vain did he affirm it in his testament; the Castilians held that the purity of the royal blood must be above suspicion. To safeguard that purity they undertook to solve a mystery of heredity. They may have committed an injustice, but they showed once again where the remedy for the uncertainties of paternity in a hereditary monarchy was to be found.

The maintenance of the scepter in the same family is a broad principle that allows of more than one interpretation. The reigning king has several sons; custom holds that the eldest should succeed. But what is to be done if he dies before his father? Should the child of the dead prince or the younger son of the living king be chosen as heir presumptive? Who is nearer the throne, the uncle or the nephew? Does the grandson inherit from his father the quality of heir presumptive, which the latter possessed while alive, by right of *representation,* or does the younger son replace his dead brother, at the expense of his nephews, by virtue of the right of *immediation?* In Spain this question received varied answers. In the Partidas, Alfonso the Sage had pronounced for the right of representation; events compelled him to follow a different doctrine. After the death of his eldest son, Don Ferdinand de la Cerda, he wanted to secure the crown to the children of the deceased; but he had another son, Don Sancho, who was brave and popular. The orphans lost out despite French support. The Castilians preferred taking for king a warrior of acknowledged bravery to exposing the crown to the hazards of a minority. The right of immediation had the better of it; uncles were preferred over nephews. This principle was consecrated at the Cortes of Alcalá de Henares (1348), when Alfonso XI caused its adoption, with revisions of the laws of the Partidas.[6] These dispositions, contrary to civil law, were in force till the reign of Isabella the Catholic; she returned to the original notion of Alfonso the Sage. She decided that nephews should be preferred over uncles. The right of representation became the law of the monarchy.

The Catholic Queen achieved in her own person the triumph of another principle, the right of women to succeed. Castile never knew the famous Salic Law, which the Bourbons imported into Spain, and which was later repudiated as a foreign custom. Enrique of Trastamara had ignored the daughters of Don Pedro; but a man capable of fratricide is not likely to have scruples of any kind. Despite this example, which could not have the authority of a precedent, the female succession was not contested. True, at the death of Enrique IV, some friends or relatives of Ferdinand of Aragón claimed that his rights were superior to those of his wife Isabella.[7] The debate ended in the rout of these excessively zealous partisans. The legists, history book in hand, had no difficulty in proving that in Castile women had always been acknowledged competent to succeed.

Nevertheless, the marriage of Ferdinand and Isabella created a special situation, and Ferdinand was not the man to be content with the role of prince consort. It was very difficult to harmonize the prerogatives of the queen, legitimate proprietor of the Kingdoms of Castile and León, with the large claims of her husband. There were three points in particular, in regard to which the Castilians displayed extreme sensitivity: Isabella alone must have the grant of graces and favors; she alone must name the governors of strongholds; she alone must administer the domains of the crown. Conjugal love settled the dispute. Isabella declared to Ferdinand that she was not less a woman for being queen, and so was ready to share with him all her goods and dignities. But it would be dangerous, said she, to establish the equality of the spouses in law. At the moment their only heir was a daughter who doubtless would marry a foreign prince. If their example should create a favorable precedent for the claims of the husband, she thought there was reason to fear that this foreigner might use it as authority for introducing troops of his nation, for occupying fortresses, and for lording it over the Castilians. Ferdinand yielded to these arguments; he consented to wield through wifely affection the influence that he had first proposed to exercise in law. Charters, privileges, orders, were issued in the name of the king and queen; there was but one royal seal bearing the joint arms of Aragón and Castile; the images of Isabella and Ferdinand were joined on the coins of the kingdom. This honorable compromise, which subordinated the rights of claimants to the duties of spouses,[8] was so successful in practice that it is difficult to separate the respective actions of the two sovereigns.

History offers no finer example of a dyarchy than this enduring accord of two persons, each possessed of a firm will and superior intelligence.

At their accession, the ceremonies that accompanied the proclamation of a sovereign were held at two points in Spain (December 13, 1474). Although one party declared for Doña Juana, the majority of the nation acclaimed Ferdinand and Isabella. The latter was in Segovia when she learned of the death of her brother Enrique IV. There was erected a scaffold on which the *caballeros,* the *regidores,* and the clergy of Segovia seated themselves. The people, whom the chronicles do not mention, were massed all about. Suddenly the Duke of Alba displayed the royal banners and the herald cried out: "Castile, Castile, for the King Don Ferdinand and for the Queen Doña Isabella, his wife, mistress of these realms!" The grandees who were present immediately approached her and kissed the sovereign's hand, then they gave the oath of loyalty in the customary form.[9] The kissing of the hand and the giving of homage were, together with the proclamation, the characteristic ceremonies of every accession. It seems that all grandees were obliged to render these solemn marks of acknowledgment; they had to appear in person or send their representatives. The prelates, the governors of fortresses, also had to swear fealty. The kings were very careful to hold the aristocracy by the bond of the plighted word. Whenever Ferdinand and Isabella reduced one of their revolted subjects to obedience, they hastened to demand homage. Refusal to swear fealty was regarded as an act of rebellion; lukewarmness in swearing was considered a portent of future defection.

The Cortes convened at the beginning of a reign also swore obedience and homage in formulas whose precise wording left no room for equivocation. Here are the terms used by the deputies of the towns in regard to

Philip the Handsome and his wife Juana (Cortes of Valladolid, 1506).

They [the deputies] say that they have and receive and hold
the said very high and very puissant sovereigns the King and the
Queen, our masters, for the sovereigns and lords of the said kingdoms and lordships, and that as such lords and kings they name,
entitle, will name and will entitle them henceforth, and that they
give and render them the obedience and subjection and vassalage
that as natural subjects and vassals they give and are obliged to
give and render them, and they promise that they will be their
good and loyal vassals and natural subjects, and that wherever
they may see and know anything harmful to them, they will pursue
it and will warn them thereof, and that they will do and perform
and keep their royal orders, and will do and perform all the rest
as their good and loyal and obedient subjects and natural vassals
should and are obliged to do and perform, as the laws and *fueros*
and ancient customs of these realms dispose.

As if this were not enough, the promises were repeated, the duties were stated more precisely, the conscience of the swearer was imprisoned in an unbreakable
ring. In addition, a new commitment was required of
each noble deputy in his private capacity.[10]

This personal character of the oath of allegiance shows
that the crown had not yet disentangled itself from feudal
traditions; at a time when the idea of the state still
seemed vague and obscure the bond of man to man appeared the best guarantee of the loyalty of subjects.

In case an oath of loyalty to the heir presumptive had
been given by the Cortes during the lifetime of his father,
it was not regarded as necessary to convene the assembly
of the kingdom a second time for this purpose. Ferdinand
and Isabella did not convoke the representatives of the
towns, of the nobility, and of the clergy until two years
after their accession (Cortes of Madrigal, 1476), and
then to secure recognition of their first daughter, Isabella.

Recognition of the heir presumptive as future king was

as important a solemnity as that of proclamation. In 1480, after the birth of the Infante Don Juan, the Catholic Sovereigns designated him as their successor at the Cortes of Toledo.[11] The grandees, the bishops, and the deputies of the towns, assembled in the Church of Santa María, came up one by one and there, before the main altar, swore hand on missal to regard as King of the realms of León and Castile Prince Don Juan, eldest son of the king and queen, immediately upon the death of the queen, the proprietor of these kingdoms. They bound themselves to do this, the lords acting for themselves and their descendants, the deputies for the towns that had chosen for them. This anticipatory homage was a wise precaution that the Catholic Sovereigns caused to be renewed in favor of each successive heir as death struck time and time again at the royal family. Adherence to this custom demonstrates that though the monarchy was hereditary in law and in fact, the crown recognized the force of public opinion, the value of the national assent; it also suggests that the sovereigns feared the tendency of factions to seize on any pretext for revolt. Once loyalty had been sworn, disobedience following the accession of a prince assumed a very special character. It was more than defiance of the rules of the hereditary monarchy; it constituted a breaking of faith, an act of treason, a felony. These personal relations between subject and sovereign probably explain the Spanish reputation for loyalty.

In France the kings sought to increase the respect in which they were held by the ceremony of religious consecration; they caused themselves to be crowned by bishops and anointed with holy oil. In Spain coronation was the rule in the Christian kingdoms throughout the Middle Ages. The rulers of Castile went to the monastery of Las Huelgas to crown themselves with their own hands. Apparently, Ferdinand and Isabella did not follow this tradition. However, Saint-Simon twice affirms that the Catholic Sovereigns were the last to use coronation. Be that as it may, contemporary chroniclers attached so little importance to the ceremony that they forgot to mention it. The Kings of Castile could dispense with the prestige of religion; they relied solely on respect for royal blood and on the binding character of the oath.

Although Aragón appears to have accorded more importance to the national assent than Castile, it is certain that the Aragonese monarchy was hereditary and not elective. Facts which may seem to establish a free choice of the kingdom prove, on the contrary, that royal power was transmitted from male to male in the same family. If the people intervened, it was to regulate the ever delicate question of succession in the collateral line. In such a case it clearly was necessary to find an arbiter if the decision was not to be left to the hazards of a civil war. Was it not natural to consult in the first place the people whose destiny was at stake?

The death of Don Martín, King of Sicily, left the King of Aragón, Martín the Humane, his father, without a legitimate heir (1409). There was more than one claimant: Jaime, the son of Louis II of Anjou, the Count of Urgel; and Alfonso de Aragón, Duke of Gardía, each of whom held rights by virtue of descent from a royal princess. The reigning king in turn proposed the candidacy of the Infante of Castile, Don Ferdinand de Antequera, son of his own sister, Doña Leonor.[12] The States-General of the crown of Aragón, composed of the deputies of Aragón, Catalonia, and Valencia, assembled to discuss the titles of the candidates. Each claimant had his party in the assembly; debate soon gave way to violence; and the Archbishop of Zaragoza, García Fernández de Heredia, was assassinated. The estates, unable to reach agreement, resolved to delegate their powers to a commission of nine electors. They were charged, properly speaking, not with choosing at will from among the several names, but with examining the titles of the different rivals; not to make a king, but to pronounce on a question of succession. The Count of Urgel was best liked by a majority of the electors; however, the Infante of Castile was found to have the best title.

The question of female succession was always a source of difficulties in the lands of the crown of Aragón.[13] It was not always the Cortes that was called upon to pronounce judgment in doubtful cases. In the twelfth century, Queen Petronilla, daughter of Ramiro the Monk, just before being brought to bed, bequeathed her inheritance in a testament to any male child that she should bear; if she bore a daughter, her husband Ramón Berenguer IV, Count of Barcelona, was to succeed. Thus she appeared to exclude women from the succession. Her son, Alfonso II, annulled this provision, and designated his sisters to succeed him. "The right of succession," says the historian Mariana, "was changed by the whim of princes in such fashion that there have been cases in the Kingdom of Aragón where daughters were excluded, while the grandchildren born of them were called to the throne." Don Juan II, father of Ferdinand the Catholic, had also changed the laws of succession at will. He had ordered that the crown should be transmittable in the descendants of his son from male to male, and that in default of such the throne should belong to the sons of this prince's daughters, to the exclusion of the women.

When the death of the Infante Don Juan deprived the Catholic Sovereigns of their only son, they wanted to secure Aragón to their daughter Isabella, Queen of Portugal, whose recognition by the Cortes of Castile they had easily obtained. If he could wring an acknowledgment from the recalcitrant Cortes of Aragón, Ferdinand would add the crowns of Aragón to the same head that already bore the crown of Portugal. In vain he protested that no formal law excluded women from the throne, and that he should have the same right as his father, Juan II, to change the law of succession. His courtiers spoke "of subjugating the land by force rather than suffer the insolence of the Cortes." Far from intimidating the Aragonese, these threats only stiffened their opposition. The death of the unfortunate Queen of Portugal left the debate up in the air. Her son, Don Miguel, was a frail and sickly child who survived his mother only a short time.

Ferdinand and Isabella now transferred to their second daughter, Doña Juana, married to the Archduke of Austria, Philip the Handsome, the hopes that they had placed in her elder. The archduke and his wife came to Spain to be recognized as heirs presumptive. The Castilians recognized them without a murmur. There was reason to fear that the Aragonese might again prove difficult; but Ferdinand must have used very persuasive and irresistible arguments upon them. Far from justifying its proverbial reputation for stubbornness, the Cortes made a sudden change of front.[14] The kingdom's representatives, who four years before had shown themselves so intractable, declared that in default of a male heir the custom and law of the country assigned the crown to Princess Juana. However, at this date (1502) Doña Juana had a two-year-old son who made a very suitable successor. Popular assemblies are very changeable, and the most die-hard intransigence will usually take into account the rewards of a graceful surrender.

The Aragonese showed themselves more unbending on other points. They regarded the presence of the sovereigns at the moment of their recognition to be indispensable. The Cortes would not render homage and swear loyalty to anyone but the king himself. In fact, they would not accord the title of king to a prince until he had appeared before them. What was more, he must appear in each of the states of the crown of Aragón. Charles I of Castile (the Emperor Charles V) had great difficulty in obtaining his recognition as king by the Aragonese Cortes while his mother (who had gone mad) was living. He went to Catalonia to ask for the same homage; he thought he could dispense with visiting the Kingdom of Valencia. The people there refused to swear obedience to an absent prince. Cardinal Adrian had no more success than Peter Martyr and Jerome Cabanillas.[15] The Valencians would grant neither homage nor *servicio*.

King Jaime I, successor of Pedro II (killed at Muret, 1213),[16] was the first ruler of Aragón whose subjects took an oath of fealty. From that day on, the oath was repeated with the accession of each prince. It has been claimed that originally the lords and later the Cortes gave their homage in these insolent terms: "We who are as good as you, and who together are stronger than you, choose you for our king if you maintain our *fueros,* and if not, not." But this insolent formula is wholly legendary.[17] It was invented by the illustrious French jurist François Hotman, and introduced into his *Franco-Gallia* to serve the needs of his cause. We should add that Aragonese obedience was not unconditional. Subjects assumed obligations toward the king, but he in turn had obligations to his subjects. When the estates (*brazos*) of the realm swore loyalty to the heir presumptive, he in turn promised to uphold the privileges, the usages, and the customs of the land. It was a kind of synallagmatic contract which bound each of the parties. The Aragonese jurisconsults regarded fidelity as conditional and made the obedience of the people depend on the loyalty of the prince. It was this reciprocity of duties that François Hotman publicized in his pamphlet.

The status of the king, then, was very different in Aragón and Castile. In both countries the principal barrier to the extension of royal power consisted of the privileges of the classes and the privileges of the towns; but whereas in Castile the aristocratic party represented an assemblage of individual wills lacking cohesion and therefore powerless, in Aragón the nobility was disciplined and united. Whereas the civil wars had ruined the municipal liberties of Castile, already weakened by royal encroachments, the Aragonese *universidades* (municipalities) remained powerful and strong, and on occasion the whole kingdom displayed an invincible attachment to its *fueros*. In Aragón, as in Castile, the king was the supreme chief of the army, the dispenser of favors and offices; but his legislative power was much more limited in the one country than in the other. Whereas in Aragón the assent of all the estates and of the king was needed to make a law, in Castile the king's legislative initiative had never been contested. The Pragmáticas, designed to supplement the laws and meet some pressing necessity, were sometimes issued on request of the Cortes, sometimes promulgated without their initiative. These ordinances were supposed to have only a provisional character; but Isabella's predecessors had already grown accustomed to giving their own decrees the force of laws voted in the Cortes, and even to declaring them superior to existing laws or previously issued pragmatic sanctions. The preamble of the Leyes de Toro[18] stated nothing new: "To the king belongs and it is in his power to make *fueros* and laws, to interpret and amend them as may to him appear convenient."

The Kings of Castile dispensed justice in person or delegated it to ministers of their choice. None, whatever his rank, could name judges or exercise any jurisdiction save with the consent of the monarch. In time of peace

the king was all-powerful; everything gave way before
his supreme power. The royal prerogative was not so extensive in Aragón. There is no example of Ferdinand
holding assizes in person, as Isabella did in Seville. The
tribunal of the *justicia,* although its role has been over-
played, intervened between governors and the governed
and offered subjects guarantees against arbitrary acts.
The Castilians had traditions and customs that were as
venerable as those of France before 1780; Aragón possessed a constitution. To achieve absolutism the Castilian monarchs had only to give full play to their prerogative; if the Kings of Aragón wished to achieve mastery,
they must begin by weakening if not repudiating the laws
of the country.

II

The Cortes

The sovereign shared the legislative power with the States-General, or Cortes, of Castile and Aragón. Hernando del Pulgar uses the characteristic expression, "the Arm [*Brazo*] of the King," as if the crown constituted an estate just like the clergy, the nobility, and the towns.

The marriage of Ferdinand and Isabella joined the crowns of Aragón and Castile but left intact the constitution of each. Each kingdom retained its assemblies, and there never were common States-General, all-Spanish chambers charged with protecting the interests of all the kingdoms. In order to have an adequate idea of these representative bodies it is necessary to study them separately, but to avoid repetition, Castile will be singled out for more ample discussion; in the case of Aragón it will do to point out the differences and peculiarities.

Castilian writers trace the origin of the *cortes generales* of the Castilian monarchy to those councils of the Gothic Empire, composed of prelates and lords, which gave their views on the major religious and political questions. According to the historian Marina, there is no doubt that these assemblies served as rule and model for the Cortes of the Kingdoms of León and Castile.[1] In the early period of the Spanish monarchy, the kings often convened the most notable personages of the country for purposes of consultation. At first only the prelates and nobles were summoned, but in the middle of the twelfth century the *Crónica general* notes the presence besides them of the deputies of the towns (Cortes of Burgos, 1169).

The representation of the clergy, regarded as the first of the estates, had a completely aristocratic character. The abbots of the great monasteries, the bishops, and the archbishops held seats in the Cortes by virtue of their titles. The nobility was represented by the great officers of the crown, by the dukes, marquises, and counts, and by those *ricos homes* who had no titles but possessed a seignorial jurisdiction. The deputies of the towns had seats beginning in the twelfth century; but the rights of the Third Estate (*estado llano, tercer estado*) in these great councils of the nation were not clearly recognized and fixed until the beginning of the fourteenth century (by a law given at the Cortes of Medina del Campo, 1328). Originally, the number of deputies was unlimited. All towns belonging to the crown could carry their complaints to the Cortes. This favor seemed very burdensome to the communes, since they had to pay the costs of such representation. Accordingly, most of the towns entrusted the management of their affairs in the Cortes to their richer and more influential members.

This show of disinterest, which at first appeared to be a wise economy, had the gravest consequences for the towns involved. When they began to appreciate the value of the privilege, it was too late to claim their rights; the right of representation had become customary. The towns which, in the time-honored expression, had voice and vote in the Cortes, rose with the utmost energy against any extension of the suffrage. Thus some very important centers and even an entire kingdom (Galicia) had no representation in the Cortes. In the fifteenth century the number of privileged places was very restricted. Hernando del Pulgar enumerates only fifteen cities and two towns in the Cortes of 1480: Burgos, León, Ávila, Segovia, Zamora, Toro, Salamanca, Soria, Murcia, Cuenca, Toledo, Seville, Córdoba, Jaén, Valladolid, Madrid, and Guadalajara. After the surrender of the Moors, Granada obtained the same privileged status. The Cortes of Valladolid (1506) requested the sovereign to make no more concessions of this kind.

In the fourteenth century the Third Estate had gained preponderance in the Cortes. The prelates and nobles generally stayed away from its meetings. It has been claimed that Charles V systematically shunted the aristocracy away from the national assemblies. It is only fair to note that the aristocracy had long before ceased to interest itself in the deliberations of the Cortes. Under the Catholic Sovereigns, only the *procuradores,* or deputies, of the towns appeared at the Cortes of Madrigal (1476). The grandees showed not the least interest in coming to the Cortes of Toledo (1480); but when the *procuradores* of the towns raised the question of revoking all the donations made to the nobility in preceding reigns, Ferdinand and Isabella decided to consult all the principal interested parties; it was necessary to summon *individually* the heads of the aristocracy. This indifference of the upper classes arose from various reasons. The Cortes was usually convoked to respond to a request for money. Since the nobility and the clergy were exempt from taxes, they left to the representatives of the taxpayers the task of voting the subsidies. However, members of the great nobility did not disdain to serve as leaders of the Third Estate. Such great personages as Pedro Lasso de la Vega and Alonso de Vega represented the city of Toledo at the Cortes of Coruña (1520).

The fortress castle of La Molina de Aragón, situated in the borderlands between Aragón and Castile. Constructed after 1139, probably under the powerful noble, Manrique de Lara.

View of Santander drawn by the Flemish artist and geographer Joris Hoefnagel during his travels in Spain between 1563 and 1567.

The Alcázar of Segovia, fortress residence of many kings and queens of Castile, was the scene of notable events in the Middle Ages. In 1474, Isabella the Catholic set forth from this castle to be proclaimed Queen of Castile.

The Cathedral of Burgos, one of the greatest structures of medieval Christendom, was begun in 1221 by St. Ferdinand. The spires and lantern (above) were completed in the early sixteenth century after the designs of Hans and Simon of Cologne. The Stations of the Cross in the *trasaltar* (below) are by Philippe Vigarni.

Above and below: The Casa de las Conchas in Salamanca, built in 1512 by Dr. Talavera Maldonado, royal councilor and ambassador to Portugal and France. The outer walls are decorated with heraldic scallop or cockle shells of the Benavente family with which the owner was connected.

Left: The church of San Juan de los Reyes in Toledo, one of the principal works of Juan Guas, is part of a convent founded by the Catholic Sovereigns to commemorate their victory over the Portuguese at Toro (1476) in the War of Succession.

Padre Eterno, a detail of the choir of the Cathedral of Toledo by Alonso Berruguete.

Below, left: Iron knocker combining the Isabelline style with Moorish decoration. The hammer is a dragon with folded wings.

Below, right: Sixteenth century dalmatic of black velvet couched in precious threads.

The Virgin and Child Enthroned, panel of a fifteenth century Catalan *retablo.*

Hispano-Moresque plateau of the fifteenth century from Valencia.

Oriens.

Septentrio.

1. S. Chr
2. S. Andre
3. Las Theat
4. El Baldio
5. Generalopsis
6. S. Helena
7. El Castillo m
8. Palacio Real
9. Palacio
10. El Cas

The city of Granada in 1563 by the Flemish artist and geographer Joris Hoefnagel, noted for his naturalism and exactitude of observation. Both this and the earlier scene of Santander appeared in *Civitates orbis terrarum* by Georgius Braun and Franz Hohenberg; first edition, Cologne, 1572.

Renaissance Gothic portal of the New Cathedral of Salamanca, begun
in 1515 by Juan Gil de Hontañón and continued by his son Rodrigo.

Left and below: The golden *retablo* and the octagonal mausoleum of
Juan II of Castile and Isabella of Portugal in the chapel of the Carthusian Monastery of Miraflores. Both by Gil de Siloe, 1489–1499.

Court of the Lions in the Alhambra, palace and stronghold of the Moorish kings until the Conquest of Granada in 1492.

Mudéjar salon of the
Casa de Pilatos in Seville,
a residence of the Dukes
of Medinaceli.

The Gardens of the Ge-
neralife, summer palace
of the Moorish kings just
above the Alhambra in
Granada.

The Casa del Cordón in Burgos, palace of Pedro Fernández de Velasco, Count of Haro and Condestable of Castile, built in 1482. A mixture of northern and Moorish styles, it is assigned variously to Simon of Cologne or Mohammed de Segovia. Named for the Franciscan knotted girdle on its facade.

Polychrome wood sculpture of St. Martin cutting off his cloak for the beggar. From Cacabelos in western León. Late fifteenth or early sixteenth century.

Plateresque façade of the University of Salamanca, designed, possibly,
by Enrique de Egas. Founded about 1215, Salamanca is the oldest
university in Spain and during the fifteenth and sixteenth centuries was
renowned throughout Europe.

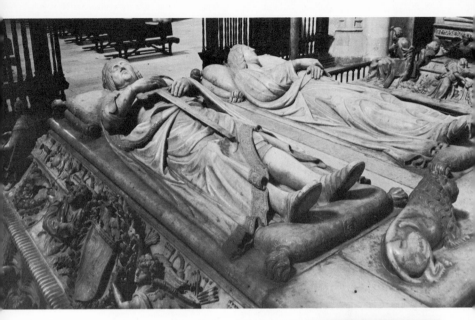

The tombs of the Catholic Sovereigns in the royal chapel of the Cathedral of Granada. Carved by Domenico di Alessandro Fancelli, 1514–1517.

The Hospital Real in Santiago de Compostela, founded by the Catholic Sovereigns. The cruciform plan was made by Enrique de Egas, 1501–1511.

The mode of election served to produce capable and honest representatives. The *procuradores* were not chosen by the people; they were named by the municipal council (*concejo* or *ayuntamiento*), which did not possess a democratic character, whatever its composition. When the royal letters summoning the States-General arrived, the members of the council gathered to conduct an election; they swore to choose the best qualified persons; the elected deputies in turn swore that they would fulfill their mandate loyally and would refuse any present or favor from the court. They were granted a daily allowance of 140 maravedís to cover their expenses. Each city or town with the right of suffrage named two deputies.[2] The Cortes of the crown of Castile, when the nobility and clergy ceased to attend, was reduced to thirty-six persons. This number was too large for a council of state, too small for a national assembly.

Under the princes of the House of Trastamara, the Cortes assembled almost every year. Generally speaking, the pretensions and frequency of these assemblies were a measure of the strength of the prince. In the troubled reigns of Juan II and Enrique IV, there were fifty-two sessions in a period of sixty-three years. There was no rule; the sovereign was free to summon or not summon the States-General; he alone was judge of the advisability of a meeting; he could postpone a summoning as long as he pleased; he had full power to set the day and place of assembly. Events might force his hand, and it sometimes happened that the Cortes met of its own accord; but in principle no law guaranteed the legitimacy of this institution. Thus we see the same sovereign pursuing opposed lines of conduct, according to circumstances.

The Catholic Sovereigns were too strongly wedded to tradition to sweep aside the States-General of the monarchy; they convoked the Castilian Cortes sixteen times during their reign, usually at intervals of about two years. It is noteworthy that they broke the regularity of these summonings during two periods. From 1482 to 1498, during a space of sixteen years, Isabella had no Cortes; after the death of his spouse, Ferdinand followed the same system for some time.[3] When the kings needed money, they summoned the Cortes regularly; when the treasury was full or when peace prevailed abroad, they permitted the institution to slumber.

The assistance of the Hermandad had enabled the sovereigns to wage their struggle with the Moslems and against anarchy without having to summon the Cortes. But the course of foreign affairs compelled a change. Relations with France heavily influenced the domestic policy of the sovereigns. It is interesting to see how greatly the ebbs and flows of foreign conflicts affected the Cortes; Italian wars had their repercussions in Castile. Under the pressure of financial need Isabella had to turn to the deputies of the towns; she returned to the practice of regular convocation of the Cortes. Her death brought another change of front. The marriage of Ferdinand with Germaine de Foix, niece of Louis XII, restored good relations between the two kings. Hostilities were suspended until the conclusion of the Holy League (1506 to 1514). During this calm Ferdinand summoned the Cortes of Castile only once; he did not convoke the Cortes of Aragón at all from 1503 to 1510. These facts indicate what liberties the crown permitted itself with regard to these assemblies, which it convened or failed to convene at its own pleasure.

The Cortes was ordinarily held in the place where the court was in residence. The presence of the Cortes excluded that of all armed forces save troops in transit. Laws guaranteed parliamentary immunity to its members. In the minority of Enrique III one of the regents, the Count of Benavente, appeared armed in the assembly hall. There was a cry of violation of privilege, and his rivals made a great thing of it, declaring that he sought to tyrannize over the nation.[4] The meeting place of the Cortes was typically a church, a palace, or a monastery. Until the time of Charles V the sovereigns opened the session in person; they made their way to the Cortes followed by a magnificent retinue, surrounded by all the glitter of royal pomp. A throne was prepared for them on an elevated stage from which they dominated the assemblage. The nobles and prelates sat on the right and the left, on the two sides of the hall; the Third Estate occupied the center. The sessions were not public. The participants were bound to keep their deliberations secret.

At the Cortes of Burgos (1515), the bishop of that town presided in the absence of Ferdinand, then confined to his bed. Before opening the proceedings, he turned toward the *procuradores:* "You others, gentlemen, do you take oath before God, the holy Virgin Mary, on this Cross, on the words of the holy Evangel, to keep secret all that should be said in this Cortes?" They replied: "I do so swear. Amen." If this obligation, which continued in force thereafter, was then assumed for the first time, Castilian authors have good reason to regard it as a grave attack on the independence of the Cortes. But there is some reason to believe that this measure considerably antedated Ferdinand's reign.

The king or, in his absence, the president explained the reasons for the summoning. The nobility, if present, gave its opinion through the mouth of an *hidalgo* (ordinarily a member of the House of Lara). The Archbishop of Toledo spoke for the clergy. When the proposed object demanded mature consideration, the *procuradores* of the towns took with them the text of the royal communication; they examined it and gave their response in writing at the next session. If it was unfavorable, the king either insisted or modified his proposals. A new examination took place; a new reply was made in the same form. The proceedings of a parliamentary commission, or, in a monarchy, the debates of the committee charged with preparing a reply to the Speech from the Throne, give a better idea of the sessions of the Cortes than our deliberative assemblies with their stormy debates. Certainly there was no place in the Cortes for that grandiloquence which the parliamentary battles of our time inspire. All was done with a calm and order that are adequately explained by the custom of written communications, the small number of the actors, and the absence of any spectators.

The jurisdiction of the Cortes was very extensive. It was consulted on the most important questions, such as foreign alliances, and on the most intimate matters, such as the marriages of the infantes. In 1515, at the Cortes of Burgos, Ferdinand presented an explanation of the state of relations between Spain and France, and justified his policy in regard to Navarre. He had submitted to the Cortes of Madrigal (1476) the plan of the Santa Hermandad, as well as the tariff of duties collected by his chancellery and by the different agents of the crown. Four years later, at the Cortes of Toledo (1480), he submitted for its examination the plan of reorganization of the royal council and the creation of the *audiencia* of Valladolid. Financial questions were of special concern to the Cortes. The development of national industry, the export of specie and precious metals, the protection of agriculture, were frequent subjects of their deliberation. But the question of taxes dominated everything else.[5] No tax could be laid without their consent. This was a fundamental law of the monarchy, or at least a right hallowed

by time. At each session the Cortes prolonged the existing taxes, duties, and *gabelles*. They voted the *servicio,* an
extraordinary contribution designed to cover unforeseen
expenses incurred by the prince. As each new need arose,
they had to render their opinion; theirs was the responsibility for finding the money needed to conduct a war.

Of all the prerogatives of the Cortes, their omnipotence in financial questions was the best established, the
least disputed. Thus they had it in their power to influence
the decisions of the sovereign by granting or denying
financial assistance. It appears that the *procuradores,* the
sole judges in this matter, did not understand the importance of this privilege and made no effort to found a parliamentary opposition on refusal of subsidies. They laid
the wishes of the country at the foot of the throne, but
did not attempt to impose those wishes.

When the deputies left their towns for the meeting of
the Cortes, they took along the most detailed and precise
instructions.[6] They knew beforehand what replies they
should make to the royal requests and what solutions
they should advance for pending questions. It was the
most imperative mandate possible. The *procuradores*
also had the mission of presenting the complaints of their
constituents. Each town could voice its wishes; the *procuradores* often assembled to draft an exposition of the
grievances of the whole nation. These memorials (*peti-
ciones, cuadernos*) often served as basis for the legislative
activity of the sovereign. The petitions were transformed
into law by the royal sanction; not that the Cortes of
Castile had the right to legislate (the historian Marina
rightly observes that it is an error to attribute legislative
power to the assembly), but the royal legislator was often
influenced by their desires and transferred their requests
without change into the domain of law.

Thus the proceedings of the Cortes are among the

most important sources for the history of Spanish legislation.[7] The sovereigns often cited at length the text of the memorials presented by the deputies; they formulated their agreement in these terms: "We hold useful to our service what is contained in your petition"; "we order that it be so done." Sometimes they also gave a general and definitive approval to all the measures that had already received their assent in detail. We see the Catholic Sovereigns close the proceedings of the Cortes of Madrigal with this declaration:

Wherefore we order all and each of you to keep and carry out, to cause to keep and carry out really and effectively the replies made by us to the said petitions and to each of them. . . . We desire and order that they should have the force and vigor of law and that none of you act or go against in any manner, on pain of our displeasure and loss of office and confiscation of goods of those who do the contrary, to the profit of our *camara*. In confirmation whereof we order the issuance of our letter signed with our names and sealed with our seals.

I the King.—I the Queen.[8]

The political decay of these assemblies, so clear under Charles V, was already visible in the time of the Catholic Sovereigns. As their reign advanced, the tone of the Cortes became ever more respectful. At the outset the Cortes dared to ask of the sovereigns and of each of them their *royal word and pledge* that they would not name any person to their council or *audiencia* save in case of a vacancy. They demanded in extremely strong terms the annulment of certain acts. "We, in the name of your said realms, protest . . . and rise against. . . ." [9] But once the royal power had been consolidated, formulas of devotion and obedience replaced these haughty protests. The sovereigns, assuming the offensive in their turn, subordinated the Cortes to the royal council of justice which they had organized. The president of this body was also

Per signũ crucis de inimicis
noſtris: libera nos do=
mine deus noſter.

president of the Cortes; the ordinary or working councilors attended its sessions as of right; after each session
they carried away the minutes of its proceedings for examination.[10] The national assembly was thus handed over
to the control and surveillance of hostile officials.

The powerlessness of the Cortes was due above all to
the abstention of the privileged orders. The aristocracy,

ever eager to form leagues, lacked the intelligence to understand the value of a wise, prudent, legal opposition. In such a case, to be sure, it would have had to concern itself with the general needs of the realm, whereas it was interested only in its own privileges. The sovereigns took skillful advantage of this disastrous posture of detachment. The towns, facing alone an all-powerful crown possessed of incomparably superior resources, were no longer capable of forcing it to respect their wishes. Ferdinand, who was impatient of all interference with his prerogative, more than once neglected to consult the estates. He did not summon the Cortes of Castile when he assumed the regency; he did not summon it when he resumed his sway following the death of his son-in-law. Thus he pursued a course of usurpation that under his successors led to the complete annihilation of the Cortes as an instrument of national representation.

Whereas the different domains of the Crown of Castile had become so intimately merged that they were all represented in the single assembly of the Cortes, the states of the Crown of Aragón had each kept their particular representation. Even when the monarchs desired to consult the deputies of the different kingdoms at one time and summoned them to meet in the same place, they came as separate groups, spoke and sat in the name of their own realm, interested themselves only in its problems, and did not meddle in the affairs of their neighbors. These general Cortes were nothing more than a juxtaposition of the individual Cortes. Valencia, Aragón, and Catalonia had nothing in common save the person of the monarch.

The Cortes of Aragón holds the greatest interest. It was composed of four arms or estates (*brazos, estamentos*): 1. The clergy. 2. The aristocracy of the nobility (*ricos hombres*). 3. The *caballeros* and the ordinary gentlemen (*infanzones*). 4. The towns.[11]

The order of the clergy was represented by the Archbishop of Zaragoza, the six other bishops of Aragón, the abbots of the principal monasteries, the grand commanders of the military orders, the priors of the cathedrals and collegiate churches, and the deputies of the chapters. Thus the lower clergy, as well as the heads of the church, were represented. The nobility had a double representation. This was one of the original features of the Aragonese Cortes, found neither in Catalonia nor Valencia. The aristocracy formed an order composed of the chiefs of "eight great houses" who sat by virtue of their preeminent position. The king joined to them as many *ricos hombres* as he pleased. The ordinary nobility composed another arm. The *infanzones* held their right to sit by royal favor. This invitation had to be renewed at each session.

The name of *universidades* was given to the centers of population that sent deputies to the Cortes. This fourth arm was composed of four cities, three confederations or *comunidades,* and eighteen towns.[12]

It appears that originally the Cortes of Aragón assembled every two years; but this rule was not always observed. From 1503 to 1510 Ferdinand did not summon the Cortes. In the case of Valencia he allowed himself even greater liberties; he summoned the States-General of this kingdom only once during his whole reign. The Sovereigns of Aragón followed more faithfully some other, less irksome prescriptions. The letter of convocation had to be sent two months before the day of the opening. It indicated the date, the place, and the reason for the summoning. The session was opened by the sovereign in person, and all the details of the ceremony were

regulated with the most punctilious etiquette. After the
speech from the throne, each arm retired into premises
especially designated for its deliberations in order to ex-
amine the royal proposals. Before replying to these proposals, the Cortes responded with an enumeration of
grievances; the deputies stated their complaints and
sought to obtain satisfaction from the Crown before all
else. They even made themselves spokesmen for private
claims. They would not vote subsidies or adopt the proposed measures save at the price of numerous concessions. This gave rise to long debates between the king
and the assemblies in which the two parties fought dog-
gedly, neither side giving an inch.

The Aragonese are celebrated for their tenacity. The
making of laws presented incredible difficulties. The
Cortes effectively shared legislative power with the king.
The agreement of the Cortes and the sovereign was
needed to make a law; and all the orders had to be persuaded of its need; the opposition of a single order
brought matters to a complete halt. Even after the Cortes
had been dissolved, the king was not free from its control. A permanent commission composed of eight persons (two for each arm), the Deputation of the Kingdom, sat at Zaragoza between sessions. It was charged
with protecting the public liberties and especially with
watching over taxes or customs duties. The Aragonese
seem to have understood the formidable weapon that the
right of voting subsidies and taxes placed in their hands.
The situation here was very different from that in Castile;
the assemblies were more numerous, demanding, and
spirited. The nobility took pride in appearing in the Cortes and in joining the defense of its class privileges with
that of the public interest. The Cortes always displayed
great sensitivity on the subject of finances; the kings pur-
chased rather than obtained the *servicio*.

Sovereigns less authoritarian than Ferdinand and Isabella might have taken umbrage at this formal and suspicious spirit. Yet who would censure this people for having defended its political liberties with such firmness and constancy? Of all the peoples of Spain, the Aragonese were most likely to give offense to a crown all too jealous of its prerogatives. Zurita calls attention to Ferdinand's aversion for the Cortes.[13] The estates always appeared more interested in submitting their complaints than in listening to his requests for money. When he was forced to summon them, he was careful to confront them with a *fait accompli*. He did not have faith in his ability to wring from the Cortes a vote of subsidy; instead he would raise soldiers for his numerous wars and then saddle the country with the cost of their support. Despite such little ruses, he was not as successful as in Castile in forcing the Cortes to do his will.

Aragón offered the stoutest and longest resistance to the lures and even the pressures of this powerful monarchy. In the long run the great weight of royal authority tipped the scales and swept away the liberties of the country. In the reign of Ferdinand and Isabella, however, Aragón, thanks to the character of its Cortes and the general tendencies of its institutions, was still capable of resisting the good as well as the bad designs of the government.

III

The Central Government: The Councils

The civil wars that agitated Europe in the fourteenth and fifteenth centuries had ruined public administration, discredited justice, and weakened the power of the crown. It is the glory of the Catholic Sovereigns that they revived these social forces in Spain.

Convinced, however, that the institutions of the past were powerless to prevent the return of anarchy, they strove to give the central government a larger, more energetic, more formidable action. Aragón, strongly attached to its traditions, was inimical to change. Castile was the principal field in which the innovating genius of Ferdinand and Isabella displayed itself. They developed its administrative organization to the point where they transformed it. From their hands the central government issued armed at all points. Isabella's predecessors overcame resistance only by the most strenuous efforts. Henceforth a gesture from on high caused the stiffest necks to bend. So formidable was the royal power that it had no need to employ all its resources. The royal councils were the most useful instruments of the crown in its struggle against both special privileges and public liberties.

The origin of the councils has sometimes been traced

back to Ferdinand III, who died in 1252. This prince had placed by his side twelve jurisconsults who were charged with assisting him in holding court, with pointing out his errors to him, and with advising him in difficult cases. It has been suggested that this body was the remote ancestor of the royal council of Castile, but this is a completely gratuitous assumption.[1] If we must go that far back, we may recall that the Kings of Castile and León always had by their side men of worth and good birth who formed the king's council and tribunal.[2] The development of government finally brought a division of functions between the members of the *curia regis.* In 1385 responsibility for Castilian affairs of state was entrusted exclusively to a commission of twelve persons chosen from the three orders.[3] To this body, as the principal organ of the supreme justiciary, the king, was also entrusted the judgment of certain cases, while the dispensation of justice was more especially reserved to the *audiencias.* Under this system, which fixed the bounds of its competence, the royal council continued without significant change until it received from the Catholic Sovereigns its definitive form.

The nature and operation of the royal council can best be studied in the proceedings of the Cortes of Toledo (1480).[4] At that date the war with Portugal had ended, civil strife had either quieted or been put down. The political weather vanes pointed to obedience. The moment was well chosen for the work of reorganization. In the future the council was to be composed of a prelate, three *caballeros,* and eight or nine legists. The predominance of this last class is remarkable. It was not so at the beginning of the reign, when the position of the sovereigns was still precarious and they disputed their crowns with the King of Portugal and an aristocratic faction. The proceedings of the Cortes of Madrigal (1476) designated as councilors Cardinal Pedro de Mendoza, the Duke of the Infantado, the Duke of Alba, the Admiral of Castile, Don Alonso Enríquez, the Count of Benavente, "and the other viscounts and *caballeros, ricos homes,* and *letrados.*" Here the legists have the last rank and are lost among a swarm of gentlemen. Four years later (1480) the proportion was reversed; now it was the legists who were most numerous. To be sure, the prelates, dukes, counts, marquises, and grand masters of the military orders continued to sit in the council by virtue of their titles,[5] but their influence was nil. Business was transacted by the ordinary councilors. The aristocracy had been driven from this strategic position, had been ousted, as it were, from the keep of the castle.

Henceforth the council belonged completely to the king, who always kept it at his side, lodged it in his palace or a neighboring house, and even assigned to it in his absence the house that he himself ordinarily occupied.[6] The careful manner in which Ferdinand and Isabella regulated the employment of its time indicates the interest they took in its labors. It was to sit every day except Sundays and holidays. Its sessions were held in the morning, from six to ten, between Easter and mid-October, and from nine to twelve during the rest of the year; they could be prolonged if the business on hand could not be finished within the appointed time. If some members were absent, their colleagues would nevertheless dispatch their business, "provided there were four councilors present, two of them being legists." In case of disagreement and division in voting, the question was submitted to the sovereign. A royal reporter and his substitute were attached to the council. The clerks who recorded the acts of the royal chancellery and the royal council had to attend all sessions on pain of being fined.

No time was to be lost in idle discussions. The reporter

was to present the subject without digression. Then the councilors must offer their opinions without repeating the content of the report or arguments previously stated. If they agreed with the view of the preceding speaker, they had best remain silent. They were to speak only if they had some new point to make. They must dispose without much palaver of matters that were simple and easy of solution, without wasting their time with tittle-tattle, anecdotes, and irrelevant matters. At the door of the hall stood two mace-bearers or porters, one to bar entrance, the other to summon petitioners. If some importunate individual forced his way and appeared in the hall without invitation, his case was mercilessly postponed to another day. To avoid large public attendance, care must be taken to post on the doors the agenda for that day. Thus only the interested parties would remain; others would go about their business. The sovereigns were so anxious to deprive the royal council of all occasion for being idle that they even exempted its members from observing the marks of respect due to royalty. They must not only refrain from paying visits, however illustrious the personages, but were even excused from coming out to meet the sovereigns.

The jurisdiction of the council was extensive; it could summon before it all persons who could enlighten it on some matter. The royal commissioners, sent to check on the administration of towns, took oath in its presence and swore to communicate to it the results of their inquiries. The cases that it had judged could be neither appealed nor annulled.[7] Its decisions were binding on all, without distinction of rank or birth. Judicial functions occupied only a small part of its time. All matters of state were submitted to its examination and criticism. Alliances, embassies, and relations with foreign powers were subjects of its particular study.

In matters of such importance the council did not limit itself to a verbal discussion in which arguments together with the incident which had given rise to them might be completely lost. The deliberations of the council had to be put down in writing in order that the king might inform himself more accurately concerning its doings. As a result there accumulated in the archives of the royal council a vast collection of memoirs, covering the entire history of Spain's foreign policy, that was available for consultation by those who came after. This supreme court, to which the king entrusted the fate of his people and state, must not permit itself to be guided by passion or selfish interest; its members were sworn, on pain of exclusion, to the most inviolable secrecy.

This notable regulation, which was promulgated in the Cortes of Toledo (1480), envisaged a council invested with both judicial and political functions. We may conclude that at this date there was as yet no clear line of separation between the council of state proper and the council of justice.

The sovereigns designated the whole number of councilors employed in their service in these varied tasks by the title of *Nuestro Consejo* (Our Council). However, there were already special sections within the royal council. The chronicler Pulgar sketches the following very interesting picture of the government as of 1480: "At the time of these Cortes, there were five councils in five separate apartments in the royal palace where the king and queen were staying. In one were the king and queen, with some grandees of their realm and other members of their council, who had cognizance of the embassies sent by foreign kingdoms to Spain, and of matters under discussion with the Holy Father at the Court of Rome, with the King of France and other kings, and of all other matters on which it was expedient to have their advice."[8]

Clearly, here we have to do with the political section of the council. "In another place were the prelates and doctors who were assigned to hear the petitions laid before them and to issue letters of justice, which were numerous and of different sorts; and also to follow the course of lawsuits that were pending before them, and to terminate such lawsuits with final judgments." This is the judicial section. "In another place were the *contadores mayores* and the officials who kept the accounts of the royal treasury and the crown domain." This is the financial section.[9]

Thus a division of labor became necessary; and in the natural course of events the royal council split up into a number of sections that tended to develop into autonomous bodies. We do not know just when particular persons were assigned to a single exclusive task. It may even be that during the reign of the Catholic Sovereigns the different sections, while independent, had at least in part a common personnel. In any case, the confusion tended to disappear, since Talavera, in a letter to Isabella (1493), clearly distinguishes the Council of State, the Council of Justice, and the Council of Finance (Consejo del Estado, Consejo de la Justicia, Consejo de la Hacienda).[10] It is plain that by that time the three sections of the royal council had each a well-defined role, a clearly delimited activity, and that although they formed part of a single body, each had its distinctive functions.

Although all these councils had equal claim to the name of royal council, this title was applied especially to the Council of Justice.[11] The reasons for this are not difficult to find. It was once said of France that she was conquered by the inkstand. The Spanish kings also employed men of law to subjugate the nation. Moreover, the Council of Justice was composed in its majority of men of middling condition who, owing everything to the crown, could not be other than its docile servants. Was it not natural for the Spanish sovereigns to regard this body as their principal support? The president of the council was the most eminent personage of the kingdom after the king. His position, which he held by royal favor, set him above the highest aristocracy.[12]

This preponderance of the Council of Justice is a capital fact of administrative history. To appreciate all its meaning we must resort to comparison, illuminating that fact in the light of French history. Everyone knows what great services the Parlement rendered the French monarchy, how much it contributed to the overcoming of feudal resistance, to the destruction of special class privileges, to the advantage of the royal power. And yet the Parlement was constituted apart from and outside the crown. Now imagine this supreme court made an immediate and direct instrument of the sovereign power, lodged in its very bosom, and drawing to itself virtually the whole state power. This was the role of the Council of Justice in Castile; it dominated the whole judicial organization and thereby dominated the whole internal life of the kingdom. Its influence was so general, so profound, that the *chancillerías* of Valladolid and Granada (with reason compared to the French provincial Parlements) never had any political importance.

The consequences for Spanish liberties were disastrous. The monarchy lacked the control and counterweight that the French king often found in the opposition of the magistrates. It is true that the Cortes could cause the complaints and grievances of the nation to be heard; but given the degree of development of the Spanish monarchy under the successors of Charles V, the remonstrances of a permanent body would have been more effective than the representations of assemblies convened by the sovereign at an hour of his choosing, at his convenience.

In Castile, the Council of Justice was the essential organ of the royal power; thus it dominated all the other councils, whatever their importance.

The Council of State, called also "secret council" (*concilium secretorum*), was presided over by the king in person.[13] Its jurisdiction comprehended foreign affairs. The aristocratic element was more strongly represented in this body than elsewhere.

The Council of Finance (Consejo de la Hacienda; *concilium regii census et omnium bonorum*) supervised the administration of the public finances. At the head of the organization stood originally three, later two *contadores mayores de la Hacienda*. They farmed out the revenues of the state and authorized their collection; they paid the pensioners and royal officials. Matters relating to the crown domain fell within their jurisdiction. They should not be confused with the *contadores mayores de cuentas*,[14] who were charged with checking the accounts of the royal functionaries, and who formed a sort of court of accounts. A *tesorero general* collected all crown receipts and issued all payments for crown expenditures.

The three councils, the Councils of State, of Justice, and of Finance, evolved from a pre-existing organization. Circumstances led to the creation under the Catholic Sovereigns of four new councils: that of the Hermandad, which had an ephemeral existence, that of the Inquisition, that of the military orders, and that of the Indies.

The Council of the Hermandad was composed of deputies from the Hermandades of the entire kingdom.[15] Together with the sovereigns, it decided on the measures necessary for the restoration of order and imposed a uniform administration and policy on the provincial associations. When the Santa Hermandad had accomplished its repressive mission, the Catholic Sovereigns, who may have feared a union of the towns against the

crown, hastened to dissolve it (1498). It had lasted twenty-four years.

The persecution of the Moriscos and the Judaizers led to the organization of the Council of the Inquisition, or Consejo de la Suprema. The grand inquisitor, who was named by the king, was its president. He was assisted by five members, three ecclesiastics and two doctors of law. The tribunal had appellate jurisdiction over all cases tried in the first instance by the ordinary tribunals of the Inquisition. The king sought to retain control over the actions of this formidable institution; but more than once the crown had to yield to it; the Council of the Inquisition defied even the Council of Justice.

After Ferdinand had taken into his own hands the grand masterships of Alcántara, Calatrava, and Santiago, he found it necessary to establish a council to administer the domains of these military orders, collect their revenues, and advise him respecting the distribution of commanderies and prebends. The king could buy a good many devoted servants with these favors. Therefore it was important for him to know the value of these gifts and how he might use them to best advantage. There is a general belief that Charles V created this council at the time Pope Adrian VI vested the administration of the military orders in him as a perpetual right. But it already existed under the Catholic Sovereigns, since Jiménez alludes to it in a letter of November 28, 1516;[16] and at the Cortes of Burgos, held while Ferdinand was still living (1515), Fernando de la Vega, Grand Commander of Castile, was named its president.

The necessity of providing a government for the New World led to the creation of a new council. The sovereigns had initiated at Seville an establishment charged with organizing the fleets and receiving the gold they brought from the Indies.[17] Juan de Fonseca, Archdeacon of Seville, was the director of this board of trade and navigation. He had two other agents under him. The prodigious development of his overseas empire obliged Ferdinand to make a place for it in the central government. Cádiz was left with the customhouse, Seville with the Casa de Contratación; but the supreme direction of the affairs of the Indies, together with an appellate jurisdiction, was entrusted to the Council of the Indies, sitting near the king and presided over by Fonseca (1511). In 1524 Charles V put the last touches to the work of colonial organization.[18]

A dependency of the Council of the Indies was the pilots' office, headed by a pilot major, which gathered information, drew maps, and traced new sea routes to challenge the daring of navigators. To this office Ferdinand summoned such experienced mariners as Pinzón, Solís, Vespucci, and Cabot.

This vast system of administration was peculiar to the crown of Castile. The Aragonese were unwilling to receive new impulses from without, would not stand for losing their identity in a united Spain. They wished to preserve their independence, their autonomy, their nationality. Ferdinand and Isabella found themselves in a strange situation. They were proprietors of two groups of states that regarded each other, not as enemies, but as foreigners. It was to humor these separatist tendencies that they had declined, at the death of Don Juan II of Aragón, to assume the title of Sovereigns of the Spains. Despite their delicacy in this matter, Castile was destined to become the center of their government; her preponderance was due to her extent and wealth; here the sovereigns habitually resided; here the major decisions were made. The opinions of the Council of State, for example, touched the destinies of Aragón as well as of Castile. The supreme tribunal of the Inquisition had jurisdiction over all cases tried in both kingdoms, irrespective of their origin.[19] However much the two peoples may have wished to live in isolation from each other, they were borne along in the general movement of the monarchy. Foreign policy, wars, alliances, exposed both crowns to the same hazards.

But the internal affairs of each state were regulated separately. Aragón continued to have its own life, as in the past; it preserved its customs, its liberties, its frontiers, its Cortes, its special justice. Ferdinand established a special council, the Council of Aragón, to direct the affairs of his hereditary kingdom. All questions relating to Catalonia, Valencia, Sicily, and the Kingdom of Naples

were reserved to it. In those lands it had the same supreme jurisdiction and supreme authority that the Council of Justice enjoyed in Castile. It followed the court
wherever it went; it was composed of native *caballeros*
and doctors of law. Each state of the crown of Aragón
was represented by two legists, the regents, presided over
by the Vice-Chancellor of Aragón, named by the king.
The addition of a crown treasurer, of a *procurador fiscal,*
and of a prothonotary completed the council.[20] Under
Charles V the affairs of Italy were entrusted (1555) to a
Council of Italy, which had control of Sicily, Sardinia,
Naples, and Milan.

All of the councils were in fact, consultative commit-
tees, designed to advise and inform the prince, to dispatch business and try cases, but incapable of taking the
initiative, of formulating a plan, of imprinting a direction on the movement of things. The impulse had to come
from elsewhere, from the sovereign himself or from the
persons to whom he had delegated his authority. Ferdinand and Isabella were their own ministers. United by a
rare community of sentiments and views, they personally
directed foreign affairs and internal administration; they
were too fond of power to relinquish it into other hands.
Nevertheless, their relations with the councils and with
foreign governments required intermediaries. They
could not personally attend all meetings, explain their
views on all questions, draft all their dispatches, and take
personal charge of the crushing burden of diplomatic correspondence. To assist them in the dispatch of business
they had secretaries, some of whom wielded enormous
influence, although they were hidden from view, as it
were, by the mighty shadow cast by royalty.

Juan de Coloma put his name to two of the most important acts of Spanish diplomacy. He signed the Treaty
of Barcelona (1493), which restored Roussillon and

Cerdaña to the crown of Aragón. He drafted the convention concluded between the Catholic Sovereigns and Christopher Columbus (April 17, 1492), those famous capitulations that were of such great consequence for Spain and the whole of the Old World.

Secretaries of Aragonese origin played the primary role in the second part of the reign. The most famous among them was Miguel Pérez de Almazán, whom Ferdinand made Lord of Maella and Knight of Santiago. He was a very astute, very able, very reliable person who was not at all puffed up by knowledge of his influence, one of those invaluable servants who render the greatest services with self-effacement, leaving to their master all the glory and credit for their common effort. Ferdinand, the craftiest man in Christendom, laid open his most secret designs to this secretary who was also his confidant.[21] Miguel Pérez de Almazán died April 10, 1514; he conducted most of the negotiations relating to Italy in the reign of Louis XII and of Ferdinand.

By no means did all secretaries enjoy the same influence. Some, like Fernán Álvarez, were no more than humble executors of royal orders. Others, like Miguel Pérez de Almazán and Pedro de Quintana, were something more than trusted clerks. They played the parts, but only parts, of true ministers of state; their role was proportionate not to their responsibility but to the royal favor, which limited or extended the sphere and importance of their functions at will. They never had a direct and personal power of action; and in the cabinet composed exclusively of the king and the queen they remained simple clerks, whose advice might or might not be heeded.

They were not the only persons consulted by the sovereigns. Jealous as they were of their power, Ferdinand and Isabella were not afraid to surround themselves with counselors. As long as he lived Cardinal Pedro González de Mendoza had the ear of the sovereigns. They took his advice on affairs of state, family problems, on alliances and the marriages of princes. His influence was so pronounced and so patent that he was called "the third king." Talavera and Jiménez enjoyed the same favor after him; but their influence had as much to do with their position as confessors as with their acknowledged ability.

No other European country assigned such a large role in government to the director of the royal conscience. In France the role of a Michel Letellier, who wielded such great influence over Louis XIV, was an exception; in Spain the intervention of the confessor was the rule. The correspondence of Talavera and Isabella does not always deal with the practices of piety, with devout confidences, with delicate problems of conscience, with comforting assurances or severe admonitions, in a word, with discussion of how the queen's spiritual welfare might be ensured. If Talavera thundered against luxury in dress, against bullfights, dances, and gallantry, this was only a part of his office; the queen employed him in many other, quite secular tasks. When in 1480 the sovereigns undertook to recover the crown domains and revenues that had been alienated in favor of the aristocracy, Isabella's confessor was assigned the task of distributing the sacrifices to be imposed on the nobility, and of making the amount of the restitutions fit the value of the royal gifts. Actually, he was not departing from his spiritual role, for the queen proposed to despoil the nobles justly and to reconcile her interests with her conscience. He was very naturally called upon to give his opinion on questions of peace and war, which exposed the Christian ruler indifferent to considerations of justice and injustice to grave hazards in the afterlife.[22]

With Jiménez, the political influence of the confessor

reached its apogee. The queen gave him the archbishopric of Toledo, the cardinal's hat, the first place in the
Church of Spain. She charged him with reforming the
discipline of the monastic orders. He intervened with an
intemperate zeal in the conversion of the Moors; though
his intolerance led to an insurrection, he managed to
ride out this storm. His influence even survived the death
of his benefactress. The expedition against Oran was his
work; he supported it with his money, directed it in person. Ferdinand, who had no love for him, on his deathbed bequeathed the regency to Jiménez.

Torquemada and Deza, the one confessor to the queen,
the other confessor to the king, did not play so brilliant a
role, but they were the first two grand inquisitors. Judges
of Judaizers and Moriscos, they held in their hands the
lives of several thousand human beings; they were true
masters of consciences, scrutinizers of sentiments and intentions, convinced representatives by the side of the king
of a jealous orthodoxy and nationality. The high situation
enjoyed by these men, the rewards offered them, show
the great value that the Catholic Sovereigns attached to
their counsels. The tribunal of penitence was more than
once transformed into a cabinet meeting. It is in the company of these monks, counselors, jurisconsults, that the
first sovereigns of modern Spain make their appearance.

The work to which the Catholic Sovereigns devoted
themselves was not done by halves. They were not content with making absolute monarchy work; they
equipped it with a personnel of devoted servants. They
not only prepared for their successors the formidable instrument of coercive institutions but left to them men
capable of applying that instrument. Yet it would be unjust to attribute to them the first use or even the idea of
despotism. They never abused their authority. Although
it was very great, they were ever careful to humor public

opinion, and they respected the customs, traditions, and privileges that were not impediments to the royal prerogative. Finally, although they made large encroachments on the public liberties, at least in Castile, they justified the power they assumed by the services they rendered their country. Absolute power can make up for its odious character by a vigilant, economical, upright conduct, by the sureness and success of its plans. This glory may not be denied to Ferdinand and Isabella. They merit the first place among all the rulers of Spain in the administrative history of the monarchy.

IV

The Royal Agents

The government of the Catholic Sovereigns, disposing of new means for attracting talent to its service, tended to choose its own servants instead of accepting the agents designated by tradition. Preponderance passed from the great dignitaries to the councils and to the men of the middle class. The modern monarchy was founded at the expense of the privileged classes. The Catholic Sovereigns sought to eliminate those elements of the past that might impede their advance. The great offices of the crown, once invested with immense prestige and power, were reduced to the status of honorific dignities.

The office of chancellor suffered this fate. Isabella conferred the title of Grand Chancellor of Castile in perpetuity on the Archbishop of Toledo.[1] She did this to place the office beyond the reach of the lay aristocracy; it allowed her to elevate to this high charge a priest, a monk sprung from the lowest social class. In the view of contemporaries, this dignitary ranked immediately after the Prince of Asturias; but influence and power passed into other hands, even though some incumbents, such as Jiménez de Cisneros, held the first place in the state. After him the office declined to an empty and pompous show.

The grand chancellor of the privy seal (*canciller*

mayor del sello de la poridad) was a powerful figure when Cardinal Mendoza held the office. On his death, its authority and influence fell, or rather returned to the royal council. The whole office of the chancellor, laconically observes Salazar de Mendoza, "consists in affixing the seals."

The notaries were charged with drafting and writing the acts of the chancellery. They had at their head several chief notaries (*notarios mayores*), two for León, one for Castile, one for Toledo, another for Andalusia. All were persons belonging to the highest nobility. Their names appeared at the foot of diplomas, together with those of the great officers and members of the aristocracy. This right of confirmation was taken away from them and assigned to a corps of special agents, the *confirmadores*. Thereafter the office of *notario mayor* was without function; the empty title was permitted to remain in the families that possessed it at the time of the reform. They had to be content with this privilege.

The new administrative system made the ancient offices useless. What was the *justicia mayor* (chief justice), compared with the president of the Council of Justice, who directed the court police with sovereign power and could on his own initiative, without an order from the king, cause the arrest of the greatest of great lords? The *justicia mayor* could, if he liked, regard himself as a great officer of the crown; in reality he was only a high palace dignitary.

This course of necessary usurpation reached to the highest command of the armed forces on land and sea. The transformation of military tactics, foreign conquests, and the creation of a maritime empire enabled the sovereigns to shatter the old system of ranks. The marshals of Castile (created in 1382) were the lieutenants of the *condestable* in the army; and, save where appeal was made to his superior jurisdiction, they exercised the right of high and low justice, of civil and criminal justice, in the camps. They still played this role in the War of Granada, but the creation of regiments brought into existence new ranks that obliterated the old ones. The office of *condestable* had been established in 1382 by Juan I, who filched this title from neighboring states. The *condestable* was the generalissimo of the army; he commanded it in the absence of the king. In 1473 a Velasco had been invested with this dignity; it remained in his family. However, the Spaniards conquered Italy under the command of other leaders.

At some time in the past the *condestable* had taken over the principal functions of the *alférez mayor* (grand standard-bearer). The *alférez* of the royal banner (*alférez del pendón real*), whose title resembled that of this great crown officer, had no other right than that of carrying the campaign standard before the king. From 1432 on, the Silvas, Counts of Cifuentes, enjoyed this distinction.

Don Alonso Enríquez, uncle of Ferdinand, was Almirante Mayor (Grand Admiral) of Castile in 1474. He had jurisdiction over seamen and over merchants engaged in maritime trade. He established his tribunal and erected his gallows in all ports and at all river towns reached by the tide. He issued letters of marque and collected a considerable part of the value of prizes. Outfitters paid him a fifth of the value of their cargoes. The king himself, if he employed a ship in some commercial enterprise, had to pay like any ordinary citizen. The outfitting and arming of the Castilian fleets were done in the name and by order of the admiral. When war broke out, he boarded a ship, raised his standard, and assumed command of all the naval forces. His was one of the most prestigious and lucrative offices.[2]

The auspicious discovery of Columbus deprived the *almirante mayor* of his jurisdiction over the navigation of the Ocean Sea; the sovereigns did the rest. They were careful to substitute their authority for his own with great demonstrations of deference. In 1479, at the beginning of their reign, when hostilities were about to recommence with Portugal, the sovereigns caused it to be announced everywhere that mariners who outfitted a ship for war would be exempt from payment of the fifth. They had taken this step without the knowledge of Don Alonso Enríquez; they informed him of it as a matter of no importance and requested him to advise his lieutenant and collectors thereof. To expedite the formation of a fleet, they had dispatched members of their council to Seville and Santander. Now it became necessary to provide the armada with a commander (*capitán mayor*) as quickly as possible. Ferdinand and Isabella did not claim for themselves the right of making the appointment; they were content to inform the admiral, "Mosén Juan de Villamarín will arrive with the galleys, and it is reasonable that he should hold the *capitanía mayor* for you." All these adroit encroachments sapped the strength of the office. Little by little the *almirante mayor*, like the *condestable*, was reduced to the role of a decorative personage in the royal entourage.

From the great offices of the crown these usurpations spread to offices of the provincial governments. The states of the crown of Castile were divided into lieutenancies general. It appears that St. Ferdinand had created the *adelantados* to replace the counts, whose functions they performed.[3] Their power was very extensive, their duties extremely varied. "In time of peace," says the law of the Partidas, "the *adelantado* is president and chief judge; in time of war he assumes command of the troops in his jurisdiction." [4] Thus he united in his hands justice, administration, and military power. The dignity of *adelantado,* following the main current of the time, tended to become hereditary and remain in the same family, although the sovereign always retained in law if not in fact the right of appointment. Under the Catholic Sovereigns there were seven great officers bearing this name. Those of León and Castile enjoyed greatest respect and were called *adelantados mayores.*

1. The *adelantado mayor* of Castile. At the beginning of Isabella's reign this office belonged to Pedro López de Padilla, who had received it by inheritance from the Counts of Santa Gadea.

2. The *adelantado mayor* of León was, in 1469, Don Pedro Manrique, Count of Treviño.

3. The *adelantamiento* of Andalusia was vested from the time of Enrique III in the house of Ribera, represented in 1486 by Don Pedro Enríquez de Ribera.

4. A Fajardo, Perianez Fajardo, governed in 1474 the *adelantamiento* of Murcia.

5. The *adelantado* of Galicia was the first Don Fernando de Pereja; he was succeeded by the Sarmientos.

6. An *adelantamiento* was created at Granada immediately after the conquest; the Catholic Sovereigns gave the investiture to the archbishopric of Toledo.

7. The *adelantado* of Cazorla was also designated by the Archbishop of Toledo. The ecclesiastical principality of which Toledo was the capital included a great number of towns and villages. To command their troops the prelates needed a lay vicar whom they chose from among the members of their family. Here there was no question of inheritance; as the seat became vacant, the office changed hands. Cardinal Mendoza had chosen his brother; Jiménez named his nephew.[5]

Asturias and Guipúzcoa were governed for the king by

two *merinos mayores* who exercised under a different title the same functions as the *adelantados*.

These great jurisdictions were superimposed on a swarm of others of every kind and extent, districts, territories of cities, governments of towns and fortresses. The greatest variety of officers reigned in this feudal world, which was organized piece by piece. Old Castile was divided into *merindades*, which were unknown in New Castile. The royal officers at the head of towns bore different names: *asistentes, adelantados, corregidores*. This last category had a brilliant future before it. All these officers had a special jurisdiction; and all worked to increase their power at the expense of the royal power.

Ferdinand and Isabella never proposed to abolish all these offices. They respected everything in the past that was compatible with the royal supremacy. They were intent only on gaining the reality of power, without hurt to old interests and habits. But the *alcaides* sought to perpetuate themselves in their charges and transmit them to their children. The sovereigns suppressed hereditary transmission of office and entrusted the guard of fortresses to persons of their choice.[6] The two *merinos mayores* disappeared, says Salazar de Mendoza, together with their privileges. The *adelantados* survived, but their authority was reduced to nothing. The Cortes of Toledo complained of the abuses committed by the tribunals of the *adelantamiento* of Castile. The sovereigns opened an inquiry and suspended the judges; then they restricted their number and their competence. It was a prelude to more radical measures. For these judicial lieutenants of the *adelantados* there were soon substituted three *alcaldes mayores,* designated *alcaldes* of Burgos, León, and Campos, who were the king's men. Only the *adelantado* of Cazorla retained his judicial jurisdiction. The military functions of the *adelantado* resisted the royal usurpations with greater success; but the political unification of Spain, the end of the civil wars, and the conquest of Granada, rendered useless if not dangerous the maintenance of large forces in the interior of the country. "All is changed," says Salazar. "What was once an office is now a *dignity*."

The system of administration inherited from medieval Spain was neither adequate nor appropriate to the needs of the reorganized state. A new personnel was needed, and agents who, if not new, were at least animated by a new spirit. The civil war had developed on all social levels a taste for disorder, lack of discipline, corruption. The officials, poorly paid, indemnified themselves at the expense of the taxpayer; they sold justice and trafficked in influence. Offices tended to become hereditary and objects of commerce, like a house or a field. The Catholic Sovereigns had to put an end to all these abuses. Venality and inheritance of office were condemned by legists in the name of Scripture, experience, and antiquity.

So great was the evil that none thought of guaranteeing the independence of the magistrate, so much do principles vary from one age to another. To guarantee tenure of office to judges would have served only to perpetuate abuses. The central government was in honest hands; it would have been a disaster to oppose entrenched privilege to its beneficial action. The Catholic Sovereigns applied themselves to finding devoted and honest servants; they displayed such zeal therein that their solicitude became legendary, and after their deaths the Cortes cited their example as a model for the negligent government of Charles V. [7] They had, said the Cortes, a register in which they noted the services of their subjects in order to reward them when the occasion arose; they also wrote therein all the information that they could gather on candidates for public office. It was rumored that one day Isabella let drop a paper on which she had written these words: "The office of public crier in the town of X . . . is reserved for such-and-such a one . . . because he has a better voice."

Even if this charming story were only an invention, it would still have value for the historian insofar as it confirms the high opinion that men had of the queen's conscientious spirit. If the people were ready to believe that she took such great care to fill the humblest of positions with the worthiest candidate, it was because she had so frequently shown her concern that the highest offices should be placed in good hands.

The *corregidores,* the *audiencias,* and the Inquisition were three great instruments employed to unify, discipline, convert, and subjugate Spain. The *corregidor* was the key officer of the administrative edifice; he was the most direct and active agent of the royal will. Earlier rulers had already understood the need of placing over the urban centers men devoted to the central government, named and recalled by the king. The towns and cities of Spain held sway over a vast territory that was subject to their jurisdiction. Each town formed an independent grouping composed of the town itself and its satellite hamlets and villages. The city united to itself several towns over which its magistrates exercised an appellate jurisdiction. Control of these powerful communes was a matter of the first interest for the crown. Isabella's predecessors had already tried, without marked success, to impose their officials as heads of the municipalities. The Catholic Sovereigns generalized this policy and, disregarding all protests, in 1480 sent *corregidores* into all the towns and cities of Castile.[8] The *corregidores,* administrators and judges at once, were the representatives of the central government, the defenders of its rights, claims, and wishes. Their mission was to establish the royal supremacy at the expense of all classes. The oath they took at the time of entering on their duties shows the extent of their powers and the services that were expected of them.[9] They swore to keep clear of all coteries and factions. To avoid entangling alliances, they were forbidden to select agents to act under their orders from among persons born in the district which they governed. They must resist all pressures and influences.

The towns had greatly suffered from the nobles, the *caballeros,* who seized their domains and transformed their communal property into private property. The towns had everything to fear should their worst enemies be put over them with the title of *corregidores*. The sovereigns, who at the Cortes of Toledo (1480) had promised never to entrust this office to members of the military orders of Santiago, Calatrava, and St. John of Jerusalem, took the strongest measures to prevent the recurrence of such abuses. If a lord dares encroach on communal lands, the royal magistrate "will make execution on the goods of the person who has thus occupied these domains." If the guilty parties proved too powerful, the magistrate was to refer the matter to the Council of Justice. He must on no account tolerate usurpation of particular jurisdictions. As concerned the clergy, the sovereigns outlined a policy for the *corregidor* that was as firm as it was respectful.

Ferdinand and Isabella undertook to engrave these recommendations on the minds of their agents by swift and energetic actions. In 1491 they recalled all the judges of the *chancillería* of Valladolid for permitting a case which they should have settled themselves to be appealed to the Roman Curia.[10]

But lack of zeal on the part of royal functionaries was less of a problem than their passion for wealth. They received presents or permitted their children and wives to receive them; their subordinates also accepted gratuities for acts of oversight or favor. The sovereigns employed every last resource of the oath against these venal practices. They sought to anticipate all the contingencies to which a frail conscience might be exposed; they sought to close off all avenues of corruption with the barricade of the plighted word. The *corregidores,* in turn, were to require the same commitments from the functionaries under their orders, *alcaldes, alguaciles,* and clerks. On top of the presents and money that royal officials received from persons under their jurisdiction, they squeezed out of their position all the financial advantage that it could yield. The issuance of diplomas and letters and the performance of acts of every kind were burdened with fees that formed part of their emoluments. Thus they raised the cost of transacting business as their greed dictated. To remedy this state of affairs, Ferdinand and Isabella drew up a schedule of fees and forbade their officials, under the most severe penalties, to demand higher sums.

The government, then, desired a devoted and honest administration; it had made wise regulations, adopted excellent measures. A constant surveillance was necessary, however, to prevent a return of the old abuses. With this end in view, the sovereigns decided at the Cortes of Toledo (1480) to send out investigative commissioners (*pesquisidores*) or inspectors (*veedores*) charged with seeing that royal agents performed their duties and that the royal ordinances were executed.[11] The *pesquisidores* visited the provinces and towns almost every year; they took secret information concerning the conduct of *corregidores*, heard complaints against them, and verified the accusations.[12] The administration of the towns, and the manner in which justice was rendered in them, were the principal objects of their inquiry. They were to display particular zeal in restoring to the towns the property of which they had been despoiled; they were not themselves to act as judges, but to indicate to the *corregidores* the suits they should institute and the wrongs to be redressed. The *pesquisidores* lent the aid of their authority to humble persons, the little people, injured by powerful men, and brought the protection of royal justice to the lowest classes of the population. Their work did not stop there; they also had oversight of the conduct of the *alcaides*, the commanders of fortresses. The king wished to know what lords were building castles and fortified houses. Finally, the maintenance of roads, the state of bridges and causeways, were commended to the attention of these commissioners; they verified if the mandatory audit of the tax levy was being made every year. They were authorized to take urgent measures on the spot; but they were obliged to send their reports to the sovereigns.

The institution of *pesquisidores* enabled the central government to watch over its own agents and hold them to their duties. The *corregidores,* who were named for only one year, lived under the perpetual threat of recall and a punishment befitting their misdeeds. They were held responsible not only to the state but to the people; the sovereigns insisted that the people should be free from oppression. They even encouraged accusations against disloyal and tyrannical administrators. At the expiration of his term, the *corregidor,* divested of all authority, had to remain thirty days longer in the seat of his jurisdiction to answer there for his acts. During this period his subjects could submit complaints against his conduct. Several commissioners opened an inquiry; if the charges against the *corregidor* were proved, he was imprisoned and sent to be tried by the Council of Justice.

The same fate awaited the *alcaldes, alguaciles,* and *merinos.* All that could be done was done to defend the rights of the central government and the interests of the people.

The weakening of the old powers left in abeyance a large part of the administrative services; the gap left by the passing of the *adelantados* and other dignitaries had to be filled. The sovereigns filled this void by means of commissions which they entrusted to men of their choice as the need arose. These temporary and revocable delegations suited their authoritarian temper. Members of the royal council were often sent on mission; they went to carry out the royal orders or the decisions they had taken in concert with their colleagues. The sovereigns entrusted the widest variety of offices to men who at first glance might seem quite unsuited for their assignments. They employed priests and monks with secular interests and tempers in the conduct of a variety of negotiations and business. The Vicar General of Villafranca de Montes de Oca, Don Juan de Ortega, was one of the principal organizers of the Santa Hermandad. Even more brilliant was the career of Juan Rodríguez de Fonseca, whose situation of Archdeacon of Seville seems a poor qualification for the direction of the admiralty. Charged at first with the organization of fleets for the Indies, and later made President of the Council of the Indies, he was a sort of minister of the navy and the colonies during the whole reign of Ferdinand and Isabella. What qualifications did Jiménez have for organizing and leading an expedition to Africa?

The will of the royal master took the place of all rank and hierarchy in the nascent administrative system; later would come the creation of those rigid frames in which talent is imprisoned. It seems likely that in Ferdinand's time the governments of the provinces were also regarded, not as regular bodies, but as extraordinary delegations without fixed duration, charged with the accomplishment of a specific object. I have in mind, not the governors general of Aragón, Catalonia, and Valencia, who occupied permanent offices, but those governors and judges sent by Ferdinand into Galicia and into other provinces of Castile to govern and pacify them. Their functions as yet had no fixed character; we sense that we are in a period of transformation. These considerations apply above all to Castile, where the sovereigns experimented with the new administrative methods, and where the process of reform can best be seen and studied.

The formation of the councils, the establishment of *corregidores* in all the towns, the creation of institutions of control, the development of the extraordinary missions, the decline of the great crown offices, constitute measures to create the different parts of a well-conceived system that tended to subordinate all classes and all wills to the royal will. However, the change was not so brusque as may appear at the first blush. We can find an origin and a model for each reform in preceding reigns. Political evolution took place without leaps; it is not always easy to distinguish the share of credit that falls to the Catholic Sovereigns in the conception of the modern monarchy. We must add that no ruler ever pursued a design with so much vigor, consistency, and success. Isabella's predecessors were jealous of their supremacy; but they failed to achieve it, sometimes because they were in advance of their times, sometimes because they lacked the men or the means. The Catholic Sovereigns, aided by circumstances and by their genius, founded the absolute monarchy on the ruins of the ancient institutions.

V

Justice

Ferdinand and Isabella were well aware of the notable services that men of law had rendered the royal cause. In his *Guerra de Granada*, Diego Hurtado de Mendoza, who wrote under Philip II, dates the new importance of the legists from their reign. This great lord understood in what class the absolute monarchs of Europe found their instruments of domination. He comprehended the origin and the creators of "this mode of governing." The judicial organization which served their absolutist political design was in large measure the work of the Catholic Sovereigns. To be sure, they proceeded with such art, linked so skillfully the present to the past, that the historian has difficulty in establishing just what their innovations were. Faithful to the principles which they had applied to the administrative reform, they seem not so much to have changed as to have transformed. They renewed and generalized the efforts of previous ages; but where their predecessors had failed, they succeeded; where others merely tried, they brought to triumphant conclusion. Without fuss or fanfare, their government achieved improvements of the greatest importance; even when they left intact the form of institutions, they very felicitously modified their spirit.

The sovereign was the supreme judge. Public opinion regarded him as the redresser of wrongs, as a disinterested arbiter, as the last recourse of the wretched, as a sort of visible and active Providence. He was not the organ of justice; he was justice itself, making and applying the law. Such was the conception that the Church and the people of Castile had of the crown in the Middle Ages. In the manner of St. Louis, seated under the oak of Vincennes or in his Paris garden, Alfonso the Sage devoted three sessions a week to hearing cases. His successors displayed less earnestness, and finally the royal audience fell into complete disuse. But the moment royalty regained a sense of its own worth it reclaimed the exercise of its noblest prerogative. Isabella proposed to justify the adage: "The best *alcalde* is the king." She personally listened to complaints; she personally pronounced final judgments. At Seville, where the time of troubles had spawned factions and crimes, she held public hearings every Friday for two months. Her secretaries read the petitions and reported to her; within the hour she rendered her decision.[1]

This spectacle captured the imagination of contemporaries, who were not accustomed to such a righteous passion. Gonzalo Fernández de Oviedo, who as a very young man witnessed these royal assizes, drew a picture of the proceedings with a great and loving fidelity: "I seem to see her in that alcázar of Madrid, together with the Catholic King Ferdinand V, that illustrious prince, her husband, seated publicly at the tribunal every Friday, giving audience to great and small, to all who would ask for justice. And on the same high platform, to which one mounted by five or six steps, in the space outside the canopy of the dais, there was on either side, to the right and the left, a bench where sat twelve *oidores* of the Council of Justice and the president of the said royal council; and in front was a clerk of the council, named Castañeda, who read the petitions in a loud voice; and at the foot of the steps was another clerk of the chamber of the council, who noted down the subject of each petition. And at the sides of the table where the petitions were deposited stood twelve mace-bearers. And at the door of the hall of this royal *audiencia* were porters who upon order let freely enter whoever wished to submit a petition. And the court *alcaldes* were there to take whatever measures were to be taken, or to redress wrongs, or to consult with the sovereigns. In fine, it was a Golden Age, an age of justice, when he who was in the right obtained his due. I have observed that since God took away the saintly queen, it is far harder to get an audience of a secretary's valet than it used to be of her and her Council, and a great deal more expensive." [2]

The sovereigns, however zealous, could listen to only a limited number of cases. To assist them, the rulers of the thirteenth century had created the court *oidores*,[3] or majordomos for petitions, who had their own jurisdiction apart from the royal council and formed the royal *audiencia* charged with judging a multitude of cases and suits in the first and last instance. The royal *audiencia,* thus first organized under Alfonso the Sage, followed the sovereigns in all their travels. These numerous changes of residence hampered the administration of justice. For the rest, this single court of appeals was not adequate to the needs of the country. The measures taken in the fourteenth and fifteenth centuries to meet the complaints of subjects, that is, the division of the royal *audiencia* and the fixing of its place of abode, were experiments without lasting effect. In 1442 King Juan II designated Valladolid as the seat of the *audiencia real;* but this ordinance proved no more effective than its predecessors.

He left to his daughter Isabella the task of a definitive organization.

The first years of her reign were so troubled by civil war that she had no time to institute changes of any kind.[4] But at the Cortes of Toledo (1480) she sanctioned a whole plan of reform, including therein the administration of justice.

All of a sudden she took a decisive step: She separated the royal *audiencia* from herself and established it at Valladolid (1485). This time the installation was definitive. The Spanish "parliament" ceased to be an ambulating court that followed in the footsteps of the sovereigns. A revenue of 500,000 maravedís levied on the *alcabalas* of Valladolid provided for its existence. However, this judicial center was too far from New Castile and Andalusia, and it became necessary to create a second *audiencia*. The sovereigns established such an *audiencia* at Ciudad Real for the southern region, but this designation was provisional. When the Moslems were finally subdued, the *audiencia* was transferred to Granada (1505).[5] The Tagus marked the boundary of the two jurisdictions. These two *audiencias* were also called *chancillerías;* they divided between them almost all the domains of the crown of Castile. The unsettled state of Galicia had obliged the sovereigns to establish an *audiencia* there.[6] The conquest of Navarre led to the creation of a fourth *audiencia* in that kingdom. However, the *chancillerías* of Valladolid and Granada, whose jurisdictions were most extensive, enjoyed the greatest prestige and authority. These were the courts of Castile.

The *chancillería* or *audiencia* (these terms were employed indifferently) was called upon to decide disputes and punish offenses, to enforce respect for private law and the laws that ensured order and maintained public security. The *oidores* judged civil affairs; they were six in number and enjoyed greater prestige than the *sala de lo criminal*, composed of three *alcaldes*. "In addition, there was an *alcalde* for the *hijosdalgo*, an *alcalde* for petitions, and eight provincial *alcaldes*, two for Castile, two for León, one for Toledo, two for Extremadura, and one for Andalusia." [7]

The crown was represented by a special prosecutor, or *procurador fiscal*.[8] The sovereigns, who regarded this magistrate as their representative on the tribunal, commanded of him an unqualified and ardent devotion. They made him take oath that he would defend their interests and that he would not aid the accused in civil or criminal cases "against us or our fisc." If he perjured himself, he lost his office and half of his goods. A charitable impulse caused the sovereigns to place on the court two persons charged with defending the rights of the poor. These were special counsel who offered judicial recourse and legal assistance to the destitute.

A passion for litigation caused some persons to exhaust the resources of all jurisdictions and to carry an appeal to the *chancillería* and even the royal council over a case involving a few maravedís. The magistrates had to be protected against the crushing burden of suits, and the litigants against the temptation to bring about their own financial ruin. Accordingly, it was provided that no case of less than 3,000 maravedís' value could be brought before the *audiencia* or the royal council.

However, it seemed unfair to deny the opportunity for an appeal to poor persons entangled in some petty suit. The royal legislators were unwilling to hand them over without recourse to the lower courts of the towns and cities, where a single magistrate heard and decided each suit. Prejudice and interest might dictate a judgment. It was necessary to find some means of review without increasing the costs to the appellant. Suitors who believed they had been wronged had five days to appeal from an adverse decision. The case was debated a second time before the judge whose finding had been impugned; but this time there were associated with him two jurors of known integrity (*buenas personas*), who in turn chose a third juror. When a suit came before a supreme tribunal or court of the last instance, the parties could reject a judge whom they suspected of partisanship. This was no trifling matter; although the superior courts were composed of three or four judges, one might draw the others after himself. The sovereigns had learned that these currents of influence often acted upon the *oidores* of the *chancillería*. In case of protest against one of the members of the tribunal, his colleagues decided on the spot, without formal act or proceeding, if the rejection was justified or not. If their decision was affirmative, the rejected judge had to withdraw. In a criminal proceeding, when the accused raised the question of the impartiality of an *alcalde*, it was up to the other *alcaldes*, assisted by an *oidor*, to decide whether they should proceed with the case.[9] At the same Cortes of 1480, where these sage ordinances were promulgated, the sovereigns carefully regulated the criminal procedure of the court *alcaldes* and the *alcaldes* of the *chancillería*.[10]

These were the principal reforms that the sovereigns introduced into the organization of the superior courts. Even as Castile issued from the chaos of civil war, Isabella provided it with well-ordered legal institutions. She made a small number of judges suffice to maintain public peace, which her predecessors vainly sought to attain with their soldiers and their aristocratic subjects. Her achievement does not end there; Isabella understood that satisfactory administration of justice was closely linked to the character of the legislation. The multitude of *fueros,* the incoherence and contradictoriness of the laws, the obscurity and barbarism of some codes, contributed as much as the study of Roman law to lead jurists away from national customs and national laws. In her reign some efforts were made to simplify and codify the laws. If she was only half-successful, the fault was of her times and contemporaries, and not of the great queen, who even on her deathbed thought of how she might place at the service of her subjects an exact, concise, intelligible code of justice.[11]

Under the Catholic Sovereigns, who united but did not merge the crowns of Aragón and Castile, all suits entered into and all offenses committed in Aragonese territory had to be tried before an Aragonese court; it was forbidden to transfer the parties to a suit or a culprit to a foreign jurisdiction. This was a formal principle of public law and one of the most cherished liberties of the inhabitants of the country. Cases, judged in the first instance by the *alcaldes,* the *zalmedinas,* and other officers of the towns, the lords, and the king, were carried in the last resort to the *audiencia real,*[12] sitting at Zaragoza and composed of Aragonese doctors of law. It was divided into chambers, one civil and the other criminal, and had at its head the regent of the *audiencia.*[13] A legist, the *procurador fiscal,* represented the interests of the treasury on the court. He is not to be confused with the *procurador regni,* who filled the office of public prosecutor in matters concerning the security of the state.[14]

There was no public action against murderers in this society where violence was the rule. Even the intervention of private individuals was limited. In general, only blood relatives or the victim's wife were entitled to bring charges against a criminal; however, in the case of sodomy, counterfeiting, or heresy, anyone could act as

Registro.

poreñde ño ouieron los antiguos cuybado de
las fazer fobre las cofas que vinieron pocas ve
3es:poz que tuuieron que fe podzia iuzgar poz
otro cafo de ley femeiante que fe fallafe efcripta
Otrofi dixicron que enlas cofas que fe fazen de
nue uo deue fer catado en cierto la pzo ollas an
te que fe parta delas otras que fueran antigua
mente tenidas poz buenas y poz derechas. E
poz que las otras palabzas quelos átiguos pu
fieron como regla de derecho las auemos puef
tas y departidas poz las leyes defte nueftro li
bzo affi como de iufo dixímos. pozéde no las q
rieuzo doblar tenemos que abozuan los en;en
p los que aqui auemos demoftrados.

C La primera partida tiene onze qüadernos. a
b.c.d.e.f.g.b.i.k.l.
La fegúda partida tiene itueue quadernos. aa.
bb.cc.dd.ee.ff.gg.bb.ii. E dos ternos. kk.
ll.
La tercera partida tiene quaderuos catozze.
aaa.bbb.ccc.ddd.eee.fff.ggg.bbb.iii.kkk.
.lll.mmm.nnn.ooo.
La quarta patiua tiene dos quinternos el pri
mero. aaaa. el poftrero. eeee. E tres ternos
bbbb.cccc.dddd.
La quita partida tiene feys quaderuos. A.B.
C.D.E.F.E vn terno. G.
La ferta partida tiene quatro quaderuos. AA
BB.CC.DD. E dos ternol. EE.FF.
La ferena partida tiene feys quaderuol. AAA
BBB.CCC.DDD.EEE.FFF.
E vn terno. GGG.

C Las fiete partidas quel fereniffimo z muy
excelléte feñoz don Alfonfo rey de Caftilla de
Leon zc. de gloriofa memoria: nono defte non
bze fizo z mando conpilar z reduzir á muy pzo
uechofa bieuedad de todas las principales fu
erças iudiciales poz muy folenne z apzobados
iurifconfultos. Fueron impzeffas enla muy no
ble z muy leal cibdad de Seuilla: poz comiffió
de Rodrigo de efcobar: z de Melchioz gurrizo
mercadoz es de libzos. Jmpzimierő las maeftre
paulo de colonia z Johánes pegniczer de nuré
berga z Magno z Thomas compañeros ale
manes. Acabaron fe de impzimir a.xxiiij. dias
de deziembze año de nueftra faluo de mill z qua
trocientos z nouenta z vn años bienauentura
dá mente. Aan enefias fiete partidas las auicio
nes z cőcozdanças fechas poz el doctoz de mon
taluo.

accuser. These restrictions naturally were very prejudicial
to the public peace; fear and lack of money were likely to
subdue a widow's hate or restrain unhappy relations without wealth or influence. In order to give a voice to the
plaints of the weak and to secure the suppression of
brigandage, in 1510 Ferdinand ordered all the towns,
cities, and *universidades* to establish *procuradores* charged
with seeking the punishment of crimes committed on their
territory. These were the *procuradores adstricti*.[15] They
substituted themselves for the individuals with the right

to bring charges and took their cases in hand. The state understood its true role of defender of society, and regarded as a duty the maintenance of public order.

Over and above the ordinary jurisdiction in Aragón there was another: the court or tribunal of the *justicia*. It must be said that Aragonese historians, contemporaries of Philip II, formed a somewhat false or exaggerated conception of this magistracy.[16] Writing at a time when their national liberties were languishing, these erudite patriots took a nostalgic pleasure in embellishing the historical role of the *justicia*. They conceived him to be a sort of tribune or ephor, created to defend the interests of all classes and ever ready to halt royal encroachments with his veto. It is unnecessary to transform the *justicia* into an outright enemy of the royal prerogative to comprehend the importance of his functions. The facts leave him with a role so attractive as to make exaggeration unnecessary. Whatever one may think of its political action, this magistracy does great honor to the Aragonese of the Middle Ages. Historians have vied with each other in praising the existence in the thirteenth and fourteenth centuries of a protective institution which safeguarded the rights of individuals against the tyranny of the king, that is, the state. Is it not remarkable that those ages of violence should have established with so many precautions, with such great care, an intermediary power, an arbiter, between the people and the crown, between the sovereign and his subjects?

The court of the *justicia* performed the same role that the French Conseil d'État performs when conflicts arise between the administration and private citizens. It acted as a supreme court when the justicia, called upon to review the sentences rendered by other tribunals, decided whether a particular judgment had been in conformity with or contrary to the laws and the *fueros*.

On such occasions it doubtless risked handing down decisions that might be unpalatable to the government—but one can easily find examples of other courts of justice that have been equally uncooperative. This in itself does not suffice to give to the *justicia* the character of a declared opposition, the character that some would ascribe to it. The great originality of this magistracy was that it had no other purpose than to guarantee the rights of each against the tyranny of all, the freedoms of the nation against the encroachments of the central government, the possessions of subjects against the greed of the treasury, individual liberty against the abuses of the seignorial, ecclesiastic, and royal jurisdictions.

The *justicia* gave effect to his protective function by one of two means: the *manifestación* and the *firma*.

The *manifestación* was especially designed to cover security of the person. When an imprisoned individual feared or claimed to fear some act of violence on the part of his jailers or judges, he invoked the protection of the *justicia*. As soon as he learned of this appeal, the magistrate issued an order to bring the detained person before him. All that happened was a change of prison; the agents of the *justicia* conducted the prisoner to the *cárcel de los manifestados*.[17] If the guards refused to obey, the *justicia* in person came with an armed force adequate to compel delivery to him of the *manifestado*. His intervention did not halt the course of the trial; it in no way prejudged the validity of the proceedings; the protection of the *justicia* expired the very hour that sentence was pronounced.

The *firma* was a letter of protection issued by the *justicia* to whoever requested it in order to safeguard his person and goods against a judgment contrary to the *fueros*. This letter suspended the procedure; and if sentence had already been rendered, it delayed its execution in order to allow the *justicia* to inquire if the proceeding or the decision were in conformity with the laws of the country.[18] During this time the goods and person of the defendant were protected from all violence. One who disobeyed the *firmas* risked incurring the most terrible punishments; the guilty party must answer for his conduct before the *justicia,* whose commands he had scorned.

These were the weapons of a magistracy especially created to safeguard individual liberty and assure all of an equal justice in conformity with customary law. To perform such a vast and delicate task exceeded the powers and intelligence of a single man. The *justicia* was assisted by two lieutenants or deputies (*lugartenientes*),[19] one of whom, from 1467 on, was chosen from among the legists, the other from persons not engaged in the practice of law. Legal knowledge was not an absolute necessity. When the lieutenants thought it opportune, they summoned the jurisconsults residing in Zaragoza and consulted them on difficult points. The deputy who presided over this consultation gathered the sense of the majority from the views expressed. "Whence it follows," as the historian Blancas says, "that at this period the deputies had more need to be attentive than to be learned." This assembly of legists was called the *consilium extraordinarium* (extraordinary council); it was a consultative committee of the rarest competence and of great independence. Its opinions formed a jurisprudence that inspired the same veneration as the laws themselves.

These free and general deliberations probably offered too little scope for the exercise of royal influence; a smaller assembly seemed better designed to receive inspiration from on high. Thus, in 1493, the dissolution of the extraordinary council began with the designation of five jurisconsults to be attached to the court of the *jus-*

ticia to advise him in the hearing of criminal cases. Zaragoza, or any other place where the court might sit, was assigned to them as their place of residence. The transformation begun by Ferdinand was completed in the reign of Charles V. In 1519 the extraordinary council was suppressed.

The five members of the extraordinary council were replaced by seven jurisconsults who formed the *ordinary council* and who, like their predecessors, were consulted in criminal cases. In 1528 there was a final reform which joined to the *justicia* five lieutenants who inherited the functions of the two lieutenants, the ordinary council, and the extraordinary council.

This magistracy, whose prestige was so great and whose power was so extensive, nevertheless had to walk softly in its dealings with the two powers of the state: the crown and the Cortes. The crown, by the mere fact of its development, had to exercise an indisputable influence upon it. Moreover, the *justicia*, being named by the king, inevitably tended to regard himself as a royal functionary of the most exalted rank; only in the gravest circumstances could he be expected to resist directly the man from whom he held his office. On the other hand, an excessive complaisance tended to arouse the suspicions and the anger of the four arms or orders of the realm, which alone had the right to judge this grand justiciary. In 1439, on the death of Martín Díaz of Aux, who was imprisoned and perhaps poisoned by orders of Alfonso V, his post was given to a Lanuza; the office became hereditary in this family, which still held it in the time of Philip II.

It may be that the Cortes found that this dynasty defended the popular rights too feebly against the royal prerogative. In any case, the various changes introduced by the Cortes into the naming of the lieutenants may be regarded as so many signs of distrust. Before this time the *justicia* had been free to choose his assistants, and this right had been regarded as completely legitimate. The Cortes of 1461 decided that in the future the lieutenants should be chosen by lot and remain in office only three years; in 1467, that they should be named for only one year. The representatives of the realm did not attack the *justicia* himself, but they assured themselves of ways and means of influencing his assistants. The annual drawing of lots increased the chances of having the lots fall to candidates agreeable to the Cortes. The intervention of the *brazos* in the designation of the lieutenants was a safeguard against partiality on the part of the *justicia* toward the crown.

There was also reason to fear that the *justicia* and his lieutenants might misuse their power for their own profit. To guard against this danger, there had been organized much earlier a control authority which in 1390 was entrusted to four inquisitors, representing the four branches of the Aragonese Cortes. Their function was to receive complaints against the conduct of the *justicia* and his agents; they opened an inquiry, collected testimony, and, having closed their inquest, left it to the Cortes to judge the incriminating facts.

The debates in this great assembly may have grown too stormy, or perhaps the multitude of judges afforded culprits too many opportunities to escape punishment. Whatever the reason, in the reign of Juan II, father of Ferdinand the Catholic, the Cortes decided to turn over these extraordinary cases to a commission of seventeen members. This commission drew up a regulation which, with some changes, was promulgated at Zaragoza in 1467: this was the *Forus Inquisitionis Justitiae Aragonum*. Four inquisitors, chosen by lot, were charged with the task of inquiry. Each year, during the first ten days of April, they installed themselves at Zaragoza in the palace of the Deputation. On the first day, the heralds went up and down the city and invited citizens with grievances to present themselves before the commissioners-inquisitors. If during those ten days no complaint was made the inquisitors declared the session closed. That year there was no occasion to cast lots for the election of the Seventeen. But if during this period any man, even of the lowest element, reported some injustice, then the inquisitors, their powers prolonged till June 10, began an inquiry into the charges that had been made.

On May 10 the Deputation of the Kingdom drew out of the urn the names of the Seventeen; each of the three highest orders had four representatives; the towns had five. This political grand jury had no lawyer members. The Aragonese justly feared that too expert a knowledge of the subtleties of procedure might play into the hands of some interested parties. However, the Seventeen had the right to attach to their number two assistants chosen among legists. On June 10 they gathered at Zaragoza and received from the hands of the inquisitors the minutes of their proceedings and all the relevant documents. Then the lawsuit began; it must be conducted expeditiously and dispatched in the space of forty days. The judges voted with white or black stones depending on whether they wished to acquit or find guilty.[20] They could choose among penalties: infamy, fine, or death.

This wealth of precautions scarcely attests that the *justicia* was regarded at this period as the chosen defender of the nation. Although the history of this royal functionary still remains to be written in a dispassionate spirit, free from national prejudices and nostalgic regret for vanished glories, we know enough about it to conclude that in the fifteenth century the *justicia* was suspect not only to the crown but to the estates of the realm.

When this magistrate first appears in the documents, it is as a functionary named by the king and chosen from the middle nobility. It is true that he had permanent tenure; but certain kings, such as Alfonso V, demanded of the appointee a written promise that he would resign his charge at the first demand. Martín Díaz of Aux, who refused to abide by his promise, paid for his disobedience with imprisonment and his life. The Lanuzas, who succeeded him, were more obliging. When we see Juan de Lanuza, *justicia* under Ferdinand the Catholic, serving at the same time as Admiral of Sicily, Viceroy of Valencia and Catalonia, it is reasonable to conclude that his relations with the king were of a fairly close character. During the time he occupied this high charge, the strongest safeguards of Aragonese liberties were suspended, apparently without the least protest on the *justicia*'s part.

Unfortunately, the *firma* and the *manifestación,* those salutary last resorts of the oppressed, often served to protect criminals, drag out lawsuits in perpetuity, and keep alive disorder and brigandage by giving hope of impunity. The Catholic Sovereigns, who had observed the salutary effects of swift retribution in Castile, wished to apply the same remedies to the same evils in Aragón. In 1488 they asked the Cortes of Zaragoza to consent to the establishment of Hermandades in the kingdom.[21] Now the success of the Hermandad was bound up with the promptness of its pursuits, with rapidity of investigation, judgment, and execution. There was every reason to fear the effect of all these instruments of legal delay, which would brake the movement of repression at every step and shatter its *élan.* Accordingly, the Cortes decided to suspend the application of the *firma* and the *manifestación* in all the cases called *de Hermandad.* The *justicia* lost the patronage of the thieves and brigands who infested the roads and the countryside. He no longer threw the cloak of his protection over the lords who offered the asylum of their castles to highwaymen. Thanks to this large concession, order was restored for some time. But these freedoms were dear to the Aragonese; there was a movement of reaction against their abandonment. In 1500 the Cortes extended the benefits of the *manifestación* to every sort of crime, and the plague of disorder began once more. Not until 1528 was the central government definitively victorious.

Although these debates excited public opinion, the *justicias* were careful not to take part in the controversy. The estates of Aragón warmly defended their rights; they preferred their bad old customs to the most salutary innovations. Lanuza did not appear at the head of the opposition. His posture of noninvolvement gives a measure of the decay of this high magistracy. The king dominated it entirely; the Cortes had only a limited confidence in it. Thus the Aragonese historian Blancas, who finds nothing noteworthy to say about Juan de Lanuza, excuses the brevity of his account with these revealing words: "All these times were entirely peaceful; in truth, all the actions of King Ferdinand and Charles V rendered this magistracy useless." By the admission of an enthusiastic commentator, the tribunes of the people remained mute.

VI

The Spanish Army

The Spanish army underwent a complete transformation under Ferdinand and Isabella. Between the beginning and the end of their reign, its armament, tactics, and mode of recruitment were changed. The war against Affonso V of Portugal (1474 to 1476) was a struggle that recalls the melees of the Middle Ages; but at the death of the Catholic Sovereigns Spain possessed a truly modern army, composed chiefly of infantry and relying not so much on individual bravery as on the solidity of its battalions, the agility of its movements, and the skill of its leaders.

To judge the importance and value of the new organization, we must picture to ourselves the feudal rout of the early days of the reign. When the sovereigns were menaced by a Portuguese invasion, or when they prepared to make an incursion into Moslem territory, they summoned their vassals to arms. The contingents of the nobility and the towns began to gather. The number of troops raised by each lord varied according to his territorial wealth and importance. Sometimes a noble commanded in person; often he placed some captain of renown at the head of his troops. The crown lands furnished levies that were led in combat by *adelantados* or other royal officers. The cities and towns sent their men under the orders of captains or of *corregidores*. These municipal militias, like the royal and seigniorial forces, included foot soldiers and horsemen, nobles and commoners. In the Spanish communes the obligation of personal service was so imperative for the nobility that a *caballero* who could not furnish arms and a horse was reduced to the condition of a taxpayer (*pechero*). He must be able to show the public registrar and swear on the Cross that he possessed "sword, lance, shield, cuisses, morion, and cuirass," and, of course, a war horse.[1]

After these troops had been assembled, the leaders divided them into a number of distinct bodies composed of infantry and cavalry and called "battles" (*batallas*). The army that gathered at Tordesillas to fight the Portuguese numbered 12,000 horse and 30,000 foot soldiers; it consisted of thirty-five battles. In 1489 great levies were made in all parts of the kingdom to attack the town of Baza. "The king [Ferdinand] held a review; his host numbered 13,000 horse and 40,000 foot soldiers, whom he ordered drawn up as follows. He commanded that in the first line there should be 150 mounted men with the Alcaide of the Young Pages, who, according to the ancient usage of Spain, must go with the marshals to prepare the cantonments. And he commanded that in the vanguard should go the Grand Master of Santiago with 1,800 lances, with whom went the men of Écija with 150 lances and 700 foot soldiers, and 150 *espingarderos* of the city of Toledo. At one wing of this battle he placed the Grand Master of Calatrava with 400 lances and 1,000 foot soldiers. And at the other wing marched Pedro López de Padilla with 200 lances of the squires who had land and received wages from the king and queen; of these men López de Padilla had been named captain. In the second battle went Don Diego López de

Haro with 150 lances and 4,000 foot soldiers of the Kingdom of Galicia, who had been given to him to command.
In the third battle went 1,000 men-at-arms and light
cavalry and 1,000 foot soldiers of the Cardinal of Spain;
its captains were Don Rodrigo de Mendoza, Lord of the
Cid, and Don Diego Hurtado de Mendoza, Adelantado
of Cazorla. In the fourth battle went the horse and foot
soldiers of the Hermandades, each squadron with its captain. In the fifth battle went Don Diego Fernández de
Córdoba, Count of Cabra, with 250 lances and 300
foot soldiers, and Martín Alonzo de Montemayor, with
160 lances and 200 foot soldiers. . . . In the tenth battle went Don Alonso, lord of the house of Aguilar, with
300 lances and 300 foot soldiers. In advance of the
royal battle went the Count of Tendilla with 460 lances
that belonged to him, to his brother the Archbishop of
Seville, and to the Count of Benavente. . . ." [2]

Does it not seem that we are reading an account by
Froissart? This chronicler's exposition gives a very clear
picture of the rudimentary organization characteristic of
feudal armies. All these groups were constituted, not according to a rational system, but according to their origin; they were unequal in numerical strength and solidity. There was no proportion between the different arms;
one battle was stronger in cavalry, another in infantry,
all according to chance or the whims of the leaders.

However, amid all this confusion one can distinguish
elements of a superior organization. The king is not at
the mercy of the nobles and the towns; he has his vassals
about him; he uses in the service of the Holy War the
archers of the Hermandades, created by him for another
purpose. There is even some indication of a force of paid
troops. The chronicler informs us that there were men-
at-arms permanently stationed in Galicia for the suppression of disorder; another small force encamped on

the frontier with the Moors.[3] The royal guard was very numerous; it included 500 men-at-arms and 500 light horse, "who were all servants of the king and queen." [4] In the expedition against Baza, Ferdinand led fifteen companies which belonged to him personally and which consisted of more than 2,000 horse. Four hundred noble horsemen were attached to his person and formed a sort of royal guard. Several reforms added to this elite group the complement necessary for the defense of the country. But before transforming the ancient military system the Catholic Sovereigns made an effort to improve it.[5] They introduced order and system into the distribution of the contingents. Instead of distributing them in small unequal groups, they formed them into battalions, divided into ten squadrons and composed of 500 men—*espingarderos,* arbalesters, and lancers. Every year they held reviews of these militias in the important centers.

The disbanding of the Santa Hermandad and foreign complications compelled the sovereigns to take more radical measures. The years following the conquest of Granada had been for Castile a time of repose, free of disturbances or alarms, during which the people gave themselves up to the enjoyment of a long peace. The inhabitants of the towns and the countryside lost the habit of assembling for the annual reviews and drills; their arms were sold or became unfit for service through lack of care and use. Spain was at the mercy of an invasion or a civil war.

To avert the harmful consequences of this neglect, an order (October 5, 1495) compelled all subjects to provide themselves with arms, each man's equipment to be proportionate to his means. The following year a census was made of all persons able to carry arms. A decree dated at Valladolid (February 22, 1496) provided that one of every twelve Spaniards between twenty and forty-five years of age would be taken by the state to serve at home or abroad.[6] These levies were not standing troops, but they formed regular reserves that received pay from the day on which they were mobilized, whence the name of "paid soldiers" (*los de los acostamientos, milites stipendarii*) applied to these fighting men.

It is likely that as long as the towns and cities furnished their quotas they could satisfy their obligations as they pleased, either by local conscription or by appealing for voluntary enlistments. Moreover, the sovereigns did not call up all the available forces of all the provinces on each occasion; there was a rotation among the different regions of Spain of which little is known, and which probably was of ancient date. At the beginning of the reign, Old and New Castile withstood almost single-handed the Portuguese assault. "The towns of Andalusia," says Pulgar, "were not summoned because they were too distant." It is probable that Andalusia was in turn more active in the conquest of Granada. These points are not yet well clarified. The Italian wars reveal Biscayan soldiers at the side of Gonzalo de Córdoba. In 1508, when Jiménez was preparing to cross over to Africa, Ferdinand summoned for this expedition the paid troops of Ávila, Arévalo, Segovia, Medina del Campo, Olmedo, Fontiveros, and Salamanca, in Castile, and of Trujillo and Cáceres in Lusitania. These men of the towns, who had to march on order of the king and who received wages while on campaign, formed the nucleus of the Spanish infantry. They recall the free-archers of Charles VII of France. The cavalry was recruited by other means. After the War of Granada the sovereigns formed a corps of 2,500 men-at-arms, the *guardas viejas* (old guards), divided into twenty-five companies of 100 lances each.

The Italian wars revealed the inadequacy of these reforms. Expeditions to distant lands did not suit militiamen. At the same time compulsory service during several campaigns made of the departed contingents the first true soldiers, attached to their standards and henceforth wanting no other homeland than the camp. The desire for booty and glory, the lure of adventure, supplied a mass of volunteers whom the sovereigns gladly recruited to lighten the burdens on the people. Military service tended to become a trade; the Spanish towns poured into Italy and America their noblest and their vilest elements, the most high-minded and the most infamous, the most generous and the greediest—in a word, the honor and the refuse of their people.

Jiménez, who tried to renew and develop the system used by the Catholic Sovereigns, encountered all manner of obstacles. He proposed to place at the disposal of the state 40,000 men who could be mobilized in case of war but would remain at home in time of peace. Each town would furnish a contingent composed of carefully selected men; a captain would hold a weekly review of the soldiers and drill them in military exercises. Certain privileges, such as exemption from taxes, were to compensate them for their exertions and loss of time. By this means, Jiménez expected to raise a considerable force without spending a maravedí. On September 27, 1516, he wrote Diego López de Ayala that the levy of the ordinance had given the king 30,000 infantrymen, making him the most powerful prince in Europe. But the European wars forced Charles V to seek other expedients. The system of Jiménez answered the new requirements no better than that of Ferdinand and Isabella.[7]

Spain's new position in Europe and her foreign policies not only affected the composition and mode of recruitment of her army but tended to transform that army's arms, to alter their relative importance, to change military technique in general. The cavalry, which formerly played the leading role, shone for the last time in the War of Granada. "It was," says Navagero, "a really lovely war. Since relatively little use was made of firearms, every gentleman could display his bravery, and hardly a day passed that was not marked by some memorable feat of arms." [8] These feats of prowess were less successful than the Venetian believed. The Spaniards suffered bloody defeats, and without the artillery of Francisco Ramírez the Moslems would long have continued to be masters of their country. When the Spaniards came to blows in Italy with French men-at-arms, they had to admit that the Spanish cavalry were much inferior to their adversaries. Improbable as the statement may seem, there was a shortage of horses. According to Bernáldez, it was actually impossible to get together more than 10,000 or 12,000 horses for the service of the army. [9] Only a small number of cavalry was equipped with heavy, resistant armor and mounted on steeds barded with iron. The Granadan mountain war had favored the development of a light cavalry; the *jinetes* or *jinetarios,* who rode with feet lightly planted in short stirrups, protected themselves with a buckler, and brandished a light lance.

The *guardas viejas,* the base of the modern cavalry, numbered only 998 men-at-arms as against 1,843 *jinetes.* In order to strengthen their cavalry, the sovereigns borrowed elements from abroad, and made several efforts to reorganize the arm. The guard of mounted archers that followed Philip the Handsome to Spain (1502) passed into the pay of the state; Ferdinand brought back a company of scouts from Naples (1507). The African wars inspired the idea of creating a corps of mounted harquebusiers (*escopeteros*). But should the reform continue in this direction, it threatened to disperse the cavalry into congeries, a collection of small groups, armed but without cohesion. An effort was made to reduce all the elements to two types: cavalry of the line and light cavalry. The first was composed of twenty-six companies of 100 men each; the second contained 1,700 scouts divided among seventeen companies. Each company had a section of *escopeteros;* all the other cavalrymen were armed with lances.

This organization did not correct the weaknesses of the arm, for these had to do, above all, with equipment. The Spanish men-at-arms did not have heavy lances that could be couched for the charge, but only "long flexible lances" (Montluc says *arces guayes*) "tipped with iron at both ends, which they cast at the enemy." [10] Because of this inferiority of their heavy cavalry, the Spaniards often had to rely on their foreign auxiliaries. Villalobos freely acknowledges the superiority of the French army in this regard. Although he pokes fun at the cavalry of François I, "whose reviews are a delightful farce, and who leave the review laughing at themselves fit to burst," his raillery does not spare the ragged *jinetes* of Andalusia, who had never mounted a horse before entering service.[11] Whoever got the fanciful idea of making good cavalrymen out of stableboys, grooms, and mule drovers! "They know nothing of war or honor; they know neither how to wait or flee. In Castile there is also a dearth of good riders." Villalobos's banter may exaggerate the weakness of the Spanish cavalry; but the strength of the army certainly resided elsewhere.

That strength was not in the artillery, although the Catholic Sovereigns were indebted to this arm for the conquest of Granada. Historians have not sufficiently noted the decisive role of the artillery in the last struggle against the Moslems. The War of Granada was above all one of sieges, with large-scale battles of secondary importance; the towns were taken one by one, and when Granada was isolated, it fell of itself. At the start of the war, Isabella summoned blacksmiths and engineers from Italy, Flanders, and Germany;[12] she imported considerable quantities of gunpowder from Sicily and Portugal; she assembled a powerful artillery, composed of pieces of varying caliber and types: *"lombardas, pasabolantes, cabratanas, ribadoquínes,* and *buzanes."* The great lombards were regarded as particularly terrible.[13] Yet these instruments of destruction, as Prescott remarks, were very crude. The lombards used in the siege of Baza decorate the square of the town, where they serve as columns; they are twelve feet long and are made of iron plates held together by rings of the same metal. These crudely made cannon hurled stone balls. It appears, however, that the Spaniards had pieces of better quality. One could not otherwise explain the remarkable effects mentioned by Pulgar, including the destruction of walls and ramparts. The same chronicler relates that at the siege of Moclín the gunners fired "a specially made ball (*pella confeccionada*) of the kind that scattered fiery sparks and rose high in the air." [14] These references raise our estimation of the Spanish artillery. The artillery pieces were very numerous. Pulgar speaks of 1,500 gun carriages; yet on this occasion the army had left its large lombards in the city of Antequera.[15]

The service of the artillery involved a multitude of secondary services. "To make munitions and equipment of the artillery, there were employed many blacksmiths, carpenters, sawyers, woodcutters, smelters, masons, stonecutters who looked for stone quarries, and other stonecutters who worked the stone, and diggers, charcoal-burners whose job it was to make charcoal for the forges, and *esparteros* who made ropes and baskets. And over each group of workers was an overseer (*ministro*) who urged on the workers and supplied them with the things they needed for their task. Moreover, a great many carts

were needed, and for each hundred carts there was an overseer, and under him artisans to whom he gave the equipment needed to keep the carts in repair. There were other artisans to make the gunpowder, which was kept in pits dug out underground by three hundred men assigned to guard them day and night. And the king ordered them to collect in the towns of Algeciras, which were then depopulated, all the lombard balls that Alfonso the Good of Aragón, his great-great-grandfather, threw against those two cities when he had them under siege." [16] This account, as precise as it is picturesque, contains the most enlightening details concerning the organization of the companies which provided the crews for the maintenance and repair of gun carriages, carts, and wagons, for the protection of gunpowder, for the making of cannon balls of stone. A town bombarded a century before was not always at hand. A quarry had to be found where the stone was suitable, hard, not friable. The stone was then turned over to a stonecutter, whose chisel turned it into a cannon ball. When the besiegers arrived before the town to be attacked, they did not have wagons full of projectiles. Instead, they had to extract them from the soil with great expense and labor; and, to protect the gunpowder, a scarce and precious material, they had to hollow out deep vaults in the ground.[17]

Long and painful labor was necessary before the batteries could be trained and fired. The pieces were serviced not by Spaniards but by Germans, more skilled in the use of these machines of war; but the supreme direction or command belonged to Francisco Ramírez of Madrid, who must be regarded as the founder of Spanish artillery and military engineering. His merit as an engineer is highly extolled in a diploma that conferred on him the señorío of Bornos: "You, my secretary," said Ferdinand, "with my approval and license, have undertaken to build and have built a road from Vis de Torre to Villanueva, where none ever thought of building a road, for travelers could with great difficulty pass through that place."

He was no less adept in the use of his formidable lombards. To judge by the language of an official document, they must have been terribly effective. They "cast down and leveled to the ground the greater part of the fortress of Alhabar." Ferdinand also comments on the great blows struck at Loja.[18] At Moclín, where Queen Isabella came to watch the spectacle of destruction, the massive walls were knocked over by Ramírez' cannon. His felicitous inventions aroused wonder: He shot a *pelota encendida* right into the middle of a tower, setting fire to gunpowder. This was probably a ball heated almost to the molten stage. At the siege of Málaga, the great artilleryman was charged with attacking two towers which covered the approaches to the place and were a great menace to the Christians. He constructed a mine and brought one to the ground. New favors repaid his audacity and skill. He was authorized to place on his escutcheon a bridge defended by two towers.

In the Letter of Concession dated Málaga, September 15, 1487, Ferdinand recalled that "In the conquest of the kingdom and Moors of Granada for the holy Catholic faith, Señor Francisco Ramírez of Madrid, his secretary and captain of artillery and a member of his council, moved by zeal for the holy faith and by the intention of a loyal subject, exposed his person to great dangers and labored in the combats and the taking of all the cities, towns, and fortresses that their Majesties gained in this war." [19] Another document gives the same testimony with enthusiasm and a kind of tender gratitude that strike a rare note in an official document, especially one from the pen of Ferdinand. "In all that, you (Ramírez), moved by your loyalty, have in your person sustained much toil and fatigue; you have rendered memorable services to God and to me. Moreover, this has redounded to the great profit and public good of all the cities, towns, and places of this frontier, which suffered a thousand evils from those fortresses."

All this proves that the Catholic Sovereigns were fully aware of the importance of the new arm. It is equally clear that the conquest of Granada was due less to the bravery of the feudal chivalry than to these fearful engines of destruction. No wall, however massive, could withstand a sustained fire. Without artillery, the struggle would have dragged on forever or would have come to nothing. Francisco Ramírez is the Jean Bureau of Spain.

The War of Granada revealed the power of artillery; the Italian Wars put on record the value and the future of the infantry. Two men prepared that brilliant future. The name of Gonzalo Fernández de Córdoba was henceforth inseparable from that of the Spanish foot soldiers. Gonzalo de Ayora, whose merits were less dazzling, also inspired great reforms. Ayora was born in Córdoba and had lived for a long time in Italy, where he could study the structure of the various European armies; he wished to introduce into Spain the order, discipline, and tactical science that he had learned abroad. He proposed to Ferdinand that the Spanish infantry should be exercised in marches, evolutions, and maneuvers, as he had seen done with the Swiss. This would end the problem of dispatching raw recruits to the armies.

Gonzalo de Ayora wanted the office, then unknown in Spain, of colonel of infantry. In the campaign of Roussillon (1503), he did not manage to convince the Duke of Alba of the advantages of the proposed changes; but he could show the Catholic Sovereigns, at Medina del Campo, a troop that had been trained according to the new theories. At that time, it seems, he obtained the title that he sought, and in that capacity fought the campaign of Oran (1509) under the superior orders of Pedro Navarro and Cardinal Jiménez. This talented man brought from abroad a swarm of new ideas. He was skilled in the art of provisioning troops, and sought to make his system not only advantageous to the soldiers but profitable to the king.[20] He pushed his reconnaissances as close as possible to the enemy camp in order to make a careful survey of its arrangement. He found it scandalous that the Duke of Alba armed himself one night to put down some brawling camp followers. It was he who persuaded the Catholic King to surround himself with a guard corps; in return for this advice, Ferdinand named him captain of the corps. He was the first man in Spain to hold this office. It is difficult to establish very precisely his part in the military reform, but we may admit with Antonio de Capmany that Gonzalo de Ayora was "the reformer of the Spanish infantry from the time of the first use of gunpowder in campaigns, and that he was the true pioneer and organizer of tactics in our armies; his arrival in Spain marks an epoch in the military history of the nation." [21]

Gonzalo de Ayora remained a theoretician, against his wishes. Gonzalo de Córdoba joined example to precept, for he organized and conquered; his glory is twofold. In his first campaign against the French (1496), he perceived that his *jinetes* were no match for the French men-at-arms, and that his infantry could not sustain the shock of contact with the Swiss. The Spanish *peones,* lightly armed, inadequately protected by bucklers, formed an agile, swift-moving body, excellent in broken terrain, but incapable of holding firm in open country against the long lances or the eighteen-foot-long pikes.

The Great Captain began to overcome this inferiority by increasing the soldier's means of defense. He covered his head with a helmet, his breast with a cuirass with neckpiece and armguards. Half the foot soldiers received pikes to break the charge of the cavalry; of the other half, two-thirds, protected by round bucklers, were armed with a short sword and a javelin, and the rest consisted of harquebusiers, who were the counterpart of the old-time slingers.

Inspired by reflection, and perhaps also by the sight of similar efforts, Gonzalo de Córdoba simultaneously carried out a radical reorganization of the army.[22] The *capitanía* (company) was the tactical unit at this time. This unit was felt to be too weak, and a beginning was made of grouping several companies under the orders of a colonel. But the number of companies joined to act together under the orders of a single leader remained variable. Once a war had ended, the elements composing this chance combination regained their independence. Gonzalo de Córdoba stabilized this indefinite organization. The *coronelía* or *escuadrón* would be composed of 6,000 soldiers, divided into twelve battalions (*capitanías, batallatas*) of 500 men. Ten battalions invariably consisted of 200 pikesmen, 200 soldiers armed with short sword, javelin, and round buckler, and 100 harquebusiers.[23] The last two battalions (*capitanías de picas extraordinarias*) were composed of pikesmen alone. A colonel commanded the whole regiment (*escuadrón*); there was a captain for each battalion, a *cabo de batalla* (company chief) for each 100 men. There were several *cabos de diez,* corresponding in function to our under-officers. A standard-bearer (*alférez*), two drummers (*tambores*), and a fifer completed this ensemble.

On the march, the pikesmen went ahead; then the short-sword-and-javelin men; then the harquebusiers. Several rows of pikesmen formed the rear. The column advanced five men abreast; it deployed in face of the enemy. Each battalion was accompanied by a maximum of twenty-four wagons. This *coronelía,* organized on the model of the Roman legion, had 600 horse, half light cavalry, half heavy cavalry.

A brigade of 12,000 infantry and 1,200 horse drew after itself twenty pieces of varying caliber, ten cannon, eight serpentines, two swivel guns, four culverins, and twenty sakers. This came to a respectable figure, but the Great Captain set little store on artillery.[24]

The Spanish infantry was organized; now it could match its strength with the Swiss. The latter, formed in a square and protected on all sides by masses of pikes, advanced on level ground with an irresistible impetus;

they presented a compact resistant front, impenetrable to a cavalry charge, and swept before them the mass of foot soldiers. But broken terrain, ravines, small hills, broke this fine order and opened up numerous breaches in these moving citadels. The Spanish infantry, thanks to its pikesmen, was solid enough to meet the Swiss onset, and its harquebusiers enabled it to make many holes in the Swiss ranks. Moreover, it possessed a more supple and mobile character, which enabled the whole to adjust itself to varying circumstances and terrain. The Spanish battalions pressed unevenly on the massive Swiss regiments, yielding here, advancing there, but always ready to profit by any disarray of the enemy. The Spanish infantryman, lightly armed, slipped in under the long pikes and engaged in hand-to-hand combat in which his poignard and short sword guaranteed his success. It was the struggle of the legion and the phalanx in a new form; once again force was overcome by skill.

Thanks to these reforms, the Spanish army was first in the world for a century and a half. How many splendid victories it won in this long period! It was the glory of the Spanish nation; it maintained Spanish supremacy in Europe during the whole sixteenth century and during the first half of the seventeenth century. It gave an example of courage, resignation, and sacrifice, of daring bravery, and cold tenacity. It had leaders worthy of its good fortune.

Yet it must not be pictured as a school of virtue, austerity, or discipline. The armies of that time did not resemble ours. They were often the refuge of gross and violent men, avid for booty and carnage. They were trailed by a horde of prostitutes. The sack of towns, murder, and rape were among their most agreeable diversions. Mutinies were frequent; arrears in pay led to terrible upheavals that endangered the commander's life, and did not spare his honor. Gonzalo de Córdoba, himself, when unable to pay his soldiers before Taranto, was threatened with death and heaped with insults. "Sell your daughter," a Biscayan captain bawled at him, "and you will find the money." Villalobos may have been thinking of such scenes when he wrote: "Unhappy the commander who must listen to such things! How often must he aspire to be a nobody! How often must he wish to live quietly at home, eating greens!" But there were such glorious compensations!

Not all the elements of the Spanish army were so bad. Great virtues made up for shameful vices. The military spirit was very powerful; it was kept alive by the *soldados viejos,* the old soldiers, who maintained the great tradition in the troops and inspired the recruits (*bisoños*) with love for the flag, with courage and honor. Many nobles enrolled in the infantry; they formed the sound part of this motley mass. They brought to it a clear conception of loyalty, a great knowledge of arms. Whereas French gentlemen disdained infantry service, the proud Castilian and Aragonese *hidalgos* gloried in fighting amid the foot soldiers. The aristocracy was aware that here resided the true superiority of the Spanish army. This infantry, superbly commanded, and exercised in continuous wars, laid down the law to Europe under Charles V. If the Catholic Sovereigns had clung to the ancient military organization and opposed Spanish men-at-arms to French men-at-arms, they would have never conquered the Kingdom of Naples, and would not have left to their grandson, together with a vast empire, the means of its preservation and expansion.

VII

Economic Policy

A government can influence the development of the national economy in two ways, one positive, the other negative. It can seek by means of well-conceived measures to develop the nation's might, encourage labor, and open up markets for commerce. The method of direct action is very potent when wisely used, but it can easily lead to errors, because economic laws are poorly understood, and a people, its mind wholly fixed upon present sufferings, frequently demands legislation opposed to its true interests and its industrial future. There is a more indirect but equally effective intervention which consists in lightening the burdens of taxpayers, in taking as little money as possible from them by way of taxes, in not discouraging production by demanding for the treasury a lion's share of profits, in raising the necessary taxes by the most painless, most discreet, least tyrannical means possible. To reduce the burdens of subjects and augment their means of enrichment is the unattained ideal of every good administration.

The reign of Ferdinand and Isabella opened in inauspicious circumstances. The sovereigns found themselves completely without revenue. Enrique IV, their predecessor, had alienated the royal domains and had pledged the crown revenues. As if this were not enough, they were at once burdened with the expense of a defensive war. After the Portuguese had been defeated and driven from Castile the country enjoyed several years of peace; but a struggle soon began against the Moslems of Granada that lasted for ten years. During this period the public coffers often ran bone dry. To secure the money needed for the maintenance of troops and the ordinary expenses of government Isabella resorted to expedients. She made forced loans;[1] she resumed the practice of alienating the royal revenues; she pawned her jewels in the towns of Valencia and Barcelona. During the war with Portugal her distress reached such a pitch that she resolved, after much hesitation, to lay hands on the plate of the Church.[2] In 1490, if Bernáldez does not exaggerate, she levied taxes every twenty days.[3] These exactions caused much complaint; but it is easy to see the extremities to which the sovereigns were reduced. The conquest of Granada gave them a breathing space in which to improve their financial situation, but they were unable to lighten the burden of taxes during their reign.

The principal sources of the public revenue at this period are listed in the proceedings of the Cortes of Toledo (1480):

1. Duties on imports and exports (*aduanas, almojarifazgos*).
2. Duties on the right of passage or circulation (*montazgo, portazgo*).
3. Duties on consumption or commercial transactions (*alcabalas, diezmos*).
4. Revenues from the royal domain (mines and salt pits).
5. Special aids or taxes (*servicio, moneda, moneda forera*).

6. Contributions for the Holy War (Bulla de la Cruzada).
7. *Tercias reales* (two-ninths of the ecclesiastical tithes).[4]

The *servicio* was a subsidy which the Cortes voted the prince for his personal maintenance and for the extraordinary needs of his government. Originally renewed at each session of the Cortes, the *servicio* tended under the Catholic Sovereigns to become annual (*servicio ordinario*). The freely made gift was transformed into a permanent tax.

The *moneda* and the *pedido* were special aids resembling the *servicio*.

The *moneda forera* was established by the prince, who levied it every seven years in witness of his sovereignty.

The state had a monopoly on mines and salt pits, and these provided an abundant source of revenue.

Other revenues were obtained by taxing the products of industry and their consumption. When a piece of merchandise entered the kingdom, it was taxed a tenth of its value; when Spanish merchandise was exported, the same duty was imposed. If the king opened the doors of his kingdom to foreign goods, there was a charge for the permission to enter; when he allowed products of national industry to leave the kingdom, he must be indemnified for his indulgence.

These customs duties were called *aduanas*, *almojarifazgos*, and *diezmos*. Having crossed this first barrier, the merchant found others in the interior of the country. The circulation of goods was taxed no less than their importation and exportation. The royal tax collector awaited the migratory flocks of sheep at certain passes in the mountains in order to collect the *montazgo*. There was also a duty for clearing port, for passing over a bridge.

Taxed on every road by agents of the king, of the towns, and of the lords, the merchants, cattle raisers, and shepherds had, one might think, paid dearly enough for the right to trade, but the treasury would not let them off so easily. It intervened in sales and purchases to extract new revenues. All commercial transactions, whether of mobile or real property, were subject to a tax of one-tenth. This was the *alcabala*, the last and most odious of devices for wringing money out of taxpayers. In Isabella's time the *alcabala* had already existed for a century.[5] It had been established as a temporary expedient; it lasted as long as the Spanish monarchy.

This tax brought the greatest revenue of all to the crown. It was most oppressive, coming as it did on top of all the others. It was the more hateful because it made the royal agent a third party to commercial transactions whose terms and amounts buyer and seller had an interest in concealing. There was a strong temptation to commit fraud; it seemed easy, assuming that the two interested parties (buyer and seller) were in collusion with each other. But the tax collectors, a suspicious lot, might find the price absurd, open an inquiry, and seek by every means possible to get at the facts of the case. The tax farmers who had farmed out the collection of the *alcabala* were determined to extract every last cent of profit from the transaction. Accordingly, the law punished false declarations with extreme rigor.

Isabella, moved by the complaints of her subjects, approved a reform project drawn up by Jiménez.[6] The commission of collecting the tax was taken away from the farmers and turned over to the towns, which were allowed to employ their ordinary tax collectors and hand over to the royal treasury a portion of the proceeds that was proportionate to their size and importance. This change did not wholly satisfy Isabella's conscience; she had misgivings concerning the lawfulness of this tax, misgivings to which she gave free expression in the codicil to her testament. In this codicil she recommended the naming of a commission to review the royal rights. But this last wish of the generous queen was no more respected than Jiménez' prayer to Charles V to abolish this odious tax. The crown at this period needed money too badly to deprive itself of a source of revenue; if anything, it was more inclined to augment than to diminish the public burdens.

The heavy expenses of the Moorish wars obliged the Catholic Sovereigns to petition the Pope for permission to levy a tax on the least taxable of objects, the consciences of their subjects.[7] The Bull of the Crusade (Bulla de la Cruzada) offered the faithful the inestimable treasure of an indulgence to redeem their sins if they paid the sovereign a certain sum. Such payment obtained for the purchaser a diminution of the penalties of Purgatory for himself and his dead parents. The money derived from this traffic in sacred things must be devoted solely to the war against the infidels. The concession was renewed several times in the reign of Ferdinand and Isabella; the African wars served as a pretext to perpetuate this subsidy. At first free and voluntary, the indulgence soon tended to become a regular source of revenue. The temptation was strong to pressure recalcitrants into buying these remissions.

The clergy displayed great zeal in serving the interests of the treasury. The Cortes of 1512 complains energetically of the preachers of the Crusade who, in the towns and especially in the villages, "keep the people in the churches one, two, and three days from morning to evening to listen to their sermons, and thus prevent them from earning their daily bread; and when they find that they cannot persuade them to take up the said Bull by

that means, they parade through the streets, asking everyone they meet if he knows his Pater Noster and Ave Ma-
ria; and if perchance they find one who does not, they
force him to take up the said Bull as penance; and if anyone refuses, they drag him around in shackles to hear
their preachments, and thus prevail on him at last by
force and threats to take up the said Bull." [8]

This inquisitorial regime spared neither the living nor
the dead. The sellers of indulgences found it intolerable
that anyone should die without having bought the precious indulgence. They attacked the validity of testaments and called on heirs and testamentary executors to
pay in place of the negligent deceased.

Ferdinand does not appear to have received favorably
the protests of his subjects. The abuses continued, and
the indulgences of the Cruzada were entered under the
heading of regular revenues.

The sovereigns would have done better to make the
privileged orders supply the money needed by the crown.
They were content, however, to take a part of the ec-

clesiastical revenues in the form of tithes. The authorization of the Pope was necessary, but this they easily obtained. These tithes, always justified by the crusade against the Moors, were often applied to other uses; for example, the clergy paid a part of the cost of the Italian expeditions.

In addition to the special taxes that they levied on the clergy for their pressing needs, the Catholic Sovereigns, like their predecessors, took one-third of the ecclesiastical tithes (*tercias reales*). They handed back one-third of the third received, to pay for the building of parish churches; thus the crown's share was reduced to two-ninths.[9]

Despite the extent of its tax burdens, Castile had its hour of prosperity under the Catholic Sovereigns. Internal peace was favorable to productive labor; public wealth increased and furnished taxpayers with the means of meeting their obligations. Crown revenues also mounted rapidly. In 1474, taxes brought in 885,000 reales *de vellón;* in 1477, 2,390,078 reales; in 1482, 12,711,591 reales; finally, in 1504, 26,283,334 reales.[10] This increase in receipts was due as much to the development of the national resources as it was to good administration of the public finances.

The great number of *pragmáticas* concerning commerce and industry issued by Ferdinand and Isabella testifies to the importance they attached to the progress of the national economy.[11] Their preoccupation with economic matters is remarkable in sixteenth-century monarchs, whom one would expect rather to be absorbed in questions of personal politics. Their solicitude was not always intelligent, for the sovereigns shared the erroneous conceptions of their time. To prevent forestalling in the market, they imposed on grain merchants a schedule of prices that must not be exceeded. They adopted a measure of the same kind in their camp before Málaga, and fixed the price of wheat and oats for a period of four years. This law of the maximum failed to provide cheap bread.

The state was powerless, as it has ever been, to control the ebb and flow of the economic tides. But this was not a self-evident truth to the men of that time. The government believed it had the right and the power to regulate everything. What alarm was raised by the flight of gold to neighboring lands! Acting in concert with the Cortes, the sovereigns swiftly adopted radical measures. They forbade the export of gold, silver, or copper money.[12] Every infraction of the law was punished, according to the gravity of the crime, with confiscation of goods or even with death. It proved impossible to suppress all relations between Spain and the rest of the world, but what extraordinary precautions were taken to prevent the nation's monetary resources from leaving the realm. When a Spanish traveler or merchant left the kingdom, he was to inform the *alcalde* or *corregidor* of the place where he resided what money he carried with him. He must declare before an *alcalde de las sacas*[13] and three other witnesses whence he came, whither he was going, how long he proposed to remain abroad, and finally what sum of money he had upon him. All was put in writing in order to furnish evidence against the deponent in case it was found that he had lied. Foreigners who came to trade in Spain were even worse treated. A *pragmática* of December 1491 forbade the English and other foreigners to take any gold or silver money from the realm.[14] Only barter was permitted; they must exchange their merchandise for Spanish fruits and products. It is difficult for us to understand how such a system could have been made to work.

The same mania for regulation is reflected in the numerous sumptuary laws of the period. A *pragmática* of 1493 regulated the degree of splendor allowed in funerals and baptisms. In 1494 the government forbade the importation into Castile of brocade and of gold and silver vessels; in 1499 it limited to certain classes the right to wear silk garments. All these measures failed to halt the advance of luxury, an advance that is inseparable from the growth of well-being, wealth, and civilization. But the sovereigns and the Cortes judged the matter as moralists and preachers; this viewpoint causes a notable contraction of mental horizons.

The economic science of the time was neither very profound nor very complicated: Limit production to consumption; ensure cheap labor by fixing salaries and cheap means of subsistence by fixing maximum prices; protect the people against its own weakness by means of sumptuary laws. These few principles governed the conduct of statesmen. However, new ideas emerged. The state felt obliged to develop and defend national industry. To bar competition with certain national products, the import of similar foreign products was forbidden. In the long run this protective system was to prove disastrous to the very people whose advantage was sought, for it created a monopoly for a privileged group; it encouraged indolence and made unnecessary all effort and progress. Yet such a policy may be necessary to help an infant industry take its first steps.

Under the sway of these patriotic preoccupations, Ferdinand and Isabella multiplied measures prohibitive to foreign goods. We must do them the justice of allowing that they were animated by the best of intentions, even when they established trade barriers between the different provinces of Castile. Murcia complained that cloth from without was taking away the market for its native cloth. Many manufacturers had given up the struggle and departed the city. Cattle raising, too, was affected by the commercial decay; only eight thousand sheep grazed in fields where once fifty thousand had grazed. The sovereigns, implored as a visible Providence, forbade the introduction of cloth into the Kingdom of Murcia for two years (1486). In 1500 they barred silk thread made in Naples because of the disastrous competition it offered to the silk industry of the Kingdom of Granada.

They had other and wiser inspirations. The mechanical arts were more advanced in Italy and Flanders; this superiority made the Spaniards dependent on those lands. To place Spanish industry on an equal footing, the sovereigns encouraged Italian and Flemish artisans to settle in Spain; they exempted them from all tax for ten years (1484). Wishing to promote trade, the life of industry, they suppressed all the internal tolls that had been established in Castile since 1464 with the acquiescence of Enrique IV.[15] The lords and the towns had levied taxes on merchants for the right of passing through the gates of a town or over a bridge; they had levied duties on droves of cattle, on flocks of sheep. These imposts, repeated at every turn in the road, were ruinous to trade.

At the same time that the sovereigns leveled these fiscal barriers, they sought to standardize weights and measures (by a *pragmática* dated at Tortosa, January 9, 1496) and, without seeking to impose an impossible uniformity, indicated the types whose use they recommended.[16]

The same desire for simplification, joined to the pursuit of an immediate interest, is revealed in the ordinances relating to the currency. Under Enrique IV, one hundred fifty mints had been founded in Castile. All and sundry assumed this royal privilege and naturally expected to be paid for their pains. The result was an extraordinary depreciation of the coins in circulation. The Spaniard lost confidence in every currency that was not foreign gold or silver. To restore the credit of the domestic coinage Isabella struck an excellent money that equaled foreign coins in value. Intent on reserving this precious privilege to the crown, she suppressed all mints except six crown institutions established at Burgos, Toledo, Seville, Segovia, Coruña, and Granada.[17] All these measures were clearly favorable to commerce, industry, and the general welfare.

Pastoral industry was also indebted for its strong organization to Ferdinand and Isabella, but the protection they accorded pasturage placed heavy burdens on agriculture. Spain was very rich in herds of cattle, both sedentary and migratory.[18] At the advent of warm weather the latter were driven from the plateaus of Castile to the mountains of León and Galicia, where they passed the summer. At the first sign of cold weather they again set out for the plains. Their coming and going caused serious inconveniences to the localities which they traversed. The animals strayed from the road to graze right and left. The sheep, above all—that voracious eater of tender plants—committed great ravages. Faced with mounting popular hostility, the graziers pooled their strength and interests, formed themselves into an association, and proclaimed their solidarity. From Alfonso X and Alfonso XI they obtained protective legislation and helpful regulations. On several occasions the Cortes (Burgos, 1315; Valladolid, 1351) protested against ravages committed by shepherds with impunity. Alfonso XI (1347) authorized the formation of the powerful association of graziers known as the Mesta. Ferdinand and Isabella displayed the same favorable attitude toward this corporation; in 1487 they confirmed the Mesta in all its privileges in exchange for certain subsidies. True, they placed a member of their council at its head (1500). The association gained in power what it lost in independence. In 1511 it commissioned the jurisconsult Palacios Rubios to codify the diplomas and charters it had received from the crown. This became the code of its privileges, which the crown promptly sanctioned.

The herds could traverse the kingdom, drinking its water, grazing on its grass, but the grazier was forbidden to allow them to injure grain, vines, meadows reserved for mowing, and the pasturage of work animals. In their passage from the winter to summer pastures the herds followed a well-defined route or sheepwalk, the *cañada,* which must not be cleared, worked, or enclosed on pain of very severe penalties. The graziers were exempt from certain taxes; they had the right to cut down trees for the construction of bridges or other needs. A severe legislation protected them from the wrath of the peasants.

Thus they had the right of free passage across the realms of Castile. Whereas the law protected them against attack, the only restraint upon them, in principle, was that they must pay for damages committed by their herds. But their powerful organization, their wealth, their official connections, allowed them to defy all protests. The Mesta attacked enclosures, and secured from a complaisant crown a prohibition against clearing and enclosing public or communal lands. It was a true government, with its own courts of first instance and appeal.[19] Its activity, always disastrous to agriculture, was to become crushing and ruinous in the reign of princes less concerned than Ferdinand and Isabella with the public welfare.

There is more to praise in the measures taken by the Catholic Sovereigns to expand Spanish shipping, so intimately linked with the success of commerce and industry. The conquest of Granada, the union of Castile and Aragón, the discovery of the New World, were potent stimulants to the prosperity of maritime trade. The central government aided shipping by ordinances that testified to its zeal, even when they happened to be contrary to the true interests of the nation. A *pragmática* of September 3, 1500, forbade the shipping of goods and comestibles in foreign vessels if a Spanish one was available in the port.[20] This measure recalls the famous navigation acts that laid the foundations of English maritime superiority. To assure themselves of ships of the line in time of war, the sovereigns offered a large premium to outfitters who built ships of six hundred tons and upwards.[21] They did more: Shippers must give preference to these large ships over small ones. As the economic historian, Goury de Roslan, observes, this monopoly had the double disadvantage of ruining the small outfitters and slowing up transport, for these bulky ships had great difficulty in completing their lading. The express authorization of the crown was necessary to sell any Spanish vessel in a foreign land.[22] The state jealously guarded the nation's merchant marine to use for its own needs, but this prudence inevitably proved disastrous to the national dockyards, deprived of all foreign customers. Other measures were worthy of high praise: the suppression of the ancient right of wrack;[23] the order restoring derelict ships to their lawful proprietors;[24] the prohibition of customs duties or any other contribution from a shipmaster who put into a port under stress of weather and without disembarking any goods. These injunctions, inspired by humanity and justice, had the additional object of attracting foreign mariners to Spanish shores.

Under the impulse of the sovereigns, and thanks above all to attendant circumstances that gave Spain a temporary sway over the Atlantic and the Mediterranean, an extraordinary growth took place in the Spanish merchant marine. At the beginning of the sixteenth century, Spain had a thousand merchant ships. The Spanish navy underwent a similar growth. In 1481 the sovereigns sent a fleet of seventy vessels to help Ferrante I of Naples drive the Turks out of Otranto.[25] Ferdinand and Isabella also made themselves masters of the sea, cutting off all communication between Granada and Africa during the decisive struggle; they blockaded the coasts of Roussillon (1496) when they declared war against Charles VIII of France. Ferreras affirms that they despatched one hundred thirty vessels, carrying twenty thousand men, to convey their daughter Juana to her future husband, Philip the Handsome.[26] If this historian does not exaggerate, Spain has never again seen such an armada.

All these facts amply prove the quality of the administration of the Catholic Sovereigns. Their economic errors they shared with the men of their time; but their sound dispositions derive almost entirely from themselves. The majority of the reforms were their own work. Despite the restrictions which they threw about foreign trade, commercial relations multiplied. The Castilians had consuls and factors in Flanders, London, Nantes, La Rochelle, and Florence. The Aragonese and the Catalans exploited the riches and markets of Naples and Sicily and pushed their trade as far as Alexandria. Navarre served as intermediary between France and Castile. English merchants and mariners visited the ports of Biscay[27] and the whole northern coast. The country was prosperous and happy. As if the very elements had conspired to smile upon the sovereigns, after their time Spain ceased to enjoy the genial seasons and abundant harvests that had favored the reign of Ferdinand and Isabella.

Part Three

SOCIAL LIFE

I

The Spaniards

The Spain of the Catholic Sovereigns lives again on that splendid page in which Michelet, the great magician, evokes the different peoples of the Peninsula, their customs, their dress, and their manners.[1] We behold the luxurious Moslems amid their orange gardens, gardens irrigated by obedient streams under the torrid heat of an African sky. Long rests in the cool shade, the siesta, warm baths—these are the pleasant diversions of the Moors as long as the demon of war does not transform these indolent shepherds and farmers into fierce warriors.

Their conquerors come from the north and the east; they are a hardy, somber, energetic race. Here is the Castilian, proud of his pure blood, proud of the purity of his faith; there the tenacious, stubborn Aragonese, inexorably attached to his customs, a race of legists and quibblers. These form the hard and enduring nucleus of the Spanish nationality. About them are grouped the diverse elements of Andalusia, Murcia, and Valencia, where Jewish and Moslem blood has penetrated the old Christian stock; these are lands of gaiety and the dance, of lively spirit, of passionate and tender souls. The

Basques, resisting all absorption, immure themselves in their independence.

On the two sides of the Peninsula swarm two laborious hives. The brave and industrious Catalans have sent colonies of busy merchants to every shore, and Barcelona disputes with Marseille the commercial supremacy of the Mediterranean. On the opposite side, the Galicians, still inflamed with their civil wars, are forming a reserve of hardy laborers, of modest and useful toilers, for the benefit of the towns of the interior.

Despite these differences, there are tendencies and sentiments common to the entire Christian population. Without any pretense of rediscovering the Spanish soul of the fifteenth century, I shall attempt a light sketch of the national character, using writings of the time to illustrate some traits that seem to me peculiarly representative of Spain, its soil, and its people.

Contemporary accounts offer good descriptions of the countryside. The plateaus of Old Castile were dry and arid. A French visitor speaks scornfully of those poor scorched fields where the shepherds had daily to change their pasture grounds. This whole region, says he, would go up in dust if the rains did not water it from time to time.[2] The streams ran in deeply embanked beds instead of meandering at the level of the plains. From the ocean in the south, to the sources of the Ebro, the westerly winds pushed the clouds that watered the earth. In Andalusia, wheat yielded twelve bushels to the acre; even the high plains were not lost to production. The horse throve in the thick pasturages of the south and in the grassy valleys of the mountains to the north; the sheep found adequate fare in the meager pastures of La Mancha and Castile. More than one proprietor possessed a herd of thirty thousand head. Agriculture was held in high esteem. Not until the reign of Charles V did poor

seasons and lack of labor begin to ruin the countryside.
The towns were neither as numerous, populous, or
fair as in France. The dwellings were not placed side by
side in regular alignment, but stood apart from each
other. Houses were built of rammed earth or mud. The
streets, innocent of paving, became muddy sewers in
the winter; in the summer, passers-by moved in a cloud
of blinding dust that obscured the sun. Without annual repairs, the walls of the castles would soon have
slid into their moats. Assuredly, Castile possessed many
strongholds (*casas fuertes*), *peñas bravas,* and other
fortified places; but these places existed to protect their
garrisons rather than to defend the country.

This description is by a scornful observer who sought
to make comparisons with France at Spain's expense, but
the things satirized could not have been pure invention.
Robert Gaguin, General of the Order of the Maturins
and historiographer, would not knowingly have perverted
the truth. It must be remembered, however, that his dark
picture dates from the reign of Enrique IV;[3] it is entirely
possible that the disorder of the times tended to diminish
and darken everything in the eyes of a prejudiced observer. Under Ferdinand and Isabella, the churches,
not at all inferior to French Gothic cathedrals, ceased to
be the only monuments of Spain. Over seven hundred
bridges were constructed. All towns received orders to
build a hall for their *concejo.* Internal peace awakened
unknown needs and tastes. Architecture, hitherto devoted exclusively to religion, was now placed at the
service of princes, towns, and private persons in the Christian lands. *Casas de contratación* (chambers of commerce) arose in the commercial centers. The Lonja, or
Exchange, of Valencia, attests to the progress of secular
architecture.

The Catholic Sovereigns had not, however, succeeded

in completely transforming their country. A journey
through Spain was accounted an expedition that, if not
dangerous, was at least rich in incidents and surprises.
For foreigners the pilgrimage to Compostela was a true
pilgrimage, all too often requiring them to mortify their
flesh and suffer various ordeals as a sacrifice to God.
The traveler must not expect to find comfortable inns,
well stocked with wine and victuals, at each stop.

Robert Gaguin does not compare Spanish hostelries
to French stables (that would be doing them too much
honor); he ranks even the pigpens of his country above
them.[4] His vivid description suggests that our good
brother was accustomed to greater comfort and convenience. Naked walls and clay dishes were all these *ventas*
offered the wayfarer. A sick or weary traveler found no
relief here. He must hunt up his own food and serve it up
himself. Robert Gaguin had to gather his own firewood,
and had to draw from his own stout chest the air to
kindle the fire. Had these barbarians never heard of bel-
lows? Could they not have cleaned the pots and caldrons?
He does not say whether he had to attend to the needs
of the mule on which he rode, but one suspects that his
delicate hands, accustomed to leafing manuscripts, were
degraded to performing the chores of a stableboy. In
addition to inns of this type, where mine host impas-
sively watched his transient guests performing their
chores, there were others, the *posadas,* whose owners
were as skilled as highwaymen in emptying a traveler's
purse. These men spared one some annoyances—but at
what a price!

Given their views in economic matters, Ferdinand and
Isabella were not disposed to tolerate this exploitation.
They forbade the owners of the *posadas,* under the most
severe penalties, to provide their guests with anything
but the most necessary services and the cooked food. The

traveler, escorted by his servant, must make his own purchases, going from shop to shop. Such bulky provisions as barley, oats, hay, and straw for the horses would be provided by the innkeeper, but he must not charge more than the current price. A sign fixed to the inn door carried the prices current, and the payment due to servants. As a result of this judicious arrangement, the traveler had some chance of departing without a wrangle with the master of the house. In small towns and villages, where neither markets nor stores were to be found, and where a general poverty kept prices moderate, innkeepers could charge for meals as they saw fit, but in all other respects they were subject to the same restrictions as their colleagues of the towns.[5]

The annoyances of the road weighed little on the natives. Where foreigners, in relating their travels, never stopped groaning concerning the abominable cuisine, the Spaniard went his way, indifferent to poor food and to lodgings crawling with aggressive vermin. When he went on pilgrimage, he cared nothing about lodgings. The venerated sanctuaries, the relics of the saints, a monument attesting to some miracle—these were the objects claiming his attention. If religion had some competition, it was not from such vulgar concerns but from the side of romance. The wayfarer mingled visits to churches and pious reveries with rambles into the world of sentiment. Even on the road to Santiago de Compostela one might find some old hermit to tell a tale of love like those that the great Cervantes, who heard them on that road, retells so pleasantly.

Climate and soil made this a people of sparing tastes. The Spaniard ate only to live; certainly he fasted heroically and more often than the Church required. *Lazarillo de Tormes*[6] reveals the misery of all classes of the population. True, this work depicts the Spain of Philip

II, ruined by frequent wars. Economic conditions were certainly better under the Catholic Sovereigns; contemporaries attest to this fact. But if living conditions were easier, the people were no more finicky when it came to the choice of food. In order to give us an idea of the fertility of the soil, Damião de Goes cites details that prove the prevailing moderation, the marvelous indifference to plenty, and even to necessities, in all that related to food. "The fertility of the land is such," he says, "that the greater part of the year the poorest laborers and the common people live very largely on the fruit of trees, honey, and wild herbs. That is why they have so little inclination to agriculture."

It was not so much poverty as virtue and indolence that kept them from seeking a more abundant diet. Southerners have always scorned that ample, fat-encumbered life that the men of the North purchase at the price of unceasing toil. No time there for promenades, for strolling about, for dreaming! When the Flemings introduced the elaborate dinners, the interminable repasts, the unquenchable thirst of the Northern courts, the Spaniards, who were so little concerned with their stomachs, felt a certain rising of the gorge against these junketings. The Italian Peter Martyr de Anghera, echoing public opinion, scourged these men "whose only god is Bacchus followed by Cytherea." [7] The spirit of the courtier reconciled the Spanish aristocracy to the delicacy, abundance, and excess of foreign tables. As a physician, Villalobos bitterly criticized this excess for its effect on health. He remained faithful to the national dishes, which may seem less than tempting to us, but which he describes with the tender passion of a gourmet: "For myself, I prefer a pot full of garlic seasoned with olive oil, and cabbages that issue from the pot exhaling savory vapors, and laborer's bread that fills one's whole mouth

and not some hollow stuff made only to please the palate." [8] His countrymen were probably quite unanimous
in sharing this preference.

These abstemious tastes made it possible for the
great lords to surround themselves with a multitude of
servitors who formed a court that, if not brilliant, was
at least faithful. These retainers lived, so to speak, not
on the crumbs of the feast but for the honor of serving a master. They continued to live in the dwellings
where their fathers had lived, occupied the same offices,
and testified by their number to the splendor of the
house to which they were attached. The existence of the
vassals blended and became one with that of their lords.
Over the long years a great familiarity came to exist between the two; the habit of seeing the same faces did
away with prejudices of rank. They were not domestics;
they were confidants, sharing all the family joys and sor-
rows; custom and affection formed indissoluble ties.
Many were nobles and followed their suzerain to war;

in time of peace, they remained in the shadow of the feudal castle, entrusted with the service of the chase or the horses: squires, majordomos, bailiffs (*alcaldes mayores*). They lived sparingly in those little courts where gold was lavished on pompous displays and feasts of almost royal style, but where the rest of the year was passed in the bleak round, the monotonous ceremonial, of a large provincial situation. Yet they never deserted those hospitable houses.

As long ago as the fifteenth century, this stubborn attachment to such unremunerative posts surprised our changeable Frenchmen. The faithful squire pictured by Robert Gaguin has become a stock type in Spanish literature.[9] Badly fed and poorly clothed in life, he finally dies in misery and need. What has he left, indeed, save a *broquel,* that is, a leather buckler, a sword, a dagger, a javelin, a lance, a quiver, an arbalest—the future patrimony of his heirs?

This impracticality was not necessarily, as Gaguin seems to think, the mark of a defective nature. These *hidalgos,* wrapped in ragged cloaks, insensible to hunger, furnished the marvelous soldiers of the wars of Italy and Flanders. The shortcomings of the Spaniard sprang, not from baseness of spirit or heart, but from a lofty pride that was not without merit. If the peasants deserted the countryside, it was to enroll in the armies or to seek adventure in the Indies. They disdained labor but exposed their lives without hesitation in the Old and the New Worlds. With a few hundred men Pizarro and Cortés overthrew empires as powerful as that of the great Inca. These marvelous enterprises, that could be conceived only by ardent spirits spellbound by their own dreams, were executed with resolution, conducted with good judgment, pursued with dazzling success by these cool-headed enthusiasts, amid infinite toils, dangers, countless enemies, the hostility of the Spanish government, revolts, and every imaginable setback.

These adventures, in which reality blended with romance, were the achievements of a noble people with a high opinion of itself and great confidence in its capacities. These men had a religion of dignity. Whether beggars or soldiers, they preserved a heroic attitude. There was no teasing skepticism here, no taste for self-deprecation. This nation had faith in itself. All this, that sensitive and jealous feeling of personal distinction, of personal worth, constitutes the Spanish sentiment of Honor. It may be that Spain has enriched the human heart with these noble sensitivities.

Even the valets of that age prided themselves on their delicacy of feeling. In France and Germany the porters of castles, the guardians of arsenals, the sacristans, held out their hands to visitors and asked for tips. What a windfall for the servants when a friend came to stay with a great lord! Well in advance of his coming, every last servant, cook, cupbearer, and scullery-maid reckoned on his or her fingers what each would get. In Spain it was difficult to make servants or workers accept a small gift. "Their greatness of soul is such that they offer their services without charge to foreigners." [10] If they accept a tip, it is done grudgingly. What then must have been the situation in the upper classes? A traveler who arrived in a Spanish town and had some connections there found many affable guides who offered to show him the sights. If he sought to acknowledge this service by some civility, the Spaniard would decline his offer up to the last moment, when to persist in refusal might constitute a slight. In Germany, says the same author, you don't have to repeat a dinner invitation twice! In fact, how many uninvited guests may one find at one's table!

There may be an element of exaggeration in these

panegyrics, but Spanish domestics at that time were capable of a dignity not found on that social level in other countries. The lowest classes of the population shared the glorious prejudices of the aristocracy. The sentiment of honor was as keen among muleteers as among *hidalgos.* Two day laborers would carve each other up as bravely as two gentlemen over some slight.[11] The vanity of these menials was unbounded; every trade scorned the others. The muleteer believed himself superior to the water carrier, the water carrier to the day laborer. The pride of the people of Guipúzcoa was such that they all called themselves *hidalgos,*[12] and a Castilian of any condition was disposed to consider himself a gentleman *whose nobility slumbers.* A muleteer in a wretched smock says that "whoever fails to honor him does him an injury, because his forefathers descended from the Infante Don Pelayo." In this matter of race they do not stand for raillery; they assign themselves ancestors and admit into their families only good Christians of pure extraction.

Catholic Spain categorically refused to admit that it was penetrated by Jewish and Moorish blood. Popular prejudice established a difference between Old and New Christians (converts or descendants of converts). The Inquisition strengthened this hostility toward the latter. Soon the universities, the military orders, the skilled trades, were closed to the grandsons of Jews and Moors. Municipalities and government departments vied with each other in proscribing persons not of pure blood (*sangre limpia*).

A story told by Villalobos offers striking testimony of this scorn among the lower ranks. This physician of the Catholic Sovereigns and of Charles V had in his service a young muleteer whom he knew to be very vain. One day, wishing to put his pride to the test, Villalobos

offered him the hand of his daughter. The young man replied that he would gladly accept the match to oblige his
master; but how should he dare return to his homeland
when his relatives learned that he was married to Villalobos's daughter? "I said to him: 'You sound like a
man who is very touchy about his honor, but I assure
you that I don't know where you keep your honor, or
where I would keep mine if that marriage took place.'"
Where the amused Villalobos saw only vanity, there
probably entered an element of religious repulsion as
well. This stableboy of pure blood considered it a *mésal-
liance* to marry the daughter of a *confeso,* even one
who was rich, influential, and the Emperor's physician.

If men subtilized concerning honor, what wonder that
they should have done the same in regard to love. Love
in Spain already had that precious character that in the
sixteenth century would become general in Europe. Passion spoke there an elevated hyperbolic language; and
gallants knew how to soften the hearts of the lovely by
making show of their devotion, by letting the inner flame
blaze forth. "They are not content with declaring that
these ladies are their mistresses and that they want to
serve them like slaves and die for them; the gentlemen
tell them that they are their goddesses and that, for them,
there are no other deities on heaven or earth; and that if
the ladies died, they would wish to be, not with God,
but where their ladies were." [12]

These pious allusions amid the tenderest protesta-
tions, this mélange of conceits and witticisms with devotion, this mingling of sacred matters and very profane
sensations, would in other places and lands have risked
being regarded as scandalous. Religious lands and
times do not have such scruples. Faith, which filled a
man all entire, changed its altar without diminution of
ardor and without varying its mode of expression; it

addressed itself now to God and now to woman without fearing to do too much honor to the creature or to outrage the Creator. Where we would be tempted to see blasphemy, amorous Spain admired the sublime delirium of passion.

"Are you not Christian?" says a servant to the young Calisto, who drowns in despair, who dies of love for Melibea. "I!" replies the lover, "I am Melibean, I believe in Melibea, I love Melibea." [14] Here is a foretaste of that precious trait of gallantry, but with an accent of sincerity that elevates and vivifies this amorous pathos.

These and many other traits are, in the domain of sentiments and ideas, the most intimate manifestation of a nationality. Spain was distinguished not so much by special qualities as by the peculiar twist that the Spanish character gave to the general sentiments of the Christian world. That character had a certain indefinable quality of exaggeration and tenseness; it was a picture without middle tints, with a profusion of colors and blinding lights. The race was hard and without a trace of softness; but it was a patient and strong race; and in no country in the world was there less of a gulf between the different social classes. There the peasant felt himself a gentleman; the great señor was free of arrogance. The prejudice of the people against labor, its vanities, its delicacy in matters of honor, its susceptibilities, were just so many signs of its nobility.

But this splendid endowment of qualities tended toward the ruin of the state; the Spaniard's indolence and disdain for labor made him subject to foreigners. A nation cannot be composed of soldiers and conquerors alone. Misery dogged the conquerors of two worlds: Spain, unconquerable by men, must succumb to the silent pressure of economic laws.

II

The Court

Within the Spanish nation the Catholic Sovereigns and their entourage formed a select society in which was centered the administrative life of the country. It was also the residence of ambassadors, the theater of festivals, ceremonies, and public solemnities. The court included the members of the central government as well as the officers attached to the persons of the sovereigns. Ferdinand and Isabella presided over the destinies of this little world.

Their royal predecessors had also had a circle of dignitaries, familiars, and domestics, but the accession of a woman to the throne of Castile enhanced the importance of the feminine element. The queen raised the daughters of great lords in her palace; she watched over their virtue with meticulous care and gave them rich dowries when the time came to marry them off. Never had there been such a numerous and select retinue of ladies under previous sovereigns. The court, if not founded, was organized at this time. To augment the splendor of this brilliant company, Isabella had four daughters of notable beauty and intelligence. "Each of the infantas had a multitude of gentlemen, gentlewomen, and other persons who had charge of their education and other matters relating to their service." [1] It was the same with the Infante Don Juan. This heir presumptive of the crowns of Aragón and Castile had a household maintained on a royal footing. Its organization is known to us from the *Libro de la Cámara Real,* in which Gonzalo Fernández de Oviedo, the former page of the prince, lists the various offices held by a swarm of gentlemen and domestics. It is an invaluable document for the intimate history of the sovereigns; for the prince's court was a small replica of that of his parents. Moreover, the author was careful to enumerate in the second part of his work the offices held by persons of rank in the court of Ferdinand and Isabella, offices which had no counterpart in the minuscule court of their son.

Masters and servitors created a world apart, with its own life, organization, laws, and judges. Wherever the sovereigns might travel, their presence in a place halted the action of ordinary jurisdictions. The court *alcaldes* replaced the royal or municipal magistrates. They had direct cognizance of offenses committed in the court and in an area of five leagues about (*rastro de corte*); it was a reserved region;[2] the town and its suburbs became a royal domain. Royal sovereignty was affirmed by the visible symbol of an extraordinary and superior justice that annulled that of all other tribunals in its sphere of action.

The court had more than its own special police; it was provided with all the other institutions necessary for its moral and material life. It was a moving city whose inhabitants were drawn from the elite of the various social classes. It could meet all its needs without having to borrow a soldier, a priest, a magistrate, or an *alguacil* from some neighboring town. The service of God and man alike was looked after with the greatest forethought. The confessor had charge of the royal consciences. The almoner (*limosnero*) distributed the royal charities, possibly applying to this use the fines imposed by the *corregidores*.³ A number of chaplains officiated in the chapel. The *sacristán mayor*, assisted by a deputy, guarded the keys of the coffer which held the sacred objects and relics.⁴ The ornaments used in worship were in the possession of the lord high chamberlain (*camarero*), who turned them over at the proper times to the choirboys (*mozos de capilla*). A chapelmaster directed the music. A number of choirboys lent their young voices; an orchestra supported their song. The string instruments joined their sounds to those of the wind instruments; the *altos de sacabuches* (trombone-like instruments), the *cornetas* (horns), the *trompetas bastardas* (bastard trumpets), and the *atabales* (kettledrums) mingled their brassy tones with the melody of the oboe (*chirimía*), viols (*vihuelas*), and clavecins (*clavecímbalos, clavicordios, claviórganos*).⁵ The son of Isabella, like the French King Robert the Pious, enjoyed singing in the choir. The service had not the magnificence of the royal chapel under the Hapsburgs, but it satisfied the most exigent spirit of devotion, although the king's service was organized on a more sumptuous footing than the service of God.

The royal house had a very large number of officers subject to a *mayordomo mayor*. This great personage, who occupied one of the first ranks in the state, kept an eye on all palace expenses and ordered all payments to be made. The *despensero* (burser) took his orders; a comptroller (*veedor*) scrutinized with him the cost of all purchases. A *contador mayor de la despensa* kept the accounts.

The service of the palate was accounted no less important. Several *maestresalas* (majordomos, stewards) presided over it. They brought the dishes in with great ceremony, preceded by mace-bearers (*ballesteros de maza*). The carvers cut up the meats; the physicians of His Majesty tasted every dish. The cupbearer (*copero*) performed the same ceremony. The kitchen was under the exclusive direction of the *cocinero mayor* (chief cook). In the house of the infante this dignitary had four *mozos de cocina* under his orders. The small number of his aides is a tribute to Spanish sobriety. The *cocinero mayor,* in whose hands rested the health and even the life of the sovereigns, had the most awful responsibility. That is why he never parted with the keys to the kitchen, which was opened only in his presence; two porters guarded the entrance to this formidable laboratory.

Two *reposteros de camas* prepared the room where the prince slept; the *reposteros de mesa* or *estrados* set his table; the *reposteros de plata* were charged with the service of the silver, which the *mozos de plata* had to clean according to established usage. The royal chandler (*cerero mayor*) looked after the lighting. At the bottom of the palatine ladder were the sweepers, whose temper was not always of the sweetest. It seems that they complained that their task was too onerous; they were generously assigned a *mozo de escoba* (a sweeper boy).

These details give the impression of a rich household tended by numerous domestics; but they also suggest a bourgeois household intolerant of waste and show, in which each servant had his task and did his duty.

The *camarero mayor* (lord high chamberlain) had the same role near the person of the king as the *mayordomo* in the palace. He was an intimate companion whose functions explain his influence. When the king rose, the chamberlain gave him his shirt; then he presented him with a silver basin that he might make his ablutions. At the court of the Infante Don Juan, when the *camarero* had finished his duties, there next entered the *zapatero*

(cobbler) and the *barbero* (barber), the one charged with fitting the prince with shoes and the other with dressing his hair. "The barber was Guttiere de Lunaar, a virtuous man and one of witty speech, who sometimes told jokes that greatly amused the prince as well as all others who heard him. But there was no malice in him, and he never said a word that would hurt anyone." [6] This account well conveys the simple and familiar character of relations and manners in the prince's household. After Figaro had taken his leave, the *mozos de la cámara*, attached to the wardrobe, brought the clothes that the prince wished to wear that day. Should he wish to buckle on his cuirass and gird on his sword, he directed himself to the *mozos de cámara de las armas,* who guarded the keys of a closet that was a kind of arsenal. If the prince wished to read, the *mozo del retrete* went to look for his favorite books.

During the night the person of the king was entrusted to the *monteros de Espinosa,* always recruited from among the noble families of the town of Espinosa. Twenty-four of these bodyguards watched over Ferdinand, twenty-four over the infante. At the close of the day they came to the palace and took possession. There were always twelve *monteros* in attendance. Some slept on the threshold of the royal chamber, in front of the door, which was never locked save by the express orders of the sovereign; the others made rounds in the corridor. Lance in hand, sword at the side, they made sure that nothing troubled the nocturnal quiet. A person who happened to be inside the palace after the closing of the doors and tried to resist this palace patrol risked losing his life for his boldness. At sunrise the *monteros* withdrew and gave up their places to the *reposteros de camas,* also chosen from among gentlemen.

At the beginning of the reign of Ferdinand and Isabella, there was no royal guard, properly speaking. The *contínuos,* who formed part of their entourage and who were their intimate associates, did not constitute a regular troop charged with escorting and protecting the sovereigns and with garrisoning the places where they stayed. Until the assassination attempt of Cañamares (1492) the sovereigns were so trustful that they never were accompanied by an armed servant. Their fear after that affair caused them to give swords to the squires of their retinue (*mozos de espuela*). After the death of Isabella (1504), Ferdinand, grown suspicious, entrusted to Gonzalo de Ayora the task of forming a guard of fifty halberdiers; their number was soon increased to one hundred. In the same period, one hundred mounted scouts were attached to this guard. A captain commanded the one hundred infantry and the one hundred horsemen.

The court, defended like a citadel, was provided with everything needed for its maintenance. There was a multitude of officers, high and low, from surgeons and physicians to washerwomen. Every kind of craft was represented there. There were butchers, pastry cooks, armorers, furbishers, harness makers, packsaddle-makers, saddlers, farriers, embroiderers, dressmakers, and even fishermen and water carriers. When the sovereigns set out on a journey, their departure resembled a tribal migration, or one of those immense and picturesque tent cities, the residences of nomad princes, which are pitched one day amid the flourish of trumpets, cries, and the neighing of horses, and disappear the next without leaving other trace than a welter of footprints and dried-up water sources. There was no capital, strictly speaking; Valladolid was nothing more than a favorite residence. For the greater part of the year the sovereigns wandered about like vagabonds through the cities and castles of Spain.

The *caballerizo mayor,* the chief of the royal stables, had direction of the cavalcade. This personage, so important in an itinerant court, was kept extremely busy. He furnished the mules, the ambling nags, the horses needed by the retinue of the court. Whoever rode must make use of his services. There were no carriages. In 1496, when Margaret of Austria came to Spain to join her betrothed, the Infante Don Juan, she brought coaches mounted on four wheels and drawn by four horses. They lasted only during the stay of the princess (1496 and 1497). This means of transport was very expensive, and, said Gonzalo Fernández de Oviedo, "these chariots travel well only on the plains." Certainly they were not made for the trackless plateaus and rugged sierras of Spain. They were abandoned in favor of the traditional litters, borne on two shafts which were raised on the backs of two mules marching one behind the other (*andas, literas duplicadas*). A *caballerizo* had charge of these carriages of an ancient style. They carried children, the infirm, and women who feared to ride horseback; some aged members of the Council of Castile also managed to find places in them. The charge of transporting baggage was no sinecure. A prominent officer, the *acemilero mayor,* directed it. The *aposentador mayor* (grand marshal of the lodging) and his lieutenants went ahead to prepare the royal quarters.

During their journeys the sovereigns were fain to leave the road to roam the mountains in pursuit of game. A grand huntsman (*montero mayor*) ruled the pack; under his orders the whippers-in led the greyhounds (*galgos*) and the deadly basset hounds to the rabbits. The sport of hawking also had its presiding officer, the *cazador mayor,* who commanded many falconers (*catarriberas*) and beaters.[7]

There were several places where the sovereigns stayed by preference. In these towns ancient palaces, built by the Moors, offered a picturesque background for the splendor of the Christian court. At Zaragoza, the old Moorish fortress of Aljafería, at Seville, the Alcázar, at Granada, the Alhambra, lured the royal guests. The town of Valladolid and its environs was their favorite place of sojourn; like their predecessor, Juan II, they liked to reside at Medina del Campo in the castle of La Mota, several of whose rooms they had decorated. La Mota, with its quadruple *enceinte,* was one of the strongest places in Castile. These *alcázares,* these castles, with their girdle of walls, symbolized a power that had just emerged from the chaos of the civil wars. They formed the setting for the court festivals with their gorgeous pomp, their rich ceremonial, their processions of ladies and gentlemen.

Isabella loved these solemn occasions in which royalty expressed itself by the splendor of its retinue and the luxury of its dress. She herself appeared there in robes of velvet, dazzling with jewels and precious stones, adorned like an Italian madonna and laden with a fortune in clothes.[8] Woman and queen, she took pleasure in those splendors of toilette that add brilliance and an ultimate perfection to female beauty. Her confessor, Talavera, did not cease to thunder against the spirit of vanity. He bitterly reproached her for her expenditures in connection with the reception at Barcelona of the representatives of Charles VIII, for the sumptuous attire of her gentlemen and ladies, and even for the dress that she wore at these diplomatic solemnities. However, on this occasion she was receiving ambassadors who brought the retrocession of Roussillon and Cerdaña. According to the confessor's agents, the queen herself took part in the dancing that marked this festive occasion. Two provinces were well worth a venial sin! But Talavera would not relent on this point; he cried abomination, and went so far as to proclaim to the queen that these scandalous receptions were calculated to corrupt the French visitors and give them a most grievous notion of the Castilian character. The queen, meek of aspect, made mild excuses; even the hardiest courage evaporated in the confessional. She undertook a timid apology: "Because it seems that people have told things that did not happen, I will tell what did happen, that I may know wherein I did wrong, for you say that a certain person danced who should not have done so. If it is meant that I danced, then this was not so, and the idea never even occurred to me." Having explained this point, she went on to her toilette: "Neither I nor my ladies wore new dresses or any new clothes at all; for all that I wore there I had already worn since coming to Aragón, and the Frenchmen had already seen me in that costume. The only thing new was a silk dress that I had made for three gold marks, the plainest thing you can imagine; that was my whole extravagance." [9] The ladies will appreciate the greatness of Isabella's sacrifice. Talavera really was too strict and got excited over a very trifling peccadillo, indeed.

To judge by the accounts of contemporaries and by the representations of the period—miniatures, paintings, and, above all, the funerary statues—display and luxury were carried very far. Ferdinand and Isabella vainly promulgated sumptuary laws; the lowest as well as the highest classes, intent on their pleasures, violated the ordinances. The mode of the time favored stuffs of velvet and silk brocaded with gold and silver and bordered with small pearls. Men and women wore very long gloves, the fingers loaded down with rings. Women were beginning to wear those pattens whose use became general in the sixteenth century. About their necks they wore gold chains and collars. A glance at the trousseau of the Infanta Isabella suggests that the future Queen of Portugal was superbly outfitted for gala occasions. Her parents gave her "500 gold marks and 1,000 silver marks, four gold collars with a profusion of pearls and precious stones, and other chains and jewels of great value. They also gave her many gold and silken tapestries and twenty robes of material figured in different colors, four robes of drawn gold thread, and six other robes of silk edged with pearls and encrusted with gold: the value of the whole is estimated to be 100,000 florins." [10]

We are momentarily overcome by this magnificence, but in reality it was heavy and gaudy. The queens of the fifteenth century would today give the impression of idols adorned to a fantastic excess.

They made an even more dazzling appearance when they participated in those processions in which the gods of the moment displayed themselves before the charmed eyes of the people. A multitude of *ricos homes* and nobles formed the splendid retinue of the sovereigns. The aristocracy spared no expense in order to shine at the side of the king. Each great lord was attended by a numerous following of pages and gentlemen whom he had richly attired at his own expense. The ladies displayed their most beautiful finery. There was a profusion of silk, velvet, jewels, and precious stones. All the nobles, following the example of the sovereigns, made show "of their great wealth and their great readiness to spend it." [11]

These grandiose ceremonies, where money flowed like water, were held only at rare intervals. The Venetian Querini said of the Spaniards that they were prodigal on the days of festivity and lived meagerly the rest of the year. This observation is as valid for the sovereigns as for the people. The day following these celebrations they resumed their simple, economical life. They needed scarcely 1,500,000 maravedís for the upkeep of their household and that of the infantes and the infantas. Whatever concessions they made to the desire to enhance the dignity of their positions, they never allowed the palace to be encumbered with officeholders without duties, with dignitaries without function. Whereas the court of the Hapsburgs[12] was cluttered with a host of useless officials and an unheard-of profusion of illustrious servants without employment, the Catholic Sovereigns managed to achieve prestige without multiplying the number of supernumeraries. The stage on which they moved was worthy of their royal majesty, but its decorative trappings were not ruinous to the nation. In this we recognize a simple grandeur, a magnificence without excess, in contrast with the showy spirit, the passion for etiquette, and the costly formality of the Hapsburgs.

III

The Clergy

It was natural for the clergy to be powerful in a land where a struggle of seven centuries against the Moslems had heated religious sentiment to an extraordinary degree. Spanish piety has always been singularly ardent and demonstrative.

Among this devout people the Church occupied a position of great influence. Not that it was safe from the eye of greed; in Spain as in other European lands the nobility looked with envy on the wealth of the clergy. In Galicia the lords had taken advantage of the time of troubles to secularize the greater part of the ecclesiastical revenues. Laymen held a multitude of benefices *in commendam.*[1] But the liberality of some atoned for the greed of others; the inexhaustible charity of the people made up all losses. Moreover, the clergy enjoyed numerous privileges. The law of the Siete Partidas had exempted the regular and secular clergy from all taxes.[2] As a result, extensive domains escaped all obligation to the royal treasury; every new acquisition, every property secured by legacy or succession, increased the extent of the property under mortmain. The clergy were also skillful in evading municipal taxes, to some of which even nobles were liable. The clergy were unwilling to contribute for the maintenance of the roads and streets, for the repair of bridges, fountains, ramparts, or any other work of general utility.[3]

The crown vainly promulgated vigorous decrees; they do not appear to have had any significant effect. The Church entrenched itself behind its rights, it invoked the protection of its sacred office. Even laymen applied for and obtained the privilege of clergy in order to evade payment of taxes.[4] Men joined the Third Order of St. Francis with the same aim. Far from giving up any of their rights, the priests tried to extend their privileges to their servants and vassals. All who lived in their houses, sat at their tables, and lived their life—relations, allies, domestics—sought to escape the burden of taxes. The Cortes protested in vain against these abuses.

In the time of troubles extending from the death of Pedro the Cruel to the accession of Isabella, the Trastamara dynasty was in no position to compel respect for the rights of the state. The Catholic Sovereigns were strong enough to subject the clergy to the common law, but they preferred not to make a frontal attack, and instead drained away the ecclesiastical riches by tithes repeated at frequent intervals. Once the disposal of benefices was securely in their hands, they gave up all idea of despoiling the Church. The compromise of 1482 gave them the patronage of the bishoprics, archbishoprics, and the richest abbeys of Aragón and Castile; in Granada and the Indies they made all appointments *proprio motu*. This supremacy amply explains their interest in leaving intact such a rich storehouse of revenues and favors.

The clergy were not content with the immense domains with which the piety of subjects and kings had endowed them. The tithe secured for the Church a part of the product of those properties which it did not possess. According to the historian Marina, until the eleventh century it apparently exercised this right only on its own properties. The authority of the false decretals, the weakness of Alfonso X (no sage, but a savant), extended this charge to the whole kingdom.[5] The tithe on harvests was levied throughout the kingdom. The kings even decreed the products of industry to be subject to this tax. This order remained a dead letter. But the personal tithe had more success and was established in several provinces. If we may believe the complaints of the Cortes, the clergy collected these dues with the utmost rigor. It hurled excommunication and anathema against those who would not pay. It collected the tithe not once but two and even three times.[6]

The sovereigns dared not meet the ecclesiastical power head-on; they acknowledged the justice of complaints but did nothing to halt the abuses. In the reign of Charles V the burdens of the tithe became so heavy and so frequent that the deputies of the towns again raised their voices. They complained that certain bishops collected a tithe on the sale of herbs in the public markets. The collection of this iniquitous tax on the food of the poor was not halted. From all these sources the Spanish Church became extremely rich. It had forty bishoprics and archbishoprics (three archbishoprics in Aragón, four in Castile)[7] drawing a revenue of 476,000 ducados.[8] However, some bishops, like those of Guadix, Túy, and Lugo, had a revenue of only 1,500 to 2,000 ducados. The average income of an archbishop was 8,000 to 20,000 ducados, but the Primate of the Spains, the Archbishop of Toledo, left all his colleagues far behind.[9] His archbishopric yielded him 80,000 ducados.

This prince of the Church ranked immediately below the king in point of power, wealth, and the extent of his dominions. We can imagine what an exalted social and political station was occupied by Archbishop Alfonso de Carrillo, who posed a threat to Isabella's succession.

Table of the Archbishoprics and Bishoprics of the Crowns of Aragón and Castile

Following, with the necessary additions, the *Paralipomenon* of Joan de Margarit, Bishop of Gerona (died 1484)[10]

ARAGÓN

† Tarragona 7 suffragan bishops	Barcelona Gerona Vich Lérida Urgel Tortosa Elne	† Zaragoza 3 suffragan bishops	Huesca Tarazona Pamplona	† Valencia erected in 1492 2 suffragan bishops	Segorbe Mayorca

CASTILE

† Toledo 6 suffragan bishops	Sigüenza Osma Burgos Segovia Cuenca Córdoba	† Compostela 13 suffragan bishops	Ávila Badajóz Salamanca Zamora Ciudad Rodrigo Plasencia Calahorra	Coria Túy Lugo Astorga Mondoñedo Palencia

† Seville	Jaén Cádiz Málaga (1486) Palma (Canaries)	† Granada 1492 2 suffragan bishops	Guadix and Baza (1493) Almería (1492)

Churches depending directly on the Apostolic Holy See

Cartagena, León, Oviedo

The prelates did not monopolize the wealth of the Church. According to Damião de Goes, who lived in the middle of the sixteenth century, the endowment of the secular clergy was two times that of the episcopate.

At that rate, the curates and ordinary priests could well scorn their surplice fees. "God grant," said this sagacious student of the causes of the Reformation, "God grant that it be not so in other lands!" There were also a great many abbeys and monasteries, whose combined revenues equaled and even exceeded those of the clergy. According to Damião de Goes, the Spanish Church had a total annual revenue of 4,000,000 ducados.[11]

The convents were as well endowed. At Las Huelgas, near Burgos, lived one hundred fifty nuns of noble birth. The abbess ruled over fourteen other convents. Her power extended over fourteen towns (*oppida*) of some renown and over fifty others of lesser importance. She had numerous ecclesiastical benefices in her gift; she named twelve commendatory abbots and appointed judges and governors for her subjects.[12] Only the queen had greater power.

The wealth of the clergy produced its natural results: ignorance and immorality. The privilege of clergy grouped about the clergy a half-lay, half-ecclesiastical following who led a licentious life in the shadow of the sanctuary and who covered the most profligate activities with the cloak of religion. These tonsured clerics, dedicated to God by their parents from tenderest infancy and entered by them in the minor orders, scandalized even the laity, and made money by exploiting the basest passions.[13] The monks showed no greater capacity to resist temptation. If Spain contained a great number of austere religious like Jiménez and of true ascetics like Juan de la Puebla, who died of his penances, if the rugged valleys of the sierras had hermits covered with the skins of beasts, rudely housed in huts of boughs, and nourished on herbs and spring water like the mountain animals, there were many more of those wayward friars who gave themselves up to worldly pleasure, lived lavishly on the revenues of their monasteries and the alms of the devout, and had no other rule than their passions.

The manners of the secular clergy were no better. Castile was the only land where under the influence of the prevailing morality the bastard of an ecclesiastic had the right of inheriting from his father in case of death *ab intestate*.[14] Concubinage was a normal, recognized, accepted state of affairs. The concubines of the clergy were detested for their ostentation rather than scorned for their misconduct; it enraged the lawful wife of a layman to see the superb attire and extravagant toilette of the curate's mistress. The Cortes of Briviesca had issued the most severe orders against this deeply rooted vice. But the clergy rejected the intervention of the civil power in its affairs. It believed or claimed that its tribunals were adequate to extirpate the evil.[15] The licentiousness continued. In 1480 the sovereigns decided that the known concubines of priests should be banished for one year from their places of residence; in case of a second offense they should be subjected to a public flogging. The civil law did not undertake to punish their accomplices.

The high clergy gave an example of laxity. The prelates were generally men of high birth who retained the manners of the world, and who remained great lords in the bishop's palace. Alonso of Aragón, bastard of Ferdinand and Archbishop of Zaragoza, was succeeded in office by his natural son. These sons and grandsons of kings sought an exalted social station in the Church; they would have no nonsense about living like monks of humble life. The younger sons of great houses were no more interested in practicing the Christian virtues; they had worldly tastes and passions. They took part in the commotions that convulsed the country;

now they followed the royal banner, now that of the aristocracy. They gave more than sympathy to the favored faction, appearing in person at the head of armies. At the battle of Olmedo, fought by Juan II against his rebellious lords, the Archbishop of Toledo, Alfonso de Carrillo, had an arm pierced by a lance and was one of the last to leave the field of battle. At Toro (1476) the same prelate fought against Isabella in the ranks of the Portuguese invaders. Facing him in the Spanish army was another archbishop, Don Pedro de Mendoza. The father of the famous Bishop of Zamora, Antonio de Acuña, one of the leaders of the *comuneros,* was a bellicose bishop who had drawn his sword for La Beltraneja against Isabella the Catholic.

The lives of these warrior-pontiffs were anything but edifying. Alfonso de Carrillo did not scruple to be buried at Toledo, the seat of his archbishopric, beside his bastard son Troilo. The Cardinal of Spain, Don Pedro de Mendoza, had three natural sons by two Spanish ladies; these sons founded powerful aristocratic families. One day a monk dared to criticize the cardinal's manners in his presence; instead of punishing the presumptuous friar he ordered some money given to him. These great lords at least had the sincerity and courage of their misconduct.

But whereas the other Churches of Christendom slumbered in blissful peace and put up with their vices till the day Luther's thunder roused them and forced them to reform on pain of destruction, Spain, which in the fifteenth century had its own heresy in the form of Judaism, was led sooner to undertake the work of reform. Even as the pyres were being lighted for the Judaizers, Isabella strove to keep her people faithful to Catholicism by restoring to the clergy the prestige of good examples and good actions. Before her time the evil was

known, the corruption avowed, the remedies prescribed; but it required her persevering will and the imperious spirit of Jiménez to make the rule triumph despite the resistance of the clergy itself, despite the indifference of an Alexander VI.

The Spanish Church had long abandoned the custom of holding those diocesan or general assemblies which have the useful function of pointing out abuses. From 1429 to 1473 no council had been held in the Peninsula; for half a century the quarrels of parties had relegated to an inferior plane the higher interests of ecclesiastical discipline. In 1473 the Archbishop of Toledo decided to convene a council in Aranda. The signatures to its acts indicate the presence of Don Juan Arias Dávila, Bishop of Segovia, Diego de Mendoza, Bishop of Jaén, and of deputies of the Bishops of Osma, Cuenca, and Sigüenza.[16] The ignorance and corruption of the clergy formed the principal subject of deliberation. The assembly noted with sorrow that some priests kept one or more concubines.

The council of Seville (1512), held under the presidency of Deza by the suffragan Bishops of Cádiz, Silves, and the Canaries, voiced the same complaints and exposed the same vices. It counseled the clergy to deport themselves decently; it forbade them to wear garments of silk or of green or violet-colored material, or belts embroidered with gold and silver. They should have their hair cut short enough to show their ears. They were forbidden to enter a tavern without good reason, or to get drunk, to attend bull fights, to swear, to go out at night "after the striking of the second bell." The chief *alguacil* had orders to arrest them if found in the streets after the curfew and to confiscate their arms, if they were armed.[17] The fathers noted with chagrin that clerics preferred censure and punishment to leaving their mistresses. The council limited itself to ordering confiscation of one year's salary of culprits; hardened sinners would be imprisoned until they had shown signs of repentance.

Concubinage was plainly the great plague of the Spanish Church. The council recommended to regular and secular clergy guilty of this grave fault that they should at least abstain from appearing at the marriages of their sons and daughters, and that they should not testify in favor of the women whom public opinion pointed out as their mistresses. In default of morality, an austere prelate like Deza proposed that the clergy should spare the humble the spectacle of scandals whose existence he admitted.

The ignorance of the clergy was as great as its corruption. The majority of the clerics knew no Latin; they neglected their preaching. Peter Martyr wrote Don Guttiere of Toledo. "You will be bishop. I have persuaded influential men that you would make a good preacher. This is the talent that one would wish especially to find in a pastor, but it is rarer among the noble prelates than a white crow." The council of Aranda had forbidden admission to orders of a candidate who did not understand the liturgical language. An assembly of the clergy held at Madrid the same year (1473) asked the Pope to authorize the bishops and chapters of the cathedral churches to reserve two prebends for learned priests, one canonist and one theologian.[18] The Pope consented and, by a bull of December 1, 1474, allowed this piece of affectation. The Spanish clergy rewarded with a tidy subsidy this show of benevolence toward learning on the part of Sixtus IV and his legate Rodrigo Borgia.[19]

Conciliar decrees and Papal bulls, however, signified nothing but good intentions. Could one expect a primate like Alfonso de Carrillo to compel respect for the clause forbidding ecclesiastics to bear arms? Could one expect this prelate and his colleagues, who had raised their own bastards with such tenderness, to punish concubinage? Other and purer hands must enforce discipline. This was the work of Isabella and Jiménez.

The queen's confessor took special charge of the regular clergy. The Franciscan Order, to which he belonged, had chosen him as its provincial. By virtue of this title, and later as Archbishop of Toledo, he pressed the reform of the convents.

Not all members of the great family of St. Francis had remained faithful to the spirit of renunciation, of abnegation, of sacrifice, which its spiritual father had bequeathed to his followers. The respect and piety of the multitude had enriched the mendicants; their discipline and their poverty had disappeared together. Whereas the founder and his first disciples would not hold any property of their own and were content to sustain life with the alms of the faithful, their latterday heirs lived on the reputation of those illustrious forerunners and founded a great propertied interest on a tradition of disinterestedness. This order, which once had carried the principle of renunciation to the point of rejecting all property, accumulated goods, domains, and revenues; it built superb convents; and it added alms-collecting to all its other means of acquisition.

Some monks, more faithful to the memory of St. Francis, broke with these worldly colleagues, whom they called *conventuales,* and, under the name of "Brothers of the Observancia," continued the ancient simplicity and revived the rule of the order. There was a lively struggle between these hostile brethren. The Popes wavered between the two parties until 1517, when Leo X subjected the conventuals to the rule of the Observancia. At the beginning of Isabella's reign the conventuals were still all-powerful, holding the majority of the monasteries. But the minority won out through its zeal, conviction, and the prestige of its virtues.

Jiménez, raised among these enthusiasts, and imperious by nature, was the declared enemy of indifference and laxity. He began to visit the monasteries, to drive out unworthy brethren; he sought to recall the conventuals to their primitive discipline. He encountered the liveliest resistance; the Franciscans of Toledo preferred to leave the convent rather than conform to the rule.[20] In 1505 it became necessary to expel the conventuals of Salamanca. The evil was so deeply embedded that four hundred monks passed over to Africa and became Moslems. Jiménez did not retreat; he ordered the imprisonment of the commendatory abbot of the Convent of Santo Espíritu at Segovia, Laurencio Vacca, who had come forward as head of the antireform party. At the menacing instances of the Catholic Sovereigns, the Pope, who displayed indifference and even hostility to all change, declared in favor of the Observancia.

The victory was complete. The majority of the religious orders accepted the reform without offering any opposition.[21] The Dominicans, the Carmelites, the Augustinians, warmly endorsed Jiménez' proposals. In his own diocese Jiménez was careful to appoint to benefices the most capable and worthy applicants; he repulsed intriguers. His large political responsibilities and cares prevented him from summoning a diocesan synod every year. He convoked only two synods, held at Alcalá de Henares and Talavera. In fact, during the whole of that long reign there was held only one Church council, that of Seville in 1512. Perhaps the Catholic Sovereigns distrusted these great assemblies of the clergy as much as those of the Cortes. Or perhaps we may ascribe the infrequency of synods to the numerous preoccupations of that crowded reign.

Nevertheless, the reform of the secular clergy was accomplished. And the principal credit for it goes to Isabella, who brought to the choice of bishops and other high ecclesiastical dignitaries the most scrupulous care, the purest considerations. She did not hesitate to cross Ferdinand, when he subordinated propriety to political calculations or private likes and dislikes. There were some compromises; but the reform of the episcopacy was carried through. The prelates were chosen among persons eminent for knowledge and piety; the great ecclesiastical offices ceased to be a monopoly of the aristocracy. The tendency was rather to select the bishops from the lower nobility and the middle class. That is why during the turbulent days of the revolt of the *comuneros* the scandalous spectacle of warrior priests occurred only by way of exception. Public opinion demanded purer manners. The Spanish clergy was not a court clergy; it held strictly to the rule of residence. For the rest, the establishment of an Inquisition directed by monks tended to consign the bishops to a secondary plane, just as the Council of Justice, controlled by legists, replaced the aristocracy in the government of the state.

Isabella and Ferdinand made themselves masters of the Church, but they used their power, Isabella above all, to raise its moral tone. The change must have been rapid and general for contemporaries to be able to note its effects. They were unanimous in praising the character of the new clergy that had been molded by the hands of the Catholic Queen. "In our times," says Oviedo, "Spain has had eminent and learned men, excellent prelates, religious, and other persons, who by their knowledge and science raised themselves to the highest dignities of the chapters and archbishoprics and to the highest posts in the Church of God."[22]

IV

The Nobility

In the reign of Ferdinand and Isabella, the Spanish nobility began to disappear from the political scene, without having lost its social importance, its privileged situation, or its territorial wealth. The aristocracy, the scourge of previous reigns, was subjected by the Catholic Sovereigns to a rule of discipline and obedience from which it would never stray again. The masters of the state, the turbulent barons and battlers, were about to be transformed into courtiers.

What had been their condition and role during the previous period? Some Spanish scholars wax very indignant and protest mightily against any comparison of the Spanish baronage with that of other European lands. Their Middle Ages, they say, do not precisely correspond to the medieval era in other lands of Western Europe; the term "feudalism" does not fit the Spanish social organization of that epoch. Step by step, the kings conquered the land from the Moors; they distributed immense domains, dignities, revenues, and subjects to their military leaders. To be sure, these donations and rewards gave rise to a powerful, a formidable aristocracy; but the origins of the feudal system are more complex than this. The wealth that was the reward of the warrior attached him to the prince who was the author of these favors; but an obligation of this kind bound only the donatory. There was not that reciprocity of duties between vassal and suzerain that appears to have been a characteristic feature of French society in the Middle Ages. Instead of being protected by a reciprocal contract, the vassal was covered only by the *fueros* of the place where he lived.[1] Besides, the feudal tie is both real and personal, whereas in Spain the relations of subject and sovereign, of vassal and suzerain, were above all personal. The customs of neighboring France influenced Spanish society to borrow some features of no particular importance. The titles of duke and marquis were of foreign importation. But Spain never knew that maze of jurisdictions and fiefs, and that hierarchy which ascended from the humblest gentleman, through a series of lords, vassals, and suzerains, to the king, the suzerain of suzerains.

Despite these differences, it would probably be something of a paradox to maintain that Spain completely escaped the influences which prevailed for a number of centuries in all the rest of Europe. The aristocracy was long preponderant; it treated royalty with contempt, and dictated terms to it. The Fuero Viejo[2] of Castile preserves traces of those times of disorder and anarchy. There we see that the *ricos hombres* (the great lords) could renounce the obedience due a king without other ceremony than that of sending to him one of their men to announce the fact: "Sir, in the name of such-and-such a *Rico Home*, I kiss your hand and, henceforth, he is no longer your vassal." [3] Freed from all ties, they departed with their servitors and companions to take service in a neighboring kingdom. How often the Cid changed his allegiance! He did not hesitate to make war on his former sovereign, either alone or with the aid of other banished men.[4] The military orders were known to sign a true defensive and offensive alliance to defend their liberties, privileges, and customs against every other man, "whatever his condition." These orders, like the feudal lords, enjoyed an almost royal authority in their domains. With the exception of the right of coining money, which throughout the Peninsula remained in the hands of the king or was exercised only by way of delegation, there was not a single royal power that the nobility had not usurped.

However, one must distinguish between the Castilian and the Aragonese nobility. The former had at its head grandees who were considerably richer and more powerful than those of Arágon. Trusting in the multitude of its vassals, the Castilian nobility regarded itself as a special caste in the state. It separated its cause from that of the nation. It scorned to appear in the Cortes and, sure of obtaining by force all that is desired, it refused to merge its privileges with the general liberties of the country. It abandoned to the king, as a contemptible ally, the people of the towns and the countryside.

The Aragonese aristocracy did not commit this mistake. Because it was weaker, it was more prudent; the nobles forged solid ties with each other, and instead of scorning the Cortes they secured the right of a double representation therein. Their victories over the crown appeared to be so many fetters placed upon royal absolutism.

In the fifteenth century this preponderance of the nobility declined. The power of the nobility was not so much broken by direct attacks as dwarfed by the extraordinary development of the royal power. The great resources of Ferdinand and Isabella made it impossible for the aristocracy to stand up to them. Besides, the repressive acts of a government are not always an accurate measure of its power; its moral influence and the degree of re-

spect and fear that it commands frequently provide a
more valid measure. Authority is often a personal trait.
In Castile, Alfonso XI struck the first blows against the
nobility; he used against them the instruments of seduc-
tion and fear. Although he sent the highest heads in the
kingdom to the block, he attracted the lords to his
court by offering them tourneys and feasts;[5] he surrounded himself with a body of paid cavalry to protect
himself against the ill will of his great vassals. Under
Don Pedro the Cruel the most illustrious blood of Castile
flowed in torrents. Under the Trastamara the high nobility
achieved all its pretensions, but its irremediable decadence
was evident from the fact that various factions disputed for the privilege of being the royal confidant.
Anarchy reached its height under Enrique IV. The accession of Isabella marks the end of the feudal aristocracy.

The crown would have had difficulty in overcoming its adversaries if the nobility had acted together;
but that multitude of nobles was composed of different
classes with the most diverse interests. The kings found
many collaborators in the ranks of privilege. The number
of simple gentlemen was considerable. Certain provinces,
such as Biscay, and certain towns, such as Simancas,
made this claim for all their sons; a comfortable living and
residence in a place exempt from taxes and enjoying liberal *fueros* were sufficient grounds for assuming the title
of *hidalgo*. The struggle against the Moors had developed
in the people a sense of dignity, the habit of bearing arms,
and a distaste for manual pursuits. From these conditions
sprang the large number of nobles.

Nobility was transmitted from father to child; in some
places, the womb ennobled. Bastardy was not regarded
as a cause of shame. The Spaniards were free of the
prejudice that punishes the child born of a woman's mis-
step while the father, the only guilty party, continues to

enjoy high position and public respect. A simple acknowledgment sufficed to place the bastard on the same footing as the legitimate child. The law forbade the father,
under penalty of making the act null and void, to use
the phrase "natural child" in this declaration. An avowal
of paternity by Christopher Columbus sufficed to legiti-
mize his son Ferdinand.[6] A number of great lords of the
time of Ferdinand and Isabella left bastards as their only
heirs.

A mass of financial and personal privileges was
attached to the quality of nobleman, be he the most
insignificant and the poorest of simple gentlemen. First
of these was exemption from all taxes, contributions, or
imposts paid to the state or to the towns. However, the
noble contributed his mite to certain charges of general
interest, such as the upkeep of fountains, bridges, and
highways and the destruction of locusts. In principle, he
had preference over commoners in the distribution of
offices, of lay and ecclesiastical dignities. Society surrounded him with a deference that constituted a confirmation of his pre-eminent position. He occupied a place
of honor in the church, in processions, in the tribunal. He
could not be imprisoned or seized for debts. If he committed some offense and was deprived of his liberty, he
was shut up in a special prison; if the crime was great
and concerned the security of the state, the culprit was
done the honor of being immured in a strong castle. A
nobleman must not be put to the torture; he must not be
hanged, but must instead have his head cut off—unless
convicted of high treason to God or King. Treason or
heresy, whatever a man's rank, led straight to the gibbet
or the stake.[7]

Not all these privileged beings were rich; the poor but
proud gentleman who combined a grand air with heroic
fasting became a fixture of Spanish literature. A con-

siderable number of gentlemen had no other possession than their good birth. Unlike French country squires, they could not show a castle, a *casa fuerte*, a *peña brava*, or even a pigeon roost that had once belonged to their ancestors; they did not have a *solar conocido* (a known estate). It is likely that the name *infanzón* was originally applied to a noble who possessed a manor, but this name became a synonym for gentleman. An *hilalgo* reduced to poverty often entered the service of some rich and powerful lord; he fought under this lord's orders and in time of peace held some domestic offices under him. Such a man was called a squire (*escudero*). This name did not denote a degree of nobility but the exercise of a function.

The same was not true of the term *caballero,* which marked a more eminent rank in the social hierarchy. A man received this title of knight when he entered a military order; but the king also made knights by virtue of his prerogative. He granted this title to gentlemen of high birth or great merit. Ferdinand and Isabella even conferred nobility on commoners.[8] The Cortes of 1480 complained that the sovereigns were constantly diminishing the number of the taxable (*pecheros*).

The ceremony of investiture entailed solemn rites which the Siete Partidas had carefully prescribed. In the face of the enemy, it seemed childish to take time out for such empty formalities. Ferdinand expressly reserved the right to make knights with or without ceremonies. He went so far as to bestow knighthood by letters, privilege, or simple royal patent. In such cases knighthood was simply a decoration accorded to *pecheros,* with dispensation from paying poll tax. However, young men of the aristocracy departing on their first campaign continued to be invested with the golden spurs if they had not already assumed the habit of the military orders.

At the head of the nobility stood an aristocracy of lords possessed of large domains and revenues. In the fifteenth century the name of *ricos homes* or *ricos hombres,* rich men, still designated the first among the nobles.[9] In order to call oneself a *rico home* it was not enough to have broad acres and many vassals. The king conferred this title at a ceremony in which he presented the recipient with a standard and a cauldron, as if to make him chief and foster parent of his soldiers. Moreover, the king alone could confer the dignities of marquis, duke, and count.

These great barons occupied an eminent situation, but there were grades even in this superior class. The holders of the most distinguished titles formed an aristocracy within the aristocracy: the grandees. The grandees enjoyed privileges that set them apart from other lords. They kept their heads covered and sat in the presence of the king; the queen rose to receive them when they entered, and caused cushions to be given to them on which to sit. Under Ferdinand and Isabella, this privilege apparently belonged to all the dukes, marquises, and counts. Philip the Handsome, accustomed to greater respect in his Flemish homeland, succeeded in getting the grandees to renounce their right to be covered in his presence. In order to spare the pride and sensibilities of the electors at the coronation of Aix-la-Chapelle, Charles V obtained the same concessions from the grandees. The Spanish lords thought they had yielded up their rights for but a single day. The prince regarded the concessions as definitive; he did not abolish the privilege, but he restricted it to a small number of families. It was to the heads of these powerful families that Charles V returned the rank of grandee with all its prerogatives. He also conferred it on two members of the Aragonese aristocracy, the Dukes of Segorbe and Montalte. This first investiture seems to have established what later came to be called the grandees of the first class. These empty distinctions grew in number even as the nobility lost its importance.

The crown dealt the nobility a dreadful blow when it assumed for itself direction of the military orders. The grand masterships with which Ferdinand caused himself to be invested placed in his hands considerable revenues and the disposal of wealthy benefices. The orders had been created in the twelfth century to make eternal war on the Moslems; there were three of these orders in Castile: Santiago, Calatrava, and Alcántara. Their militias, composed of nobles, had a religious character, and like the monastic orders followed a rule into which a great deal of laxity had gradually entered. The young man who aspired to become a knight made his novitiate in a convent, a sort of retreat where he was instructed in his duties. Upon taking the habit, he pronounced vows of poverty and obedience. Alcántara and Calatrava, which remained faithful for a longer time to the letter of their original institutions, added to these vows that of chastity. However, these pledges were poorly observed by men whose military mode of life and wealth encouraged every sort of debauchery.

List of the Greatest Spanish Lords in the Reign of Ferdinand and Isabella[10]

Family Names (Apellidos)	Titles	Date of Erection of These Dignities	
Pimentel	Count of Benavente	1398	
Enríquez	Admiral, Lord of Medina de Río Seco, Count of Melgar	1438	
Osorio	Count of Lemos	1457	
Guzmán	Duke of Medina Sidonia	1460	
La Cueva	Duke of Alburquerque	1464	
Pacheco	Duke of Escalona	1469	
Toledo	Duke of Alba	1469	
Mendoza	Duke of the Infantado	1475	
Manrique de Lara	Duke of Nájera	1482	
Zúñiga	Duke of Béjar	1486	Duchies erected in the reign of Ferdinand and Isabella
Velasco	Constable-Duke of Frías	1488	
Córdoba	Duke of Sessa	1486	
La Cerda	Duke of Medina Celi	1491	
Ponce de León	Duke of Arcos	1498	
Cárdenas	Duke of Maqueda		

As the Moslems fell back toward the south, the possessions of the orders, swollen by the Reconquest, continued to expand; meanwhile the services of the knights, thanks to the growing weakness of the infidels, became less and less necessary. When Granada fell, these warrior congregations ceased to have any reason for existence. The sovereigns preserved them, but in the time of Charles V, the crown secured for itself in the capacity of perpetual administrator (1523) the disposition of the orders and their immense properties: Santiago possessed seven hundred thousand souls; Calatrava, two hundred thousand; Alcántara, one hundred thousand.[11] The three together ruled over one-third of the population of Castile. From its subject population Santiago extracted an annual tribute of 60,000 ducados; the two others together, 95,000 ducados.

The Order of St. John of Jerusalem, absorbed in the war against the Turks, played no political role and thus inspired no distrust, although its revenues were as large as those of Calatrava and Alcántara. The crown of Aragón, in which the Castilian orders had commanderies, had its own national order, Our Lady of Montesa; it was founded after the destruction of the Templars (1316), and inherited all their property in the Kingdom of Valencia. It was a dependency of Calatrava, and as such, was subject to the visits and correction of the Cistercian abbots of Valdagno and Sainte-Croix. We note the remarkable fact that three of the Spanish military orders accepted the spiritual tutelage of a French center like Cîteaux.

The Orders of Montesa was probably too weak to disquiet the Catholic Sovereigns; they may have also feared the lively opposition of their Aragonese subjects if they interfered with it. Not until the reign of Philip II was the grand mastership abolished and the king proclaimed perpetual administrator.

Knights and nobles ruled a multitude of subjects living upon their lands. There were free men who enjoyed liberties freely given or wrung from their lords. The condition of these men was much harder than that of their fellows in the royal domain. That is why the crown towns protested and even rose in revolt when a royal caprice caused them to pass under the domination of some lord.

The aristocracy, however, had recognized the necessity of granting the towns liberal charters.[12] The lord's domain was cultivated by *solariegos* who made fixed payments. Their original condition must have been quite miserable. The Fuero Viejo of Castile declared that "the lord can take the body of a *solariego* and all that he has in the world." This was slavery in all its rigor. It is true that the same *fuero* distinguished between different regions; it set apart from this enslaved class the men who peopled Castile from the Duero up to Old Castile. It was impossible to reduce to serfs the valiant colonists who, following in the footsteps of the soldiers, pushed into the plains recently wrested from the Moors. These men could leave the soil when their lot became too rigorous and look for a more humane master. The lord could not prevent their departure; he could only distrain the chattels that they were carrying away. Thus there seem to have remained in the inferior category of *solariegos* only the serfs and the inhabitants of the conquered territories. We know little about the slow progress of this rural population, but the fifteenth century saw its emergence to personal liberty. A *pragmática* of October 28, 1480, permitted the inhabitants of a locality to leave with their chattels, flocks, and harvests in order to settle in another place, and annulled all contrary dispositions.[13] With the reign of Isabella, serfdom disappeared completely from Castile.[14]

The condition of the serfs of Aragón was much harder. In Catalonia, in the valleys of Vich, Gerona, and Ampurdán, the *payeses de remensa* could not abandon or alienate their land or even marry without permission of their lord. It even seems that the lord enjoyed with regard to his vassals the same shameful rights that existed in some other valleys of the Pyrenees. It was the glory of Ferdinand that he abolished the *malos usos;*[15] in 1486 he rendered an arbitral sentence that replaced each of these customs with a payment of six dineros.[16] He could not destroy all existing abuses. "The Aragonese nobles and other lords of places who are not of the Church," say the Observancias of Aragón, "can treat badly or well, at their pleasure, their vassals of servitude (*vassalos servitutis*) and can take away their goods, without any appeal, and the king cannot meddle in these lordships."[17] These were the subjects of *signi servitii,* whose condition was most miserable. There were others who claimed better treatment, saying they were not *vassalos servitutis.* But the aristocracy rejected these distinctions and sought to reduce them all to the same level. It exercised the right of life and death in all its fullness. As late as the seventeenth century, in the reign of Philip III, a lady of high birth, widow of Don Martín of Alagón, caused one of her servants, Pedro Salaverte, to be killed because he refused to obey her. In the same period, the Duke of Híjar ordered some inhabitants of Belchite to be strangled for some trivial reason without a trial of any kind.[18] The king, angered by these executions, wanted to punish the responsible parties. The Council of Aragón, having been consulted, replied that the *fueros* authorized such acts.

In the time of the Catholic Sovereigns the nobility was equally cocksure as to the extent of its power. Despite his exalted opinion of his prerogatives, Ferdinand had much less freedom of action in Aragón than in Castile. Insurrections broke out frequently in the oppressed countryside, and the struggle between master and subjects

sometimes lasted for several years, with the crown helpless to intervene. Don Guillén Palafox, Lord of Ariza,
having been besieged in his castle by his own serfs,
ordered some to be hanged and the rest whipped.[19] The
royal agents, always hostile to the feudal power, had rejoiced at the difficulties and embarrassment in which he
was involved. He complained of this in an arrogant letter which did not spare Ferdinand himself: "It seems that
your Highness has blamed (my conduct) because I have
not afforded (the defeated rebels) a trial." Don Guillén found it strange that he should be criticized for putting his subjects to death without a judicial process. The
king yielded, and, by the Decree of Celada, acknowledged the baronial claims.[20] But the revolt ceased at one
place only to break out at another with redoubled violence. The vassals of the barony of Monclus accused
their master of tyranny. Denied relief by royal justice
(1507), they appealed to arms, and as late as 1517
disorders continued. Thus the Constitution of Aragón,
so liberal in other respects, tolerated the existence of a
servile class at the base of the social ladder.

Whereas in Aragón all these serfs were attached in
perpetuity to the same master, in Castile there were districts in which they could freely choose their lord.[21]
These were called *behetrías*. The condition of these people represented a compromise between personal liberty
and the medieval principle that could not conceive
of land without a master. Sometimes the exercise of this
right of choice was unlimited; those of the *behetrías de
mar a mar* could seek a protector among all the families
and regions of the Peninsula. Sometimes the choice was
limited to members of a single family (*behetrías de fami-
lia*). In either case, the obedience of such vassals was
bounded by the limits of their patience or by their whims.
If the lord's protection became a tyranny, they might try

a new master. In some *behetrías* they were free to make this experiment seven times a day, though, no doubt, they never went to such lengths. During the continuance of his functions, the lord received certain feudal dues in money and kind to compensate him for his trouble and the cares of government.

Thanks to its large domains and numerous subjects, the nobility disposed of considerable resources. "I believe," says Lucius Marineus Siculus, "that the revenues of all Spain are divided into three nearly equal parts, of which one belongs to the king, the second to the grandees, the third to the clergy." The Castilian aristocracy stood in the first rank. In the time of Charles V, its twelve dukes, thirteen marquises, and thirty-six counts collected annually from their domains 1,254,000 ducados,[22] wrung from a population that Alonso de Quintanilla estimated, in 1482, at 1,500,000 *vecinos* (6,000,000 to 7,000,000 persons). The distribution of income in Castile was completely unbalanced. Add to the lay nobility the ecclesiastical aristocracy, also generously endowed, and the military orders, and it becomes clear what a mass of money flowed into the hands of the privileged class to the prejudice of the laboring class.

In Aragón, a poorer country, and one whose soil was less equitably divided, three dukes and the Condestable of Navarre together had a revenue of 87,000 ducados; three marquises collected 32,000 ducados in revenue; twelve counts and viscounts received 61,000 ducados. This comes to a total of 180,000 ducados for nineteen persons.[23]

Among these prosperous families there were some, like the Velascos, the Mendozas, the Guzmáns, who enjoyed a truly princely situation. The Condestable Don Pedro Fernández de Velasco, Count of Haro, was regarded as the greatest lord of Old Castile: "Of all the *caballeros* who lived beyond the ports he had the largest number of vassals.[24] The Duke of Medina Sidonia needed one hundred ships to transport his people and the necessary provisions to the camp before Málaga.[25] When Philip the Handsome was preparing to come to Castile to wrest his kingdom from Ferdinand, the duke offered the husband of Juana the Mad a port, two thousand horsemen, and 50,000 ducados if he would disembark in Andalusia. But of all these noble families, the Mendozas were the greatest, by reason of their wealth, the number of their dignities, their entailed estates, and their vassals. The head of the house was the Duke of the Infantado; his brothers were Cardinal Mendoza, Archbishop of Toledo, Primate of the Spains and Grand Chancellor of Castile, and the Count of Tendilla, Viceroy of Granada and Governor of the Alhambra. In the list of the grandees of Castile, we note two marquises and five counts who bear this illustrious name. Among them was the *adelantado* of Galicia. Oviedo draws a brilliant picture of the magnificence of the Duke of the Infantado, of his palaces furnished with tapestries, gold, jewels, and silver plate. His chapel contained accomplished singers and musicians; his falcons, his pack of hounds, his hunting equipment, his stud, put the luxury of the other grandees in the shade. In the time of Philip III the senior branch of the family possessed eight hundred villages and ninety thousand vassals in different parts of the kingdom; it was no less powerful half a century earlier. In 1574 it was estimated that the head of the Mendozas could summon twenty allies or relations, each capable of raising twenty companies of three hundred noble dependents.[26]

One may ask why, having such great wealth and so many men at their disposal, the grandees allowed themselves to be annihilated politically without a struggle. The fact is that at the very moment when the establishment of primogeniture and substitution (Leyes de Toro, 1505) was about to concentrate in a few hands the fortunes and domains hitherto divided and diminished at each succession, the crown became strong enough to overcome all resistance. When the crown became master of the Peninsula, Italy, and the New World, the aristocracy grew very weak. Moreover, the kings did not abuse their power; they respected all privileges that caused them no offense. The grandees kept their immense domains, their vassals, their prestige; they lived surrounded by almost royal honors in the obscurity of the provinces. But obedience was obligatory; the period of feudal violence had closed. At the death of Ferdinand there remained only a handful of survivors of the civil wars, and this turbulent and intractable generation left few heirs.

It is here that we bid farewell to the medieval nobility. Rodrigo Ponce de León, whose living portrait Bernáldez drew in the style of a funeral oration,[27] may be regarded as the prototype of those proud gentlemen who were not yet become courtiers. The man he depicts, pious, jealous of his power and the honor of his vassals, vindictive, combative, devoted to his own and hard to his enemies, exemplifies the best of that feudal aristocracy which triumphed over the Moors but had to give way before the irresistible advance of the monarchy.

V

The Towns

The towns played an important role in Spain during the Middle Ages. They represented political centers of major importance; they united into associations which resisted the violence of the nobles and the caprices of the kings. The insurrection of the *comuneros,* (1520 to 1521), directed against both the aristocracy and the crown, was the last and supreme manifestation of a power that presumed too much on its strength, but which had its time of brilliance and glory, and which contributed significantly to the liberation of the Christian kingdoms and the defeat of the Moors. Conquest of land from the Moslems promoted municipal development; the privileges bestowed on the towns by the kings and lords were made necessary by the part the cities played in the national crusade. The municipal militia made a good showing on the field of battle, and contributed to the growth of municipal territorial possessions as well as the national domain. With each advance the number of the privileged places increased: Every important town taken from the Moslems was immediately transformed into a free commune.

As soon as the fortune of arms delivered a piece of Moslem territory into the hands of a Christian king, he hastened to establish his own soldiers there, and to attract thither immigrants of his own religion. It was like a colony founded on conquered soil; that is why the Spaniards gave such a place the name of *población*. The newcomers, united with the Old Christian population which had lived under Moslem rule, formed the nucleus of a Spanish and Christian group. The Moslems were either expelled, reduced to slavery, or tolerated; but even the most favored Moors, if they did not adopt the religion of their conquerors, were relegated sooner or later by the logic of things to the status of a foreign minority without influence, unesteemed, condemned to be scorned and hated by their neighbors. Only conversion to Christianity could restore to them the advantages they had lost.

The manner in which the Catholic Sovereigns dealt with the Moors of Granada sheds light on an obscure page of earlier Spanish history. After the fall of Málaga they took possession of the whole territory and its inhabitants.[1] A certain number of Moors were exchanged for Christian captives detained in Africa. Ferdinand presented one hundred young people to the Pope; fifty young girls to the Queen of Naples; Isabella also made largesse of human cattle to ladies of her court. The soldiers received their quota of slaves as part of the booty. Then the sovereigns induced Spaniards to come to the town by the gift of fields and houses. The same thing had happened at Ronda, which the conquered abandoned, and was then occupied by the people of Seville and Córdoba.[2] The houses and lands of Marbella, Cártama, Casarabonela, Setenil, and many other places, were distributed to Christian colonists in the same way.

Ferdinand and Isabella were only following in the path of tradition. The organization of the conquered territory also is reminiscent of the origin of the Spanish municipalities. Málaga was chosen as the political center of the surrounding region, to which the mountainous districts of Ajarquía and Algarbia were also attached. This annexation was a mere administrative act without importance, whereas in the high Middle Ages this grouping would have constituted a city in the Roman sense of the word, with a large measure of autonomy, a capital, and towns and hamlets having the status of dependencies or members of the political body.

That was, in effect, the importance of the Spanish municipalities; they were true small states. To ensure the triumph of the Reconquest, the kings granted numerous and tempting concessions and liberties to whoever would come to live within their limits; the citizens were permitted to surround the towns with ramparts, and to construct an *alcázar* to defend themselves against a possible return of the enemy. In order to form a stronger unit, more defensible and capable of energetic action, the kings did not limit the city to its own walls but joined to it other towns, villages, and hamlets; they gave the city's internal administration into its own hands, under the surveillance of a royal delegate; they authorized it to maintain a militia; they conceded to it in whole or in part the right of electing its magistrates; they reduced its financial charges to one or two light tributes. They resigned to the men of the community the responsibility of taxing themselves to pay for the needs of their city. Finally, they guaranteed the safety of these persons against their own royal agents, and sometimes they even assured immunity to malefactors who came to seek refuge and made their homes in this asylum. Personal liberty, financial prerogatives, administrative autonomy—these were the principal franchises inscribed in the municipal *fueros* or charters.[3] The towns with *fueros* did not receive exactly the same concessions, but all received a measure of independence. The movement of independence began in the eleventh century and increased thereafter. León received its *fuero* in 1020; in 1076 came the turn of Nájera and Sepúlveda. It was in the twelfth and thirteenth centuries that concessions of this kind became most numerous.[4] Some of these *fueros* became celebrated as model charters. The kings no longer granted such-and-such privileges, but such-and-such a *fuero*. Thus the *fuero* of Sepúlveda was extended to many other places. The *fuero* of Logroño (1095) enjoyed the greatest authority in Castile. Ferdinand III gave the *fuero* of Toledo with amplifications (1222) to the towns which he had conquered: Córdoba, Seville, Murcia, Niebla, Carmona. The charter of Cuenca (1190), which is a legislative monument of these ages, served as the model for many other *fueros* (which borrowed from it the majority of their provisions). However, this famous *fuero* appears to have been only a copy of the *fuero* granted by Alfonso II to the town of Teruel.[5] Aragón followed the same course as Castile. In 1064, Don Sancho Ramírez granted to Jaca its *fuero*, which was confirmed and expanded in 1087. Alfonso the Battler granted very extensive privileges to Zaragoza in 1125; and he did even more, the following year, in favor of Belchite (1126). In 1025, Barcelona obtained from Count Ramón Berenguer a charter of privileges.

Under the influence of this liberal legislation, the towns became a veritable power in the state. The militias of Soria, Almazán, Atienza, Medinaceli, Cuenca, Huete, and Alarcón fought at the celebrated battle of Las Navas de Tolosa (1212).[6] This urban feudalism presented an unyielding front to seigniorial feudalism. The communes contracted alliances among themselves for the defense of their rights and their territory. The stormy reigns of Alfonso the Sage and his successors offer numerous examples of these brotherhoods.[7] Their boldness extended to the point of attacking even the king. These ancient associations disappeared with the Catholic Sovereigns.

There were distinctions of importance and rank among the towns. To begin with, some were designated "cities," others simply "towns." The cities had an honorific pre-eminence; in official documents they are cited as "very noble." Some ruled a vast territory over which they exercised jurisdiction. The towns were most often limited to the area bounded by their walls and to the neighboring countryside. Fifteen cities and two towns had a right of representation in the Cortes; but those two towns were Valladolid and Madrid. The Italian humanist Lucius Marineus Siculus calls Valladolid a very great and noble *oppidum* (city). "What towns or cities would I prefer to this stronghold? I know not." With some exceptions, the cities were the most important centers of Spain, being the capitals of regions that comprised towns (*villas*) and villages (*aldeas*) subject to their justice.

The composition of the municipal assemblies was much the same everywhere. The mode of election varied from one place to another; here the inhabitants had the right of electing all magistrates; there the choice belonged to the king; elsewhere there was a division of powers between the sovereign and the commune. A sort of municipal bourgeoisie (the *vecinos*) formed the political body. The council, which governed in its name, was composed of *alcaldes,* charged with the civil and criminal justice; *regidores,* who administered the affairs of the city; and an *alguacil mayor,* who commanded the militia. There was also a great number of officers of all kinds, like the *fieles almotacenes* (controllers of weights and measures); the *alarifes* (controllers of the building crafts); the *montañeros* or *caballeros de monte* (foresters); intendants of communal property (*mayordomos*). *Alguaciles, corredores,* and *rayones ejecutores* (constables, policemen, bailiffs) maintained order and executed the laws.

The magistrates charged with the conduct of the communal affairs formed the *ayuntamiento.*

The general assembly of the heads of families (*vecinos*), the electoral body, bore the name of *concejo.*

With some variations, this organization existed in all the towns. Toledo had three *alcaldes,* one being an *alcalde mayor;* Seville had four *alcaldes mayores,* thirty-six *regidores,* two *alcaldes ordinarios.* These were only formal differences; the magistrates who administered justice and carried on municipal government were the same everywhere. Their authority extended to every class of persons. The *hidalgos* residing in the territory of a city were subject to its jurisdiction. The lords who possessed castles and lands there could maintain *mayordomos* to collect their rents, but they must not appoint political agents, *alcaldes,* or notaries public, because the sovereign rights belonged to the *concejo.*

At Toledo the king named the *alcalde mayor;* the citizens elected the ordinary *alcaldes.* At Seville the king reserved for himself the designation of *regidores* and *alcaldes mayores;* the other judicial officers were chosen by the council itself. Other towns had preserved the right of election to all offices.

The voting, to use a modern expression, was not by party ticket. The Spanish communes emerged from a movement that was at once national and religious. In Spain, where war had always the character of a crusade, the Cross grouped the combatants; the Cross grouped the population. The parish was the religious and political unit; the union of several parishes within a given area constituted a city. These primary groupings (*barrio,* ward; *parroquia* or *colación,* parish) had united without merging and losing their own individuality. After the renewal of a municipal council, the first thing done was to distribute the municipal offices among the different wards by casting lots.[8] At Madrid, for example, the lot gave the seal and the banner (*guía*) to the parish of San Juan; San Nicolás received a *fieldad* (inspection of weights and measures); San Pedro received another *fieldad;* San Salvador, the office of *mayordomo.* These last two parishes obtained the right of choosing all the foresters. The lot also decided the designation of the offices of *alcaldes* of appeal (*alcaldías de las alzadas*). The towns remained divided into quarters that divided the municipal functions among themselves by lot.

The offices of *regidores* were generally divided between *caballeros* and ordinary *vecinos.* Prosper Mérimée was wrong to assert that the municipal councils were closed to the *hidalgos.* His mistake probably stems from the royal ban on the construction of castles by powerful men in the territory of a town.[9] But no law denied them the benefits of *vecindad* if they accepted its obligations and if they agreed to submit to the local *fuero.* Actually, they enjoyed, as of right, half of the municipal offices. Even *ricos homes* were not excluded. The Admiral of Castile sat by virtue of his office among the *veinticuatro* of Seville.[10] Personages as eminent as Francisco Maldonado and Juan de Padilla appeared at the head of the insurrection of the *comuneros.* The appointment of such gentlemen brought the cities added strength. This municipal aristocracy was most often drawn from the great landed proprietors, whom the *fueros* obliged to possess a saddle horse and to serve in the cavalry. Thus the richest, most independent, and

most active element had the direction of the city's affairs. The *fuero* of Molina assigned to this element all the municipal dignities; but most often, the ruling group shared them with the ordinary *vecinos*. Whatever the role assigned to this chivalry, there is no doubt that this equestrian order maintained among the urban population a spirit of audacity and resolution, generally incompatible with the tendencies of an industrious bourgeoisie. The combative, ardent temper of the Spanish towns was formed under this influence. The lords, in turn, sought to dominate the cities—that was the danger of an alliance that offered many advantages.

The municipal organization of Aragón presented some interesting peculiarities. The communes bore the name of *universidades;*[11] these were territories at the head of which stood a city or town. They were administered by magistrates called *jurados*. Several *justicias* or *zalmedinas* administered justice. There was no election; the names of candidates were put in a purse, and the officeholders were chosen by lot. Zaragoza, capital of the Kingdom of Aragón, shone among all these universities. The *jurado en cap*, who, with four colleagues, administered the town, marched on the right of the king after his solemn entry if the governor of Aragón was absent. In 1486 the vice-chancellor of the Council of Aragón was elected *jurado en cap*. He regarded it as an honor, despite his high position, to exercise this municipal function. These five *jurados* formed a genuine executive directory which managed current affairs. In very grave circumstances they united with themselves an assembly of thirty-five citizens, also chosen by lot. Together they formed the chapter or council of the city (*capítulo, concejo de la ciudad*). Finally, the *jurados* sometimes assembled all the citizens of Zaragoza; these extraordinary assemblies, where the presence of one hundred persons sufficed to legalize the voting, bore the name of *concejos generales*.[12]

The *universidades* thus constituted important centers, but Aragón had an even more extensive grouping, the *comunidad*, a confederation with a capital, revenues, and vassals. There were three of them: Daroca, Calatayud, and Teruel. Teruel headed an association of eighty-nine villages of some importance. Some notion of the extreme diversity of the municipal regime in Spain is obtained from the fact that the *fuero* of Sepúlveda, a Castilian town, governed Teruel and Albarracín. These were also the only towns of Aragón where the king named the judges, called captains or presidents at Teruel, and superior judges at Albarracín. The king could even choose these officials among foreigners, something completely at variance with the customs of this kingdom. The stormy life of the *comunidades* often made necessary the king's intervention. Teruel, for example, attempted to lay down the law to the rest of the territory, and the other localities offered armed resistance to its pretensions. Bloody struggles then arose, massacres that compelled Juan II of Aragón to intervene. He decided that the town and the countryside should each in turn have the privilege of filling the municipal offices.

The towns and cities of the Middle Ages, with their vast territories, their revenues, their militias, and their vassals, constituted an urban feudalism alongside the lay and ecclesiastical feudalism. The liberties they enjoyed were of remote origin; in what concerns the development of municipal autonomy, Spain took the lead over other European lands. The Third Estate wielded great influence there from an early date; the Cortes of Castile admitted the deputies of the towns to its midst a century before the communes were represented in the English Parliament, and two centuries before Philip the Fair convoked the first French States-General. The thirteenth and fourteenth centuries marked the most brilliant epoch in the history of the Spanish towns. The struggles between the nobles and the people, the encroachments and growing power of the crown, contributed to the ruin of the proud structure of the municipal constitutions.

The *caballeros* formed an ambitious group which sought to win full control for itself. In the fourteenth century this class rivalry degenerated into brawls and riots at Córdoba, Segovia, and Seville.[13] These disorders often provoked royal intervention at the expense of local liberties. Great lords had established themselves in the cities. There they waged armed struggles for power; they formed *alianzas* or *bandos,* attracted soldiers and criminals to their service, and transformed the streets into battlefields.

The inhabitants and *vecinos* were the victims of these struggles between hostile factions. At Córdoba, Don Diego Fernández de Córdoba, Count of Cabra, made war on Don Alonso de Aguilar, Lord of Montilla. At Seville, the Ponce de Leóns and the Guzmáns engaged in bloody combats; a burned church, a devastated territory, a starving city, murders, testified to the cruelty and irreconcilable hatreds of the parties. An anonymous poet gave voice to the misery caused by these conflicts:

"Unhappy Seville, bathed in the blood of thy children and *caballeros*. . . . Where are the men who maintained thee in peace and justice, where are they, those severe *alcaldes?* Where are those brave *regidores* who never bent the knee before a *rico home?* Where thy *jurados,* those zealous hearts who kept thee safe from all evil and hurt? Why hast thou made thy *vecinos* thy masters and why does thy glory abase itself before their ambition? The Ponce de Leóns and the Guzmáns resided within thy walls, but never of yore did they place a yoke on thy neck." [14]

The age of happy independence had passed; the towns must either obey the grandees or submit to the king. The latter choice was certainly the wiser of the two. The kings had intervened in municipal elections at an early date. Alfonso XI first employed this policy of encroachment.[15] To restrain the *concejos,* whose independent spirit annoyed him, he introduced into many towns *corregidores,* royal agents who presided over the *ayuntamiento* and administered justice. The elections often caused disturbances; the renewal of the councils periodically threw out the majority and docile councilors were succeeded by turbulent men. To eliminate this instability, Alfonso XI hit on the idea of perpetual *regidores.* At Madrid, for example, he named in 1346 twelve *regidores* who should hold office at the king's pleasure.

He did the same in many other towns. The Catholic Sovereigns pursued the same policy. They generalized the institution of *corregidor,* suppressed elections wherever they could, and arrogated to themselves insofar as they could the appointment of municipal magistrates. The legislative code known by the name of the Ordenancias of Montalvo, drafted under their inspiration, declared that the king had supreme jurisdiction over all towns and cities, and compelled grandees and bishops who were *señores justicieros* to establish their authority by valid titles. The naming of *alcaldes* and judges belonged to the king of right, but he agreed to respect practices consecrated by usage.[16]

Thus the factionalism of the nobles and the encroachments of the crown brought to an end the brilliant career of Spain's urban feudalism. An omnipotent central government could not long put up with the prejudices, pretensions, and liberties of the towns. Moreover, order and prosperity compensated for the loss of autonomy. As its only memorial of that glorious past in which the cities formed veritable small republics, modern Spain preserves a very zealous and narrow local patriotism, a faded image of the ardent passions and generous enthusiasms of a vanished time.

Part Four

INTELLECTUAL LIFE ·

I

Literature and Letters

The reign of Ferdinand and Isabella was a period of literary transition. The Spanish Middle Ages closed with the fifteenth century; and a new era opened, an era of prosperity and grandeur in which Spain would awe the world not only by the talent of its generals and statesmen but by the genius of its writers. It was the glory of Isabella to have aided this brilliant flowering of Spanish talent by the attention that she paid to learning and by the favor with which she surrounded scholars, poets, and artists. Without repudiating the past, she summoned to her court the men of the Renaissance; she encouraged the study of ancient letters. Italian masters, Alessandro Geraldini, Lucius Marineus Siculus, and Peter Martyr de Anghera, and such Spaniards as Antonio de Nebrija, sought to inspire in their students a veneration and a taste for the ancients. New influences fertilized the national genius and caused it to give more abundant and savory fruit. To be sure, the age of Isabella did not produce a work of perfect beauty, but her reign was a glorious promise.

During the Middle Ages, Aragón, Catalonia, and even Castile had imitated the troubadours; the defeat of Pedro II of Aragón by Simon de Montfort at Muret

(1213) and the ensuing decay of Provençal culture had their repercussions across the Pyrenees. Although the Spanish sisters of the Provençal literature had their days of triumph and brilliance in the fifteenth century, the language in which wrote Auziàs March, who died about 1460, and Jaume Roig, who died in 1478, was doomed to wane to the rank of a dialect. Castilian established itself decisively as the national language of the Peninsula. The literary influence of Provence declined with the decay of Catalan and Valencian, which had served as its intermediaries and as its means of penetration. The poets of the sixteenth century would go in search of models to Italy. The Marquis of Santillana and his contemporaries were the last writers of a double inspiration, Italian and Provençal. Their successors were more exclusive.

When Isabella and Ferdinand came to power, death had just removed the great names of the fifteenth century. Juan de Mena had closed the literary period of Juan II. His reign, so troubled by the strife of factions, was ennobled by the cultivation of letters; this inept monarch was himself a poet at odd hours, and took more pride in being the collaborator of Juan de Mena than of Álvaro de Luna.[1] He bequeathed his taste to his daughter Isabella, who could harmonize the highest intellectual aspirations with her duties toward the state. The revolts and scandals that marked the reign of Enrique IV gave a lively impulse to the Castilian genius; for the spectacle of so much agitation developed a critical spirit and invited reflection. The uncertainty of the times aroused in a poetic soul the sadness and despair that have inspired so much beautiful verse. A Spanish poet dead in the flower of his age (1479) mourned the death of his father, not with cries of embittered sorrow, but in the tender accents of resignation. This descendant of an illustrious family in which a taste for letters was joined with nobility of blood is at his best when he is despairing the loss of all that was great, all that was good.

Who does not remember the ballad of Villon?

> Dites-moi où, en quel pays
> Est Flora, la belle Romaine,
> Archipiada, ni Thais
> Qui fut sa cousine germaine?
> Écho parlant quand bruit on mène
> Dessus rivière ou sur étang,
> Qui beauté eut trop plus qu'humaine?
> Où sont-ils, Vierge souveraine?
> Mais où sont les neiges d'antan? [2]

Jorge Manrique strikes the same melancholy note in his *Coplas que fizo por la muerte de su padre*:

> ¿ Qué se fizo el rey don Juan?
>   Los infantes de Aragón,
>   qué se fizieron?
> ¿ Qué fué de tanto galán?
> ¿ Qué fué de tanta invención
>   como truxieron?
>   Las justas y los torneos,
>   paramentos, bordaduras,
>   y cimeras
> ¿ fueron sino devaneos?
> ¿ Qué fueron sino verduras
>   de las eras?
>
> ¿ Qué se fizieron las damas
>   sus tocados, sus vestidos,
>   sus olores?
> ¿ Que se fizieron las llamas
>   de los fuegos encendidos
>   de amadores?
> ¿ Qué se fizo aquel trobar,
>   las músicas acordadas
>   que tañían?
> ¿ Qué se fizo aquel dançar,
>   aquellas ropas chapadas
>   que traían? [3]

Where Villon lavishes the resources of a somewhat
frigid erudition, the imagination of the Spanish poet
evokes the vision of a brilliant society, and perhaps some
more intimate regret inspires in the poet the tenderness
that characterizes his verses.

Another member of the aristocracy, Pedro de Urrea,
whose *Cancionero* was published in 1513, wrote verses
remarkable for their lively accents of passion and sincerity. He celebrates charmingly the pleasures of marriage,
just as he sings with rapture of the bloody pleasures of
war; he reveals to us his misfortunes and hates. Such confidences are the very soul of lyric poetry. Two monks,
Íñigo de Mendoza and Juan de Padilla, placed their inspiration at the service of morality and religion. Fray
Íñigo de Mendoza published a lively satire against cour-
tesans, in which he praises the honest woman; "angel and
woman in her life and in her beauty." His *El Dechado
de la reina doña Isabel* (*Model of Queen Isabella*) is a
poetic treatise on the art of government. Fray Juan de
Padilla, writing in the retreat of a Carthusian convent,
composed *El Retablo de la vida de Cristo* (*The Retablo
of the Life of Christ*) and the *Los Doze Triunphos de
los doze apóstoles* (*Twelve Triumphs of the Twelve
Apostles*), in which good intentions do not always make
up for lack of inspiration and a dull sermonizing tone.[4]

None of those names, or still other names that could
be drawn from the anthology known by the name of the
Cancionero General (1511), rises above the level of
mediocrity.[5] Juan del Encina, who does shine in the
first rank, interests us less as a poet than as a founder of
the Spanish theater. If the origins of that theater are uncertain, it is because they are complex. An ingenious erudition may lead one to seek the elements of the drama,
the first indications of action and dialogue, in the popular

festivals, the masquerades, and the farces in which appeared the greatest personages of state. On Epiphany, for example, one might see the Condestable Miguel Lucas, disguised as an Eastern potentate, and followed by his pages, solemnly receiving in his palace a woman who carried an infant in her arms and represented the Virgin Mary.[6] Or again one might behold a procession of Moorish cavaliers, commanded by the King of Morocco. These infidels defied the Christian knights and fought with them. The battle ended with the conversion of the Moslems.

It is unnecessary to seek so far for the origins of an art which had already found its complete form in the mystery plays. The Spanish theater issued from the Church. To celebrate the presence of the Catholic Sovereigns at Zaragoza, in December 1487, the archbishop and the chapter staged before them a Nativity of Christ in which appeared six angels, some shepherds, the prophets, the Child Jesus, the Virgin Mary, St. Joseph, and the Eternal Father. The representation was interspersed with dances and song.[7] One of the two authors who collaborated in the play had been especially charged with writing the couplets and the music. The Middle Ages thus possessed a theater which the censures of the Church and the progress of time were to secularize. The novelty consisted in substituting profane for religious subjects; it was in this way that the drama first set itself apart from the mystery play. We may regard as a first effort the anonymous satirical dialogue (*Coplas de Mingo Revulgo*) in which two shepherds, Gil Arribato and Mingo Revulgo, lash the vices of King Enrique IV and deplore the unhappy condition of a flock entrusted to the care of this incompetent shepherd. The drama found its scenic form, without any search on its part, in the romance of *La Celestina*

(1499), which seems written for the theater. It would play better than the *Églogas* of Juan del Encina—but we must allow to each the merit of his design.

Juan del Encina was born in the village whose name he took, about 1469; he studied at Salamanca. When he went to Rome, where he was chapelmaster of Leo X, he had already published his works (1496). He was a musician and a poet. Although we have two or three descriptive poems from his pen, he would be known to only a few scholars were it not for his dramatic compositions.[8]

These are nine eclogues in dialogue form to which Juan del Encina himself gave the title of "representations." They were played before the Catholic Sovereigns, the Admiral of Castile, and the Duke of Alba. Some of these compositions, designed to enhance the effect of the great solemnities of Christmas and Easter, drew their subjects, like the mystery plays, from the New Testament. The secular subjects are of greater interest as evidence of an evolution in art. The *Auto del Repelón* depicts peasants and students at Salamanca who vie with each other in jesting. In the *Antruejo* appear four shepherds who on Shrove Tuesday, so popular in the Midi, recount to each other the struggle between Carnival and Lent, and the shameful flight of Carnival. The conversation ends with a dinner at which the four rustics gorge themselves. The farce is grossly spiced. A composition of more delicacy presents a squire who takes the shepherd's crook and shepherds who become courtiers.

In all these compositions, sacred or profane, there is hardly any action; the style is rude, either because Encina's language lacks suppleness or because the writer wished to fit the expression to the condition of his characters. But some of the lyrical pieces are full of freshness, grace, and sentiment; such is the *villancico* in which a shepherd describes with affecting charm the sweetness of the countryside, the fresh mornings, the silence of the nights broken by the chirping of crickets, and the pleasure of drinking long draughts from wellspring or brook in the parching heat of summer. Although Encina's talent is above all lyrical, we must acknowledge that he brought the drama out of the temple and adapted it to the imitation of everyday life. His students, his shepherds, his hermits, and his squires have an enduring vitality. One of his contemporaries, Gil Vicente, transported the Castilian innovations into Portugal. The *Auto* of the sibyl Cassandra presents a bizarre amalgam of sacred and profane antiquity. Cassandra, sought in marriage by Solomon, insists on remaining a maid. Moses, Abraham, and Isaiah, appealed to by the scorned lover to dissuade her from this design, precede their argument with a wild dance. *O Viudo* (*The Widower*), played in 1514, the *Rubena*, and the *Don Duardos* have a semblance of plot.[9] Gil Vicente wrote many of his dramas in Castilian; the presence of Spanish queens at the Portuguese court inspired poets to write in a language made easy for them by its great affinity with their own.[10]

It was given to a Spaniard, Bartolomé de Torres Naharro, who lived in Italy, to sketch the first rules of the new art and to compose in conformity with these principles true comedies in which the plot is clearly delineated, in which manners are well observed, in which Italian and Spanish life are rendered with fidelity. Torres Naharro had studied his Horace, and he interpreted him intelligently. Although Torres Naharro evidently did not know that Trissino had written, in 1515, the first formal tragedy in Italian,[11] his acquaintance with the ancients and the taste shown by the Italians for scenic representations greatly aided the development of his talent. It does not appear that the *Amphitruo* of Plautus, published in 1515 by Villalobos, could have had the least influence on the genius of Torres Naharro.

The language was in the process of formation, of acquiring force and precision. In addition to these first essays at dramatic poetry, there appeared a truly remarkable prose work, *La Celestina,* written in dialogue form and divided into acts. The first act seems to have been written by Rodrigo Cota of Toledo and the rest by Fernando de Rojas of Montalván. It is possible, however, that the *Celestina* was composed by Rojas alone.[12] The author had first entitled it *La Comedia de Calisto y Melibea;* he published it in Burgos in 1499. It is the moving story of a young girl who begins by repelling the advances of a lover, yields to the suggestions of a go-between, La Celestina, and upon learning that her lover has been killed by a fall, commits suicide in despair. Almost all the actors in the drama are involved in her ruin. Thus the romance has its moral lesson. But what a strange world Rojas shows us, a world of loose women, debauched servants, dissolute monks! La Celestina is enthroned as queen of this world by her evil genius; none is more skilled in dispelling scruples, in arousing desires, in embellishing a shameful act with good intentions. She glides into every home with some fair-seeming pretext, and wherever she goes, she leaves temptation in a woman's heart, disquiet in the imagination of a young girl. Rojas does not recoil before the most realistic and revolting details. His ribald fancy respects neither society nor the Church. His prose is lively, alert, colorful; he ranks among those classics that have no place on a child's shelf. He wrote the literary masterpiece of the reign of Ferdinand and Isabella.

In all epochs, in all literatures, an idealistic current skirts this dark shore of reality. Men's souls seek escape in superb flight toward those happy regions where love, heroism, all the human virtues, have not only their day of suffering and effort, but their morrow of triumph. The romances of chivalry satisfied those high aspirations of our nature. The year 1508 saw the appearance in all the radiant brilliance of his youth of that Amadís de Gaula who was the ancestor of Esplandián, Palmerín, and so many other Amadís'.[13] It required all the genius of Cervantes to kill off or rather bring to a bad end this prodigious line of perfect knights. It matters little that the first author of these incomparable heroes, Garcí Ordóñez de Montalvo, a *regidor* of Medina del Campo, took for his model the lost work of a Portuguese. For posterity, which has no basis for comparison, his imitation has the value of an original work. Amadís remains a model of courage and chastity. After a thousand trials, love leads him to the altar.

Sentimental literature, of which this is the most brilliant specimen, furnished many other works. It would take a volume to enumerate all the Combats, Testaments, Wars, Castles, Ladders, Professions, Hours, Judgments, and Prayers of Love produced by the writers of the court of Juan II.[14] The vein was not exhausted under Ferdinand and Isabella: Diego San Pedro wrote the *Cárcel de amor* (*Prison of Love*) and a short treatise debating this delicate point: Who suffers more than the lover who beholds death robbing him of his mistress, or more than the lover who serves without hope a beloved mistress?[15] Here we are led back into the ways of love.

Other prose writers treated of graver subjects. Alonso Ortiz, Canon of Toledo, wrote a *Treatise of Consolation* for the Infanta Isabella, daughter of the Catholic Kings, who had just lost her husband. This learned courtier also addressed to Ferdinand and Isabella, after the fall of Granada, a congratulatory discourse in which

a most ardent and exclusive patriotism sometimes found expression in a true eloquence. Another ecclesiastic, Diego de Almela, composed a *Valerio de las escolásticas y de España* (1487), a moralistic work in which examples drawn from antiquity were coupled with the great deeds of national history.[16] Where deeds supply a solid basis for thought, the style rises as if sustained by its matter.

That is why chroniclers are among the best prose writers of the time. Diego de Valera, who was born in Cuenca in 1412 and held responsible posts at the court of Juan II, published under that sovereign and under the Catholic Sovereigns some works, such as the *Tratado de las armas* and the *Ceremonial of Princes,* in which he showed a profound acquaintance with the past.[17] His letters are very precious for the history of the time. Diego Enríquez del Castillo and Alfonso de Palencia told of the acts of Enrique IV from opposite points of view.

Two chroniclers treated the reign of Ferdinand and Isabella. One was Andrés Bernáldez, better known as the Curate of Palacios, who was secretary of the Grand Inquisitor Deza and shared his intolerance. His hatred for Jews and Moors, his cruelty, go hand in hand with a great goodness. This very contradiction throws a strange light on the Spanish mentality of the fifteenth century. Bernáldez' chronicle is especially rich in events that concern Andalusia. It was probably during his stay in Seville that the Curate of Palacios made the acquaintance of Columbus. He devotes to him four chapters containing intimate details of great interest for the biography of the illustrious navigator.

By all these chroniclers the story is unfolded year by year. The most notable of them all, Hernando del Pulgar, also followed this somewhat dry annalistic method. A man of action first and foremost, Hernando del Pulgar was a writer only during his leisure hours. As secretary and counselor of the Catholic Sovereigns, he was dispatched to the court of Louis XI to negotiate the retrocession of Roussillon and Cerdaña. During the struggle between Portugal and Castile he took up his pen several times to rebuke the rebel archbishop, Alfonso de Carrillo, or to recall the Portuguese monarch to respect for treaties. His experience in public business gave him special qualifications for the role of historian. Taking for his model a work written by Fernán Pérez de Guzmán, who died about 1460, he wrote a series of biographies in which he drew with a sure hand portraits of the Admiral, Don Fadrique Enríquez, the Count of Haro, the Marquis of Santillana, and Alfonso de Carrillo.[18] He may have flattered his subjects a bit.

Pulgar's masterpiece is the *Crónica de los reyes católicos*. He seems to me to be much superior to his forerunners. His discourses, of which Ticknor speaks with some scorn, are by no means second-rate; they have a good deal of interest for the reader who will take the trouble to disentangle the truth of Pulgar's observations and reflections from their conventional form. As a statesman, Hernando del Pulgar delights in detailing the organization of the public powers; he tells of negotiations, the conduct of wars, legislative reforms, and the Cortes, information that one seeks in vain in other works, notably in his abbreviator, Antonio de Nebrija, who probably judged these facts unworthy of the majesty of history. Ticknor acknowledges that his "style is dignified," but says that it is a historical style and not that of the chronicle.[19] He deserves to be complimented rather than reproached on this account. Certain of Pulgar's discourses show that this statesman was aware of the political and social transformations of his time, transformations that escaped the eye of less attentive or perspicacious observers.

It is to be regretted that the *Crónica* covers only nineteen years of the reign. This was not the fault of the author, who died in 1491 or 1492. He has sometimes been confused with a writer of the same name, Hernando Pérez del Pulgar, who about 1526 wrote the *Hazañas de Gonzalo de Córdoba*, a rough and vigorous sketch of the life of the Great Captain. Hernando del Pulgar, last of the annalists, foreshadows Diego Hurtado de Mendoza, the historian of the revolt of Granada.[20]

New influences hastened the passing of the Middle Ages and stimulated the intellectual development of Christendom. This general progress, which found expression in all the manifestations of human genius, had the cultivation of ancient letters for its instrument. The study of Greek and Roman civilization fertilized all the branches of learning. In the school of the Greek and Roman masters the world learned to think and feel; the human spirit gained in penetration, extent, and force what it perhaps lost in naïveté and freshness. Italy had never completely forgotten its traditions and the incomparable models offered by its past. The Middle Ages were at their height when Dante, the great Florentine, was nourished on the reading of the ancients. The fall of Constantinople in 1453 and the emigration of Byzantine scholars added to the lessons of the Latins the immeasurably richer teaching of Greek literature.

Spain, in constant communication with Italy, followed its example from afar. Although results did not always correspond to efforts, a generous passion impelled the peoples of the Peninsula to multiply their centers of study. The University of Salamanca, so celebrated in the Middle Ages, and that of Valladolid, no longer sufficed to meet the general needs. The Archbishop Don Alonso de Fonseca at Compostela (1462), the Archdeacon of Almazán, Juan López de Medina, at Sigüenza (1471), and Don Francisco Álvarez at Toledo (1490) founded colleges that were genuine universities, although they did not receive this title until the next century.

Even at Salamanca and Valladolid the generous piety of illustrious ecclesiastical patrons established, by the side of the old university, *colegios* where students led a monastic life, working and praying together. Where ordinary students returned from their classes to the independence and often to the dissipation and disorders of worldly life, these houses were so many seminaries, as it were, closed to the temptations of freedom.[21] Don Diego Anaya de Maldonado had founded at the beginning of the fifteenth century the Colegio de San Bartolomé, surnamed the Old, at Salamanca. In 1492 the last stone was placed in the great Colegio de Santa Cruz, built by Cardinal Mendoza at Valladolid. When Jiménez created the center of Alcalá de Henares (1508), he united the two systems and founded a college-university from which he banished the study of civil law, placing on the first plane the teaching of the Sacred Scriptures, but not neglecting grammar, philosophy, and medicine, which were provided with master's chairs.

Whereas in Castile it was the Church that endowed the universities with their revenues, in Aragón the development of higher studies was indebted only to the crown and the towns. In this kingdom, Lérida held the place that Salamanca occupied in Castile. Huesca, which had flourished initially, suffered an eclipse at the beginning of the fifteenth century; but it regained its pristine brilliance under Don Juan II, father of Ferdinand. Valencia certainly went through the same phases of greatness and decadence, since a bull of Alexander VI re-established there in 1500 a *Studium Generale* whose creation went back to 1412.[22] In the reign of the Catholic Sovereigns other towns increased their educational facilities; in 1507 Barcelona assigned premises to the university whose foundation Alfonso the Magnanimous had decreed. Although Zaragoza did not obtain a university establishment till 1541, beginning in 1474 it had an Arts faculty whose chancellor granted degrees. At Mallorca, the memory of Ramón Lull kept alive the study of the natural sciences.[23]

These facts show that Spain did not lack centers of study, and that the kings, the towns, and, above all, the Church made generous provision for educational needs. But classical studies did not occupy the first place in the numerous universities. At Salamanca, which graduated "jurisconsults, theologians, physicians, doctors of science of every kind," the humanities were probably relegated to the second plane. Lucius Marineus Siculus, in a book that he composed to the glory of Spain, complained that the Spaniards did not possess a disinterested passion for study.[24] Students had barely acquired a light tincture of letters when they hastened to desert the school and exploit their fund of learning as lawyers, judges, or governors. "They do not toil to acquire knowledge," he said, "but with a view to speculation."

If we may believe the humanist Arias Barbosa, the professors were hardly of a quality to inspire a taste for antiquity in their students: "There are barely two or three of us at Salamanca who speak Latin, a larger number speak Spanish, and the rest, jargon." When a man like Antonio de Nebrija, trained in the school of the Italians, proposed to introduce philology, he encountered everywhere the most strenuous resistance. At Valencia he was riddled with mockery by Luis Vives, who, while still almost a child, attacked the reactionary grammarians with his aggressive pen. At Salamanca, where Nebrija taught for some years, the students, called upon to select a professor, preferred one of his worst students to this conscientious teacher. Aside from some illustrious examples, the clergy both high and low was undeniably ignorant. The ecclesiastical aristocracy, drawn from the great families, included some able statesmen, influential counselors, and even some patrons of letters, but talent for preaching was as rare among them as a "white crow." Cardinal Jiménez reproached the universities with neglecting Holy Scripture and theology. It appears that the only study honored in Spain was that of law, because it led to office and fortune. It was the age of the legists.

It is the glory of Isabella that she dreamed of something better than a nation of lawyers. From her father she had inherited a strong intellectual taste; she knew Latin and read Cicero, Seneca, and Livy in their native tongue. Ferdinand had received only an elementary education, but his mind was receptive to ideas.[25] If Spain was not to be regarded as a barbarian people, the Spaniards, like the Italians, must assimilate the culture of antiquity. Neither Aragón, Portugal, nor Castile possessed the instruments of intellectual renovation. "If there is [in Spain] a man well taught and versed in Latin, one may safely affirm that he is not a Spaniard, or that he is a Spaniard raised in Italy from tenderest infancy." So the sovereigns looked for teachers where teachers could be found. Several Italian savants crossed the sea and came to live in Spain. The brothers Antonio and Alessandro Geraldini were charged with the education of the four infantes. Lucius Marineus, a Sicilian, brought up Alonso de Aragón, Ferdinand's bastard. Peter Martyr de Anghera, the last to come, directed the palace school where the queen had Latin, history, and grammar taught to the young pages, children of the greatest houses of Spain. It was to be hoped that an example come from so high would make its influence felt in teaching circles, and that the ancient universities would be honored to add to their traditional courses the glorious complement of the ancient literatures.

These noble efforts were in some measure crowned with success. If we cannot without qualification assign to Spain the glory of Luis Vives, that rival of Erasmus who, though born in Valencia, spent most of his life abroad, it seems only fair to assign to her the credit for works written in Latin by foreigners, since she provided the subject matter. What would Peter Martyr have been without the prodigious events of which he was a spectator as counselor and dependent of the Catholic Sovereigns? His talent would have functioned in a void if the genius of Ferdinand and Isabella had not furnished him with great matter to work upon and polish. From one point of view his *Opus epistolarum* and his *Decades de orbe novo* are as much the work of those great actors as of the writer himself. How much more forcibly and justly does this observation apply to Lucius Marineus Siculus! His letters draw upon day-to-day occurrences and incidents in the literary life of Spain.[26] His major work, *De Rebus memorabilibus Hispaniae,* is a summary of the history and geography of the Peninsula. All the talent of these expatriates was devoted to the glorification of their adopted country.

Beside these Italians stands a Spaniard who had studied in Italy, Antonio Martínez de Cala, better known under the name of Antonio de Nebrija. He was above all a grammarian. His *Decades,* which Hefele declares to be one of the most precious documents for the history of Ferdinand and Isabella, are said by contemporaries to be a free translation into Latin of the chronicle of Hernando del Pulgar.[27] But Nebrija's reputation as an educational reformer remains intact. We must not, however, exaggerate the influence of this Spanish master and compare it to that which a Guillaume Budé, a Muret, a Turnèbe, or a Casaubon exercised in France.

Having cited these celebrated names, we must mention some other talented men: the Portuguese Arias Barbosa, who taught Greek at the University of Salamanca; Lucius Flaminius, who occupied the chair of Latin rhetoric there. A student of Arias Barbosa, the Commander Hernán Núñez de Guzmán, was the true introducer of

Greek studies into Spain. Unfortunately, knowledge of Greek in this country was always limited to a few choice spirits.[28] Some converted Jews, such as Alfonso de Zamora, left a reputation for being profound exegetes and able Hebraists.

A Greek, Demetrius Ducas of Crete, came to Alcalá at the request of Jiménez. Pedro Ciruelo, who taught mathematics there, was called to the University of Paris because of his fame for knowledge.

Philology had some loyal disciples. Erasmus praised Complutum, or Alcalá de Henares, for making its name renowned by the teaching of languages. His allusion was to the project, set in motion by Jiménez, for publishing a polyglot Bible. Three *confesos,* Alfonso, physician of Alcalá, Pablo Coronell of Segovia, and Alfonso of Zamora, were charged with establishing the Hebraic text; Demetrius Ducas of Crete, López de Zúñiga, and Hernán Núñez de Guzmán worked on the Greek text; the badly garbled Vulgate was also in need of revision. These scholars had to collate the manuscripts to find the best text among a multitude of variants.

A collaborative work which dealt with both the Old and the New Testament, it had no model. Despite the difficulties of the task, the New Testament, forming the first part of the Polyglot, appeared in 1514. It was a grandiose work, worthy of the genius who conceived it. However, it raises a good many questions. The most enthusiastic of its panegyrists, the German historian Hefele, does not hide his serious misgivings.[29] The critical remarks of the linguists of Alcalá were limited to four remarks. They never indicate the variants; they do not say who are their authorities for the single text offered to the reader. One must take their word for it when they affirm that they used the most ancient and correct manuscripts (*antiquissima et emendatissima*). Although it is true that Leo X sent them Greek manuscripts from the Vatican, we must note that this Pope was elected March 11, 1513, and that the first part of the Polyglot was printed January 10, 1514. How could a serious effort at collation have been made between these two dates? "The text," says Hefele, "conforms throughout to the most recent manuscripts, whenever these disagree with the older ones, almost never giving preference to the older versions." [30] If we would be just, we must measure the merits of the enterprise, not by its results, but by its novelty and boldness. Spain, in any case, has the honor of having published the first polyglot Bible.

These labors, encouraged by Cardinal Jiménez, and the protection accorded to scholars by Ferdinand and Isabella, created a very strong movement of opinion in favor of ancient letters. The greatest lords had received a classical education in the school of the Italians; some did not scorn to appear in university chairs. Spain even possessed some distinguished women who added to the brilliance of birth or beauty the charm of a superior education. Some of them were even admitted to the schools: Doña Lucia de Medrano lectured at Salamanca on the classics of the Augustan Age; and the aged Nebrija, that Nestor of grammarians, as Erasmus called him, saw the honor of Alcalá de Henares reborn in his daughter Doña Francisca de Nebrija.

Unfortunately, these noble aspirations and generous enthusiasms were confined to a small elite. Spain did not enter as profoundly as France and Germany into the study of ancient letters. The compliments of Erasmus, on which some Spaniards preen themselves, are very flattering, but they are only compliments. Whoever reads attentively his letter to Francisco Vergara and his letter to Juan Vergara will perceive that this ancestor of Voltaire merely reproduces in the form of a eulogy the information that Juan Vergara had just sent him. "With what joy," he writes Juan Vergara, "did I read in your letter that languages and belles lettres are progressing in Spain, once the fecund mother of illustrious spirits." Erasmus's true thought emerges in a letter to a certain Nicolás, a poet and probably an imitator of Pindar. "I exhort, I urge you to continue your course toward the goal that you have fixed, and to restore the ancient glory of your Spain." After some comment on the elegance of Pindar, he adds: "It will be all the easier for you to revive those virtues of wit, of knowledge, of eloquence, wherein Spain was not at all inferior to Italy, and to make disappear the solecisms produced by the invasion of the Goths and the Saracens." These counsels prove that the writer appreciated the efforts of individuals and of the nation, but let it be known that they were still far from their goal.

All things considered, Spain had no cause for dissatisfaction. If, in these times, she produced no scholar comparable to the great savants of France and Germany, a Joseph Justus Scaliger or a Henri Estienne, for example, that was no reason for Spaniards to feel chagrin or for foreigners to exult. There are two ways of studying the ancients. One can study the ancients themselves and sometimes by an excess of erudition destroy one's native originality. In such case their influence does not reach beyond the bounds of academe. Surely it is better to take them as teachers and spiritual guides. These old books diffuse, as it were, a fecund dust into the air. It was in this beneficial way that the ancient letters exercised their influence in Spain. They cleansed tastes, revived benumbed minds, offered perfect models for the imitation of writers. The stimulus of the ancients was felt in all directions. They renovated history; for the chronicle would soon give way to works like the *Guerra de*

Granada of Diego Hurtado de Mendoza. The drama was born, developed, and found its tongue. Great poetry was about to be written. The novel appeared under a double aspect, realist and idealist, but definitely superior in the presentation of reality.

II

The Fine Arts

The close of the Gothic period and new beginnings in painting were the salient artistic events of the reign of Ferdinand and Isabella. During the half-century that the royal pair occupied the throne, medieval styles in architecture and sculpture were blended with Renaissance orders. Spanish artists tried to reconcile old traditions with national tastes and with the spirit of innovation. Painters, hitherto slaves to Flemish and Italian influences, produced some primitives that are worthy of being placed beside the masters. Although these achievements were only a beginning, they gave promise of a true national school. The Gothic style in architecture was about to disappear, but its last exponents produced a multitude of masterpieces as the supreme manifestation of its greatness.

The Catholic Sovereigns loved to build. Although very economical, they were ready to spend lavishly in a good cause. Using the plans of Anton de Egas and Alfonso Rodríguez, Juan Gil de Hontañón began the new Cathedral of Salamanca. The Cathedral of Segovia was built on the same model. The completion of the great religious structures that required the labors of several centuries was also pressed; such work of the ages were finished at Burgos and Seville. The Carthusian Convent of Miraflores, begun under Enrique III (1441), was finished in 1488 by Simon of Cologne. To celebrate the happy issue of the war with Portugal, Ferdinand and Isabella charged Juan Guas with the construction of the church of San Juan de los Reyes at Toledo. They enlarged and beautified the Hospital de Santa Cruz in Toledo, opened in 1494 as a home for foundling children.[1]

The aristocracy and the church followed their example. Cardinal Mendoza entrusted to Enrique de Egas the construction of the superb Colegio de Santa Cruz (1494) at Valladolid, while Alonso de Cartagena, Bishop of Burgos, raised in that town the Dominican Colegio de San Gregorio (1488). Jiménez enlarged the proportions of the *capilla mayor* of the Cathedral of Toledo. The Velascos ornamented Burgos with two monuments of unequal value: the *capilla del Condestable,* their tomb in the cathedral, and the Casa del Cordón, which served as their palace. Design in civil architecture attained perfection with some of the first efforts. The Exchange of Valencia (Casa Lonja), begun about 1482, is a marvel of lightness and elegance.

These structures are in the pointed or Gothic style, but in the decoration new tendencies already appear. The architect Enrique de Egas, whose talent beautified Valladolid and Toledo, boldly inaugurated the style of the future. Spain, proud of its triumphs, placed the seal of its good fortune and power on the fronts of its palaces. Whereas the churches bore the severe stamp of the past, other monuments of the same epoch astound us by the richness of their ornamentation. The artists gave their imagination completely free rein, mingling arabesques, flowers, and foliages with inspirations of the classical Renaissance. All parts of the stone are worked or chiseled like a piece of jewelry, whence the name Plateresque style, used to designate this exuberance of fantasy and ornamentation.

The façade of the Hospital de Santa Cruz offers one of the first examples of an alliance between the new forms and the traditions of Gothic art. "The portal consists of a double semicircular arch supported on each side by two baluster columns. The intercolumniation and the archivolt are ornamented with a series of statuettes on *dais*, reminiscent of the Gothic style, and this style reappears in the bas-relief of the tympanum of the arch; it represents Cardinal Mendoza, founder of the hospital, adoring the Cross and attended by St. Peter and St. Paul. Above the arch, a second element is occupied by another sculptured group representing the Visitation. Two pierced windows at the level of this second element are flanked, like the portal, by baluster columns supporting a semicircular arch surmounted with a triangular fronton." [2] The portal, as well as the two pierced windows, displays richly sculptured candelabra. The artist seems to have risked an effect of heaviness and encumberment in order to prove the wealth of his invention.

The Colegios of San Gregorio and Santa Cruz reveal still better this curious mixture of different elements. "The Renaissance is more evident in the brilliant decoration of the arcades than in any particular detail." On the other hand, "the torso columns and the fantastic crests, the division of the arcades by interior dwarf columns, the archivolt displaying dense garlands of foliage and cordons of fruit, the exuberant and overflowing ornamentation—all this forms a fantastic amalgam of the Christian and Moorish Middle Ages." [3] However, many structures preserve their homogeneity. Even the façade of San Gregorio is as Gothic as the cloister of San Juan de los Reyes. The Plateresque style triumphed under the successors of the Catholic Sovereigns, but in their time it was still in its infancy; its pretensions were modest, and it claimed for itself, as a rule, only the façades and the patios.

Sculptors, like the architects, were no longer content with simplicity; for the serene impression of great lines, they substituted the dazzling effect of a thousand details. To the artist nothing was secondary; everything was treated with the greatest care. The modeling of cloth held no secret for these sculptors; all the richness, all the refinements of costume were reproduced in the stone, and the daring of the artisan was such that he might add to the caprices of style the fantasies and dreams of his own imagination. Alabaster and marble were pierced in open work like lace, fashioned and made soft like silk and velvet. This sumptuous art was at its height in the mausoleums that members of great families erected out of love or vanity. Its design displayed there all the brilliance, invention, and superfluous luxury of the flamboyant Gothic.

To be sure, at the portals of churches[4] we find evidence of a more sober spirit, but the majority of the tombs and effigies and funeral cortèges exhibit an astounding magnificence. Gil de Siloe is the most illustrious representative of this school. We owe to him the superb mausoleum that Isabella raised in the Carthusian Convent of Miraflores for Don Juan her father, her mother Isabella, and her brother the Infante Don Alfonso. The effigy of Don Juan II ranks above the others. The costume of the dead king is of an unheard-of richness. The technical perfection of the bas-reliefs and the great number of scenes represented therein recall the tombs of the Dukes of Burgundy.[5] "These works," said the archaeologist Carderera, "although less notable than those of the preceding period as regards good taste, arouse admiration by the magnificence of the decoration and by the great delicacy of the carving." [6] He attributes to the same sculptor the effigy of a youth, Don Juan de Padilla, killed in 1491 in battle against the Moors. The artist lavished marvels of elegance and richness on the showy robe in which he dressed the young hero. The tomb of Don Alonso de Cartagena, Bishop of Burgos (built in 1450), reveals the same qualities. "Nothing could be more sumptuous or finer than the pontifical habits of the prelate." The chasuble represents "Gothic arcades with exquisitely detailed *dais*." [7]

The mausoleum of Álvaro de Luna in the Cathedral of Toledo is by another artist, Pablo Ortiz, who executed it in 1489. It represents the constable couched, covered with the capitulary mantle. His face, somewhat severe, is full of life. Another grand master of Santiago, Don Juan Pacheco, Marquis of Villena, reposes in the monastery of El Parral near Segovia. The work is by Sebastián de Almonacid or by Jorge de Contreras; it shows Pacheco on his knees, armed from head to foot. His marble cuirass is a model of delicate carving.

We do not know for certain to whom we should attribute the tomb of Count Íñigo López de Mendoza and his wife in the church of San Ginés in Guadalajara. The angels that were so characteristic of the monuments of the preceding period here give place to a page seated at the feet of the count, to a serving woman seated at the feet of his wife. None of these productions of Spanish art suffers by comparison with the works of contemporary Italian artists, already touched by the breath of the Renaissance.

The mausoleum of Ferdinand and Isabella in the royal chapel of the Cathedral of Granada was probably erected by foreign hands. "The base, placed above a plinth of black marble, is ornamented with flowerwork, with foliage, and supports a series of small columns between which

are niches with statues in half relief of the twelve apostles. At the four angles are sphinxes with eagles' heads
and lions' legs, and above them four lovely statues of
doctors of the Church, some seated and meditating,
others writing at the feet of the sovereigns. The two royal
effigies, executed with great art, are couched on the
sarcophagus on rich tapis and cushions of velvet. Ferdinand V is clad in armor; the royal mantle is over his
shoulders, the crown on his head; he holds his sword in
his hands. Isabella also wears her crown, is dressed in
court garments, and holds her scepter. Two lions are
couched at their feet and seem to be watching over their

slumber." [8] Another Italian, Domenico di Alessandro Fancelli, executed at the Monastery of Santo Tomás de Ávila the tomb of the son of the Catholic Sovereigns, a less sumptuous work but of more perfect composition.[9]

Alabaster and marble were not the only materials on which the sculptors of that period stamped the mark of their talent. In their skillful hands, wood, that intractable material, lent itself to the rendering of the forms, contours, and images of things, and even to the expression of life. Perhaps the Spaniards borrowed from the Germans the idea of constructing those enormous wooden *retablos* decorated with painting, with polychrome statues, with bas-reliefs, such as the superb edifice erected by Bernardo Ortega and Maestre Dancart on the high altar of the Cathedral of Seville (1482 to 1497);[10] certainly the Arabs, and the Spaniards after them, knew how to use wood for purposes of ornamentation.[11] The art of the *entalladores* blossomed at the end of the fifteenth century in the choir stalls (*sillerías de coro*) that are the ornament of Spanish churches. Dancart worked with Nufro Sánchez on the stalls of the Cathedral of Seville; Francisco Gomar decorated the choir of Tarragona.

But the prince of sculptors in wood was that Philippe Vigarni whom the Spaniards call Felipe de Borgoña. He was born in Langres, on the confines of the Burgundian land, but lived in Castile. Equally skillful in carving marble and wood, he had no rival before Alonso Berruguete returned from Italy. He was the head of a school; he directed the work of numerous pupils. In 1505, he was at Palencia, where the canons entrusted him with the execution of the choir stalls and inserted in the contract the curious clause "that the heads and hands shall be done by his own hand, in smooth walnut and without painting." At Granada, Vigarni did the great *retablo* of the royal chapel, whose bas-reliefs in sculptured and painted wood represent the surrender of Granada and the baptism of the Moors.[12] His masterpiece is regarded as being the *sillería de coro* of Burgos, the loveliest stalls in Spain.[13] He worked there from 1507 to 1513. With his rival Berruguete, he later did in the Cathedral of Toledo those "three ranks of stalls in wood, sculptured, detailed, carved out in a marvelous manner," that elicited from Théophile Gautier a cry of admiration. Alonso Berruguete had spent many years in Italy in extended and rich association with the Italian masters, and on his return to Spain represented another generation.

These great artists produced sculptures that will never be equaled. Their art can be renewed, transformed; it cannot be surpassed. We cannot say the same of painting,[14] which was barely in its infancy, and which steered an uncertain course between Flemish and Italian art. These two influences mingled and crossed on Spanish soil. The lands of the crown of Aragón had been in more intimate communication with Italy, and Castile had greater opportunity to assimilate the Gothic style of the North; however, Luis Dalmau, the Catalan painter, composed his famous tableau the *Virgin of the Counselors,* in the Flemish style, after Van Eyck, whereas Antonio del Rincón,[15] founder of the Toledo School, was certainly a student and disciple of the Italians. If Roger van der Weyden and Petrus Christus (Peter Christophsen) furnished the Spanish churches with numerous masterpieces, many Italians, like Gherardo Starnina in the fourteenth century and the painter-sculptor Dello Delli, established schools on Spanish soil. Therefore it is not always easy to distinguish the sources of inspiration, to establish the precise contribution made to Spanish painting by the masters of the two countries.

Even as she imitated, Spain asserted her originality,

now in technical procedures, now in tendency. Charles Blanc has admirably defined the great Spanish art that begins toward the end of the fifteenth century "as devoted to religious ideas as it is faithful to the realities of nature; Catholic and colorist." This painting is essentially sacred painting; the convents and churches absorb almost the totality of the work of the sixteenth century. In all times, the Spaniards have excelled in expressing religious emotion and in giving their devotional tableaux a profound pathos.

This unconscious aptitude already appears in the illuminators, the remote ancestors of the painters. Without going back to the manuscripts of the tenth and eleventh centuries, or even to the Bible of the thirteenth century painted by Pedro de Pamplona for Alfonso the Sage, there are in the Escorial, and in Madrid and Seville, miniatures on parchment that are reminiscent of the school of Van Eyck or the Italian schools, though the whole has an entirely Spanish character. The *Pontifical* of Alonso de Fonseca, Archbishop of Seville, who died in 1473, the missal of Cardinal Mendoza, who died in 1495, and the two Books of Hours of Isabella, to be seen in the Escorial, are particularly interesting.

At this time painters began to enlarge their horizons; artists began to try their hand at painting in distemper on coarse cloth called *sargas,* until Luis de Vargas (1502 to 1568), a disciple of the Italians, introduced the more sophisticated procedure of painting in fresco and in oil.[16]

The artistic movement started in certain favored centers where students gathered about foreign or native masters, and where schools arose. In Valencia, which like other provinces of Aragón had a more precocious development than Castile, two Italians, Francesco Neapoli and Paolo Aregio, painted the *retablo* of the master altar of the Cathedral of Valencia and set a tradition. Seville and Toledo also had their established painters, but it is probably impossible to distinguish the methods and style of each group. The majority of the paintings of the primitives have disappeared; the works that have survived have not yet been studied closely enough to permit a strict classification.[17] We are frequently reduced to listing a few names. In 1498, Juan of Segovia, Pedro de Gumiel, and Sancho of Zamora painted in the chapel of Santiago, in the Cathedral of Toledo, the fourteen figures on a background of gold that surround the equestrian statue of the Apostle of Compostela.[18] Pedro of Córdoba did an *Annunciation* for the Cathedral of Córdoba. These painters are less celebrated than Fernando Gallego, who has left a *Decapitation of St. John the Baptist*[19] (Museum of the Prado), a *Madonna between St. Christopher and St. Andrew* in the Clementine Chapel of the Cathedral of Salamanca, and a *retablo,* which is regarded as his masterpiece, in the Cathedral of Zamora.

Of Antonio del Rincón[20] nothing authentic remains except his reputation. He was the favorite painter of the Catholic Sovereigns.[21] He had studied in Italy under Andrea del Castagno or Domenico Ghirlandajo. Carderera attributes to him a painting representing the royal family that he was commissioned to do by Torquemada. Pedro Berruguete, father of Alonso Berruguete, also enjoyed great renown. He died in 1500. He worked with Santa Cruz and Juan de Borgoña on the great *retablo* of the main altar of the Cathedral of Ávila. The ten principal panels represent scenes from the life of Christ. The Flagellation, the Resurrection, the limbs of the figures, are by Pedro Berruguete.[22]

The school of Seville especially distinguished itself in the period. Of Juan Sánchez de Castro, its founder, who lived in the second half of the fifteenth century, there remains a colossal *St. Christopher* bearing forty pilgrims suspended at his belt (1484). Juan Sánchez, like other painters of his time, commits singular anachronisms: "He paints," says M. de Latour, "the Virgin with spectacles, St. Gabriel with a chasuble." He knows nothing of perspective, of the arrangements of groups. His figures have no expression; from the mouths of his personages issues a streamer on which is written the thoughts that the faces of these personages are incapable of rendering. His pupil Juan Núñez, who flourished about 1500, is not subject to these reproaches. His *Pietà* or *Descent from the Cross* (in the Sacristía de los Cálices in the Cathedral of Seville), although cold and dull, evidences a certain talent for arrangement.

Núñez, however, is not the equal of Alejo Fernández, who broke with the hieratic coldness of the Byzantine models. The arms of his figures have mobility, their eyes are animated. The saints retain their golden halos, but they have life and movement.[23] His principal works are in the Cathedral of Seville; the most remarkable ones are the *Adoration of the Kings* and the *Purification of the Virgin*. Another work attributed to him is a picture of St. Anne in the church of that name, at Seville. St. Anne, dressed in a splendid robe of gold brocade, is seated on a throne. She holds a rose in her hand. Angels prostrate themselves before the child Mary. The luxury of the material reminds one of Flemish paintings, but the style of the heads, says Woltmann, suggests northern Italy rather than Florentine models.[24]

In addition to these native artists, a foreigner, Juan de Borgoña (flor. 1495 to 1523), like his compatriot Vigarni, made a large contribution to the progress of Spanish art. He was a good colorist, whose frescos in the Sala Capitular in the Cathedral of Toledo, undertaken on the orders of Jiménez, are much admired. Juan de Borgoña also worked on the decoration of the University of Alcalá de Henares; there he painted a part of the *paraninfo,* the great amphitheater in which degrees were conferred. The works of Juan de Borgoña are among the loveliest of the beginning of the sixteenth century.

Foreigners or natives, all these artists contributed to giving the reign of Ferdinand and Isabella that brilliance which is a fitting complement to power and glory. The union of Aragón and Castile, the conquest of Granada, a policy as fortunate at home as abroad, inspired in Spaniards a just pride in the national genius and spurred them to seek excellence in every sphere of artistic activity. This confidence in the capacity of the sovereigns and in the future of the nation underlay all strivings, animated all talents.

It is from this point of view, above all, that the Catholic Sovereigns were the Maecenases of the art of the past and of the future. Their strong government, succeeding centuries of anarchy, allowed agitation only of that fertile kind in which minds commune with and stimulate each other. Furthermore, they did not neglect the important and rewarding task of protecting creative talent in the person of the artist. The Cartuja of Miraflores, with its superb mausoleums, testifies to Isabella's happy aptitude for employing, in the glorification of filial piety, the most skillful hands, the finest, most patient, most delicate carvers. Ferdinand, although untaught, had a very genuine sensitivity to artistic beauty. He was the protector of painters. He brought to Castile and heaped favors on the Aragonese Pedro de Aponte; he made Antonio del Rincón a knight of Santiago. With these acts he placed talent and birth on an equal footing.

Conclusion

Conclusion

The reign of Ferdinand and Isabella may be summed up in a few words. These sovereigns wielded very great power, and they used that power for the greatest possible good of the Spanish people. In their hands sovereign authority was an instrument of progress and prosperity. Influence without, peace within, were the first fruits of absolute monarchy.

Absolute monarchy! Theirs is the honor and the responsibility of its creation. When they succeeded Enrique IV, anarchy reigned everywhere, not only in central Spain but in all parts of the country. The crown, weakened by the incapacity of their predecessor, at the mercy of factions, had neither the means nor the servants required for its defense. The provinces, thrown back into their old isolation, were the prey of brigands and the theater of savage struggles. The government retained its feudal character. Great lords sat in the royal council; the affairs of state, all the relations of the sovereign with his subjects and with foreign countries, were subject to the control of this aristocratic body. Dispensations, favors, diplomas, privileges, bore the signatures of the heads of the nobility together with that of the king. Nothing was done without their consent and participation.

These dubious if not hostile collaborators Ferdinand and Isabella replaced with agents drawn from the middle class, men without a past and without attachments, necessarily devoted to their master. In the royal council, or council of justice, which dominated the whole administration, influence and numerical preponderance passed to the legists. The lords and prelates continued to have seats in the body; but the dispatch of business, the work of deliberation and decision, was reserved to the ordinary councilors, that is to say, the men of law. To bar all interference with their actions, the sovereigns took away from the *ricos homes* and assigned to a corps of functionaries the confirmation of all diplomas.

The great crown offices were reduced to the status of honorific dignities, used by their owners merely to make a show at court. The Almirante of Castile, who had had command of all naval forces, was reduced by the capitulations of Sante Fe with Columbus, and by royal usurpations, to the status of an unemployed seaman. The Condestable of Castile played no part at all in the Italian Wars. Men of merit chosen by the sovereigns won battles, conquered kingdoms and empires, administered provinces and towns. The ancient dignitaries were surrounded with respect, heaped with honors, invited to all the festivities; they played brilliant parts in the comedy of monarchical prestige, but in the last analysis they had nothing but titles and some satisfactions in the way of vanity or money.

The royal power grew on the ruins of special privilege. The Roman Curia had to yield its supremacy in the disposal of large and small benefices in the Spanish Church. By a mixture of firmness and diplomacy, Ferdinand and Isabella obtained a right of petition which amounted to a right of designation of their candidates (1482). Now they could select the bishops. Isabella displayed such zeal in searching for the worthiest candidates, not in the aristocracy, but in the cloistered orders, that more than once she drew a refusal from these solitary and saintly figures and had to appeal to the Pope for help in overcoming their scruples, as rare as they were admirable. The new clergy was more moral, more learned, more patriotic, and less independent than the old one. The Inquisition placed the civil power at the service of orthodoxy and the fanaticism of the Spanish clergy at the service of Spanish nationality. Church and state worked hand-in-hand on a project that concerned both the future of the nation and the purity of its faith.

The crown sought to assure its preponderance everywhere. The cities and towns were surrounded by vast territories which they administered and over which they exercised undisputed sway. With the pretext of safeguarding order in the towns, the Catholic Sovereigns placed royal officers at their heads and reduced them to a condition of tutelage. The sovereigns even claimed the right to name their magistrates. In certain places the municipal offices became life tenures, and the crown arrogated to itself the right of filling each vacancy. The towns which retained free elections were forbidden to choose their *regidores* from among the most powerful lords; thereby the municipalities were detached from the patronage of the grandees as well as deprived of the free initiative and impulses of communal autonomy, so that they were absolutely subject to the action of the central government.

Wherever the crown sensed resistance, it sought means of breaking it. It even took precautions against its own agents. It suppressed venality and inheritability of office, which protected magistrates; it held over the heads of its *corregidores* the threat of frequent investigation and accusation by the people.

THE FOUR INHERITANCES
OF CHARLES V

Inheritance from his paternal grandfather Maximilian of Austria

Inheritance from his paternal grandmother Marie of Burgundy

Inheritance from his maternal grandfather Ferdinand of Aragón

Inheritance from his maternal grandmother Isabella of Castile

KINGDOM OF DENMARK

LÜBECK

HAMBURG

BREMEN

BRANDENBURG

MAGDEBURG

BERLIN

Elbe

Oder

KINGDOM OF POLAND

THE

LEIPZIG

MÜHLBERG

LUSATIA

DRESDEN

BRESLAU

COLOGNE

ERFURT

SAXONY

SILESIA

River

MAINZ

WORMS

NUREMBERG

PRAGUE

BOHEMIA

METZ

LORRAINE

EMPIRE

RATISBON

MORAVIA

River

STRASBOURG

ULM

Danube

PRESBURG

Tisza

River

BASEL

AUGSBURG

BAVARIA

SALZBURG

VIENNA

AUSTRIA

KINGDOM

OF

SWITZERLAND

INNSBRUCK

TYROL

CARINTHIA

STYRIA

HUNGARY

GENEVA

DUCHY

REPUBLIC

CARNIOLA

TRIESTE

Drave

DUCHY OF MILAN

MILAN

PAVIA

OF VENICE

Save

River

Danube

OF SAVOY

Po River

VENICE

BOSNIA

River

River

GENOA

PARMA

BOLOGNA

FLORENCE

ANCONA

SARAJEVO

OTTOMAN EMPIRE

MARSEILLE

STATES

OF THE

CHURCH

ADRIATIC

RAGUSA

CORSICA

ROME

SEA

DURAZZO

KINGDOM

NAPLES

OF

NAPLES

ALBANIA

ALGHERO

SARDINIA

CAGLIARI

CORFU

PREVESA

IONIAN

SEA

PATRAS

MEDITERRANEAN

PALERMO

MESSINA

SICILY

BÔNE

BIZERTE

GOLETTA

ALGERIA

TUNIS

SEA

This concentration of authority, this weakening of provincial and communal life, indicate the tendencies of the new reign. The Catholic Sovereigns advanced toward absolute power; in Castile they achieved their goal. They were as much masters as Charles V and Philip II. If we are deceived concerning the nature and degree of their power, it is because they governed with intelligence, with moderation, with a constant care for the true interests of the country. Their generosity or genius placed limits on the exercise of their omnipotence. But in the last analysis they were the masters.

It must be said in their defense that when they began to reign, Spain needed a strong hand. Many believed, with Pulgar, that all the evils of Castile stemmed from the effacement and impotence of the king. Ferdinand and Isabella could not defer to class privileges or traditions or habits if they wished to repress disorder. For the rest, the civil war had ruined everything: The aristocracy displayed nothing but greed; the clergy was devoid of morality; the municipalities had become battlefields for aristocratic factions; the commune oppressed the countryside; the lords devastated the towns. The monarchy was falling apart at every joint; the Catholic Sovereigns restored it on a new plan, but they proposed to be its absolute owners, without obligations of any kind; they claimed for themselves all the credit and advantage of the restoration.

Could they have established that order without destroying what remained of public liberties? Some generous spirits think so and mingle praise for the internal policy of the sovereigns with certain reservations. One might reproach them with greater reason for having attacked only those abuses which thwarted them. All those which did not stand in the way of their designs they carefully respected. They neither dared nor wished to reform the tax system or abolish the financial exemptions of the clergy and the nobility. They were too sensitive to the abuses that obstructed them and not enough to those that weighed heavily on the people. Despite these just reservations, we must admit that the institutions Ferdinand and Isabella destroyed were either full of decay or of little value, and that their reforms were beneficial to the nation. In place of its liberties it gained peace at home, glory abroad. Absolute monarchy created the conditions for a flowering of Spanish culture. The country came to know economy and honesty in public administration, rapidity in the dispatch of business and justice.

The sovereigns displayed a genuine parsimony in the provision of state services. They were very careful not to create more offices than were needed. Twelve magistrates, says the historian Sempere, assured good order in all of Castile. The strongest measures were taken against corruption. Peace, security on the roads, the suppression of banditry, promoted the growth of public wealth. Commerce and industry prospered; the towns grew rich and beautified themselves. The discovery of America gave a new stimulus to navigation.

A foreign policy that was quite unscrupulous, but ever adroit, rounded out the united kingdoms of Aragón and Castile at the expense of the Moslems of Granada and the Christians of Navarre. From France, the sovereigns obtained Cerdaña and Roussillon; from the same power they wrested Milan and Naples, and established Spanish domination in Italy. To consolidate his conquests Ferdinand married his daughters to Henry VIII of England and to Philip the Handsome, son of Marie of Burgundy and Maximilian of Austria. To prepare the day of a definitive union of all the states of the Spanish Peninsula, the Infanta Isabella married, one after the other, the two heirs presumptive of the crown of Portu-

gal. A series of misfortunes defeated this project but gave the succession of the Catholic Sovereigns to the Archduke Charles, who already possessed the domains of the Houses of Burgundy and Austria. The ruler of Spain was to have sway over half of western Europe.

This unheard-of good fortune probably exceeded Ferdinand's expectations. A ruler of his practical temper was not prone to dreams of universal monarchy. He may have feared that the resources of Castile and Aragón might be employed to support the ambitions of a cosmopolitan monarchy. It would be unjust to reproach him for having subordinated Spanish to Austrian interests. But we may justly express some reservations about his foreign policy. It was too violently anti-French in character; it perceived only a single enemy in Europe, and began a struggle against that enemy which lasted two centuries and ended in disaster for Spain. Ferdinand, animated by Aragonese resentments, drew Isabella into the Italian conflicts and committed his successors to following him down that fatal road. Although he was ever skillful and fortunate in his negotiations and his conquests, the reverses and misfortunes of the seventeenth century had their origin in the tradition of hostility to France that he had created. Those Italian rivalries were a fatal legacy which inevitably engendered many others.

Much the same commentary may be made on the domestic policy of Ferdinand and Isabella. The Hapsburg despotism was nothing more than the development of the principles established by the Catholic Sovereigns. We hesitate to censure their usurpations when we consider what great evils they eliminated, what great services they rendered. But so well did they destroy privilege, weaken all classes, and strengthen the crown, that their successors encountered no obstacle, met with no further resistance. But it will not do to let an absolute monarchy fall into incompetent hands. When a man of genius establishes such a monarchy for the advantage of his family, he should be sure of his descendants. The Spain which under Ferdinand and Isabella had known the advantages of personal power soon learned that the omnipotence of kings does not necessarily produce the prosperity of the people.

Notes

Editor's Preface

1 The story is retold by R. B. Merriman, *Rise of the Spanish Empire* (New York, 4 vols., 1918-1934), III, 189.
2 The quotations from Quevedo, Gracián, and Clemencín are taken from Américo Castro, *The Structure of Spanish History*, tr. by E. L. King (Princeton, New Jersey, 1954), pp. 299-300.
3 William H. Prescott, *History of the Reign of Ferdinand and Isabella the Catholic* (10th ed., New York, 3 vols., 1851), I, 248 n.
4 Ramón Ménendez Pidal, *Los Reyes católicos según Maquiavelo y Castiglione* (Madrid, 1952), pp. 60-61.
5 See, for example, L. B. Wright, *Middle-Class Culture in Elizabethan England* (Chapel Hill, North Carolina, 1935); A. L. Rowse, *The England of Elizabeth* (New York, 1951); Wallace Notestein, *The English People on the Eve of Colonization, 1603-1630* (New York, 1954); Allardyce Nicoll, *The Elizabethans* (Cambridge University Press, 1957); Lu Emily Pearson, *Elizabethans at Home* (Stanford University Press, 1957).
6 Mariéjol, born at Antibes in 1855, taught at the Universities of Lyon and Paris and wrote widely in the fields of French and Spanish history. In addition to the present book, he is the author of a standard work on *Pierre Martyr d'Anghera* (Paris, 1887), and of lives of Catherine de Medici, Marguerite de Valois, and Philip II of Spain.
7 G. M. Dutcher and others, eds., *A Guide to Historical Literature* (New York, 1931), p. 655.
8 *Rise of the Spanish Empire*, II, 8.
9 *History of the Reign of Ferdinand and Isabella*, I, 66.
10 *Ensayo biológico sobre Enrique IV de Castilla y su tiempo* (Madrid, 1930).
11 Ferrara, *L'Avènement d' Isabelle la Catholique*, p. 286.
12 Ferrara, *L'Avènement*, p. 32.

[13] *History of the Inquisition of Spain* (New York, 4 vols., 1906-1907), I, 55 ff.

[14] Manuel Jorge Aragoneses, "Los Movimientos sociales en la baja edad media," *Estudios de historia social de España*, I (Madrid, 1949), pp. 275-423.

[15] Lea, *History of the Inquisition*, I, 131-132.

[16] Lea, *History of the Inquisition*, I, 135.

[17] "The Decline of Spain," *Economic History Review*, VIII (1938), 168-179.

[18] The distinguished Spanish historian Jaime Vicens Vives has neatly summarized the economic consequences of the Inquisition. "The first great Spanish purge . . . eliminated from social life the only groups in Castile that could have received the impulse of dawning capitalism, undermined the basis of the prosperity of many towns, and mobilized an enormous quantity of wealth, a large part of which was applied to the financing of the foreign policy of the Catholic Sovereigns, while another part was dissipated in the hands of the aristocracy." *Aproximación a la historia de España* (Barcelona, 1952), p. 111.

[19] Jaime Vicens Vives, *Manual de historia económica de España* (Barcelona, 1959), p. 277.

[20] J. M. Batista i Roca, "The Hispanic Kingdoms and the Catholic Kings," in *The New Cambridge Modern History* (Cambridge University Press, 2 vols., 1957), I, 338.

[21] In my survey of the economic policies of the Catholic Sovereigns I have been chiefly guided by two recent works of synthesis, Jaime Vicens Vives, *Manual de historia económica de España* (Barcelona, 1959); and Santiago Sobrequés Vidal, "La Época de los reyes católicos," in Jaime Vicens Vives, ed., *Historia social y económica de España y América* (Barcelona, 3 vols., 1957), II, 408-492.

[22] Julius Klein, *The Mesta: A Study in Spanish Economic History* (Cambridge, Massachusetts, 1920), pp. 321-322.

Introduction

[1] [The Cortes of Lamego, supposed to have been held by Affonso Henriques, is now regarded as a fiction. See H. V. Livermore, *A History of Portugal* (Cambridge, England, 1947), p. 138 n. Ed.]

[2] [A great code of law combined with moral maxims and reflections, in seven parts or sections, compiled between 1256 and 1265 by a number of jurists at the direction of Alfonso the Sage, and promulgated in 1348 by Alfonso XI as the law of Castile. Ed.]

[3] [A special judge in Aragón, appointed by the king, who had jurisdiction over cases involving violation of privileges by any person or complaints against officials for violation of the law. For an extended discussion of the office of *justicia*, see Part II, Chapter V. Ed.]

Part I. THE REIGN OF FERDINAND AND ISABELLA

1. The End of Anarchy

1 Letter of Hernando del Pulgar to the Bishop of Coria, dated 1473, in *Epistolario español* (Madrid, 2 vols.; Vol. 13, 1850), and Vol. 62, 1870, of the *Biblioteca de Autores Españoles**, I, 56.

2 Hernando del Pulgar, *Crónica de los señores reyes católicos* (BAE, Vol. 70, pp. 225-511, Madrid, 1878), Part II, Ch. xcviii.

3 Pulgar, *Crónica,* Part II, Ch. lxx. Andrés Bernáldez, *Historia de los reyes católicos D. Fernando y D. Isabel* (Seville, 2 vols., 1870), Ch. xxix.

4 Bernáldez, *Historia,* Ch. iv.

5 Pulgar, *Crónica,* Part II, Ch. lxx.

6 Diego Clemencín, *Elogio de la reina doña Isabel,* in *Memorias de la Real Academia de Historia,* Vol. VI (Madrid, 1821), p. 135. Pulgar, *Crónica,* Part II, Ch. li. Lucius Marineus Siculus, *De Rebus Hispaniae Memorabilibus,* in Andreas Schott, Johann Pastorius, and Franciscus Schott, *Hispaniae illustratae, seu rerum urbiumque Hispaniae, Lusitaniae, Aethiopiae, et Indiae scriptores varii* (Frankfurt, 4 vols., 1603-1604), I, 477.

7 Lorenzo Galíndez Carbajal, *Anales breves* (BAE, Vol. 70, pp. 533-565, Madrid, 1878), p. 541, nn. 6 and 9.

8 *Cortes de los antiguos reinos de León y Castilla, publicadas por la Real Academia de la Historia* (Madrid, 5 vols., 1861-1903), IV, 5 ff.

9 Albert Du Boys, *Histoire du droit criminel en Espagne* (Paris, 1870), p. 455.

10 *Los Problemas de Villalobos,* in *Curiosidades bibliográficas* (BAE, Vol. 36, Madrid, 1871), p. 429.

11 Pulgar, *Crónica,* Part III, Ch. xii.

12 Clemencín, *Elogio,* p. 137.

13 The Hermandad was established in Aragón in 1488; it continued in existence until the Cortes of Monzón in 1510. Pulgar, *Crónica,* Part III, Ch. xcv.

14 José Amador de los Ríos, *Historia de la villa y corte de Madrid* (Madrid, 4 vols., 1860-1864), I, 300.

15 *Cortes de los antiguos reinos,* IV, 97.

16 Pulgar, *Crónica,* Part II, Ch. xcv.

17 Pulgar, *Crónica,* Part II, Ch. lxix.

18 Amador de los Ríos, *Historia de Madrid,* II, 226.

19 Pulgar, *Crónica,* Part II, Ch. xcv.

20 Pulgar, *Crónica,* Part III, Ch. lxvi.

21 Pulgar, *Crónica,* Part III, Ch. liii.

22 On the ecclesiastical jurisdiction, see F. M. Marina, *Ensayo histórico-crítico sobre la legislación y principales cuerpos legales de los reinos de León y Castilla* (Madrid, 1845).

* Hereafter cited as BAE.

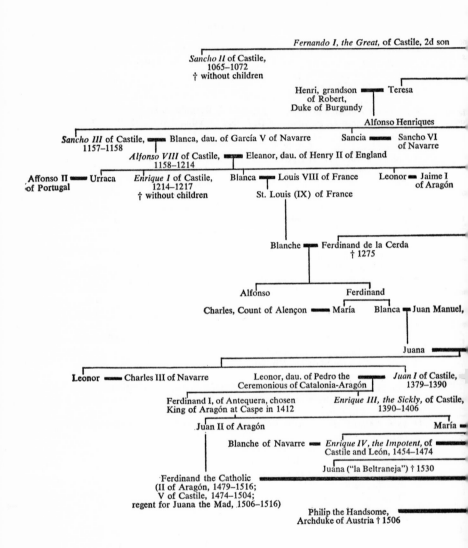

Fernando I, the Great, of Castile, 2d son

Sancho II of Castile,
1065–1072
† without children

Henri, grandson ━━ Teresa
of Robert,
Duke of Burgundy

Alfonso Henriques

Sancho III of Castile, ━━ Blanca, dau. of García V of Navarre   Sancia ━━ Sancho VI
1157–1158   of Navarre
Alfonso VIII of Castile, ━━ Eleanor, dau. of Henry II of England
1158–1214

Affonso II ━━ Urraca   Enrique I of Castile,   Blanca ━━ Louis VIII of France   Leonor ━ Jaime I
of Portugal   1214–1217   St. Louis (IX) of France   of Aragón
                         † without children

Blanche ━━ Ferdinand de la Cerda
† 1275

Alfonso   Ferdinand
Charles, Count of Alençon ━━ María   Blanca ━ Juan Manuel,

Juana ━━

Leonor ━━ Charles III of Navarre   Leonor, dau. of Pedro the ━━ Juan I of Castile,
                                     Ceremonious of Catalonia-Aragón   1379–1390
Ferdinand I, of Antequera, chosen   Enrique III, the Sickly, of Castile,
King of Aragón at Caspe in 1412   1390–1406
Juan II of Aragón   María ━
Blanche of Navarre ━━ Enrique IV, the Impotent, of ━━
Castile and León, 1454–1474
Juana ("la Beltraneja") † 1530
Ferdinand the Catholic ━━
(II of Aragón, 1479–1516;
V of Castile, 1474–1504;
regent for Juana the Mad, 1506–1516)
Philip the Handsome, ━━
Archduke of Austria † 1506

RULERS OF LEÓN AND CASTILE

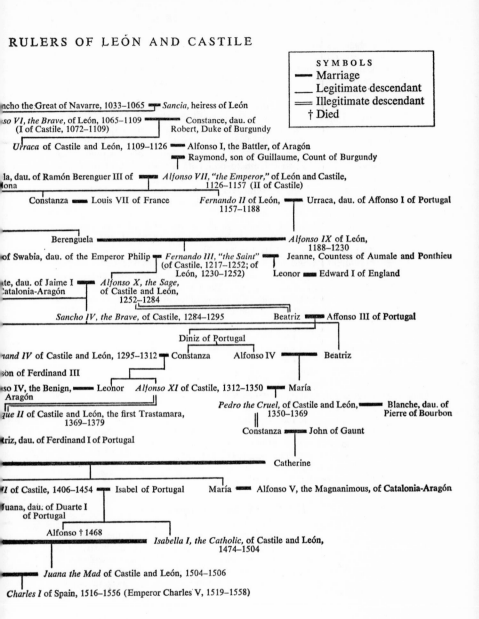

ncho the Great of Navarre, 1033–1065 — Sancia, heiress of León

so VI, the Brave, of León, 1065–1109 — Constance, dau. of
    (I of Castile, 1072–1109)   Robert, Duke of Burgundy

Urraca of Castile and León, 1109–1126 — Alfonso I, the Battler, of Aragón
                                      — Raymond, son of Guillaume, Count of Burgundy

la, dau. de Ramón Berenguer III of — Alfonso VII, "the Emperor," of León and Castile,
lona   1126–1157 (II of Castile)

Constanza — Louis VII of France   Fernando II of León, — Urraca, dau. of Affonso I of Portugal
                                             1157–1188

Berenguela — Alfonso IX of León,
                                    1188–1230

of Swabia, dau. of the Emperor Philip — Fernando III, "the Saint" — Jeanne, Countess of Aumale and Ponthieu
                                          (of Castile, 1217–1252; of
                                           León, 1230–1252)   Leonor — Edward I of England

te, dau. of Jaime I — Alfonso X, the Sage,
atalonia-Aragón   of Castile and León,
                              1252–1284

Sancho IV, the Brave, of Castile, 1284–1295   Beatriz — Affonso III of Portugal

                                    Diniz of Portugal

nand IV of Castile and León, 1295–1312 — Constanza   Alfonso IV — Beatriz

son of Ferdinand III

so IV, the Benign, — Leonor   Alfonso XI of Castile, 1312–1350 — María
   Aragón

que II of Castile and León, the first Trastamara,   Pedro the Cruel, of Castile and León, — Blanche, dau. of
       1369–1379   1350–1369   Pierre of Bourbon

triz, dau. of Ferdinand I of Portugal   Constanza — John of Gaunt

                                                  Catherine

I of Castile, 1406–1454 — Isabel of Portugal   María — Alfonso V, the Magnanimous, of Catalonia-Aragón

Juana, dau. of Duarte I
   of Portugal

        Alfonso † 1468   Isabella I, the Catholic, of Castile and León,
                                           1474–1504

— Juana the Mad of Castile and León, 1504–1506

Charles I of Spain, 1516–1556 (Emperor Charles V, 1519–1558)

23 Pulgar, *Crónica,* Part III, Ch. lxvi.
24 Pulgar, *Crónica,* Part II, Ch. civ.
25 Wilhelm Maurenbrecher, *Studien und Skizzen zur Geschichte der Reformationszeit* (Leipzig, 1875), p. 13. Vicente de la Fuente, *Historia eclesiástica de España* (Madrid, 5 vols., 1873-1875), V, 150, correctly asserts that the right of presentation was not definitely yielded up to the Kings of Spain until the time of Charles V. It is equally certain, however, that Isabella and Ferdinand enjoyed a right of supplication that in the last analysis was a genuine right of presentation. However, the term "Concordat," used by Maurenbrecher and Prescott, is too solemn to designate a concession of uncertain duration. Maurenbrecher committed an even graver error: He took for the text of the agreement Ferdinand's instructions to his ambassador to Rome; that is, he confused Ferdinand's claims with the concessions of the Papal court.
26 William H. Prescott, *History of the Reign of Ferdinand and Isabella the Catholic of Spain* (London, 2 vols., 1858), II, 401.
27 Pulgar, *Crónica,* Part III, Ch. xxxviii.
28 Ferdinand caused the same policy to prevail in the states of the crown of Aragón. In Sicily, the totality of rights that guaranteed the supremacy of the state over the Church was designated by the name of *Monarchia sicula.* On the manner in which Ferdinand used these rights in relation to the Papacy, see Prescott, *History,* II, 402, n. 4.
29 Pulgar, *Crónica,* Part II, Ch. c.
30 Pulgar, *Crónica,* Part III, Ch. lxvii.
31 Pulgar, *Crónica,* Part III, Ch. xcix.
32 Clemencín, *Elogio,* pp. 142-146.
33 Pulgar, *Crónica,* Part II, Ch. xcv.
34 Clemencín, *Elogio,* Ilustración v.
35 Pulgar, *Crónica,* Part II, Ch. lxiv.
36 Pulgar, *Crónica,* Part II, Ch. xcvi.
37 Maurenbrecher, *Studien und Skizzen,* p. 52.
38 Amador de los Ríos, *Historia de Madrid,* II, 154.
39 *Cortes de los antiguos reinos,* IV, 191-192.
40 Pulgar, *Crónica,* Part II, Ch. iv.
41 Pulgar, *Crónica,* Part II, Ch. lxxix.

II. The Spanish Inquisition

1 If one considers the difficulties being prepared for the future by the presence in Algiers, side by side with French colonists, of a Moslem group ten times as numerous, he will judge less severely the conduct of Ferdinand and Isabella. I have neither the wish nor the intention to justify the Inquisition; I leave this task to others. My only wish is to show, without eulogy or censure, the true character of events, to show things as they happened.
2 Concerning the aristocratic houses that were stained with bastardy or that descended from a Jewish or Moorish ancestor, see the memoir presented to Philip II and attributed to Cardinal Mendoza

(*El Tizón de la nobleza española o máculas y sanbenitos de su linaje* (Barcelona, 1880).

3 Andrés Bernáldez, *Historia de los reyes católicos D. Fernando y D. Isabel* (Seville, 2 vols., 1870), Ch. xliii.

4 Antonio María Fabié, *Vida y escritos de Francisco López de Villalobos* (Madrid, 1886), p. 8.

5 Bernáldez, *Historia,* Ch. xliii.

6 Orthodox Jews eat animals that have been slaughtered and not beaten to death. The meat of an animal killed according to the rites is kosher. [More specifically, "Kosher" is applied to the meat of an animal not prohibited by Jewish dietary laws and slaughtered by cutting the windpipe so as to produce instantaneous loss of consciousness, after which the meat is salted to remove the blood and the carcass critically examined for physical blemishes. Ed.]

7 It may be that even "Old Christians" were seduced by a belief that had all the attraction of mystery. Bernáldez notes the sympathy felt for the new sect by the lawyers, the bishops, the monks, the canons, and the royal functionaries (*contadores, secretarios, e factores*). Judaism was the great heresy of Spain.

8 Pulgar, *Crónica,* Part II, Ch. lxxvii.

9 Bernáldez, *Historia,* Ch. xliv.

10 Juan de Mariana, *Historia de España* (Madrid, 1854), p. 17.

11 G. A. Bergenroth, ed., *Calendar of Letters, Dispatches, and State Papers Relating to the Negotiations between England and Spain* (London, 2 vols. and supplement, 1862-1867), I, xlv.

12 Oropesa had composed a memoir in which he complained, in the name of the Evangel, of the distinction that the Spaniards sought to establish between Old and New Christians. Albert Du Boys, *Fernando de Talavera,* p. 2.

13 *Cortes de los antiguos reinos de León y Castilla, publicadas por la Real Academia de Historia* (Madrid, 5 vols., 1861-1903), IV, 149-50.

14 Bernáldez, *Historia,* p. 330, says that the sovereigns decided to banish the Jews "because it was there that the heretical Mosaic wickedness (*pravedad*) had its nourishment (*nudrimento*).

15 Bernáldez, *Historia,* Chs. cx-cxiii.

16 J. H. Mariéjol, *Pierre Martyr d'Anghera* (Paris, 1887), p. 64.

17 Álvaro Gómez de Castro, *De Rebus gestis Francisci Ximenii,* in Andreas Schott, Johann Pastorius, and Franciscus Schott, *Hispaniae illustratae, seu rerum urbiumque Hispaniae, Lusitaniae, Aethiopiae, et Indiae scriptores varii* (Frankfurt, 4 vols., 1603-1604), I, 961.

18 [For a somewhat different account of this conversion, more flattering both to Jiménez and the Moor Zegri, see Walter Starkie, *Grand Inquisitor, Being an Account of Cardinal Ximénez de Cisneros and His Times* (London, 1940), pp. 257-258. Ed.]

19 Not until 1526 was a special tribunal established at Granada.

III. The Spanish Supremacy

[1] William H. Prescott, *History of the Reign of Ferdinand and Isabella the Catholic of Spain* (London, 2 vols., 1858), I, 239.

[2] [The following table will help to clarify the relations between Aragón and Naples in the period covered by this chapter.

Table of the Aragonese House of Naples

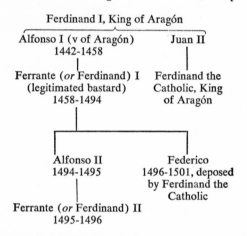

Ferdinand I, King of Aragón

Alfonso I (v of Aragón)
1442-1458

Juan II

Ferrante (*or* Ferdinand) I
(legitimated bastard)
1458-1494

Ferdinand the
Catholic, King
of Aragón

Alfonso II
1494-1495

Federico
1496-1501, deposed
by Ferdinand the
Catholic

Ferrante (*or* Ferdinand) II
1495-1496

[3] Louis XI took the initiative; he did a bad turn to Isabella, spouse of Ferdinand of Aragón, by recognizing as King of Castile, Affonso V of Portugal, husband of Doña Juana, the alleged daughter of Enrique IV (Treaty of Senlis, September 8, 1475).

[4] Hernando del Pulgar, *Crónica de los señores reyes católicos* (BAE, Vol. 70, pp. 225-511, Madrid, 1878), Part II, Ch. liii.

[5] Pulgar, *Crónica*, Part II, Ch. lxxxiv.

[6] This is the thesis solidly established by H. F. Delaborde in his book *L'Expédition de Charles VIII en Italie* (Paris, 1888). [Compare, however, Henry Lemonnier, in Ernest Lavisse, ed., *Histoire de France* (Paris, 9 vols., 1900-1911), V (1), "Les Guerres d'Italie," pp. 13-16. Ed.]

[7] Delaborde, *L'Expédition de Charles VIII*, p. 385, following Jerónimo Zurita y Castro, *Anales de la corona de Aragón* (1562-1579).

[8] [Certain towns (Paris, Rouen, Lyon, Poitiers, Angers, Orléans, Amiens, Tournay) that served as guarantors of treaties entered into by the French king. Ed.]

[9] Delaborde, *L'Expédition de Charles VIII*, p. 545, does not believe this dramatic story, told by Paulus Jovius and Zurita.

[10] Delaborde, *L'Expédition de Charles VIII*, p. 591.

[11] The marriage of Philip the Handsome and Doña Juana produced

a son, Charles of Luxembourg, born February 24, 1500, who became Charles V.

12 Delaborde, *L'Expédition de Charles VIII*, p. 688.

13 André Joseph Ghislain Le Glay, *Négociations diplomatiques entre la France et l'Autriche durant les trente premières années du XVI ème siècle* (Paris, 2 vols., 1835), I, xlvi.

14 Le Glay, *Négociations*, I, lii.

15 G. A. Bergenroth, ed., *Calendar of Letters, Dispatches, and State Papers Relating to the Negotiations between England and Spain* (London, 1862-1867, 2 vols. and supplement), I, 305.

16 [A district lying between French Abruzzi, and Spanish Apulia, important because of its fertility and because of the profits derived from the tolls levied on the cattle going to and fro between summer and winter pastures. Ed.]

17 Le Glay, *Négociations*, I, lx.

18 Three treaties were signed at Blois (September 22, 1504). [The first of these treaties between Louis XII, on the one hand, and Maximilian of Austria and Philip of Castile, on the other, related to the marriage of Claude of France with Charles of Luxembourg (Charles V). The second provided for the restoration of peace between Louis and Maximilian and Philip. The third bound Louis, Maximilian, and Philip in an alliance and confederacy against the Venetians. Ed.]

19 Le Glay, *Négociations*, I, lxi.

20 J. H. Mariéjol, *Pierre Martyr d'Anghera* (Paris, 1887), p. 75

21 Le Glay, *Négociations*, I, xci.

22 Bergenroth, *Calendar*, I, xxxvii; November 1509.

23 Bergenroth, *Calendar*, II, lxvi.

24 Bergenroth, *Calendar*, II, lxxvi.

25 Wilhelm Maurenbrecher, *Studien und Skizzen zur Geschichte der Reformationszeit* (Leipzig, 1875), p. 74.

26 Bergenroth, *Calendar*, II, xxv ff.

27 Lorenzo Galíndez Carbajal, *Anales Breves* (BAE, Vol. 70, pp. 533-565, Madrid, 1878), anno 1516, Ch. ii.

28 Zurita even denies that Ferdinand intended to leave to his younger grandson the administration of the military orders, but Galíndez, Ferdinand's contemporary and official chronicler, seems to me worthier of credence on this point.

IV. The Indies

1 Henry Harrisse, *Additions à la Biblioteca América Vetusta* (Paris, 1866-1872), pp. xvi-xviii.

2 Harrisse, *Christophe Colomb, Études d'histoire critique* (Paris, 2 vols., 1884), I, 248-249. [I have used, with slight changes, the translation made from the original Latin text of Toscanelli's letter by John Fiske in his *The Discovery of America* (Boston, 2 vols., 1892), I, 356-361. The italics are Mariéjol's. Ed.]

3 [Columbus was born in the city of Genoa sometime between August

25 and the end of October 1451. Quinto and Terrarossa were villages in the Republic of Genoa. Ed.]

4 Harrisse, *Colomb*, I, 360.

5 [This traditional belief rests on a slight foundation: three youths who had been sentenced to life imprisonment for helping a condemned murderer to break jail were released on condition of shipping with Columbus. Samuel E. Morison notes that they "turned out to be trustworthy men and went with the Admiral on later voyages." *Christopher Columbus, Master Mariner* (New York, 1956), pp. 31-32. Ed.]

6 It is more than 100 degrees between Panama and the mouth of the Mekong.

7 Harrisse, *Colomb*, II, 53.

8 Harrisse, *Colomb*, II, 89.

9 M. F. de Navarrete, *Colección de los viajes y descubrimientos* (2d ed., Madrid, 5 vols., 1858-1859), I, 303.

10 Harrisse, *Colomb*, I, 100.

11 Harrisse, *Colomb*, II, 103, n 1.

12 Valeriu Marcu claims that the name America is Indian and has nothing to do with Amerigo Vespucci. His brochure *Nouvelles Recherches sur l'origine du nom d'Amérique* (Paris, 1888) is curious; but it has not convinced me.

13 Was it really the 40th degree of latitude? See William Robertson, *Histoire d'Amérique*, ed. J. A. C. Buchon (Paris, 1836), p. 495.

14 Navarrete, *Colección*, II, 11, n 5.

15 Navarrete very ably defends the Catholic Sovereigns against the charge of injustice.

16 Harrisse, *Colomb*, II, 238, n. 4.

17 Navarrete, *Colección*, II, 390.

18 Navarrete, *Colección*, II, 389.

19 Robertson, *Histoire*, p. 492.

20 Navarrete, *Colección*, II, 316, order of January 20, 1503; p. 375, order of June 15, 1510; p. 383, May 18, 1511. Robertson, *Histoire*, p. 740.

21 Navarrete, *Colección*, II, 378.

22 Harrisse, *Colomb*, I, 398.

23 Harrisse, *Colomb*, II, 45-47.

24 Robertson, *Histoire*, p. 484.

25 Robertson, *Histoire*, p. 490.

26 Letter of the Catholic Sovereigns of April 16, 1495. Navarrete, *Colección*, I, 193.

27 Navarrete, *Colección*, II, 34, 29.

28 The Franciscans, established in America since 1502, were more accommodating, and accepted, if they did not approve, the existing state of affairs.

29 Antonio María Fabié, *Vida y escritos de Fray Bartolomé de Las Casas* (Madrid, 2 vols., 1879), I, 13-14. What Fabié says of Las Casas could be said with even greater truth of the Dominican monks.

30 Fabié, *Vida*, I, 35.

31 The instructions are given in Antonio Herrera y Tordesillas, *Décadas de las Indias* (Madrid, 4 vols., 1601-1615), II, Book 2, Ch. iii *et seq.* C. J. von Hefele, *Vie du Cardinal Ximénes* (Paris, 1869), p. 402 ff.

Part II. THE INSTITUTIONS

I. The Crown

1 [A codification or summary of all existing *fueros*, whether of local or national scope, promulgated by Alfonso I in 1254-1255. Ed.]
2 Albert Du Boys, *Histoire du droit criminel en Espagne* (Paris, 1870), p. 328.
3 Du Boys, *Histoire*, p. 325.
4 Juan de Mariana, *Del Rey y de la institución real* (Madrid, 1854), Ch. vi.
5 F. M. Marina, *Ensayo histórico-crítico sobre la legislación y principales cuerpos legales de los reinos de León y Castilla* (Madrid, 1845), p. 73.
6 Marina, *Ensayo*, p. 363.
7 Ferdinand was the great-grandson of King Juan I of Castile.
8 Despite Isabella's precautions, Philip the Handsome became King of Castile and not prince-consort, but Isabella could not foresee that her daughter Juana would be a madwoman incapable of governing.
9 Hernando del Pulgar, *Crónica de los señores reyes católicos* (BAE, Vol. 70, pp. 225-511, Madrid, 1878), Part II, Ch. i.
10 *Cortes de los antiguos reinos de León y Castilla* (Madrid, 5 vols., 1861-1903), IV, 220-221.
11 Pulgar, *Crónica*, Part II, Ch. xcvi. The King of Castile, Juan II, gave the heir presumptive the title of Prince of Asturias after the marriage of his son with the daughter of the Duke of Lancaster, in imitation of the English, who called the heir to the throne the Prince of Wales.
12 Juan de Mariana, *Historia de España* (Madrid, 1854), Book XIX, Ch. xx.
13 Mariana, *Del Rey y de la institución real*, Book I, Ch. iv.
14 William H. Prescott, *History of the Reign of Ferdinand and Isabella the Catholic of Spain* (London, 2 vols., 1858), II, 184.
15 J. H. Mariéjol, *Pierre Martyr d'Anghera* (Paris, 1887), p. 128.
16 [The battle of Muret ended Aragonese influence and interests north of the Pyrenees and destroyed the brilliant Provençal culture. Ed.]
17 J. M. Antequera, *Historia de la legislación española* (Madrid, 1874), p. 297. [R. B. Merriman regards this oath as genuine; see his *Rise of the Spanish Empire* (New York, 4 vols., 1918-1934), I, 458-459, and the references listed there. Ed.]
18 [A group of laws promulgated at the Cortes of Toro in 1505 that reflected, especially in the field of civil law, the strong influence of Roman and Canon Law. Ed.]

II. The Cortes

1 F. M. Marina, *Ensayo histórico-crítico sobre la legislación y principales cuerpos legales de los reinos de León y Castilla* (Madrid, 1845), p. 29, nn. 16 and 17. J. M. Antequera, *Historia de la legislación española* (Madrid, 1874), pp. 114-115, denies this relationship.

2 Antequera, *Historia,* p. 209. This rule was not absolute. At the Cortes of Madrid (1390), Burgos and Salamanca each had eight deputies, Seville three, Cádiz two, Badajóz one. But under Ferdinand and Isabella, each town sent two *procuradores.*

3 The following table of the Cortes of Castile is drawn from Antequera, *Historia,* pp. 543-544.

Cortes of Castile under the Catholic Sovereigns

1.	Valladolid	1475	9. Toledo	1502-03
2.	Madrigal	1475-76	10. Toro	1505
3.	Toledo	1480	11. Salamanca-Valladolid	1506
4.	Madrid	1482	12. Burgos	1506
5.	Toledo	1498	13. Madrid	1510
6.	Ocaña	1499	14. Burgos	1511
7.	Seville	1499	15. Burgos	1512
8.	Seville	1501	16. Burgos	1515

4 Juan de Mariana, *Historia de España* (Madrid, 1854), Book XVIII, Ch. xv.

5 William H. Prescott, *History of the Reign of Ferdinand and Isabella the Catholic of Spain* (London, 2 vols., 1858), I, 14 and n. 5.

6 Prescott, *History,* I, 14, n. 3.

7 For the period of the Catholic Sovereigns, see Vol. IV of *Cortes de los antiguos reinos de León y Castilla, publicadas por la Real Academia de la Historia* (Madrid, 5 vols., 1861-1903).

8 *Cortes de los antiguos reinos,* IV, p. 97, n. 3.

9 *Cortes de los antiguos reinos,* IV, p. 108.

10 Juan Sempere y Guarinos, *Histoire des Cortes d'Espagne* (Bordeaux, 1815), p. 198.

11 The Cortes of Valencia and Catalonia were composed of only three branches.

12 Antequera, *Historia,* p. 295.

If we may trust this list below, prepared by Antequera on the basis of the works of the Academia de Historia de Madrid, it appears that there were only three general Cortes of all the states of the Crown of Aragón (1484, 1510, 1512). Moreover, Valencia seems to have been singularly mistreated, since there was only one session (Orihuela-Valencia) of the particular Cortes of that kindom.

It will also be noted that there was a period of six or seven years in the reign of Ferdinand during which he did not summon Cortes. This is the period that extends from the death of Isabella to 1510, the year when his quarrels with Louis XII were renewed.

Cortes of the Crown of Aragón under Ferdinand

Aragón		Valencia		Catalonia	
1481	Calatayud, Zaragoza	1484-88	Tarazona Valencia Orihuela	1480-81	Barcelona
1484	Tarazona			1484	Tarazona
1488	Zaragoza			1485	Barcelona
1493-94	Zaragoza			1493	Barcelona
1495-97	Zaragoza			1495-96	Tortosa
1497-99	Zaragoza			1503	Barcelona
1502-03	Zaragoza				
1510	Monzón	1510	Monzón	1510	Monzón
1512	Monzón	1512	Monzón	1512	Monzón
1515	Zaragoza, Calatayud			1515	Lérida

13 Jerónimo Zurita y Castro, *Anales de la corona de Aragón* (Zaragoza, 6 vols., 1561-1580), Part VI, fol. 96.

III. The Central Government: The Councils

1 José Amador de los Ríos, *Historia de la villa y corte de Madrid* (Madrid, 4 vols., 1860-1864), II, 213.
2 F. M. Marina, *Ensayo histórico-crítico sobre la legislación y principales cuerpos legales de los reinos de León y Castilla* (Madrid, 1845), fol. 55, n. 6.
3 J. M. Antequera, *Historia de la legislación española* (Madrid, 1874), p. 374.
4 *Cortes de los antiguos reinos de León y Castilla* (Madrid, 5 vols., 1861-1903), IV, 112.
5 *Cortes de los antiguos reinos,* IV, 120.
6 *Cortes de los antiguos reinos,* IV, 112.
7 *Cortes de los antiguos reinos,* IV, 117-118.
8 Hernando del Pulgar, *Crónica de los señores reyes católicos* (BAE, Vol. 70, pp. 225-511, Madrid, 1878), Part II, Ch. xcv.
9 Pulgar also mentions the Council of Aragón and the Council of the Hermandad, to be discussed below. (*Crónica,* Part II, Ch. xcv.
10 *Epistolario español* (Madrid, 2 vols.; Vol. 13, 1850, and Vol. 62, 1870, of the BAE) II, 19.
11 *Concilium justitiae, quod regale vocant,* says Lucius Marineus.
12 Lucius Marineus, in Andreas Schott, Johann Pastorius, and Franciscus Schott *Hispaniae Illustratae, seu rerum urbiumque Hispaniae, Lusitaniae, Aethiopiae, et Indiae scriptores varii* (Frankfurt, 4 vols., 1603-1604), I, 321.

13 Schott, I, 221.
14 *Cortes de los antiguos reinos*, IV, 68.
15 Pulgar, *Crónica*, Part III, Ch. xcv.
16 *Epistolario español*, II, 261.
17 Andrés Bernáldez, *Historia de los reyes católicos D. Fernando y D. Isabel* (Seville, 2 vols., 1870), Chs. cxviii, cxx.
18 J. H. Mariéjol, *Pierre Martyr d'Anghera* (Paris, 1887), pp. 156-157. [The year 1524, not 1511, is the true date of the creation of the Council of the Indies; see Ernesto Schäfer, *El Consejo real y supremo de las Indias* (Seville, 1935), pp. 24-32. Ed.]
19 Aragón had its own grand inquisitor for only a very short time.
20 Antequera, *Historia*, p. 292.
21 G. A. Bergenroth, ed. *Calendar of Letter, Dispatches, and State Papers Relating to the Negotiations between England and Spain* (London, 2 vols. and supplement 1862-1867), I, xvi ff.
22 The office of confessor was a genuine institution in Spain. Villalobos, inveighing against the ambitions of the French kings, noteɛ that they had no confessor to reproach them for acts of injustice.

IV. The Royal Agents

1 Salazar de Mendoza, *Orígen de las dignidades seglares de Castilla y León* (Toledo, 1618), Book II, Ch. xiii, fol. 61.
2 M. F. de Navarrete, *Colección de los viajes y descubrimientos* (2d ed., Madrid, 5 vols., 1858-1859), Appendix.
3 F. M. Marina, *Ensayo histórico-critico sobre la legislación y principales cuerpos legales de los reinos de León y Castilla* (Madrid, 1845), p. 267.
4 Salazar de Mendoza, *Orígen de las dignidades seglares,* Book II, Ch. xiii, fol. 61.
5 One may compare to the *adelantados* of Cazorla the *caudillos mayores* (chief captains) of the Bishopric of Jaén, who had command of the troops of all the cities comprised in this diocese.
6 *Cortes de los antiguos reinos de León y Castilla* (Madrid, 5 vols., 1861-1903), IV, 161-162.
7 *Crónicas de los reyes,* III (Vol. 70 of BAE, Madrid, 1878), 533-534, 533, n. 2. (Petition 66 of the Cortes of Valladolid of 1537).
8 Hernando del Pulgar, *Crónica de los señores reyes católicos* (BAE, Vol. 70, pp. 255-511, Madrid, 1878), Part II, Ch. xcv.
9 Oath of the corregidores. Pulgar, *Crónica,* Part III, Ch. xxxix.
10 Lorenzo Galíndez Carbajal, *Anales breves* (BAE, Vol. 70, pp. 533-565, Madrid, 1878), anno 1491.
11 Pulgar, *Crónica,* Part II, Ch. xcv.
12 Pulgar, *Crónica,* Part III, Ch. c.

V. Justice

1 Hernando del Pulgar, *Crónica de los señores reyes católicos* (BAE, Vol. 70, pp. 225-511, Madrid, 1878), Part II, Ch. lxx.

2 Gonzalo Fernández de Oviedo, Las *Quinquagenas de la nobleza de España* (Madrid, 1880), *Quinquagena III*, Part II, cited by José Amador de los Ríos, *Historia de la villa y corte Madrid* (Madrid, 4 vols., 1860-1864), II, 165-166.

3 Albert Du Boys, *Histoire du droit criminel in Espagne* (Paris, 1870), p. 430.

4 J. M. Antequera, *Historia de la legislación española* (Madrid, 1874), p. 218.

5 Francisco Bermúdez de Pedraza, *Antiguedad y excelencia de Granada* (Madrid, 1608), fol. 140.

6 Pulgar, *Crónica*, Part III, Ch. lxvi.

7 Antequera, *Historia*, p. 397.

8 Antequera, p. 397, holds there were two of them.

9 *Cortes de los antiguos reinos de León y Castilla* (Madrid, 5 vols., 1861-1903), IV, 127.

10 *Cortes de los antiguos reinos,* IV, 125.

11 F. M. Marina, *Ensayo histórico-crítico sobre la legislación y principales cuerpos legales de los reinos de León y Castilla* (Madrid, 1845), p. 434. Compare Antequera, *Historia*, p. 393.

12 The royal audiencia judged in the first instance certain cases stipulated in the *fueros*.

13 Jerónimo de Blancas, *Commentarii rerum Aragonensium*, in Andreas Schott, Johann Pastorius, and Franciscus Schott, *Hispaniae illustratae, seu rerum urbiumque Hispaniae, Lusitaniae, Aethiopiae, et Indiae scriptores varii* (Frankfurt, 4 vols., 1603-1604), III, 753.

14 Du Boys, *Histoire*, p. 480.

15 Du Boys, *Histoire*, p. 480.

16 Pedro José, Marquis de Pidal, *Philippe II, Antonio Pérez et le royaume d'Aragón*, tr. J. G. Magnabal (Paris, 2 vols., 1867), I, 40.

17 This prison was constructed by order of the Cortes in 1461.

18 Blancas, *Commentarii*, in Schott, *Hispaniae illustratae*, III, 721. Du Boys, *Histoire*, pp. 529-530.

19 Blancas, *Commentarii*, in Schott, *Hispaniae illustratae*, III, 758.

20 Blancas, *Commentarii*, in Schott, *Hispaniae illustratae*, III, 581.

21 Pulgar, *Crónica*, Part III, Ch. xcv.

VI. The Spanish Army

1 José Amador de los Ríos, *Historia de la villa y corte de Madrid* (Madrid, 4 vols., 1860-1864), II, 163.

2 Hernando del Pulgar, *Crónica de los señores reyes católicos* (BAE, Vol. 70, pp. 225-511, Madrid, 1878), Part III, Ch. xciv.

3 Pulgar, *Crónica*, III, Ch. xiv.

4 Pulgar, *Crónica*, Part III, Ch. xxi.

5 R. de Sotto, Conde de Clonard, *Historia orgánica de las armas de infantería y caballería españolas* (Madrid, 16 vols., 1851-1859), II, 165.

6 *Memorias de la Academia de Historia* (Madrid, 1796-), VI, Appendix 13.

[7] Alvaro Gómez de Castro, *De Rebus gestis Francisci Ximenii*, in Andreas Schott, Johann Pastorius, and Franciscus Schott, *Hispaniae illustratae, seu rerum urbiumque Hispaniae, Lusitaniae, Aethiopiae et Indiae scriptores varii* (Frankfurt, 4 vols., 1603-1604), I, 1025. *Epistolario español* (Madrid, 2 vols.; Vol. 13, 1850, and Vol. 62, 1870, of the BAE), II, 219.

[8] William H. Prescott, *History of the Reign of Ferdinand and Isabella the Catholic of Spain* (London, 2 vols., 1858), II, 434.

[9] Prescott, *History*, II, 52, n. 2.

[10] Jean Baptiste Dubos, *Histoire de la ligue de Cambrai* (Paris, 2 vols., 1728), I, 53; Blaise de Montluc, *Commentaires et lettres*, ed. Ruble (Paris, 5 vols., 1864-1872), I, 51, 53.

[11] *Los Problemas de Villalobos*, in *Curiosidades bibliográficas* (BAE, Vol. 36, Madrid, 1871), pp. 412-413.

[12] Prescott, *History*, I, 276.

[13] As Auguste Jal observes, the historian Du Cange falls into the error of confusing lombards with bombards.

[14] Pulgar, *Crónica*, Part III, Ch. lxi.

[15] Pulgar, *Cronica*, Part II, Ch. lxxi.

[16] Pulgar, *Crónica*, Part III, Ch. lxxvi.

[17] Letter cited by Amador de los Ríos in his *Historia de la villa y corte de Madrid*, II, 189 n. 1.

[18] Amador de los Ríos, *Historia de Madrid*, II, 192

[19] Amador de los Ríos, *Historia de Madrid*, II, 208, n. 1.

[20] *Epistolario español*, I, 62.

[21] *Epistolario español*, I, 62.

[22] Clonard, *Historia orgánica*, II, 486.

[23] Clonard, *Historia orgánica*, II, p. 487.

[24] In 1505 all the Spanish forces were divided into twenty *coronelías*, under the superior orders of a *coronel general*.

VII. Economic Policy

[1] Hernando del Pulgar, *Crónica de los señores reyes católicos* (BAE, Vol. 70, pp. 225-511, Madrid, 1878), Part III, Ch. lxiv.

[2] Pulgar, *Crónica*, Part II, Ch. xxiv.

[3] Andrés Bernáldez, *Historia de los reyes católicos D. Fernando y D. Isabel* (Seville, 2 vols., 1870), Ch. xxiv. Should we take this to mean that the tax was levied fifteen or sixteen times?

[4] We find in Aragón the taxes borne by the Castilians under different names. Goury de Roslan, *Essai sur l'histoire économique de l'Espagne* (Paris, 1888), p. 346, lists some duties which, according to him, were peculiar to that country (Aragón); but the *quinto de los presos* existed in Castile.

[5] Juan de Mariana, *Historia de España* (Madrid, 1854), Book XVI, Ch. ix.

[6] Alvaro Gómez de Castro, *De Rebus gestis*, in Andreas Schott, Johann Pastorius, and Franciscus Schott, *Hispaniae illustratae, seu rerum urbiumque Hispaniae, Lusitaniae, Aethiopiae, et Indiae scriptores varii* (Frankfurt, 4 vols., 1603-1604), I, 954.

7 Pulgar, *Crónica,* Part III, Ch. xiv.

8 *Cortes de los antiguos reinos de León y Castilla* (Madrid, 5 vols., 1861-1903), IV, 236-237.

9 Goury de Roslan, *Essai,* p. 325.

10 Diego Clemencín, *Elogio de la reina doña Isabel,* in *Memorias de la Real Academia de Historia,* Vol. 6 (Madrid, 1821), pp. 147-149; Goury de Roslan, *Essai,* p. 335.

11 There is a succinct analysis of these pragmáticas in Clemencín, *Elogio,* pp. 243-258.

12 *Cortes de los antiguos reinos,* IV, 157.

13 One of these officials was stationed in every place where a main road crossed the frontier.

14 Clemencín, *Elogio,* p. 245.

15 *Cortes de los antiguos reinos,* IV, p. 173.

16 José Amador de los Ríos, *Historia de la villa y corte de Madrid* (Madrid, 4 vols., 1860-1864), II, 226. Clemencín, *Elogio,* p. 249.

17 Clemencín, *Elogio,* pp. 236-237.

18 In 1482, after a census of the migratory herds, their number was put at 2,694,032 animals of all kinds. Goury de Roslan, *Essai,* p. 232.

19 In Aragón, despite strenuous efforts, the Mesta could only obtain a simple right of passage.

20 M. F. de Navarrete, *Colección de los viajes y descubrimientos* (2d ed., Madrid, 5 vols., 1858-1859), I, Intr., pp. 47 ff.

21 Ordinance of Álfaro (Nov. 10, 1495). Goury de Roslan, *Essai,* p. 291.

22 Granada, August 11, 1501. Juan Ramírez, ed., *Las Pragmáticas del reyno* (1520), fol. 301.

23 [That is, the right to possess remnants of or goods from a wrecked vessel driven or cast ashore. Ed.]

24 Navarrete, *Colección,* I, 46.

25 Pulgar, *Crónica,* Part II, Chap. xciv. Navarrete wrongly gives the number of ships as "fifty." *Colección,* I, 54.

26 See some other facts cited by Navarrete, *Colección.*

27 G. A. Bergenroth, ed., *Calendar of Letters, Dispatches, and State Papers Relating to the Negotiations between England and Spain* (London, 2 vols. and supplement, 1862-1867), I, cxxxiii.

Part III. SOCIAL LIFE

I. The Spaniards

1 Jean Michelet, *Tableau et précis de l'histoire moderne* (2d ed., Paris, 1826), "Précis," Chap. ii, §3, p. 41.

2 Robert Gaguin, in Edmond Martène and Ursin Durand, *Thesaurus novus anecdotorum* (Paris, 5 vols., 1717), I, 1835 B.

3 The letter is dated 1468. Moreover, Gaguin was familiar only with northern Spain.

4 Martène and Durand, *Thesaurus novus anecdotorum,* I, 1839 A.

5 Damião de Goes, in Schott, *Hispaniae illustratae, seu rerum urbi-umque Hispaniae Lusitaniae, Aethiopiae, et Indiae scriptores varii* (Frankfurt, 4 vols., 1603-1604), I, fol. 1170.

6 [*The Life of Lazarillo de Tormes,* a Spanish picaresque novel issued anonymously about 1554 and regarded as a masterpiece of Spanish prose. Ed.]

7 Peter Martyr d'Anghiera, *Opus Epistolarum* (Alcalá de Henares, 1530), Epistola 608.

8 *Los Problemas de Villalobos,* in *Curiosidades bibliográficas* (BAE, Vol. 36, Madrid, 1871), p. 426.

9 Alfred Morel-Fatio, *Études sur l'Espagne* (Paris, 4 vols., 1888-1925), I, 18-19.

10 Damião de Goes, in Schott, *Hispaniae illustratae,* I, 1171.

11 *Los Problemas de Villalobos,* in *Curiosidades bibliográficas,* p. 425.

12 Pulgar, in *Epistolario español* (Madrid, 2 vols.; Vol. 13, 1850, and Vol. 62, 1870, of the BAE), I, 59.

13 *Los Problemas de Villalobos,* in *Curiosidades bibliográficas,* p. 417.

14 *La Comedia de Calisto y Melibea,* known as *La Celestina,* published in 1499 in Burgos.

II. The Court

1 Hernando del Pulgar, *Crónica de los señores reyes católicos* (BAE, Vol. 70, pp. 225-511, Madrid, 1878), Part III, Ch. cliii.

2 *Cortes de los antiguos reinos de León y Castilla* (Madrid, 5 vols., 1861-1903), IV, 125.

3 Pulgar, *Crónica,* Part III, Ch. xxxix. Fines imposed as sentences might be recovered through his good offices.

4 Gonzalo Fernández de Oviedo, *Libro de la cámara real del príncipe don Juan* (Madrid, 1870), p. 170.

5 Oviedo, *Libro de la cámara real,* p. 170.

6 Oviedo, *Libro de la cámara real,* p. 27.

7 An interesting description of the court of Navarre may be found in the work of G. Desdevises du Dezert, *Don Carlos d'Aragon, prince de Viane* (Paris, 1889), p. 150 ff.

8 Bergenroth, *Calendar,* I, xxxv.

9 *Epistolario español* (Madrid, 2 vols.; Vol. 13, 1850, and Vol. 62, 1870, of the BAE), II, 16-19.

10 Pulgar, *Crónica,* Part III, Ch. cxxix.

11 Pulgar, *Crónica,* Part III, Ch. cxxviii.

12 Antonia Rodríguez Villa, *Etiquetas de la casa de Austria* (Madrid, 1875).

III. The Clergy

1 *Cortes de los antiguos reinos de León y Castilla* (Madrid, 5 vols., 1861-1903), IV, 186.

2 See also F. M. Marina, *Ensayo histórico-crítico sobre la legislación*

y principales cuerpos legales de los reinos de León y Castilla (Madrid, 1845), p. 168, on the engagement made by King Ferdinand IV in 1311 not to demand *pechos* (taxes) of the clergy without their consent.

3 Marina, *Ensayo,* p. 329 ff.

4 Marina, *Ensayo,* p. 331.

5 Marina, *Ensayo,* p. 336. [The "false decretals" refer to the famous fictitious "Donation of Constantine," assigning territorial sovereignty to the Popes. Ed.]

6 Marina, *Ensayo,* p. 355.

7 See the table.

8 The share of the Castilian bishops came to 385,000 ducats; the Aragonese prelates were not so well fixed.

9 Lucius Marineus Siculus, in Andreas Schott, Johann Pastorius, and Franciscus Schott, *Hispaniae illustratae, seu rerum urbiumque Hispaniae, Lusitaniae, Aethiopiae, et Indiae scriptores varii* (Frankfurt, 4 vols., 1603-1604), I, 321-322. Compare p. 308.

10 In Schott, *Hispaniae illustratae,* I, 13.

11 Damião de Goes, in Schott, *Hispaniae illustratae,* I, 1162.

12 Lucius Marineus Siculus, in Schott, *Hispaniae illustratae,* I, 313.

13 The assembly of the clergy of Seville (1478) forbade them to be "public ruffians and procurers (*públicos rufianes nin tengan mugeres públicas a ganar*)."

14 Juan de Mariana, *Historia de España* (Madrid, 1854), Book XXXII, Ch. xviii.

15 *Cortes de los antiguos reinos,* IV, 143. The assembly of the clergy of Seville (1478) called for repressive measures.

16 Philippe Labbé, *Sacrosancta concilia* (Paris, 1671-1672), XIII, col. 1464.

17 J. Sáenz de Aguirre, *Collectio maxima conciliorum omnium Hispaniae et novi orbis* (Rome, 6 vols., 1753-1755), IV, 11 ff.

18 Sáenz de Aguirre, *Collectio,* III, 671.

19 Mariana, *Historia de España,* Book XXIII, Ch. xviii.

20 Álvaro Gómez de Castro, in Schott, *Hispaniae illustratae,* I, 936-952; C. J. von Hefele, *Vie du Cardinal Ximénes* (Paris, 1869), pp. 25, 148.

21 Cîteau had been reformed in the course of the fifteenth century. Cluny held out till 1520. Aragón followed a little later the example set by Castile.

22 Oviedo, cited by William H. Prescott, *History of the Reign of Ferdinand and Isabella the Catholic of Spain* (London, 2 vols., 1858), II, 402.

IV. The Nobility

1 The word *fuero* may refer to a law that regulates the privileges of a class, the freedoms of a town, the customs of a region. *Fuero* sometimes designates a code, sometimes a charter, and again a legislative enactment.

2 [A code of privilege of the Castilian aristocracy. Ed.]

3 Antonio de la Escosura y Hevia, *Juicio crítico del feudalismo en España* (Madrid, 1856), p. 53.

4 Reinhart Pieter Anne Dozy, *Recherches sur l'histoire et la littérature de l'Espagne au moyen âge* (Leyden, 1860), p. 116.

5 Escosura, *Juicio crítico*, p. 90.

6 Henry Harrisse, *Christophe Colomb, Études d'histoire critique* (Paris, 2 vols., 1884), II, 351-352.

7 B. Moreno de Vargas, *Discursos de la nobleza de España* (Madrid, 1636), pp. 64 ff.

8 *Cortes de los antiguos reinos de León y Castilla* (Madrid, 5 vols., 1861-1903), IV, 78.

9 Salazar says that from the time of Ferdinand and Isabella no more *ricos homes* were made.

10 According to the Duke of Saint-Simon, *Mémoires,* ed. P. A. Cheruel and Adolphe Reynard (Paris, 30 vols., 1873-1877), XVIII, 4, 83, 112 ff. Compare Lucius Marineus Siculus, in Andreas Schott, Johann Pastorius, and Franciscus Schott, *Hispaniae illustratae, seu rerum urbiumque Hispaniae, Lusitaniae, Aethiopiae, et Indiae scriptores varii* (Frankfurt, 4 vols., 1603-1604), I, 322.

11 Vicente de la Fuente, *Historia eclesiástica de España* (Madrid, 5 vols., 1873-1875), V, 79.

12 Escosura, *Juicio crítico*, p. 72.

13 Diego Clemencín, *Elogio de la reina Isabel,* in *Memorias de la Real Academia de Historia,* Vol. VI (Madrid, 1821), p. 243. This pragmática, which dissolved all ties between man and land, may have only reproduced previous ordinances.

14 [This statement requires qualification. There is evidence that the pragmática of October 28, 1480, was frequently violated, especially on seignorial lands. "We cannot therefore make a simple inclusive statement to the effect that by the end of the fifteenth century all field laborers had achieved *de facto* a situation comparable to that of renters on the land . . . or of proprietors tilling their own fields." Rafael Altamira, *A History of Spain,* tr. Muna Lee (New York, 1949), p. 268. It may be added that a slave class, consisting chiefly of Moorish prisoners of war, continued to exist in Spain well into the period after the reign of the Catholic Sovereigns. Ed.]

15 ["Bad Customs." The six dues owed by the *payeses de remensa* to their feudal lords in medieval Catalonia, the principal one being the stipulation that the peasant could not leave his land without purchasing personal redemption from servile status at a price satisfactory to his lord (*remensa personal*). The *malos usos* included unofficially the practice of the *jus primae noctis* (*derecho de pernada*). Ed.]

16 Escosura, *Juicio crítico,* pp. 40 ff., and the notes to which these pages refer.

17 Albert Du Boys, *Histoire du droit criminel en Espagne* (Paris, 1870), p. 583.

18 Escosura, *Juicio crítico,* p. 80, nn. 100 and 107.

19 Pedro José, Marquis de Pidal, *Philippe II, Antonio Pérez, et le*

royaume d'Aragón, tr. J. G. Magnabal (Paris, 2 vols., 1867), I, 53 n. 1.

20 Pidal, *Philippe II* . . . , p. 61.

21 This privilege was entitled *behetría,* and the name was also applied to the district enjoying this privilege.

22 Compare C. R. von Höfler, *Quellen der Geschichte Philipps des Schoenen* (Vienna, 1883), pp. 251-262.

23 On a population of 50,931 households or 230,000 persons for Aragón alone. The total population of Spain, including Valencia, Catalonia, Navarre, and Granada, may be reckoned at 1,800,000 *vecinos* (8 to 9 million inhabitants).

24 Hernando del Pulgar, *Crónica de los señores reyes católicos* (BAE, Vol. 70, pp. 225-511, Madrid, 1878), Part II, Ch. li.

25 Pulgar, *Crónica,* Part III, Ch. lxxxviii.

26 Gaspar Muro, *La Princesse d'Eboli* (Paris, 1878), p. 11, n. 1.

27 Andrés Bernáldez, *Historia de los reyes católicos D. Fernando y D. Isabel* (Seville, 2 vols., 1870), Ch. xcxiv.

V. The Towns

1 Hernando del Pulgar, *Crónica de los señores reyes católicos* (BAE, Vol. 70, pp. 225-511, Madrid, 1878), Part III, Ch. xciv.

2 Pulgar, *Crónica,* Part III, Ch. xlv.

3 For an analysis of the principal *fueros,* see F. M. Marina, *Ensayo histórico-crítico sobre la legislación y principales cuerpos legales de los reinos de León y Castilla* (Madrid, 1845), pp. 93-137 and 138-155; and J. M. Antequera, *Historia de la legislación española* (Madrid, 1874), pp. 137-152.

4 See the list prepared by Antequera, *Historia,* Appendix 8, p. 553.

5 Antequera, *Historia,* pp. 186 ff.

6 Fermín Gonzalo Morón, *Curso de historia de la civilización* (Madrid, 6 vols., 1841-1846), I, 256.

7 Antequera, *Historia,* p. 212.

8 Marina, *Ensayo,* p. 154, on the *fuero* of Soria.

9 Marina, *Ensayo,* pp. 158-159. However, these prescriptions generally remained a dead letter.

10 However, Ferdinand and Isabella, in order to protect the towns from aristocratic influence, forbade the towns which retained the right of election to choose their *regidores* from among the grandees.

11 Aragón also had a division into towns and cities; there were ten cities and eighteen towns. Antequera, *Historia,* p. 295, n. 6.

12 Pedro José, Marquis de Pidal, *Philippe II, Antonio Pérez, et le royaume d'Aragón,* tr. J. G. Magnabal (Paris, 2 vols., 1867), I, 53.

13 Morón, *Curso de historia de la civilización,* I, 283.

14 Alonso Ortiz de Zúñiga, *Anales eclesiásticos y seculares de la ciudad de Sevilla* (Madrid, 1677), anno 1468.

15 For Madrid, see José Amador de los Ríos, *Historia de la villa y corte de Madrid* (Madrid, 4 vols., 1860-1864), II, 309. Morón, *Curso de historia de la civilización,* I, 280-281.

16 Antequera, *Historia,* p. 396.

Part IV. INTELLECTUAL LIFE

I. Literature and Letters

1 Comte de Puymaigre, *La Cour littéraire de Don Juan II, roi de Castille* (Paris, 1873).

2 [Tell me now in what hidden way is
    Lady Flora the lovely Roman?
Where's Hipparchia, and where is Thais,
    Neither of them the fairer woman?
    Where is Echo, beheld of no man,
Only heard on river and mere,
    She whose beauty was more than human?
But where are the snows of yester-year? (Translation by A. C. Swinburne)]

3 [Where is the king Don Juan? Where
Each royal prince and noble heir
    of Aragón?
Where are the courtly gallantries?
The deeds of love and high emprises,
    In Battle done?

Tourney and joust, that charmed the eye,
And scarf, and gorgeous panoply,
    And nodding plume.
What were they but a pageant scene?
What but the garlands, gay and green
    That deck the tomb?

Where are the high-born dames, and where
Their gay attire and jewelled hair,
    And odors sweet?
Where are the gentle knights, that came
To kneel, and breathe love's ardent flame,
    Low at their feet?

Where is the song of the troubadour?
Where are the lute and gay tambour
    They loved of yore?
Where is the mazy dance, of old,
The flowing robes, inwrought with gold,
    The dancers wore? (Translation by H. W. Longfellow)]

4 José Amador de los Ríos, *Historia crítica de la literatura española* (Madrid, 7 vols., 1861-1875), VII, 270. George Ticknor, *History of Spanish Literature* (New York, 3 vols., 1854), I, 413.

5 Ticknor, *History*, I, 443.

6 Amador de los Ríos, *Historia crítica*, VII, 477.

7 Amador de los Ríos, *Historia crítica*, p. 484, n. 1.

8 Ticknor, *History*, I, 275.

9 Ticknor, *History*, I, 290.
10 I may call attention, for the history of the origins of the Spanish drama, to a text drawn from the *Opus epistolarum* of Peter Martyr de Anghera, which I have cited in my study of this Italian scholar, p. 231, n. 1.
11 *La Sophonisba*, written in 1515 and, moreover, published much later.
12 Ticknor, *History*, I, 268. Compare Léopold Alfred Gabriel Germond de la Vigne, *La Celestine* (Paris, 1873), Preface, p. ix. [The authorship of *La Celestina* remains a subject of scholarly dispute. The prevailing but not unanimous viewpoint is that Rojas composed all the acts except the first, which he himself assigned to an unknown author, and which presents considerable divergencies of language and sources. There is no good reason, however, for attributing the first act to Rodrigo Cota. See Ángel del Río, *Historia de la literatura española* (New York, 3 vols., 1948), I, 112-114. Ed.]
13 Ticknor, *History*, I, Chaps. xi and xii. [Ángel del Río in his *Historia de la literatura española*, I, 109, says that "to judge from an allusion in the prologue to this work," Montalvo started the Amadís shortly after 1492. The earliest extant edition, however, was printed in Zaragoza in 1508.]
14 Amador de los Ríos, *Études politiques et littéraires sur les Juifs d'Espagne* (Paris, 1861), p. 358, n. 3.
15 Ticknor, *History*, I, 426.
16 Amador de los Ríos, *Historia crítica*, VII, 310-311.
17 Amador de los Ríos, *Historia crítica*, pp. 298, 305.
18 Palgar's work is entitled *Los Claros Varones de Castilla* (1486).
19 Ticknor, *History*, I, 178.
20 Amador de los Ríos also singles out Micer Gonzalo de Santa-María, who, at the suggestion of Ferdinand, wrote a life of Don Juan II of Aragón and tried to imitate Livy. He has nothing in common with his model and is not always impartial.
21 The sciences honored in the colleges were theology and canon law; other studies gained entrance only as a favor.
22 In J. Sáenz de Aguirre, *Collectio maxima conciliorum omnium Hispaniae et Novi Orbis* (Rome, 6 vols., 1753-1755), III, 682. February 1560. The subjects studied there were civil and canon law, medicine, the liberal arts, and Greek and Latin letters; the degrees conferred were those of master, doctor, and licentiate.
23 Vicente de la Fuente, *Historia eclesiástica de España* (Madrid, 5 vols., 1873-1875), V, 86 ff.
24 Lucius Marineus Siculus, *De Rebus Hispaniae memorabilibus*, in Andreas Schott, Johann Pastorius, and Franciscus Schott, *Hispaniae illustratae, seu rerum urbiumque Hispaniae, Lusitaniae, Aethiopiae, et Indiae scriptores varii* (Frankfurt, 4 vols., 1603-1604), I, 306.
25 J. H. Mariéjol, *Pierre Martyr d'Anghera* (Paris, 1887), p. 34.
26 Lucius Marineus Siculus, *Epistolarum familiarum libri decem et septem* (Valladolid, 1514).
27 Lorenzo Galíndez Carbajal, *Anales breves* (BAE, Vol. 70, pp. 533-565, Madrid, 1878), *Proemio*, p. 537.

28 C. H. Graux minimizes the role of Spaniards in the field of Greek philology.
29 C. J. von Hefele, *Vie du Cardinal Ximénes* (Paris, 1869), pp. 121 ff. Concerning this whole question, see the notable chapter in Hefele.
30 Hefele, p. 121.

II. The Fine Arts

1 The hospital had been founded by Cardinal Mendoza and built by Enrique de Egas.
2 Germond de Lavigne, *Itinéraire de l'Espagne et du Portugal* (Paris, 1860), p. 271.
3 Wilhelm Lübke, *Geschichte der Architektur* (Leipzig, 2 vols., 1884-1886), II, 400.
4 As at San Juan de los Reyes, at Santa Cruz de Segovia, at the Portal of the Lions of the Cathedral of Toledo.
5 In the museum of Dijon.
6 Valentín Carderera y Solano, *Iconografía española. Colección de retratos, estátuas, mausoleos, y demás monumentos inéditos de reyes, grandes, capitanes, escritores, desde el siglo XI hasta el XVII copiados de los originales* (Madrid, 2 vols., 1855-1864), folios xlviii, lxxxiii.
7 Carderera, *Iconografía española*, folio lvi.
8 Germond de Lavigne, *Itinéraire*, p. 333.
9 Carderera, *Iconografía española*, folio lxii.
10 Wilhelm Lübke, *Geschichte der Plastik* (3d ed., Leipzig, 2 vols., 1880), II, 791.
11 Jean Charles Baron Davillier, *Les Arts décoratifs en Espagne au moyen âge et à la Renaissance* (Paris, 1879), p. 31.
12 Baron Davillier and Gustave Doré, *Tour du monde* (Paris, 1864), p. 399.
13 Baron Davillier, *Les arts décoratifs*, p. 34.
14 [Since the publication of Mariéjol's book (1892), Spanish medieval and Renaissance painting has been subjected to intensive study by several generations of scholars. As a result, knowledge of the general tendencies of this period and of the work of individual artists has been vastly expanded. For a detailed recent survey of the artists and movements briefly touched on by Mariéjol, see the monumental set of C. R. Post, *A History of Spanish Painting* (Cambridge, Mass., 11 vols. to date, 1938-1953). Ed.]
15 [Modern criticism has "practically, if not entirely" reduced the very existence of Antonio del Rincón to a myth. He is now generally identified with the painter Fernando del Rincón del Figueroa, "who is conclusively proved to have lived by a series of references to him in documents of the end of the fifteenth and early years of the sixteenth century." See Chapter V, " 'Antonio' and Fernando del Rincón," in Vol. IX, Part I, *The Beginning of the Renaissance in Castile and León* (1947), of C. R. Post's *History of Spanish Painting*. Ed.]

16 Antoine de Latour, *Études sur l'Espagne* (Paris, 2 vols., 1855), II, 151.
17 [This statement must be qualified in the light of the intensive research in Spanish art history of the past seventy years. See, in particular, C. R. Post's *History of Spanish Painting* for a major effort to classify and attribute a vast body of material by the use of external and internal evidence. Ed.]
18 A. Woltmann and K. Wörmann, *Geschichte der Malerei* (Leipzig, 2 vols., 1879-1882), II, 356.
19 [C. R. Post does not include this picture among the works attributed to Fernando Gallego. Ed.]
20 [See above, note 15. Ed.]
21 Charles Blanc says that a *retablo* of his survives in the church of Robledo de Chavela, but Woltmann asserts that all his works have perished.
22 Woltmann and Wörmann, *Geschichte der Malerei,* II, 359.
23 De Latour, *Études sur l'Espagne,* II, 151.
24 [C. R. Post does not include this picture among the works attributed to Alejo Fernández. Ed.]

Editor's Bibliographical Note

Bibliographies and Guides

B. Sánchez Alonso, *Fuentes de la historia española e hispano-americana* (3d ed., Madrid, 3 vols., 1952), is an immense repository of titles, arranged according to subject and period, but without annotation. The critical bibliographies in Roger Bigelow Merriman, *The Rise of the Spanish Empire in the Old World and in the New* (New York, 4 vols., 1918-1934), adequately cover the printed materials, both collections of sources and secondary materials, up to the time of the book's writing. Antonio Ballesteros y Beretta has a useful survey of the pertinent literature in his chapter on the Catholic Sovereigns in Volume III (1922) of *La Historia de España, y su influencia en la historia universal* (Barcelona, 8 vols., 1919-1936). Ballesteros speaks highly of Mariéjol's book, terming it the only important foreign work on the reign as a whole since William H. Prescott's *The Reign of Ferdinand and Isabella the Catholic* (1838). "The account of events," says Ballesteros, "is dispassionate, and Mariéjol's judgments in general are remarkable for their sagacity and good sense." Fernán Soldevila, *Historia de España* (Barcelona, 7 vols., 1952-1957), gives in footnotes a running commentary on important new titles and opposed viewpoints. Since 1953 the quarterly *Índice Histórico Español,* published by the Centro de Estudios Internacionales, Universidad de Barcelona, has been giving brief critical notices of recently published materials on Spanish history. C. J. Bishko, "The Iberian Background of Latin American History: Recent Background and Continuing Problems," *Hispanic American Historical Review,* XXXVI (1956), 50-80, is a bibliographical essay of great value.

The Reign of Ferdinand and Isabella

The principal narrative sources for the reign are the chronicles of Hernando del Pulgar, *Crónica de los reyes católicos,* in the *Biblioteca de Autores Españoles,* LXX, 215-511 (Madrid, 1878), and in a new edition by Juan de Mata Carriazo, based on a hitherto unpublished version (2 vols., Madrid, 1943); Andrés Bernáldez, *Historia de los reyes católicos D. Fernando y D. Isabel* (Seville, 1870); and Diego de Valera, *Crónica de los reyes católicos,* ed. by Juan de Mata Carriazo (Madrid, 1927). The books of Prescott and Merriman, discussed in my preface, are standard secondary works. The New History, stressing economic, social, and intellectual developments, made its entry into Spain with Rafael Altamira's profound *Historia de España y de la civilización española* (Barcelona, 4 vols., 1913-1914); see the chapters on the reign of the Catholic Sovereigns in this work, in the equally weighty work of Ballesteros, and in the very meritorious set by Soldevila (cited above). See also the articles by various authorities on topics relating to the reign of Ferdinand and Isabella in the *Diccionario de historia de España desde sus orígenes hasta el fin del reinado de Alfonso XIII* (Madrid, 2 vols., 1952). There is a good summary treatment by J. M. Batista i Roca, "The Hispanic Kingdoms and the Catholic Kings," in Volume I of *The New Cambridge Modern History* (Cambridge University Press, 2 vols., 1957).

The most important recent work on Isabella is Orestes Ferrara's revisionist study, *L'Avènement d'Isabelle la Catholique* (Paris, 1958), discussed in my preface. The leading authority on the Aragonese background of the reign is Jaime Vicens Vives; his works include *Fernando el Católico, príncipe de Aragón, rey de Sicilia* (Madrid, 1952), *Juan II de Aragón (1398-1479)*: *Monarquía y revolución en la España del siglo XV* (Barcelona, 1953), a study of the Catalan revolution against Juan II and its social and economic content; and *Els Trastamares, Segle XV* (Barcelona, 1956), which contains a masterful brief account of the reign of the Catholic Sovereigns.

The approach of the 500th anniversary of the birth of Isabella (1951) inspired the writing of a number of books dealing with her reign. Unfortunately, the dispassionate spirit that marks Professor Vicens's writings is missing from most of these productions. One of the better of these books, Manuel Ballesteros Gaibrois,

La Obra de Isabel la Católica (Segovia, 1953), is conventional in interpretation and generally eulogistic in tone. However, it conforms to modern canons of historical writing. The same cannot be said of Luis Fernández de Retana's sprawling *Isabel la Católica, fundidora de la unidad nacional española* (Madrid, 2 vols., 1947). The homiletic and anecdotal tone of much of the book calls to mind some of the picture-biographies that adorned American homes in the late nineteenth century. Yet it must be said that this author has brought together a vast quantity of facts concerning Isabella, her circle, and her times.

H. C. Lea, *History of the Inquisition of Spain* (New York, 4 vols., 1906-1907), remains, in Merriman's words, "one of the greatest monuments of American historical scholarship." Efforts on the part of apologists for the Inquisition to diminish the book's stature by diligent search for flaws have so far yielded trifling results. For a good example of the apologetic approach to the Inquisition, see Bernardino Llorca, S. J., *La Inquisición en España* (Barcelona, 1936). The best modern life of Jiménez de Cisneros is Walter Starkie, *Grand Inquisitor, Being an Account of Cardinal Ximénez de Cisneros and His Times* (London, 1940), very favorable to its subject. Older works on the Spanish Jews should be supplemented by Abraham Neuman, *The Jews in Spain* (Philadelphia, 2 vols., 1942). Based in large part on the *responsas* or court decisions in epistolary form of Jewish rabbis, it sheds much light on Jewish culture and activities in medieval Spain. Américo Castro, *España en su historia: Cristianos, moros, y judíos* (Buenos Aires, 1948) (Eng. tr., *The Structure of Spanish History* [Princeton University Press, 1954]), is a learned, entertaining, but highly speculative work whose dubious thesis is that certain fixed traits of the Spanish character or mentality reflect the enduring stamp of Moslem and Jewish cultural influence. The distinguished Spanish medievalist Claudio Sánchez-Albornoz rejects Castro's determinism in a work that appears to be more solidly rooted in economic and social realities, *España, un enigma histórico* (Buenos Aires, 2 vols., 1957). However, in his Chapter 14, "Lo judáico en la forja de lo español," Sánchez-Albornoz presents some dubious notions of his own; he believes that the expulsion of the Jews from Spain was not only justified but overdue (*tardío*), and ascribes an entirely negative significance to the Jewish economic role in Spain.

The works of Prescott and Merriman remain standard accounts

of the diplomatic and military phases of the reign of the Catholic Sovereigns. José M. Doussinague, *La Política internacional de Fernando el Católico* (Madrid, 1944), is very eulogistic in spirit; it credits Ferdinand with being guided in his diplomacy by the high ideal of an all-Christian war against the infidel and acquits him of having a basically anti-French orientation. However, the book has a valuable documentary appendix and contains much useful material, especially on the North African campaigns. The international agreements of the Catholic Sovereigns have been conveniently brought together in *Tratados internacionales de los reyes católicos* (Madrid, 2 vols., 1952). Émile G. Léonard, *Les Angevins de Naples* (Paris, 1954), is a massively documented study. For Spain in Naples, see Francisco Elías de Tejada, *Nápoles hispánico (la etapa aragonesa, 1442-1503)* (Madrid, 1958).

The splendid biography of S. E. Morison, *Admiral of the Ocean Sea: A Life of Christopher Columbus* (Boston, 2 vols., 1942), superseded all previous accounts. The best recent Spanish work is Antonio Ballesteros y Beretta, *Cristóbal Colón y el descubrimiento de America* (Barcelona, 2 vols., 1945). *The Life of the Admiral Christopher Columbus by His Son Ferdinand*, tr. and ed. by Benjamin Keen (Rutgers University Press, 1959), is the first modern English version of a source of fundamental importance. C. H. Haring, *The Spanish Empire in America* (rev. ed., New York, 1952), is a standard work on the institutions of the Indies. An extensive literature has grown up on the juridical and moral problems raised by the Spanish Conquest and on the development of Spain's Indian policy. Silvio Zavala, *New Viewpoints on the Spanish Colonization of America* (University of Pennsylvania Press, 1943), ably summarizes modern insights into the evolution of land and labor systems in the Indies. On Las Casas, see the writings of Lewis Hanke, especially *The Spanish Struggle for Justice in the Conquest of America* (University of Pennsylvania Press, 1948); *Bartolomé de Las Casas. An Interpretation of His Life and Writings* (The Hague, 1951); and *Aristotle and the American Indians* (New York, 1959), a study of the great debate between Las Casas and Juan Ginés de Sepúlveda over the nature and capacities of the Indians. An older life of popular character is F. A. MacNutt, *Bartholomew de Las Casas* (New York, 1909). A full-scale biography by Manuel Giménez Fernández, *Bartolomé de Las Casas* (Seville, 1953-   ), projected in eight volumes, is in progress.

The Institutions

The works of Merriman, Altamira, Ballesteros, and Soldevila are all useful for the institutional side of the reign of the Catholic Sovereigns. Important recent monographs in this field include Fernando Hebí, *El Corregidor en el municipio español bajo la monarquía absoluta* (Madrid, 1943); Rafael Gilbert y Sánchez de la Vega, *El Concejo de Madrid* (Madrid, 1949); J. M. Font Rius, *Instituciones medievales españolas* (Madrid, 1949); Claudio Sánchez-Albornoz, *España, un enigma histórico,* is also useful for institutional developments; see particularly Chapter 12, "Inmadurez del feudalismo español," on the mooted subject of Spanish feudalism. Consult also the special articles in the *Diccionario de historia de España.*

Economic history was until lately neglected by Spanish scholars, but typical recent monographs on the era of the Catholic Sovereigns include E. Ibarra y Rodríguez, *El Problema cerealista en España durante el reinado de los reyes católicos (1475-1516)* (Madrid, 1941-1942); Leopoldo Piles Ros, "La Expulsión de los Judíos en Valencia. Repercusiones económicas," *Sefarad,* XV (1955), 89-101, and "Situación económica de las aljamas aragonesas a comienzos del siglo XV," *Sefarad,* X (1950), 73-114, 367-384; and María del Carner Carlí, *Mercaderes en Castilla (1252-1512),* in *Cuadernos de Historia de España,* XXI-XXII (1954), 146-328. American scholars have made serious contributions to Spanish economic history; their studies include Julius Klein's admirable work, *The Mesta: A Study in Spanish Economic History* (Cambridge, Massachusetts, 1920); E. J. Hamilton, *American Trade and the Price Revolution in Spain, 1501-1660* (Cambridge, Massachusetts, 1934), and *Money, Prices and Wages in Valencia, Aragón, and Navarre, 1351-1500* (Cambridge, Massachusetts, 1936); and R. S. Smith, *The Spanish Guild Merchant: A History of the Consulado, 1250-1700* (Duke University Press, 1940). R. S. Smith has a chapter on Spanish medieval agriculture in Vol. I of *The Cambridge Economic History of Europe* (1942).

The increase in monographic research on Spanish economic history has made possible improved efforts at generalization and synthesis in this area. Two recent studies for the era of the Catholic Sovereigns are Jaime Vicens Vives, *Manual de la historia económica da España* (Barcelona, 1959), Chapter 22, "La Economía de la época de los reyes católicos"; and Santiago Sobrequés Vidal, "La Época de los reyes católicos," in Jaime Vicens Vives, ed., *Historia social y económica de España y América* (Barcelona, 3 vols., 1957), II, 405-492.

Social Life

The profusely illustrated works of Ballesteros and Soldevila, and the above-cited contribution of Sobrequés Vidal to the *Historia social y económica de España y América,* are especially useful for the life and manners of the different classes in the age of the Catholic Sovereigns. On the Spanish character or mentality, see, in addition to the works of Américo Castro and Sánchez-Albornoz, cited above, Rufino Blanco-Fombona, *El Conquistador español del siglo XVI* (Madrid, 1922); J. L. Romero, "Sobre la Biografía española del siglo XV y los ideales de vida," *Cuadernos de historia de España,* I-II (1944), 115-138; Carmelo Viñas y Mey, "El Espíritu castellano de aventura y empresa y la España de los RR CC," *Archivo de derecho público,* V (1952), 13-83.

M. J. Aragoneses, "Los Movimientos y luchas sociales en la baja edad media," *Estudios de historia social de España,* I (Madrid, 1949), 275-423, perceptively analyzes class alignments and struggles in medieval Spain; L. Redouet y López-Doriga, "El Latifundio y su formación en la España medieval," *Ibid.,* pp. 139-203, deals chiefly with the early medieval period. On the agrarian question in Catalonia, the older work of Eduardo de Hinojosa, *El Régimen señorial y la cuestión agraria en Cataluña* (Madrid, 1905), should be supplemented by J. Vicens Vives, *Historia de los remensas en el siglo XV* (Barcelona, 1945). An interesting contribution is Francisco Torrella Niuhó, "Vida económico-social de un gremio textil en una villa catalana en los siglos XV y XVI," *Hispania,* July-Sept. 1952.

Intellectual Life

Three leading works on Spanish literature, containing useful discussions of the literary production of the era of the Catholic Sovereigns, are J. Fitzmaurice Kelly, *A New History of Spanish*

Literature (New York, 1926); A. Valbuena Prat, *Historia de la literatura española* (3d ed., Barcelona, 3 vols., 1940); Gerald Brenan, *The Literature of the Spanish People* (New York, 1951). The prose masterpiece of the era, *La Celestina,* has been repeatedly translated into English. A recent version is by L. B. Simpson, *The Celestina: A Novel in Dialogue* (University of California Press, 1955). However, the classic and probably still the best translation is that of James Mabbe; it can be found conveniently in Eric Bentley, ed., *The Classic Theatre,* Vol. III, *Six Spanish Plays* (New York, 1959). The same volume also contains an excellent English version by Roy Campbell of Lope de Vega's powerful *Fuente Ovejuna,* a play which suggests the reverence and affection felt by the Spanish people for the Catholic Sovereigns a century after their death.

For philosophical trends in the reign of the Catholic Sovereigns, see Marcial Solana, *Historia de la filosofía española: Época del renacimiento* (Madrid, 3 vols., 1940-1941). On the humanists at the court of Ferdinand and Isabella, see the encyclopedic first chapter in A. F. Bell, *Luis de León* (Oxford, 1923). Caro Lynn, *A College Professor of the Renaissance* (Chicago, 1937), is a truly delightful as well as informing account, not only of the attractive figure of Lucius Marineus Siculus but of the whole educational and humanistic environment in which he moved. More technical is R. B. Tate, "Italian Humanism and Spanish Historiography of the Fifteenth Century. A Study of the Paralipomenon Hispaniae of Joan de Margarit, Cardinal Bishop of Gerona." *Bulletin of the John Rylands Library,* XXXIV, 1 (Manchester, 1951), 137-165; *Speculum,* XXVI (1952).

The literature on Spanish art is abundant. A standard survey is Marqués de Lozoya, *Historia del arte hispánico* (Barcelona, 5 vols., 1931-1949). Enrique Lafuente Ferrari, *Breve Historia de la pintura española* (Madrid, 1953), is a recent introduction. Much more ambitious in scope and aim is C. R. Post, *A History of Spanish Painting* (Cambridge, Massachusetts, 11 vols. to date, 1938-   ). For the sculpture of the era of the Catholic Sovereigns, see B. I. Proske, *Castilian Sculpture: Gothic to Renaissance* (New York, 1951). Bernard Bevan, *History of Spanish Architecture* (London, 1938), is a readable survey of the subject. Enrique Lafuente Ferrari provides an extensive bibliography on all phases of Spanish art at the close of his article on this topic in the *Encyclopedia Americana* (1955 edition). Of outstanding interest is the handsomely illustrated, multi-volume *Ars Hispaniae: Historia universal del arte hispánico,* published by Editorial Plus-Ultra in Madrid, under the direction of José Gudiol, each volume by the appropriate specialist in the field.

Glossary of Terms

Terms that occur only once, and are glossed or defined in the text, are not included in this list. Only senses applicable to this book are covered.

adelantado or *adelantado mayor*. The governor of a large district in medieval Castile, having military, judicial, and administrative functions, especially that of captain general of the armed forces of the district in time of war.

adelantamiento. The office, charge, or jurisdiction of an *adelantado*.

aduana. Customs duty.

alcabala. A tax on commercial transactions: sales tax.

alcaide. The governor and commander of a fortress or castle, entrusted with its guard and defense.

alcalde. Judge; especially, a municipal judge having civil and criminal jurisdiction and also certain administrative duties.

alcalde mayor. (1) A chief or presiding municipal judge in a municipality having several *alcaldes*. (2) The chief justice and governor of a district. (3) The bailiff of a lord having seignorial jurisdiction.

alcázar. (1) A fortress. (2) A royal palace, fortified or unfortified.

aldea. Village.

alfaquí. A Moslem spiritual leader and teacher of the Koran.

alguacil. A municipal officer charged with maintenance of public order, apprehension and detention of criminals, and similar duties.

almojarifazgo. Import duty.

almojarife. Tax gatherer.

audiencia. A royal court having supreme jurisdiction over a kingdom or province.

auto. A judicial decree or sentence.

ayuntamiento. The governing body of a Spanish municipality: the whole body of municipal magistrates.

bando. Edict or proclamation.

barrio. Ward or quarter of a town or city.

bisoño. A new soldier: a fresh recruit.

brazo. One of the estates or orders having representation in the Cortes.

broquel. A small shield.

caballero. A member of the nobility of the second class: knight, *hidalgo;* especially, a knight whose privileges and noble status were originally based on the fact of having brought horse and arms to battle.

cámara. Royal treasury.

casa fuerte. Castle: stronghold.

chancillería. Audiencia.

comunero. A member of the party that rose in defense of municipal liberties against the absolutism of Charles V (1520-1521).

comunidad. A grouping of several Aragonese towns and villages around an urban center which gave the grouping its name and had jurisdiction over it.

concejo. A Spanish municipal council, consisting in the early Middle Ages of an assembly of the citizens or householders, and later of a smaller body, the *ayuntamiento.*

condestable. The highest military officer in medieval Castile, being commander-in-chief of the royal army; under the Catholic Sovereigns the office became merely honorific.

confeso. A converted Jew or a descendant of one.

Consejo de Justicia. The supreme royal council of Castile, having large judicial, legislative, and administrative powers—called also Consejo Real, Consejo de Castilla.

contínuo. One of a body of 100 yeomen who kept guard over the Spanish king's person and palace.

corregidor. A representative of the crown placed at the head of a Castilian municipality, being president of the *ayuntamiento* and having extensive judicial, administrative, and financial powers.

Cortes. A periodic assembly of representatives of the clergy, the nobility, and certain towns of a Spanish kingdom; summoned by the king for purposes of consultation and especially to respond to a royal request for money.

diezmo. (1) Ecclesiastical tithe. (2) Customs duty.

dinero. A Spanish coin used especially in the realm of Aragón; 1 dinero = 1.5 maravedís.

ducado. A Spanish gold coin of the value of $2.32 in U.S. pre-1934 gold dollars.

escopetero. A harquebusier: musketeer.

escribano. Notary or scrivener.

escudero. A member of the nobility of the second class: squire.

espingardero. A soldier armed with an *espingarda,* a long Moorish musket.

estado llano. The order of commoners: Third Estate.

estamento. Estate: order.

fiel almotacén. Municipal inspector of weights and measures.

fieldad. The office or charge of a *fiel almotacén.*

fuero. A constitution or code of laws or privileges, often applying to a particular locality or group; specifically, the charter of a medieval Spanish municipality.

galgo. Greyhound.

grande. A Spanish nobleman of the most elevated rank: grandee.

greuge or *greuje.* A wrong done by the King of Aragón, his officials, or an estate to some individual or group of individuals in violation of the law.

hildalgo or *hijodalgo.* A member of the nobility of the second class: gentleman.

infanta. A legitimate daughter of a Spanish king.

infante. A legitimate son of a Spanish king.

infanzón. A member of the nobility of the second class: *hidalgo.*

jinete. Light cavalryman.

jurado. Any of several officials of the Spanish medieval municipality.

letrado. Lawyer: legist

maestresala. Mayordomo or steward.

maravedí. A Spanish copper coin of the value of $.007 in U.S. pre-1934 dollars.

Marrano. A Jewish convert to Catholicism who secretly practices Judaism.

merindad. The office, charge, or jurisdiction of a *merino.*

merino. The governor of a district in medieval Castile, often appointed by and serving under a *merino mayor.*

merino mayor. The governor of a large district or province in medieval Castile, having military, judicial, and administrative functions, especially that of captain general of the armed forces of the district in time of war; the office was abolished by the Catholic Sovereigns.

Morisco. A Moslem convert to Catholicism.

mosén or *mossén.* A honorific title or address used in Valencia and Aragón, equivalent to the Castilian "Don."

oidor. Judge.

payese de remensa. A Catalan peasant who could not leave his land without purchasing personal redemption from servile status at a price satisfactory to his lord (*remensa personal*).

pechero. Taxpayer: taxable.

peña brava. A castle held by a lawless noble: a castle used for brigandage or illegal warfare.

peón. Foot soldier.

posada. Inn.

pragmática. A royal ordinance: pragmatic.

procurador. A deputy to the Cortes of a town having the right of such representation in the national assembly.

real or *real de vellón.* A Spanish silver coin of the value of $0.133 in U.S. pre-1934 gold dollars.

regidor. Councilman.

repartimiento. A distribution of conquered territory and population among the Spanish conquerors; also, an individual allotment of such territory and persons.

rico hombre or *rico home.* A Spanish noble of the first class: one on whom the title of *rico hombre* has been conferred by the king.

servicio. An extraordinary contribution by the Cortes, designed to cover unforeseen expenses incurred by the prince.

shohet. A person who slaughters according to a prescribed ritual animals or fowls to be used by Jews.

solariego. A Castilian peasant who worked the land of another and had a servile or semiservile relationship to the lord of the land.

tercia real. The royal third of the ecclesiastical tithe.

universidad. An Aragonese city or town, usually having jurisdiction over an extensive territory, that sent deputies to the Cortes of Aragón.

vecindad. Citizenship of a town.

vecino. A citizen of a town: householder.

veinticuatro. A councilman or magistrate of medieval Seville and some other towns of Andalusia.

villa. Town.

villancico. A Spanish verse form resembling the madrigal.

venta. Inn.

zalmedina. A petty judge in Aragón.

Glossary of Persons

This glossary contains basic biographical facts about persons mentioned in the text. The names of the Catholic Sovereigns and a few well-known figures such as Christopher Columbus have been omitted. For members of the royal houses of Castile and Aragón, see also the appropriate genealogical table.

Abul Hassan, Muley. King (as Mohammed X) of Granada (1462-1482, 1483-1485); brother of El Zagal; father of Boabdil, the last Moorish king of Granada.

Acuña, Antonio de (?-1526). Archdean of Valpuesta and later Bishop of Zamora (1507-1522); leader in the revolt of the *comuneros*.

Acuña, Fernando de. Spanish soldier; son of the Count of Buendía; named Governor (Justicia Mayor) of Galicia by the Catholic Sovereigns; active in suppressing baronial disorders in the province.

Adrian VI (1459-1523). Dean of Louvain, Bishop of Tortosa, and Grand Inquisitor of Aragón (1516); of Flemish origin; named Cardinal by Leo X (1517); for a short time regent of Spain (1520); Pope, 1522-1523.

Affonso V, the African (1432-1481). King of Portugal; in 1471 invaded Africa, capturing Arcila and Tangier; invaded Castile in support of La Beltraneja's claims to the throne; defeated at Toro (1476) by Ferdinand the Catholic.

Affonso Henriques (1111-1185). First King of Portugal, son of

Count Henri of Burgundy; expelled the Moors from Portuguese territory.

Aguilar, Alonso de. *See* Aguilar y de Córdoba, Alonso Fernández de.

Aguilar y de Córdoba, Alonso Fernández de, Marquis of Aguilar, Lord of Montilla (?-1501). Distinguished Spanish soldier, elder brother of Gonzalo de Córdoba; killed in battle against Morisco rebels in the Sierra Bermeja of Granada.

Aisha. *See under* Zoraya.

Alaminos, Antonio. Spanish navigator who accompanied Columbus on voyages in 1499 and 1502; chief pilot of early expeditions to Mexico (1517-1520).

Alba, Duke of. *See* Álvarez de Toledo, Fadrique.

Albión, Juan de. Alcaide of Perpignan and diplomat; played important role in Italian negotiations.

Albret, Jean d'. King of Navarre (1484-1516) by his marriage with Catherine de Foix.

Alburquerque, Duke of. *See* Cueva, Beltrán de la.

Alexander VI. *See* Borgia, Alexander.

Alfonso I, the Battler. King of Aragón and Navarre (1104-1134); conquered Zaragoza and other important towns from the Moors.

Alfonso II, the Chaste. King of Aragón (1162-1196); son of Berenguela and Ramón Berenguer IV; first ruler of a single Aragonese-Catalan realm.

Alfonso IV, the Good (1299-1336). King of Aragón (1327-1336); his reign was dominated by war with Genoa over possession of Corsica and Sardinia.

Alfonso V, the Magnanimous (1394-1458). King of Aragón (1416-1458), of Sicily (as Alfonso, 1416-1458), and of Naples (as Alfonso I, 1443-1458); conquered Naples (1443); spent most of the rest of his life there and made it one of the brilliant literary courts of the period.

Alfonso VI, the Brave (1040-1109). King of Castile and León (1072-1109); reconquered Toledo (1085), a decisive event in the Christian advance against the Moors.

Alfonso X, the Sage (1221-1284). King of Castile and León (1252-1284); patron of arts and sciences; directed preparation of a great law code (Las Siete Partidas).

Alfonso XI (1312-1350). King of Castile and León; subdued rebel lords and fostered political authority of the towns; won battles of Salado (1340) and the Palmones River (1343), decisive in the Reconquest.

Alfonso (1453-1468). Son of Juan II and half-brother of Enrique IV of Castile; proclaimed lawful heir of the throne by rebellious nobles in place of La Beltraneja; died, perhaps by poisoning, July 5, 1468.

Alfonso de Alcalá. Jewish physician of Alcalá la Real, of the last part of the fifteenth century; convert to Catholicism; employed by Cardinal Jiménez in revision of the Polyglot Bible; with Pablo Coronell translated into Latin the Hebrew books of the Old Testament.

Alfonso de Aragón. *See* Aragón, Alfonso de.

Alfonso de Zamora (?-1532). Spanish rabbi, converted to Catholicism in 1506; first professor of Hebrew in the University of Salamanca; charged by Cardinal Jiménez with correction of the Hebrew text of the Polyglot Bible and translation into Latin of the Chaldean paraphrase.

Alfonso Henriques. *See* Affonso Henriques.

Almazán, Miguel Pérez de. *See* Pérez de Almazán, Miguel.

Almela *or* Almella, Diego Rodríguez de (1426-1492). Spanish priest and historian; chaplain to Isabella the Catholic.

Almohades. Moslem dynasty in North Africa and Spain which overthrew the Almorávides in the middle of the twelfth century.

Almonacid, Sebastián de. Spanish sculptor of the late fifteenth and early sixteenth centuries.

Almorávides. Moslem sect and dynasty established in Spain in 1091 and overthrown by the Almohades in the middle of the twelfth century.

Alonso de Aragón. *See* Aragón, Alonso de.

Alonso de Cartagena. *See* Cartagena, Alonso de.

Álvarez de Toledo, Fadrique, second Duke of Alba (?-1531). Spanish noble and soldier; served with distinction in the War of Granada; led Spanish forces in the conquest of Navarre (1512).

Anaya de Maldonado, Diego (c. 1360-1442). Spanish prelate; named Bishop of Salamanca in 1401; founded there a college providing free education and devoted to this establishment almost his entire fortune.

Anne of Brittany (1477-1514). Wife (1) of Charles VIII of France, (2) of Louis XII; through her Brittany was united to crown of France.

Antequera, Ferdinand of. *See* Ferdinand I, of Antequera.

Aponte *or* Ponte, Pedro de. Spanish painter of the fifteenth century; in 1479 appointed court painter of Ferdinand the Catholic.

Aragón, Alfonso de, Duke of Gandía and Count of Denia (?-1412). Unsuccessfully claimed the throne of Aragón on the death of Martín the Humane.

Aragón, Alonso de, Duke of Villahermosa (?-1485). Natural son of Juan II of Aragón and thus brother of Ferdinand the Catholic; admired for his bravery and knightly character.

Aragón, Alonso de (1470-1520). Natural son of Ferdinand the Catholic; Archbishop of Zaragoza.

Arias Dávila, Juan (1410-1497). Bishop of Segovia and foe of the Inquisition.

Aubigny, Robert Stewart, Count of Beaumont-le-Roger, Seigneur d' (?-1544). Marshal of France; distinguished himself in the Italian wars, taking part in the sieges of Bologna (1506) and Genoa (1507) and the battles of Marignano (1515) and Pavia (1525).

Ayala, Diego López de. *See* López de Ayala, Diego.

Ayora, Gonzalo de. Spanish military writer and reformer under the Catholic Sovereigns; introduced the tactical theory and practice of the Swiss and German infantry into the Spanish army.

Balboa, Vasco Núñez de (c. 1475-1517). Spanish conquistador; discoverer of the Pacific (1513); explored northern coast of South America with Rodrigo de Bastidas (1500); spent several years on Española; quarreled with Ojeda's lieutenant in New Andalusia and with the newly appointed governor of the colony, Pedrarias (Pedro Arias de Avila), who had him tried and beheaded.

Barbosa, Arias *or* Ario (?-1530). Portuguese scholar; studied at Salamanca and Florence; taught at Salamanca where he and Nebrija introduced a new method of grammatical instruction.

Beltraneja, La. *See* Juana, Doña.

Benavente, Rodrigo Pimentel, Count of. Spanish grandee, partisan of Isabella in struggles over the succession to the throne of Castile; prominent in the wars and politics of Castile under the Catholic Sovereigns.

Berenguela (1180?-1246). Queen of León and Castile, daughter of Alfonso VIII of Castile; wife of Alfonso IX of León;

regent during the minority of her brother Enrique I; later occupied the throne and abdicated in favor of her son Ferdinand (III, of Castile and León).

Bergenroth, Gustav Adolf B. (1813-1869). German editor of a major collection of Spanish diplomatic correspondence, based on research in the Archives of Simancas, still important despite editorial flaws discovered by modern scholarship.

Bernáldez, Andrés, Curate of Palacios (?-1513). Spanish priest and chronicler; author of the important source *Historia de los reyes católicos*.

Berruguete, Alonso (1488-1561). Spanish sculptor, painter, and architect; court painter and sculptor to the Emperor Charles V; spent many years studying in Italy; remembered especially for his altars in Valladolid and the choir stalls of the Cathedral of Toledo.

Berruguete, Pedro (?-c. 1500). Spanish painter; father of Alonso; with Rincón del Figueroa painted (1483-1488) the sanctuary of the Chapter of Toledo.

Blanc, Charles (1813-1882). French art critic.

Blanca of Castile (1183-1252). Queen of France; married (1200) the future Louis VIII of France.

Blancas y Tomás, Jerónimo de (?-1590). Aragonese historian who succeeded Zurita as official chronicler of Aragón.

Blanche of Navarre (1385-1441). Queen of Aragón; daughter of Charles III of Navarre; wife of (1) Martín I of Sicily, (2) Juan II of Aragón; mother of Don Carlos de Viana.

Boabdil (Abu 'Abdullah) (?-1527). Last Moorish king (as Mohammed XI) of Granada, 1482-1483, 1486-1492; driven from Granada (1492) by the Catholic Sovereigns; crossed to Africa and retired to Fez.

Bobadilla, Francisco de (?-1502). Spanish officer sent to Española to investigate charges against Columbus, whom he succeeded as Viceroy of the Indies; sent Columbus and his brothers home in chains; was himself relieved and sent home under arrest, but went down at sea.

Boil *or* Boyl, Bernardo. Spanish priest employed by the Catholic Sovereigns on diplomatic missions; accompanied Columbus on Second Voyage to Española but quarreled with the Discoverer and returned to Spain in November 1494; abbot of Benedictine abbey of San Miguel de Cuxa in Roussillon (1503-1507).

Borgia, Alexander (1431-1503). Better known as Alexander VI, Pope, 1492-1503.

Borgia, Rodrigo. Original name of Alexander VI.

Borgoña, Juan de (c. 1470-c. 1536). Distinguished painter of Toledo; brother of Felipe Vigarni; painted in 1493 the amphitheater of the University of Alcalá de Henares and employed from 1508 to 1511 in the Cathedral at Toledo, where he executed the fresco of the taking of Oran by Cardinal Jiménez.

Budé, Guillaume (1468-1540). French humanist, friend of Erasmus, who fostered rise of interest in Greek language and literature; one of the founders of the Bibliothèque Nationale.

Bureau, Jean (?-1463). French military engineer who served with distinction in the wars of Charles VII and Louis XI; named marshal of the French artillery in 1430.

Cabot, John (1450-1498). Italian navigator in the service of Henry VII; his discoveries in 1497 and 1498 (mostly in what is now Canadian territory) formed the basis for English claims to North America.

Cabot, Sebastian (1476?-1557). Italian navigator; son of John Cabot; chief pilot to Charles V (1519-1526, 1526-1534); explored La Plata region (1526-1530).

Cabra, Count of. *See* Fernández de Córdoba, Diego.

Cabral, Pedro Álvares (c. 1460-c. 1526). Portuguese navigator and explorer; sent by Manoel I to establish trade with East Indies (1500-1501) but was carried westward by current and winds to the coasts of Brazil, of which he took possession in the name of Portugal.

Cádiz, Marquis of. *See* Ponce de León, Rodrigo.

Capmany, Antonio de (1742-1813). Spanish philologist, historian, and man of letters.

Cárdenas, Alonso de (?-1499). Spanish nobleman; Grand Master of the Order of Santiago.

Carderera y Solano, Valentín (1796-1880). Spanish archaeologist, writer, and painter.

Cardona, Ramón de. *See* Folch de Cardona, Ramón.

Carlos de Viana (1421-1461). Son of Juan II by his first wife, Blanche of Navarre; disputed with his father the succession to the throne of Navarre.

Carrillo, Alfonso de (1410-1482). Archbishop of Toledo; prominent in the wars and politics of his time; first supported

Isabella's claims to the throne of Castile but later sided with La Beltraneja.

Cartagena, Alonso de (1396-1456). Bishop of Burgos, patron of art, and historian, of Jewish origin; his principal work is a history of Spain in Latin from early times to 1456.

Casas, Bartolomé de las. *See* Las Casas, Bartolomé de.

Casaubon, Isaac (1559-1614). French theologian and classical scholar.

Castagno, Andrea del (1397-1457). Florentine painter.

Castillo, Diego Enríquez del. *See* Enríquez del Castillo, Diego.

Castro, Juan Sánchez de. *See* Sánchez de Castro, Juan.

Catherine of Aragón (1485-1536). Queen of England. Youngest child, fourth daughter of the Catholic Sovereigns; first queen of Henry VIII of England (1509); abandoned by Henry (1531).

Cavour, Camillo Benso, Conte di (1810-1861). Italian statesman, Prime Minister of Kingdom of Sardinia (1852-1859, 1860-1861), and leading figure in movement of Italian unification.

Cerda, Alfonso de la (1271?-1333?). Son of Ferdinand de la Cerda and grandson of Alfonso X; his hereditary right to succeed his father as heir apparent to the throne of Castile was set aside by the Cortes of 1276 in favor of the Infante Don Sancho.

Cerda, Ferdinand de la (?-1275). First-born son of Alfonso X, King of Castile and León; his death gave rise to a dynastic struggle over the succession to the throne.

Cerda, Luis de la. *See* Medina Celi, Duke of.

Charles V (1500-1558). Emperor of the Holy Roman Empire and King of Spain (as Charles I); as son of Philip the Handsome and Juana the Mad, inherited vast dominions including Spain, the Netherlands, Naples, North Italy, central Europe, and the Spanish colonies in America.

Charles V (1337-1380). King of France (1364-1380); strengthened the crown at the expense of the nobility; initiated the Franco-Castilian alliance.

Charles VII, the Victorious (1403-1461). King of France (1422-1461); his reign was marked by struggles to recover French domains in the north and southwest from the English.

Charles VIII (1470-1498). King of France (1483-1498); son of Louis XI; began Italian wars by his invasion of Naples.

Charles I, of Anjou (1220-1285). King of Naples and Sicily (1226-1285); driven from Sicily by Pedro III of Aragón.

Chinchilla, Garcí López de. Prominent legist and member of the royal council of the Catholic Sovereigns; sent with Fernando de Acuña to suppress baronial disorders in Galicia.

Christus *or* Cristus, Petrus (c. 1400-c. 1473). Flemish painter.

Cid, the, called *El Cid Campeador* (The Lord Champion) (c. 1040-1099). National hero of Spain; identified with the historical personage Rodrigo Díaz de Vivar, famous for exploits against the Moors; captured Valencia from the Moors (1072); subject of twelfth century epic poem *Cantar de Mio Cid* (Song of the Cid).

Ciruelo, Pedro. Spanish scholar of the sixteenth century; taught at Universities of Alcalá and Paris; author of numerous works on philosophy and mathematics.

Cisneros, Francisco Jiménez de. *See* Jiménez de Cisneros.

Claude of France (1499-1524). Oldest daughter of Louis XII and Anne of Britanny; first wife of François I.

Coloma, Juan de, Baron of Aljaferín. Secretary to the Catholic Sovereigns; signed Treaty of Barcelona (1493); drafted Capitulations of 1492 with Columbus.

Columbus, Bartholomew (1455?-1514). Brother of Christopher Columbus and his collaborator in the Enterprise of the Indies and other projects; founded Santo Domingo (1496).

Columbus, Diego (1480?-1526). Son of Christopher Columbus; second Viceroy and Admiral of the Indies.

Columbus, Ferdinand (1488-1539). Natural son of Christopher Columbus; humanist, cosmographer, and author of an invaluable life of his father.

Columbus, Luis (c. 1521-1572). Grandson of Christopher Columbus; third Admiral of the Indies.

Córdoba, Diego Fernández de. *See* Fernández de Córdoba, Diego.

Córdoba, Gonzalo Fernández de. *See* Fernández de Córdoba, Gonzalo.

Córdoba, Pedro de. Spanish painter active in Córdoba in the second half of the fifteenth century.

Córdoba, Pedro de (1483-1525). Spanish Dominican, vicar of the first community of his order on Española; friend of Las Casas and active in the struggle against Indian slavery.

Coronell, Pablo. Spanish Jew, convert to Catholicism, of the late fifteenth century; employed by Cardinal Jiménez in revision of the Polyglot Bible; with Alfonso de Alcalá translated into Latin the Hebrew books of the Old Testament.

Cortés, Hernando (1485-1547). Spanish conquistador; came to Española (1504); participated in the conquest of Cuba (1511-1512); founded Veracruz in Aztec territory (1519); pushed into the highlands over Aztec objections and entered their capital of Tenochtitlán without resistance; driven out by Aztec uprising (1520), but returned with reinforcements to besiege Tenochtitlán, which fell after a desperate struggle (1521); extended conquest into Central America and organized various exploring expeditions; heaped with honors and rewards by the crown, but later fell under suspicion, was stripped of his authority, and spent last years in vain efforts to gain redress at the Spanish court.

Cosa, Juan de la (c. 1460-1510). Spanish navigator and map-maker; sailed with Columbus as master of *Santa María* in 1492 and on voyage of exploration of Cuba (1498); made at least five voyages to northern coast of South America between 1499 and 1509; his map of the New World, made in 1500, is the oldest known.

Cota, Rodrigo (?-1470). Spanish poet sometimes cited, without good reason, as the author of the first act of *La Celestina*.

Cueva, Beltrán de la, Duke of Alburquerque (?-1492). Spanish nobleman, favorite of Enrique IV; asserted by the king's enemies to be the father of La Beltraneja.

Dalmau, Luis. Spanish painter of the fifteenth century; court painter of Alfonso V of Aragón.

Dancart, Maestre (?-1487). Flemish woodcarver active in Seville.

Dávila, Juan Arias. *See* Arias Dávila, Juan.

Delli, Dello (1372-1421). Florentine painter and sculptor active in Spain; court painter of Juan II of Castile.

Denia, Count of. *See* Aragón, Alfonso de.

Deza, Diego (1444-1523). Spanish Dominican; Archbishop of Seville; protector of Christopher Columbus; Inquisitor-General of Castile, 1499-1506.

Díaz de Aux, Martín. Justicia of Aragón (1433-1440); murdered in prison at orders of Alfonso V.

Dorset, Marquis of. *See* Grey, Thomas.

Du Cange, Charles du Fresne, Sieur (1610-1688). French historian and philologist.

Ducas, Demetrius. Cretan professor of Greek at Alcalá de Henares; worked on revision of Greek text of the Polyglot Bible.

Du Guesclin, Bertrand (c. 1320-1380). Constable of France; distinguished himself in campaigns against the English and Pedro the Cruel of Castile and León.

Egas, Antón de. Flemish sculptor and architect in Spain; in 1509 with Alfonso Rodríguez prepared plan for the new Cathedral at Salamanca.

Egas, Enrique de (c. 1455-c. 1534). Flemish architect in Spain; with his brother, Antón de Egas, especially active in Toledo; his most notable design is the Hospital Real in Santiago de Compostela.

El Zagal. *See* Mohammed XII.

Encina *or* Enzina, Juan del (1469?-1529). Spanish poet and musician, whose dramatic works marked a transition from religious to secular drama in Spain; a collection of his dramatic and lyric pieces, *Cancionero,* was first published in 1496.

Enrique I (1204?-1217). King of Castile and León (1214-1217) under tutelage of Doña Berenguela.

Enrique II (1333-1379). King of Castile and León (1369-1379); founder of Trastamara dynasty.

Enrique III, the Sickly (1379-1406). King of Castile and León (1390-1406); attempted to restore royal authority by punishing lawless nobles and revoking grants made by his predecessors.

Enrique IV, the Liberal *or* the Impotent (1425-1474). King of Castile and León (1454-1474), in whose reign feudal disorder reached its climax; he struggled vainly to uphold the rights of his daughter Juana (La Beltraneja) to the throne against Isabella.

Enríquez. Noble Castilian family in which the title of Admiral of Castile was hereditary.

Enríquez, Alonso. Admiral of Castile (1473-1485); son of Fadrique Enríquez I and thus uncle of Ferdinand the Catholic.

Enríquez I, Fadrique (?-1473). Admiral of Castile and grandfather of Ferdinand the Catholic.

Enríquez II, Fadrique (?-1537). Admiral of Castile from 1485; son of Alonso Enríquez.

Enríquez, Juana (1425-1468). Daughter of Fadrique Enríquez I and wife of Juan II of Aragón.

Enríquez del Castillo, Diego (1434-1504?). Chaplain and chronicler of Enrique IV; his *Crónica de Enrique IV* is very favorable to the king.

Enríquez de Ribera, Pedro. Spanish noble; cousin of Ferdinand the Catholic; Adelantado of Andalusia under the Catholic Sovereigns.

Estienne *or* Étienne, Henri (1528-1598). One of a distinguished French family of scholars and printers; edited and printed numerous editions of Greek and Latin classics.

Eyck, Jan van (c. 1386-1440). Flemish painter; court painter of Philip the Good, Duke of Burgundy; the works of Jan and his brother, Hubert, greatly influenced the art of northern Europe.

Fancelli, Domenico di Alessandro (1469-1519). Florentine sculptor in Spain; his most noted works are the tombs of Diego Hurtado de Mendoza, Archbishop of Seville, of the Infante Don Juan in Santo Tomás de Ávila, and of the Catholic Sovereigns in Granada.

Federico I (1451?-1504). King of Naples (1496-1501); deposed by Ferdinand the Catholic.

Ferdinand I (1503-1564). Emperor of the Holy Roman Empire (1556-1564); son of Philip the Handsome and Juana the Mad.

Ferdinand I, the Great (?-1065). King of León, Castile, and Asturias; united León and Castile under his rule; compelled surrender of Coimbra by the Moors (1064).

Ferdinand III, the Saint (c. 1200-1252). King of Castile and León; prominent in the Reconquest, capturing Córdoba (1236), Jaén (1246), Seville (1248); a strong supporter of the Church, he was canonized by Clement X in 1671.

Ferdinand IV, the Summoned (1285-1312). King of Castile and León (1295-1312); son of Sancho IV and grandson of Alfonso the Sage; his reign was marked by great anarchy.

Ferdinand I, of Antequera (1379-1416). King of Aragón (1412-1416); succeeded to the throne on the death of Martín the Humane, defeating a rival claimant, the Count of Urgel.

Fernández *or* Hernández, Alejo (c. 1470-1543). Spanish painter of the school of Seville; known for his work on the main altar of the Cathedral and for the altar of the Colegio de Maese Rodrigo.

Fernández de Córdoba, Diego, Count of Cabra (1438-1487). Spanish noble and soldier who served with distinction in the Moorish Wars, being rewarded with the title of Count of Cabra (1458).

Fernández de Córdoba, Gonzalo (1453-1515). Spanish general whose brilliant victories in the Italian wars won him the sobriquet of *El Gran Capitán* (The Great Captain).

Fernández de Heredia, García (?-1411). Archbishop of Zaragoza; assassinated at the Parliament of Caspe by a partisan of the Count of Urgel.

Fernández de Oviedo y Valdés, Gonzalo. *See* Oviedo y Valdés, Gonzalo Fernández de.

Fernández de Palencia, Alonso. *See* Palencia, Alonso Fernández de.

Fernández de Velasco, Pedro, Count of Haro. Spanish noble and Condestable of Castile; son of a notable political and military figure of the same name and office who was known for his virtues as "the good Count of Haro."

Ferrante (*or* Ferdinand) II (1469-1496). King of Naples; forced to flee by French invaders but regained his throne with the aid of Ferdinand the Catholic.

Ferreras, Juan de (1652-1735). Spanish historian; his principal work is the *Historia de España* (Madrid, 16 vols., 1700-1727).

Flaminius, Lucius (c. 1450-1509). Sicilian philologist and teacher of literature at the University of Salamanca.

Foix, Catherine de (1468-1518). Queen of Navarre (1483-1514); Catherine and her husband Jean d'Albret were the last rulers of Navarre, conquered and annexed by Ferdinand the Catholic.

Foix, Gaston de, Duke of Nemours (1489-1512). French general; brother of Germaine de Foix; conducted brilliant campaign against Spaniards in Italy (1512); killed in pursuit after the battle of Ravenna (April 11, 1512).

Foix, Germaine de (1488-1538). Queen of Aragón; niece of Louis XII of France; second wife of Ferdinand the Catholic.

Foix, Leonor de (?-1479). Queen of Navarre; daughter of Juan II of Aragón and Blanche of Navarre; proclaimed queen and died in 1479.

Folch de Cardona, Ramón (?-1522). Spanish general and

governor; served under the Great Captain, Gonzalo de Córdoba, in second Italian campaign; named Viceroy of Naples by Ferdinand the Catholic; distinguished himself in the Italian campaigns of the Holy League.

Fonseca, Alonso de (1418-1473). Archbishop of Seville; of great political influence in the reign of Enrique IV.

Fonseca, Antonio de. Spanish diplomat and *maestresala* of Isabella the Catholic; brother of Juan Rodríguez de Fonseca; played important part in Italian negotiations.

Fonseca, Juan Rodríguez de (1441-1524). Spanish ecclesiastic (successively Archdeacon of Seville, Bishop of Badajóz, Palencia, and Condé, Archbishop of Rosario in Italy, and Bishop of Burgos) and public official; first head of the Casa de Contratación; organizer and first president of the Council of the Indies.

François II. Duke of Brittany (1458-1488); succeeded by daughter Anne, who married (1497) Louis XII of France.

François I (1494-1547). King of France (1515-1547); in 1515 reconquered lost French possessions in Italy but had to surrender them in exchange for his liberty (1525).

François Phoebus (de Foix). King of Navarre (1479-1483).

Froissart, Jean (1338-1410). French chronicler whose major work is the *Chronique de France, d'Angleterre, D'Écosse, et d'Espagne.*

Gaguin, Robert (c. 1425-1502). French priest, writer, and teacher at the University of Paris; employed on diplomatic missions by Louis XI, Charles VIII, and Louis XII.

Gallego, Fernando (c. 1440-c. 1507). Spanish painter in the Hispano-Flemish manner whose style dominated the greater part of northern and western Spain.

Gandía, Duke of. *See* Aragón, Alfonso de.

Gautier, Théophile (1811-1872). French poet, critic, and novelist, chief exponent of movement of "art for art's sake"; traveled extensively in Spain.

Geraldini, Alessandro (1455-1525). Italian humanist employed as tutor at the court of the Catholic Sovereigns; in 1520 appointed bishop at Santo Domingo.

Geraldini, Antonio. Italian humanist, brother of Alessandro Geraldini, employed as tutor at the court of the Catholic Sovereigns.

Ghirlandajo, Domenico (original name, Domenico Bigordi)

(1449-1494). Florentine artist distinguished for his facile manner and thorough mastery of painting technique.

Gil de Hontañón, Juan (c. 1480-1531). Spanish architect known especially for the New Cathedral in Salamanca; his son, Rodrigo, designed the Plateresque façade of the University of Alcalá de Henares.

Girón II, Pedro. Grand Master of the Order of Calatrava (1445-1466) and suitor for the hand of the Infanta Isabella.

Goes, Damião de (1501-c. 1573). Portuguese humanist, historian, and traveler; his principal work is the *Chronica do felicissimo rei D. Manoel* (1565-1567).

González de Mendoza, Pedro. *See* Mendoza, Pedro González de.

Graux, Charles Henri (1852-1882). French classical philologist.

Grey, Thomas, second Marquis of Dorset (1477-1530). Commander of English expeditionary force sent to the conquest of Guienne.

Guas, Juan (?-c. 1497). French architect and sculptor in Spain; his principal works are the church of San Juan de los Reyes in Toledo, the Palace of the Infantado in Guadalajara, and the Colegio de San Gregorio in Valladolid.

Gumiel, Pedro de. Spanish architect; active until about 1516 as architect to Cardinal Jiménez de Cisneros at Alcalá de Henares; worked on the Cathedral of Toledo with Sancho de Zamora and Juan de Segovia.

Guzmán, Enrique de. *See* Medina Sidonia, second Duke of.

Guzmán, Fernán Pérez de. *See* Pérez de Guzmán, Fernán.

Guzmán, Hernán Núñez de. *See* Núñez de Guzmán, Hernán.

Haro, Diego López de. *See* López de Haro, Diego.

Haro, Count of. *See* Fernández de Velasco, Pedro.

Hefele, Karl von (1809-1893). German Catholic bishop, professor, and historian; his biography of Cardinal Jiménez defends the Spanish Inquisition.

Henri of Burgundy, Count (1057?-1112). French noble who aided Alfonso VI in the conquest of Toledo and received the county of Portugal; his son, Affonso Henriques, became first King of Portugal.

Henry VII (1457-1509). King of England (1485-1509), first of Tudor line; his eldest son Arthur married Catherine of Aragón (1501); following Arthur's death, Henry, wishing to preserve the Spanish connection, made other efforts to match

Catherine, who eventually married Arthur's younger brother, Henry, after he ascended the throne (1509).

Henry VIII (1491-1547). King of England (1509-1547); had himself proclaimed head of the Church of England following Pope's refusal to grant him a divorce from Catherine of Aragón.

Heredia, García Fernández de. *See* Fernández de Heredia, García.

Hontañón, Juan Gil de. *See* Gil de Hontañón, Juan.

Hotman, François (1524-1590). French jurist, writer, and Huguenot leader; his principal work, *Franco-Gallia,* was a plea for representative government and an elective monarchy.

Hurtado de Mendoza, Diego, Duke of the Infantado. Spanish grandee whose title was created in his favor by the Catholic Sovereigns (1475).

Hurtado de Mendoza, Diego (1503-1575). Spanish soldier, diplomat, poet, and historian; author of a major historical work, the *Guerra de Granada.*

Infantado, Duke of the. *See* Hurtado de Mendoza, Diego.

Innocent VIII (original name, Giovanni Batista Cibó) (1432-1492); Pope, 1484-1492.

Isabella (1470-1498). Eldest child, first daughter of the Catholic Sovereigns; wife (1) of Affonso of Portugal (1490), (2) of King Manoel I of Portugal (1497).

Jaime I, the Conqueror (1208-1276). King of Aragón; conquered the Balearic Islands and captured Valencia (1238).

Jal, Auguste (1791?-?). French man of letters and historian.

Jiménez de Cisneros, Francisco. Spanish prelate prominent in the religious, political, and intellectual life of Spain under the Catholic Sovereigns; appointed confessor to Isabella (1492); made Archbishop of Toledo and Primate of Spain (1495); in 1507 appointed Cardinal in Castile and later Inquisitor-General; provisional regent of Castile (1506-1507); regent of Castile (1516-1517).

Jiménez de Urrea, Pedro Manuel (1486?-c. 1536). Spanish noble, poet, and novelist.

Jiménez, Francisco Roldán. *See* Roldán Jiménez, Francisco.

Joanna II (1371-1435). Queen of Naples (1414-1435); during a turbulent reign, she was married three times; warred with the Angevins, Aragón, and the Pope.

João II (1455-1495). King of Portugal; weakened power of

nobility and promoted voyages of exploration; signed with Ferdinand the Catholic, Treaty of Tordesillas (June 7, 1494), establishing line of demarcation for their respective claims in the New World.

Juan II (1398-1479). King of Aragón and Navarre; contended with his son Carlos de Viana, claimant of throne of Navarre, and with Catalan rebels.

Juan I (1358-1390). King of Castile and León; son of Enrique II, the first Trastamara; suffered great defeat at Portuguese hands at Aljubarrota (1385).

Juan II (1405-1454). King of Castile and León; son of Enrique III; his entire reign was dominated by the masterful personality of the king's adviser and favorite, Álvaro de Luna.

Juan, Don (1478-1497). Only son of the Catholic Sovereigns; married Margaret of Austria (1497).

Juana, Doña, called La Beltraneja (1462-1530). Daughter of Enrique IV of Castile and his second wife, Juana of Avis; rebellious nobles considered her illegitimate and opposed her as lawful heiress to the throne of Castile; died in exile in Portugal after defeat in war of succession.

Juana, the Mad (1479-1555). Queen of Castile; second daughter of the Catholic Sovereigns; married Philip, Archduke of Austria (1496); mother of Emperors Charles V and Ferdinand I; ruled jointly with Philip, 1504-1506; spent rest of her life in retirement.

Juana of Avis (1439-1475). Queen of Castile (1455-1474); second wife of Enrique IV and mother of La Beltraneja.

Julius II (original name, Giuliano della Rovere) (1443-1513). Pope, 1503-1513; joined the League of Cambrai against Venice in 1508; re-formed the Holy League against France in 1511.

Lanuza. Noble Aragonese family in which the title of Justicia Mayor of Aragón was hereditary.

Lanuza I, Juan de (?-1507). Aragonese Justicia Mayor who was also Viceroy of Valencia, Catalonia, and Naples.

La Palisse *or* La Palice, Jacques de Chabannes, Seigneur de (?-1525). French soldier who distinguished himself in the Italian wars.

Lara. A powerful Castilian noble family which played an important role in medieval Castile.

Las Casas, Bartolomé de, called the Apostle of the Indies (1475?-1566). Spanish Dominican, defender of the American Indians against the conquistadores; author of a monumental *Historia de las Indias,* first published in 1875-1876.

Lasso de la Vega, Pedro. Spanish noble, leader in the revolt of the *Comuneros.*

Letellier, Michel (1643-1719). French Jesuit who as royal confessor had great influence over Louis XIV.

Llorente, Juan Antonio (1756-1823). Spanish priest, secretary of the Inquisition (1789-1792), and historian; his principal work, commissioned by Joseph Bonaparte, is the *Histoire critique de l'Inquisition d'Espagne* (Paris, 4 vols., 1817-1818).

Llull, Ramón (*or* Raymond Lully) (1233-1315). Catalan scholar and missionary; wrote religious, philosophical, and poetic works characterized by intense mysticism; various works on alchemy and magic were also assigned without foundation to him.

López de Ayala, Diego. Canon of the Cathedral of Toledo, Vicar-General and confidant of Cardinal Jiménez de Cisneros; patron of art in Toledo and translator of Boccaccio.

López de Chinchilla, Garcí. *See* Chinchilla, Garcí López de.

López de Haro, Diego. Spanish soldier and poet in the reign of the Catholic Sovereigns.

López de Mendoza, Íñigo, Count of Tendilla. Spanish grandee and hero of the War of Granada.

López de Mendoza, Íñigo. *See* Santillana, Marquis of.

López de Padilla, Pedro. Spanish noble and soldier; Adelantado Mayor of Castile under the Catholic Sovereigns.

López de Villalobos, Francisco. *See* Villalobos, Francisco López de.

Louis, St. (1214-1270). King of France (Louis IX); famed for exemplary qualities; canonized after death.

Louis VIII (1187-1226). King of France; married (1200) Blanca of Castile; warred against English power in France; took active part in suppression of the Albigenses.

Louis XI (1423-1483). King of France (1461-1483); extended frontiers of France almost to its present limits (except for Brittany and Lorraine); obtained Cerdaña and Roussillon from Juan II of Aragón as security for a loan of 300,000 crowns.

Louis XII (1462-1515). King of France (1498-1515); continued Italian policies of Charles VIII; recognized Spanish claims to Naples (1504).

Louis XIV, called "the Sun-King" (1638-1715). King of France (1643-1715) under whom royal absolutism reached its height.

Louis of Anjou, Duke of Calabria. Son of Louis II of Anjou; unsuccessfully claimed the throne of Aragón on the death of Martín the Humane without succession.

Lucas de Iranzo, Miguel (?-1473). Condestable of Castile; killed in anti-Jewish riots at Jaén.

Lúcero, Diego Rodríguez. Inquisitor of Córdoba (1499-1509) who established a reign of terror in that city.

Luna, Álvaro de (1388-1453). Spanish nobleman who enjoyed great influence over Juan II of Castile, becoming Grand Master of the Order of Santiago; having lost the king's favor as a result of the jealousy of court nobles, he was arrested and executed at Valladolid.

Lyra, Nicolas de (c. 1270-1340). French Franciscan theologian and philosopher.

Madeleine of France (1443-1486). Daughter of Charles VIII and Marie of Anjou; married (1462) Gaston de Foix, Prince of Viana; their son, François Phoebus, inherited the Kingdom of Navarre.

Maldonado, Diego Anaya de. *See* Anaya de Maldonado, Diego.

Maldonado, Francisco (?-1521). Spanish noble, leader in the revolt of the *comuneros* against Hapsburg absolutism; executed after the battle of Villalar, April 24, 1521.

Manoel I, the Fortunate (1469-1521). King of Portugal (1495-1521); his reign was marked by the great voyages of Vasco de Gama (1498) and Cabral (1500); married (1) Isabella, eldest daughter of the Catholic Sovereigns, (2) María, third daughter of the Catholic Sovereigns, (3) Eleanor, sister of Charles V.

Manrique. A noble Castilian family distinguished in the fifteenth and sixteenth centuries for its military and literary achievements.

Manrique, Gómez (1412?-1491). Spanish soldier, politician, and poet; supported Isabella's claims to the throne of Castile; governor of the Alcázar of Toledo; the first Spanish dramatic author whose name is known.

Manrique, Jorge (c. 1440-1479). Distinguished Spanish poet and soldier; nephew of Gómez Manrique; killed in battle defending Isabella's cause; his best-known verses are the *Coplas* written on the death of his father.

Manrique, Rodrigo (?-1476). Spanish noble, first Count of Paredes, and Grand Master of the Order of Santiago; brother of Gómez Manrique.

Manrique de Lara, Pedro. *See* Nájera, Duke of.

March, Auzías (1395?-c. 1460). Valencian poet called the Petrarch of Catalonia because of the brilliance of language and the formal perfection of his verses.

Margaret of Austria (148?-1530). Daughter of the Emperor Maximilian; married the Infante Don Juan of Spain (1497); guardian of the future Emperor Charles V.

Margarit, Joan de. Spanish prelate and historian of the fifteenth century; Bishop of Gerona, later made Cardinal; author of a Latin history of Spain, *Paralipomenon Hispaniae Libri X* (1481-1484).

Mariana, Juan de (1536-1623). Spanish Jesuit historian; his major work is the *Historia general de España* (1601).

Marie of Burgundy (1457-1482). Duchess of Burgundy. Daughter of Charles the Bold; on his death lost Burgundy, Picardy, Artois, and Franche-Comté to Louis XI of France; married Maximilian of Austria (1477); through their son Philip her domains, some of which were recovered by Maximilian, descended to Charles V.

Marina, Francisco Martínez. *See* Martínez Marina, Francisco.

Marineus Siculus, Lucius (1444?-1533?). Italian humanist and historiographer of Ferdinand the Catholic; his principal work is *De Rebus Hispaniae memorabilibus* (Spanish translation, 1530).

Martín I, the Humane (1356-1410). King of Aragón and Sicily (1396-1410); son of Pedro IV and brother of Juan I, whom he succeeded on the throne; his reign was troubled by efforts at invasion by the Count de Foix, husband of Juana, Daughter of Juan I, who claimed the throne of Aragón.

Martín I, the Young (1374-1409). King of Sicily (1391-1409); conducted military campaigns in North Africa and Sicily.

Martínez Marina, Francisco (1754-1833). Spanish priest and constitutional historian.

Martins, Fernão. Councilor and chaplain of Affonso V of Portugal; corresponded with Toscanelli on subject of a western route to the Indies.

Martyr de Anghera, Peter (Italian, Pietro Martire d'Anghera) (c. 1457-1526). Italian humanist and historian; in 1487 went to Spain and remained in the service of the Catholic Sovereigns as tutor to young Spanish nobles and princes; in 1524 made member of the Council of the Indies; his major work, *Decades de orbe novo* (Seville, 1511), deals with the first thirty years of the Spanish Conquest.

Mary of France, originally called Mary Tudor (1497-1534). Queen of France; daughter of Henry VII of England and Elizabeth of York; married Louis XII of France (October 1514), who shortly died (January 1515); secretly married the Duke of Suffolk (March 1515).

Mary Tudor *or* Mary I (1516-1558). Queen of England and Ireland (1553-1558); only surviving child of Henry VIII and his first wife, Catherine of Aragón; married Philip of Spain (later Philip II) (1554); in her reign Parliament restored papal power, and the penal laws against heresy were revived and enforced with vigor.

Maurenbrecher, Wilhelm (1838-1892). German historian.

Maximilian I (1459-1519). Emperor of the Holy Roman Empire (1493-1519); married Marie of Burgundy (1477); elected King of the Romans (1486) and founded the Hapsburg Dynastic empire; his son Philip married Juana, daughter of the Catholic Sovereigns; Charles, heir of Philip and Juana, became first Hapsburg King of Spain (1516) and Holy Roman Emperor (1519).

Medina Celi, Luis de la Cerda (?-1501), Count, later Duke of. Spanish grandee who befriended Columbus and proposed to support his Enterprise of the Indies.

Medina Sidonia, Enrique de Guzmán, second Duke of. Spanish grandee and soldier active in the War of Granada.

Mena, Juan de (1411-1456). Spanish author of didactic and allegorical verse.

Mendoza, Diego de. *See* Hurtado de Mendoza, Diego.

Mendoza, Fray Íñigo de. Minor poet of the reign of the Catholic Sovereigns.

Mendoza, Íñigo López de. *See* López de Mendoza; Santillana, Marquis of.

Mendoza, Pedro González de (1428-1495). Spanish prelate and statesman; made Cardinal under Enrique IV; named Archbishop of Seville and later of Toledo by Isabella the Catholic; enjoyed great influence with the Catholic Sovereigns.

Merimée, Prosper (1803-1870). French novelist, archaeologist, historian, and literary critic.

Merlo, Diego de. Spanish soldier and royal official of the second half of the fifteenth century.

Michelet, Jules (1798-1874). French romantic historian.

Miguel (1498-1500). Son of Manoel I, King of Portugal, and Isabella, daughter of the Catholic Sovereigns.

Milan, Duke of. *See* Sforza, Lodovico.

Mohammed XII, El Zagal (the Valiant). King of Granada (1485-1487); uncle and rival of Boabdil; defeated by Ferdinand the Catholic; surrendered his dominions and retired to Africa.

Montalvo, Garcí Ordóñez, *or* Rodríguez, de. Spanish novelist of the late fifteenth and early sixteenth century; author of famous romance of chivalry, *Amadís de Gaula* (1508).

Montesino, Fray Antonio (?-c. 1526). Spanish Dominican who began the struggle against Indian slavery in the New World.

Montfort, Simon de (c. 1160-1218). French soldier, leader in war against Albigenses of southern France; noted for the ruthless ferocity with which he conducted the war.

Montluc, Blaise de Lasseran-Massencome (c. 1503-1577). French soldier and military historian; distinguished himself in the wars of François I and Henri II; his *Commentaires* are a valuable account of the wars from 1521 to 1574.

Muret, Marc Antoine (1526-1585). French humanist; teacher of classics at Bordeaux, Paris, and other places.

Nájera, Pedro Manrique de Lara, Count of Treviño, Duke of. Spanish grandee, made Adelantado Mayor of León under Enrique IV; the title of Duke of Nájera was created in his favor by the Catholic Sovereigns (1482).

Navagero, Andrea (1483-1529). Venetian historian and poet who traveled widely in Spain; his *Viaggio* is a major source of information on Spanish political and social life of the period.

Navarro, Pedro. Spanish captain who served with distinction as soldier and engineer in the Italian wars; later commanded Spanish forces in the conquest of Oran and other North African victories.

Neapoli, Francesco (1446-1536). Italian painter in Spain, believed by some critics to be the father of the Valencian school.

Nebrija *or* Lebrija, Antonio de (1444-1522). Spanish humanist and grammarian; reformed teaching of Latin in Spain; author of first scientific Castilian grammar (1492).

Nemours, Duke of. *See* Foix, Gaston de.

Nicuesa, Diego de (c. 1465-1511). Spanish conquistador; attempted unsuccessfully to colonize Castilla de Oro, a region extending along the coast of Central America from the Gulf of Darién to Cape Gracias a Dios, Honduras, granted him in 1508.

Núñez, Juan (c. 1455-c. 1534). Spanish painter.

Núñez de Balboa, Vasco. *See* Balboa, Vasco Núñez de.

Núñez de Guzmán, Hernán (1478?-1553), called "el Comendador griego" because he was a commander in the Order of Santiago and a Greek scholar; taught Greek at the University of Salamanca and edited many classicial texts.

Ocampo, Sebastián de (c. 1465-c. 1509). Spanish navigator; in 1508 circumnavigated Cuba, proving its insular character.

Ojeda, Alonso de (c. 1498-1514 or 1515). Spanish nobleman who accompanied Columbus on his Second Voyage; with Juan de la Cosa and Amerigo Vespucci explored coast of Guiana and Venezuela (1499-1500); granted a strip of coast from Cap de la Vela to Gulf of Darién, known as New Andalusia; founded Darién colony (1509), leading to the eventual discovery of the Pacific Ocean and Peru.

Ommiads. Dynasty of caliphs who ruled at Córdoba from 756 to 1031.

Ordóñez de Montalvo, Garcí. *See* Montalvo, Garcí Ordóñez de.

Ortega, Bernardo. Spanish sculptor of the late fifteenth and early sixteenth centuries.

Ortiz, Alonso. Spanish theologian and historian of the time of the Catholic Sovereigns; employed by Cardinal Jiménez in revision of the Mozarabic liturgy.

Ortiz, Pablo. Spanish sculptor of the fifteenth century; carved tombs of Álvaro de Luna and his wife in the Capilla de Santiago of the Cathedral of Toledo.

Ovando, Nicolás de (c. 1460-c. 1518). Spanish colonial administrator; governor of Española (1502-1509).

Oviedo y Valdés, Gonzalo Fernández de (1478-1557). Royal

chronicler of the Indies; his principal work is the vast *Historia general y natural de las Indias* (1535-1557).

Pacheco, Juan, Marquis of Villena (?-1474). Spanish nobleman; favorite of Enrique IV; prominent in the wars and politics of Castile.

Padilla, Juan de (?-1521). Spanish nobleman; leader of the revolt of the *comuneros;* executed after the battle of Villalar, April 24, 1521.

Padilla, Pedro López de. *See* López de Padilla, Pedro.

Palacios Rubios, Juan López de. Spanish jurisconsult and writer of the fifteenth century; member of the royal council of the Catholic Sovereigns and employed by them in many important tasks.

Palencia, Alonso Fernández de (1423-1492). Spanish scholar and historian whose *Crónica de Enrique IV* is very biased against the king.

Pamplona, Pedro de. Spanish miniaturist of the thirteenth century; known for his Bible in two volumes, on fine vellum, which he wrote for King Alfonso the Sage.

Pardo de Cela, Pedro (?-1483). Spanish nobleman, enemy of Isabella the Catholic, and leader in baronial disorders in Galicia; captured by royal officers and executed, December 17, 1483.

Pedro II. King of Aragón (1196-1213); defeated and slain in the battle of Muret (1213), with the result that the crown of Aragón lost its predominant position in southern France.

Pedro III (1236-1285). King of Aragón (1276-1285); expelled French from Sicily in 1282, beginning the struggle between Angevins and Aragonese.

Pedro IV, the Ceremonious (1319-1387). King of Aragón (1336-1387); son of Alfonso IV; annexed Balearic Islands in 1343; conquered Sicily (1377) and ceded it to his son Martín.

Pedro, the Cruel *or* the Just (1334-1369). King of Castile and León (1350-1369); son of Alfonso XI; defeated and captured at Montiel (1369), and slain by his brother Enrique de Trastamara, who ascended the throne.

Pedro de Córdoba. *See* Córdoba, Pedro de.

Pedro de Pamplona. *See* Pamplona, Pedro de.

Pelayo. Visigoth noble of the eighth century whose victory over the Moors at Covadonga initiated the Reconquest and led to the formation of the Kingdom of Asturias.

Pérez, Juan. Franciscan monk of the Monestery of La Rábida; interested himself in Columbus's project and urged its acceptance on Isabella the Catholic.

Pérez de Almazán, Miguel, Lord of Maella (?-1514). Secretary and confidant of Ferdinand the Catholic.

Pérez de Guzmán, Fernán (1378?-1470?). Spanish politician, historian, and poet.

Pérez del Pulgar, Hernando (1451-1531). Spanish soldier and author of a chronicle relating the deeds of Gonzalo de Córdoba.

Pessagno (in Portuguese, Peçanha). Genoese family of seamen and statesmen; in the fourteenth and fifteenth centuries the Pessagno held important naval charges in Portugal.

Petronilla. Queen of Aragón (1137-1162); daughter of Ramiro II; married Ramón Berenguer IV, Count of Barcelona, giving rise to the union of Aragón and Catalonia; succeeded by their son Alfonso II of Aragón (1162-1196); Berenguela, their daughter, became Queen of León and Castile by her marriage to Alfonso VII (1128).

Philip I, the Handsome, Archduke of Austria (1478-1506). King of Castile (1504-1506) through marriage with Juana, daughter of the Catholic Sovereigns.

Philip II (1527-1598). King of Spain (1556-1598); son of the Emperor Charles V; waged resolute struggle to crush Protestantism and maintain Spanish hegemony in Europe; briefly wielded large influence in England through marriage with Mary Tudor; in his reign conflict of interests between Spain and England erupted into open warfare; sent the Invincible Armada against England and to catastrophic defeat (1588).

Philip III (1578-1621). King of Spain (1598-1621); son of Philip II; in his reign Spain's internal economic decay and external weakening became strongly marked.

Philip IV (1605-1665). King of Spain (1621-1665); in his reign the process of Spain's internal and international decline was greatly accelerated.

Pinzón, Martín Alonso (c. 1441-1493). Spanish navigator and shipowner who accompanied Columbus on voyage of 1492 as commander of the *Pinta*.

Pinzón, Vicente Yánez (1460?-1524). Spanish navigator and explorer; commanded the *Niña* on Columbus's First Voyage in 1492; discovered the mouth of the Amazon River (1499);

with Juan Díaz de Solís explored coast from Honduras to eastern point of Brazil (1508-1509).

Pizarro, Francisco (c. 1471-1541). Spanish conquistador; with Balboa in the discovery of the Pacific (1513); settled in Panama (1519); with Diego de Almagro and Fernando de Luque schemed to conquer legendary empire to the south (1522); after initial failures succeeded in invading and conquering Inca Empire (1531-1535); quarreled with Almagro and had him executed (1538); assassinated by adherents of Almagro (1541).

Ponce de León, Juan (c. 1460-1521). Spanish explorer and administrator; accompanied Columbus on Second Voyage; made governor of Puerto Rico (1510); discovered Florida (1513).

Ponce de León, Rodrigo, Marquis of Cádiz (?-1490). Spanish grandee and soldier noted for heroic deeds in the War of Granada.

Prescott, William Hickling (1796-1859). American historian of the romantic school; author of *History of the Reign of Ferdinand and Isabella the Catholic* (1838).

Priego, Pedro de Córdoba, Marquis of. Spanish grandee, nephew of Gonzalo de Córdoba; led rising against the Inquisitor Lúcero in Córdoba; punished by Ferdinand the Catholic for affront to royal officer by heavy fine, surrender of fortresses to the crown, and banishment from the kingdom.

Pulgar, Hernando del (c. 1430-1491?). Secretary and official chronicler of the Catholic Sovereigns; his *Crónica de los reyes católicos* is a major source for the events of their reign.

Pulgar, Hernando Pérez del. *See* Pérez del Pulgar, Hernando.

Querini, Vincenzo (c. 1479-1514). Italian humanist and diplomat.

Quintana, Pedro de. Cousin of Miguel Pérez de Almazán and his successor as secretary of Ferdinand the Catholic.

Quintanilla, Alonso de (1420? *or* 1430?-1500). Chief Royal Auditor and trusted agent of the Catholic Sovereigns; played large part in the organization of the Santa Hermandad, the restoration of the royal finances, and the reform of the Spanish army.

Ramírez y Ramírez, Francisco (?-1501). Spanish general and organizer of the Spanish artillery.

Ramiro, the Monk (?-1154). King of Aragón (1134-1137); abdicated in 1137 and retired to a monastery.

Ramón Berenguer IV (1115?-1162). Count of Barcelona (1131-1162); his marriage with Queen Petronilla of Aragón established a union of Aragón and Catalonia.

René I, the Good (1409-1480). Count of Provence and titular King of Naples; patron of arts and letters and himself a writer of some note.

Renée of France (1510-1576). Duchess of Ferrara; daughter of Louis XII of France and Anne of Brittany; successively promised in marriage to Charles V and Henry VIII of England; married (1527) Hercule d'Este, Duke of Ferrara.

Ribera, Pedro Enríquez de. See Enríquez de Ribera, Pedro.

Rincón, Antonio del. Erroneous for Rincón del Figueroa, Fernando del, *which see.*

Rincón del Figueroa, Fernando del. Spanish painter of Guadalajara, active between 1491 and 1518.

Robert II, the Pious (971-1031). King of France (996-1031); son and successor of Hugh Capet.

Rodrigo (?-c. 711). Last Visigothic king of Spain; defeated and probably slain by the Moors under Tarik in 711.

Rodríguez de Almela, Diego. See Almela, Diego Rodríguez de.

Rodríguez de Fonseca, Juan. See Fonseca, Juan Rodríguez de.

Rodríguez Lúcero, Diego. See Lúcero, Diego Rodríguez.

Roig, Jaume (1409-1478). Valencian writer of didactic verse.

Rojas, Fernando de (?-1541). Spanish novelist, probably of Jewish descent; author of all or a part of *La Celestina* (*Comedia de Calisto y Melibea*) (1499).

Roldán Jiménez, Francisco (1462-1502). Spanish conquistador; accompanied Columbus on Second Voyage to America; led a revolt against Columbus on Española; went down at sea while returning to Spain.

Roselly de Lorgues, Count Antoine-François Félix (1805-1898). French writer on religious and historical subjects; wrote on Columbus and sought his beatification; his principal work is *Christophe Colomb* (1856).

Rubios, Juan López de Palacios. See Palacios Rubios, Juan López de.

Saint-Simon, Louis de Rouvroy, Duke of (1675-1755). French soldier, diplomat, and writer of memoirs.

Salazar de Mendoza, Pedro (c. 1549-1629). Spanish priest and writer.

San Pedro, Diego. Spanish novelist and poet of the late fifteenth century; wrote highly rhetorical novels of courtly love.

Sánchez, Nufro (?-1478). Flemish woodcarver in Spain.

Sánchez de Castro, Juan. Spanish painter, founder of the Sevillian school (fl. 1454-1484).

Sancho IV, the Brave (?-1295). King of Castile and León (1284-1295); son of Alfonso the Sage; designated by the Cortes as heir apparent to the crown instead of the legal heir, the Infante Alfonso; warred against Aragón and the Moors.

Sancho de Zamora. *See* Zamora, Sancho de.

Sancho Ramírez (1040?-1094). King of Aragón (1064-1094) who gained major victories over the Moors.

Santa Cruz (?-c. 1508). Spanish painter in the Hispano-Flemish manner; with Pedro Berruguete and Juan de Borgoña worked on the *retablo* over the high altar of the Cathedral at Ávila.

Santillana, Iñigo López de Mendoza, Marquis of (1398-1458). Spanish soldier and poet; introduced the Italian sonnet form into Castilian literature.

Scaliger, Joseph Justus (1540-1609). French classical scholar, son of J. C. Scaliger; pioneered in modern textual criticism of classics; founder of modern chronology.

Sempere y Guarinos, Juan (1754-1830). Spanish constitutional historian.

Sforza, Lodovico (called *il Moro*, "the Moor") (1451-1508). Duke of Milan (1481-1499); expelled from Milan by Louis XII of France (1499); regained throne briefly, but was taken prisoner in 1500 and removed to France.

Siloe, Gil de. German sculptor, one of the greatest of the wandering artists of the Middle Ages; like Hans of Cologne, brought to Burgos by Bishop Alonso de Cartagena; best known for the golden *retablo* and the tomb of Juan II and Doña Isabel de Portugal in the Cartuja de Miraflores; Gil's son Diego (c. 1495-1563) was chief architect and designer of the Cathedral of Granada and the Escalera Dorada of the Cathedral of Burgos, strongly influenced by the Italian High Renaissance.

Simon of Cologne (?-1511). Architect of German descent; with his father, Hans, built the central lantern and twin open spires of the Cathedral of Burgos and also the Cartuja de Miraflores;

the Chapel of the Condestable Don Pedro Fernández de Velasco at Burgos is also their work.

Sixtus IV (original name, Francesco della Rovere) (1414-1484). Pope from 1471 to 1484; patron of art and learning, he built the Sistine Chapel in the Vatican, but was notorious for his nepotism.

Solís, Alonso de (according to some sources, Pedro Fernández de Solís). Bishop of Cádiz and governor of the archbishopric of Seville for Cardinal Pedro González de Mendoza; attempted to reconcile the feuding houses of the Duke of Medina Sidonia and the Marquis of Cádiz (1476).

Solís, Juan Díaz de (c. 1470-1516). Spanish navigator; with Vicente Yáñez Pinzón explored coast from Honduras to eastern point of Brazil (1508-1509); succeeded Amerigo Vespucci as chief pilot of Spain (1512); killed by Indians while exploring Río de la Plata (1515-1516).

Starnina, Gherardo (1354-c. 1410). Florentine painter in Spain.

Suárez de Figueroa, Lorenzo. Spanish ambassador to Venice during the Italian wars; exerted decisive influence on the course of diplomatic negotiations.

Talavera, Hernando de (1428-1507). Jeronymite friar and confessor to Isabella the Catholic, over whom he had much influence; appointed Archishop of Granada (1492).

Tendilla, Count of. *See* López de Mendoza, Iñigo.

Ticknor, George (1791-1870). American literary historian and professor of literature; his major work was *A History of Spanish Literature* (1849).

Torquemada, Tomás de (c. 1420-1498). Dominican prior, made first Inquisitor-General for Castile in 1483; organized the Inquisition in Spain and became symbol of its cruelty; framed the plan for the expulsion of the Jews from Spain in 1492.

Torres Naharro, Bartolomé de (c. 1476-1531). Spanish dramatist and poet, one of the founders of the Spanish theater.

Toscanelli, Paolo dal Pozzo (1397-1482). Renowned physician, mathematician, astronomer, and geographer of Florence.

Treviño, Count of. *See* Nájera, Duke of.

Trissino, Giangiorgio (1478-1550). Italian writer and literary reformer; author of *La Sophonisba* (1524), the first formal tragedy in modern literature.

Turnèbe, Adrien (1512-1565). French humanist; one of the leading classical scholars of his age.

Urgel, Jaime, Count of (?-1433). Claimant of the crown of Aragón following the death of Martín the Humane; defeated in armed struggle by Ferdinand de Antequera and condemned to life imprisonment.

Urrea, Pedro de. *See* Jiménez de Urrea, Pedro Manuel.

Valera, Mosén Diego de (1412-1487?). Spanish chronicler, letter writer, and poet.

Vargas, Luis de (1502-c. 1568). Spanish painter, last important mannerist at Seville; noted for his frescoes in the Cathedral.

Vega, Pedro Lasso de la. *See* Lasso de la Vega, Pedro.

Velasco, Pedro Fernández de. *See* Fernández de Velasco, Pedro.

Velásquez, Diego (c. 1465-1523). Spanish conquistador and administrator; sent by Diego Columbus to conquer Cuba (1511); organized expeditions of Francisco Fernández de Córdoba, Juan de Grijalva (his nephew), and Cortés to Mexico (1517-1519).

Vergara, Francisco. Spanish humanist; brother of Juan Vergara; professor of Greek at Alcalá de Henares for twenty years; editor of Spain's first Greek grammar.

Vergara, Juan (?-1557). Spanish humanist; secretary to Cardinal Jiménez and his collaborator on the Polyglot Bible; translator of Aristotle.

Vicente, Gil (c. 1465-c. 1537). Portuguese poet and dramatist who created the Portuguese theater with his *autos,* comedies, and farces.

Vigarni, Philippe (Felipe de Borgoña) (c. 1470-1543). French sculptor and architect in Spain; collaborated with Alonso Berruguete and Diego de Siloe, notably on the Capilla del Condestable in Burgos, the choir stalls at the Cathedral of Toledo, and the polychrome *retablo* in the Capilla Real at Granada.

Villalobos, Francisco López de (1473?-1549). Spanish physician and writer of Jewish descent; personal physician to Ferdinand the Catholic and Charles V.

Villon, François (1431-c. 1463). French poet of supreme poetic genius; regarded as the fountainhead of modern French poetry.

Visconti, Valentina (1336-1408). Daughter of Gian Galeazzo; married (1387) Louis, Duke of Orléans; through descent from her, Louis XII based his claims to Milan.

Vittorio Emanuele II (1820-1878). King of Italy; son of Charles Albert, King of Sardinia; made Cavour his chief political adviser; assumed title of "King of Italy" in 1861; complete union

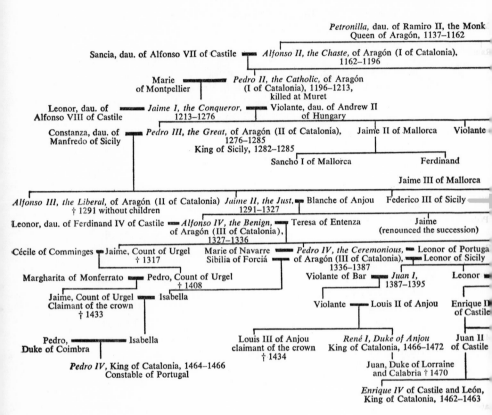

Petronilla, dau. of Ramiro II, the Monk
Queen of Aragón, 1137–1162

Sancia, dau. of Alfonso VII of Castile ▬▬ *Alfonso II, the Chaste,* of Aragón (I of Catalonia),
1162–1196

Marie ▬▬▬▬ *Pedro II, the Catholic,* of Aragón
of Montpellier (I of Catalonia), 1196–1213,
killed at Muret

Leonor, dau. of ▬▬▬ *Jaime I, the Conqueror,* ▬▬ Violante, dau. of Andrew II
Alfonso VIII of Castile 1213–1276 of Hungary

Constanza, dau. of ▬▬ *Pedro III, the Great,* of Aragón (II of Catalonia), Jaime II of Mallorca Violante
Manfredo of Sicily 1276–1285
King of Sicily, 1282–1285

Sancho I of Mallorca Ferdinand

Jaime III of Mallorca

Alfonso III, the Liberal, of Aragón (II of Catalonia) *Jaime II, the Just,* ▬▬ Blanche of Anjou Federico III of Sicily ▬▬
† 1291 without children 1291–1327

Leonor, dau. of Ferdinand IV of Castile ▬▬ *Alfonso IV, the Benign,* ▬▬ Teresa of Entenza Jaime
of Aragón (III of Catalonia), (renounced the succession)
1327–1336

Cécile of Comminges ▬ Jaime, Count of Urgel Marie of Navarre ▬▬ *Pedro IV, the Ceremonious,* ▬ Leonor of Portugal
† 1317 Sibilia of Forciá ▬▬ of Aragón (III of Catalonia), ▬▬ Leonor of Sicily
1336–1387

Margharita of Monferrato ▬▬ Pedro, Count of Urgel Violante of Bar ▬▬ *Juan I,* Leonor ▬
† 1408 1387–1395

Jaime, Count of Urgel ▬▬ Isabella Violante ▬▬ Louis II of Anjou Enrique III
Claimant of the crown of Castile
† 1433

Pedro, ▬▬▬▬ Isabella Louis III of Anjou *René I, Duke of Anjou* Juan II
Duke of Coimbra claimant of the crown King of Catalonia, 1466–1472 of Castile
† 1434

Pedro IV, King of Catalonia, 1464–1466 Juan, Duke of Lorraine
Constable of Portugal and Calabria † 1470

Enrique IV of Castile and León,
King of Catalonia, 1462–1463

THE RULERS OF ARAGÓN

Union with Catalonia

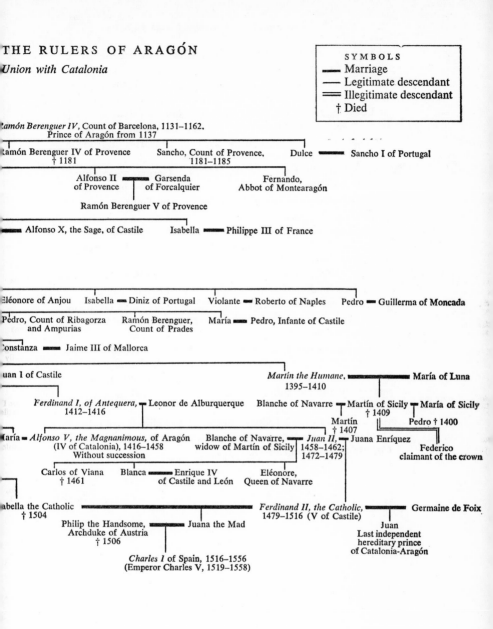

Ramón Berenguer IV, Count of Barcelona, 1131–1162,
Prince of Aragón from 1137

Ramón Berenguer IV of Provence
† 1181

Sancho, Count of Provence,
1181–1185

Dulce ━━ **Sancho I of Portugal**

Alfonso II
of Provence
━━ **Garsenda**
of Forcalquier

Fernando,
Abbot of Montearagón

Ramón Berenguer V of Provence

━━ **Alfonso X, the Sage**, of Castile

Isabella ━━ **Philippe III of France**

Éléonore of Anjou

Isabella ━━ **Diniz of Portugal**

Violante ━━ **Roberto of Naples**

Pedro ━━ **Guillerma of Moncada**

Pedro, Count of Ribagorza
and Ampurias

Ramón Berenguer,
Count of Prades

María ━━ **Pedro**, Infante of Castile

Constanza ━━ **Jaime III of Mallorca**

Juan I of Castile

Martín the Humane, ══ **María of Luna**
1395–1410

Ferdinand I, of Antequera, ━ **Leonor de Alburquerque**
1412–1416

Blanche of Navarre ━ **Martín of Sicily** ━ **María of Sicily**
† 1409

Martín
† 1407

Pedro † 1400

María ━ *Alfonso V, the Magnanimous*, of Aragón
(IV of Catalonia), 1416–1458
Without succession

Blanche of Navarre, ━━ *Juan II*, ━ **Juana Enríquez**
widow of Martín of Sicily   1458–1462;
1472–1479

Federico
claimant of the crown

Carlos of Viana
† 1461

Blanca ══ **Enrique IV**
of Castile and León

Éléonore,
Queen of Navarre

Isabella the Catholic ══════════════ *Ferdinand II, the Catholic*, ══════ **Germaine de Foix**
† 1504   1479–1516 (V of Castile)

Philip the Handsome, ══ **Juana the Mad**
Archduke of Austria
† 1506

Juan
Last independent
hereditary prince
of Catalonia-Aragón

Charles I of Spain, 1516–1556
(Emperor Charles V, 1519–1558)

of Italy under Vittore Emanuele was effected by occupation of Rome in 1870.

Vives, Luis (1492-1540). Spanish humanist, probably of Jewish descent; studied in Paris and Oxford, and became professor at Louvain; friend of Budé, Erasmus, and More; wrote on a wide variety of theological and philosophical topics; his philosophical outlook anticipated the views of Descartes and Bacon in some respects.

Waldseemüller, Martin (c. 1470-c. 1522). German geographer; in 1507 published his *Cosmographiae introductio*, in which he proposed giving the name "America" to the lands discovered by Amerigo Vespucci.

Weyden, Roger van der (c. 1400-1464). Noted Flemish painter; a triptych of his was presented to the Cartuja de Miraflores by Juan II of Castile and León.

Woltmann, Alfred M. (1841-1880). German art historian.

Zamora, Sancho de. Spanish sculptor of the fifteenth century.

Zegri Azaator. Moorish warrior belonging to the noble family of Aben Hamar; converted to Christianity and renamed Gonzalo Fernández Zegri.

Zoraya (original name, Doña Isabel de Solís). Second wife of Muley Abul Hassan, favored by him over the Sultana Aisha, who, together with supporters of her son Boabdil, took advantage of the old king's absence from the capital to seize the Alhambra.

Zurita, Jerónimo (1512-1580). Secretary to Philip II and official chronicler of Aragón; his principal work is the *Anales de la Corona de Aragón* (1562-1579).

Note on the Illustrations

Title page and page 1.
The coat of arms of the Catholic Sovereigns, often used as decoration by the Spanish printers of their reign, bears the quarterings of Castile and León and Aragón and Sicily, and the pomegranate of conquered Granada, the whole displayed on the eagle of St. John.

page 8
Title page of the first edition of the *Crónica del Rey Don Rodrigo,* relating the conquest of Spain by the Moors. Seville? 1499.

page 13
The Catholic Sovereigns accepting Fray Ambrosio de Montesino's translation of the *Vita Christi* by the Carthusian Ludolphus de Saxonia. Alcalá de Henares: Lançalao Polono (Stanislao Polono), for García d'Rueda, 1502.

page 24
Oliveros, son of the King of Castile, departs from the land, after rejecting the illicit love of his stepmother, the Queen of Algarbe. From *La Historia de los nobles cavalleros Oliveros de Castilla y Artus de Algarbe.* Burgos: Fadrique de Basilea, 1499. This anonymous classic, possibly written by David Aubert in Latin, was revised and translated into French by Philippe Camus, then translated into Castilian by an unknown person. Fadrique's cutter copied many of the blocks from the French editions but added and changed details to suit the Spanish scene.

page 49
Title page of the *Coplas de los siete pecados mortales hechas por el famoso poeta Juan de Mena.* Salamanca: unknown printer, 1500.

page 66
Woodcut from the *Coronica del muy esforçado & invencible cavallero*

el Cid Ruy Díaz, Campeador de las Españas. Toledo: Miguel de Eguia, 1526. The first known edition of this chronicle appeared at Seville, 1498, from the press of the "Tres compañeros alemanos."

page 100
Map on recto of the nineteenth leaf of Antonio de Nebrija's edition of the *Cosmographia* of the first century geographer Pomponius Mela. Salamanca, 1498. The first edition of this work had appeared in Milan in 1471.

page 113
One of the cuts in the first illustrated Latin edition of Columbus's First Letter Concerning America, usually called "Columbus's Letter to Rafael (or Gabriel) Sánchez," treasurer of the Kingdom of Aragón. Basel: Bergmann de Olpe? 1493.

page 121
Title page of the second edition of the *Doctrina e instrucción de la arte de cavallería,* the oldest Spanish compilation of rules governing knight-errantry, made by Bishop Alfonso de Cartagena. Burgos: Fadrique de Basilea, 1497.

page 141
One of the marks used by Arnaldo Guillén de Brocar, the famous printer who executed the six-volume Complutensian Polyglot Bible for Cardinal Jiménez de Cisneros at Alcalá de Henares from 1514 to 1517. This baffling design seems to contain emblems of the Passion surmounted by medallions of St. Peter and St. Paul. One authority surmises that the kneeling figure may be that of the printer himself.

page 154
The wooden block for the Legend of the Knight of Cologne in the *Contemplaciones sobre el rosario* by Gaspar de Gorricio de Novaria was taken to Mexico and used in the second half of the sixteenth century by Pedro Ocharte, successor of Juan Pablos, the first active printer in the New World. Gorricio's book was printed in Seville in 1495 by Meynardo Ungut and Stanislao Polono. The copy from which this cut is reproduced states that it was presented by the author to Ferdinand Columbus.

page 167
Coat of arms of Don Fadrique Enríquez de Cabrera, High Admiral of Castile, which appeared on the title page of the rare first edition of the Spanish translation of Petrarch's *Trionfi* by Antonio de Obregón, chaplain to Charles V. Logroño: Arnaldo Guillén de Brocar, 1512.

page 183
Colophon and printer's mark in a 1491 Seville edition of *Las Siete Partidas* of Alfonso X. The printers were Pablo de Colonia, Iuan

Pegnitzer of Nuremberg, Magnus Herbst of Fils, and Tomás Glockner.

page 201
Title page of the Castilian translation of *Tirant lo Blanch* by Johanot Martorell. Valladolid: Diego de Gumiel, 1511. This famous Catalan romance of chivalry, first published in Valencia in 1490, recounts the exploits of the Catalans and Aragonese in the East and the heroic deeds of Roger de Flor.

page 214
The labors for October from Fadrique de Basilea's edition of the *Reportorio de los tiempos,* Andrés de Li's adaptation of the almanac of Bernardo Granollachs, physician at Barcelona. Burgos, 1493.

page 223
Oliveros, having been shipwrecked near the coast of England, enters the tournaments at London and jousts with great success. As prizes, Oliveros receives a collar of gold and the hand of the Princess Helena, daughter of the King of England. (See p. 24 for an early scene in this romance of chivalry.) From *La Historia de los nobles cavalleros Oliveros de Castilla y Artus de Algarbe.* Burgos: Fadrique de Basilea, 1499.

page 231
Detail of the view of Xerez de la Frontera made by the Flemish artist and geographer Joris Hoefnagel between 1563 and 1567. Hoefnagel, the son of a diamond merchant of Antwerp, was a pupil of the painter Jan Bol and was closely associated with the geographer Abraham Ortelius, with whom he spent many years traveling in the Low Countries, France, Spain, England, Italy, Germany, and Bohemia. Hoefnagel's views of the many cities through which he passed were collected in the monumental *Civitates orbis terrarum* by Georgius Braun and Franz Hohenberg, first published in Cologne in 1572 by P. Gallaeum. Hoefnagel was noted for the naturalism of his plants and animals and for the exactitude with which he portrayed the people and their dress. For some cities, his scenes are the earliest known.

page 241
From the *Missale montis regii, s. Auriense.* Monterrey: Gonzalo Rodríguez de la Pasera, 1494.

page 256
Woodcut of the Day of Judgment in the *Viola anime* by the Majorcan theologian Raymundus de Sabunde. Printed in Toledo in 1500, probably by Pedro Hagenbach.

page 267
Title page of an old edition of the *Amadís de Gaula* by Garcí Ordóñez de Montalvo. The first extant edition of this prototype of the

romance of chivalry is that of 1508, but Montalvo probably started his work of writing and "compiling" about 1492. The romance of Amadís, possibly based on Portuguese and French sources, reached Spain at least as early as 1450.

page 285
Title page of the first Spanish edition of the *Lilio de medicina* by Bernardus de Gordonio, professor of medicine at Montpellier. Seville: Meynardo Ungut and Stanislao Polono, 1495.

page 291
The first woodcut in the text of the first edition of *La Comedia de Calisto y Melibea* by Fernando de Rojas. Burgos: Fadrique de Basilea, 1499.

page 302
Frontispiece of Diego de San Pedro's sentimental novel, *Cárcel de amor,* written about 1465 and first published in 1492. Barcelona: Juan Rosenbach, 1493.

page 319
From the *Libro de Música, de Vihuela de Mano. Intitulado, el Maestro . . .* of Don Luis Milán, one of the most valuable of the early works on instrumental music. It is the oldest known Spanish *cancionero* with musical notation. Valencia, 1536.

page 327
Detail of the border of a page in the first edition of *Tirant lo Blanch* by Johanot Martorell. Valencia: Nicolás Spindeler, 1490.

page 336
One of the marks used by Fadrique de Basilea, the celebrated first printer of the cathedral town of Burgos. His books are remarkable for the beauty of their execution, and he attempted illustration on a much larger scale than any other printer of his time on the Peninsula.